Nr.	Name	Klasse	Datum
	Nicola Pearson	10H	32,59,43,10,72,91, 86,22,97,06,101,29 86,72,53,93

Titles available from Malvern Language Guides

GCSE French - Your Vocabulary Guide
GCSE French - Your Speaking Test Guide
French Grammar - Your Guide
Your French Dictionary

Standard Grade French (Scotland) - Your Vocabulary Guide
Common Entrance 13+ - Your French Guide

GCSE German - Your Vocabulary Guide
GCSE German - Your Speaking Test Guide
German Grammar - Your Guide
Your German Dictionary

GCSE Spanish - Your Vocabulary Guide
GCSE Spanish - Your Speaking Test Guide
Spanish Grammar - Your Guide

GCSE Italian - Your Vocabulary Guide
GCSE Italian - Your Speaking Test Guide
Italian Grammar - Your Guide

Key Stage 3 French - Your Guide
Key Stage 3 German - Your Guide
Key Stage 3 Spanish - Your Guide

Mon Echange Scolaire
Mein Austausch
Mi Intercambio Escolar
Ma Visite en France

German - English, English - German

Your

GERMAN

Dictionary

Val Levick
Glenise Radford
Alasdair McKeane

ACKNOWLEDGEMENTS

We are grateful to Anne, Mick and John for editorial, moral, typographical and technical support, to Claire, Jonathan, John, Andrew and James for their tolerance of the whole process of writing and publishing this book, and to Mike Nightingale and Gail Wilson for proof-reading.

Published by Malvern Language Guides
PO Box 76
Malvern
WR14 2YP

Tel: 01684 893756 (for price enquiries only)
01684 577433 (for other enquiries)

Further copies can be obtained by completing the order form at the back of the book.

Typeset by Malvern Language Guides

Printed by Aldine Press Ltd
Barnards Green Road
Malvern
WR14 3NB
Tel: 01684 562786

ISBN: 1 898219 51 6

CONTENTS

HOW TO USE A DICTIONARY

All learners of a foreign language will find knowing how to use a dictionary a really useful skill. From 1998 onwards dictionaries will be permitted in some parts of the GCSE exam, so it is sensible to learn how to look up words and to understand the abbreviations.

Alphabetical order

Dictionaries are arranged in alphabetical order. So all words beginning with the letter *a* come before all those beginning with the letter *b*, and so on. Within the section for each letter, the same applies. So the words which start with the letters *ab* come before those starting *ac*, and so on. In the same way, words starting *aba* come before those starting *abb*. If you are not totally sure of your alphabet, write it on a bookmark which you keep with your dictionary.

In German, the Umlaut does not affect the alphabetical order.

Abbreviations

All dictionaries contain abbreviations for convenience. However, they are only convenient if you know what they mean! In this dictionary there are reminders of the most frequent abbreviations at the foot of each page. The full list of abbreviations we have used is given on page xi.

Looking up a German word

When you look up a **German** word, it is possible that you may find a number of English translations given, listed with the most common first. You will then need to work out which meaning is most likely in the context.

You may find that a word is not listed. This may mean that it is a past participle, or some other part of an irregular verb. Check the verb table on page 210.

Adjectives and Adverbs

In German adjectives can usually be used as adverbs. Therefore in this dictionary most adverbs are listed as adjectives only.

Nouns

Nouns are identified as masculine, feminine or neuter.

Example: **man** – Mann (Männer) *nm*

woman – Frau (-en) *nf*

girl – Mädchen (-) *nnt*

Some nouns can be either masculine or feminine.

Example: **adult** – Erwachsene *nmf* ‡

Some masculine nouns and *das Herz* are irregular (weak). They are identified as *nm wk*.

Example: **boy** – Junge (-n) *nm wk*

German nouns have a number of ways of forming the plural. In each case where there is a plural form in common use we have listed the modification which needs to be made to form the plural.

Example:		
girl – Mädchen (-) *nnt*	Plural: Mädchen (no change)
woman – Frau (-en) *nf*	Plural: Frauen
fish – Fisch (-e) *nm*	Plural: Fische
face – Gesicht (-er) *nnt*	Plural: Gesichter
man – Mann (Männer) *nm*	Plural: Männer
car – Auto (-s) *nnt*	Plural: Autos

Verbs

Verbs are classified as regular (*v reg*), irregular (*v irreg*), reflexive (*v refl*) and as verbs with slight variations (†). Additionally, verbs of all kinds can be separable *(sep)* or inseparable *(insep)*.

Regular verbs are verbs which follow a regular pattern in all tenses. They form the past participle by adding **ge** before the stem of the verb and adding **t** to the stem.

Example: spielen   **ge**spiel**t**

These are identified as *v reg*.

Irregular verbs are verbs which just have to be learned individually. They may be regular in the present tense but may not follow the pattern of regular verbs in other tenses.

Example: trinken, fahren, schreiben

These are identified as *v irreg*. Look in the verb table on page 210 for help with these verbs. To find the changes in irregular verbs with a prefix, first remove the prefix and then look for the verb. Remember that * is the symbol used to show that a verb takes **sein** in the perfect and other compound tenses.

Reflexive verbs are verbs with an extra pronoun.

Example: sich waschen

They are identified as *v reg refl* if they are regular, as *v irreg refl* if they are irregular and as *v reg refl* † if they are verbs with variations.
A small number of reflexive verbs require a dative reflexive pronoun. These are identified as *v irreg dat refl*.

You will not find every irregular reflexive verb listed in the verb table. If you cannot find the one you want, remove any prefix and look it up without **sich**.

Verbs with variations are verbs which broadly follow the regular pattern with some variations:

Example:	arbeiten	er arbeitet, sie hat gearbeitet
	reparieren	ich habe repariert
	besuchen	er hat besucht

These are identified as *v reg* †. Look at page 229 for help with these verbs.

Separable verbs are verbs with prefixes which often separate from the verb and move to the end of the sentence or clause. The past participle of a separable verb is formed by fitting the **ge** between the prefix and the main part of the verb.

Example: **ab**fahren   sie fährt **ab**   sie ist **ab**gefahren

These are identified as *v reg sep, v irreg sep,* or *v reg sep* †

Inseparable verbs are verbs with prefixes which do not separate from the main part of the verb.

Example: **unter**suchen   sie **unter**sucht   sie hat **unter**sucht

Looking up an English word

When you look up an **English** word to find the German equivalent, it is important to know if you are looking for an adjective, a noun, a verb, an adverb, etc. (Adjectives, nouns and verbs are all identified in both parts of the dictionary. See page vi if you are unsure of any of these terms.) When you have found the German word, look that up in the German-English section. You should get the same English word you started with in the English-German section, or a word which means the same in the same situation.

In the English-German section of the dictionary, words which could be misleading have an explanation in brackets to clarify the meaning.

Example: **square** – (in town)

                    square – (on paper)

                    square – (shape)

What else is in the dictionary?

There is a **table of German irregular verbs** at the end of the dictionary. If a verb is described as *v irreg*, you will find it in the verb table on page 210. To save space, verbs which are compounds are not given.

So **ausgehen** will behave in exactly the same way as **gehen**.

There is information about **how to write letters**, both formal and informal, on page 231.

There is a **list of instructions** in German which you might see in text books, together with translations of these instructions. These will be found on page 235.

This dictionary also contains **simple explanations of grammatical terms**, with examples on pages vi - x, and a reminder of **simple grammar points** on pages 216 - 230.

GRAMMATICAL TERMS EXPLAINED

acc   **Accusative (Akkusativ)**

The accusative case is most common for direct objects and after certain prepositions.

adj   **Adjectives (Adjektive)**

These are words which describe or tell you more about a noun.
There are many kinds of adjectives:

    Example: **big** – groß *adj*

                  green – grün *adj*

                  intelligent – intelligent *adj*

                  German – deutsch *adj*

but they all serve to give extra information about their noun. If the adjective comes between an article and the noun the adjective almost always adds an ending.

adv   **Adverbs (Adverbien)**

These are words which are added to a verb, adjective or another adverb to tell you how, when, where a thing was done:

    Example: **quickly** – schnell *adv*

                  soon – bald *adv*

                  there – dort *adv*

In German adverbs are usually identical to adjectives. Adverbs are therefore only listed where the adverb is distinct or has no equivalent adjective.

art   **Articles (Artikel)**

There are two kinds of articles mentioned in this dictionary:

    def art: **definite (bestimmt)**   **the** – der, die, das, die

    indef art: **indefinite (unbestimmt)**   **a, an** – ein, eine, ein

coll   **Colloquial (Umgangssprachlich)**

These are words used in spoken German but which are perhaps not always suitable for written German.

co-ord conj   **Co-ordinating Conjunctions (Nebenordnende Konjunktionen)**

These are words used to join sentences and clauses, which do not affect word order at all.

    Example: **and** – und *co-ord conj*

dat   **Dative (Dativ)**

The dative case is used for the indirect object and after certain prepositions and verbs.

dem pron   **Demonstrative Pronouns (Demonstrativpronomen)**

These words are used to establish contrast between two things or people:

> Example   **this one** – dieser *dem pron*

excl   **Exclamations (Ausrufe)**

These are phrases and words which are often used with an exclamation mark:

> Example: **help!** – Hilfe! *excl*

gen   **Genitive (Genitiv)**

The genitive case is used to denote possession and after certain prepositions.
An **-s** (or **-es** for one syllable nouns) is added to masculine and neuter nouns.

inv   **Invariable (Unflektiert)**

These nouns or adjectives do not change their spelling or take any endings.

> Example: **pink** – rosa *adj inv*

nm, nf, nnt, nmf, npl, nmf ‡, nm wk, nnt wk   **Nouns (Substantive)**

These are names of people, places or things. There are three genders in German:
masculine *nm*, feminine *nf* and neuter *nnt*. All nouns fit into one of these
categories. Plural forms are shown in brackets.

> Example: **spoon** – Löffel (-) *nm*
>   **fork** – Gabel (-n) *nf*
>   **knife** – Messer (-) *nnt*

Some nouns are not found in the singular. They are listed as *npl*

> Example: **sore throat** – Halsschmerzen *npl*

Some adjectival nouns can be either feminine or masculine. Information about them
can be found on page 220.

> Example: **adult** – Erwachsene   *nmf ‡*

Weak nouns are shown as *wk*. Information about them can be found on page 221.

> Example: **boy** – Junge (-n) *nm wk*

nom   **Nominative (Nominativ)**

The nominative case is used for the subject of the sentence or clause.

pers pron   **Personal Pronouns (Personalpronomen)**

This is the general name given to subject, direct object and reflexive pronouns:

    Example: **he** – er *pers pron*

                         him – ihn *pers pron*

                         himself –sich *pers pron*

pl   **Plural (Plural)**

Nouns can be singular or plural. Plural forms of singular nouns are shown in brackets after the noun

    Example: **·boy** – Junge (-n) *nm wk*

                         holidays – Ferien *npl*

                         town – Stadt (Städte) nf

Some nouns have no plural and are shown as *no pl*

    Example: **vegetables** – Gemüse *nnt, no pl*

poss adj   **Possessives (Possessivum)**

These adjectives show ownership.

    Example: **my** – mein *poss adj*

pref   **Prefix (Präfix)**

A prefix is a syllable on the front of a word which alters its meaning.

    Example: **anti~** – *pref* anti

prep   **Prepositions (Präpositionen)**

These are words placed in front of nouns and pronouns to show position and other relationships:

    Example: **with** – mit (+ dat) *prep*

                         before – vor (+ acc/dat) *prep*

pron   **Pronouns (Pronomen)**

Pronouns are short words used to stand in the place of a noun to avoid repeating it. In German they must agree with the gender of the noun they are standing for:

    Example: **he** – er *pron*

rel pron   **Relative Pronouns (Relativpronomen)**

These are words which join two phrases or ideas which are linked by meaning:

    Example: **which** – der, die, das, die *rel pron*

                         The book **which** *is on the table is interesting*

                         Das Buch, **das** auf dem Tisch liegt, ist interessant

sub conj   **Subordinating Conjunctions (Unterordende Konjunktionen)**

Subordinating conjunctions introduce a subordinate clause. The verb is placed at the end of the clause. Further information can be found on page 220.

    Example: **if** – wenn *sub conj*

v reg, v reg †, *v irreg, v refl, v sep, v insep*   **Verbs (Verben)**

A verb will tell you the actions and events in a sentence.

    Example: *I am playing football*   Ich **spiele** Fußball

The form of the verb which is listed in this dictionary and verb table is called the infinitive. It means "to".....

    Example: **sehen** – see *v irreg*

v reg   **Regular Verbs (Regelmäßige Verben) (also called Weak Verbs)**

Many verbs belong to this group and they are identified as *v reg* in the dictionary.

v reg †   **Regular Verbs † (Regelmäßige Verben †)**

These regular verbs have slight variations. Further information about these verbs can be found on pages 229.

v irreg   **Irregular Verbs (Unregelmäßige Verben) (also called Strong Verbs)**

These verbs, which do not follow the regular pattern in all tenses, are set out for you in the verb table on page 210. They are verbs which are frequently used and which you **must** know. They are listed as *v irreg*

    Example: **eat** – essen *v irreg*

                    be able to – können *v irreg*

                    come – kommen* *v irreg*

* is the symbol used to show that a verb takes **sein** in the perfect and other compound tenses.

v refl   **Reflexive Verbs (Reflexive Verben)**

These are verbs which have an extra pronoun. You must remember to use the correct reflexive pronoun.

    Example: *I wash myself* – Ich wasche **mich**

                   She gets dressed – Sie zieht **sich** an

v dat refl   **Reflexive Verbs (Reflexive Verben)**

A reflexive verb where the pronoun is in the dative case is marked *v dat refl*

    Example: *I wash my hair* – Ich wasche **mir** die Haare

v sep   **Separable Verbs (Trennbare Verben)**

Separable verbs have a prefix which often separates from its verb and moves to the end of the clause. More information about them can be found on page 228.

      Example: **depart** – abfahren *v irreg sep*

v insep   **Inseparable Verbs (Untrennbare Verben)**

Inseparable verbs have a prefix but this prefix never separates from its verb.

      Example: **examine** – untersuchen *v reg insep*

More details about Grammar can be found on pages 216 - 230.

LIST OF ABBREVIATIONS

*	verb takes *sein* in perfect tense (page 228)	*no pl*	no plural
†	regular verb with variations (page 229)	*npl*	noun found only in the plural
acc	accusative	*nt*	neuter
adj	adjective	*nm/nnt wk*	weak noun (page 221)
adv	adverb	*o.s.*	oneself
art	article	*pers pron*	personal pronoun
coll	colloquial	*pl*	plural
co-ord conj	co-ordinating conjunction	*poss adj*	possessive adjective
dat	dative	*pref*	prefix
def	definite	*prep*	preposition
dem pron	demonstrative pronoun	*pron*	pronoun
excl	exclamation	*rel pron*	relative pronoun
f	feminine	*sing*	singular
gen	genitive	*s.o.*	someone
indef	indefinite	*sthg*	something
inv	invariable	*sub conj*	subordinating conjunction
jdm	jemandem (dative)	*v dat refl*	verb, reflexive with dative pronoun
m	masculine	*v insep*	verb, inseparable
n ‡	adjectival noun (see page 220)	*v irreg*	verb, irregular; details in the verb table (page 210)
nf	noun, feminine	*v refl*	verb, reflexive
nm	noun, masculine	*v reg*	verb, regular
nnt	noun, neuter	*v sep*	verb, separable
nom	nominative		

GERMAN

DICTIONARY

A

ab (+ dat) – *prep* from (date, prices)
  ab und zu – *adv* from time to time
  ab morgen – from tomorrow
abbauen – *v reg sep* to take down
  ein Zelt abbauen – *v reg sep* take down a tent
abbiegen – *v irreg sep* turn (off road)
Abend (-e) – *nm* evening
  Bis heute abend! – See you this evening!
  jeden Abend – every evening
  Guten Abend! – *excl* Good evening!
  Einen schönen Abend! – *excl* Have a nice evening!
  gestern abend – last night, yesterday evening
Abendbrot (-e) – *nnt* evening meal, tea (cold)
Abendessen (-) – *nnt* dinner, evening meal
abends – *adv* in the evening
Abenteuer (-) – *nnt* adventure
Abenteuerfilm (-e) – *nm* adventure film
Abenteuerroman (-e) – *nm* adventure story
aber – *co-ord conj* but
abfahren* – *v irreg sep* depart, go, leave
Abfahrt (-en) – *nf* departure
  vor der Abfahrt – before leaving
Abfahrtsplan (-pläne) – *nm* departure board
Abfahrtszeit (-en) – *nf* departure time
Abfall – *nm* litter, rubbish
Abfalleimer (-) – *nm* rubbish bin
abfliegen* – *v irreg sep* to depart (plane)

Abflug (Abflüge) – *nm* flight departure
Abgase – *npl* exhaust fumes
abgeben – *v irreg sep* hand in (book, ticket)
Abgemacht! – *excl* Agreed!
abhängen von (+ dat) – *v irreg sep* depend on
abhauen – *v reg sep coll* go away
  Hau ab! – *excl coll* Clear off!
abholen – *v reg sep* meet, pick up
Abitur – *nnt* A level (-s)
Abiturient (-en) – *nm wk* Upper Sixth form student
Abiturientin (-nen) – *nf* Upper Sixth form student
Abkürzung (-en) – *nf* abbreviation
ablegen – *v reg sep* put aside
ablehnen – *v reg sep* decline, refuse
abnehmen – *v irreg sep* lose weight
  den Hörer abnehmen – *v irreg sep* pick up phone
Abonnement (-s) – *nnt* subscription
abräumen – *v reg sep* clear away
Abreise (-n) – *nf* departure
abreisen* – *v reg sep* depart
Absatz (sätze) – *nm* paragraph, heel
abschicken – *v reg sep* send away
abschleppen – *v reg sep* tow away
Abschleppwagen (-) – *nm* breakdown lorry
abschließen – *v irreg sep* lock
Abschlußprüfung (-en) – *nf* final exam
Abs./Absender (-) – *nm* sender (letter)
Absicht (-en) – *nf* purpose, intention
absichtlich – *adv* on purpose
abstauben – *v reg sep* dust
Abstellplatz (-plätze) – *nm* parking space
absurd – *adj* absurd

---

adj - adjective	*v reg* - verb regular	*v sep* - verb separable	† - see verb info
prep - preposition	*v irreg* - verb irregular	*v refl* - verb reflexive	* - takes sein

Abtei (-en) – *nf* abbey
Abteil (-e) – *nnt* compartment
Abteilung (-en) – *nf* department
abtrocknen – *v reg sep* † dry dishes
abwaschen – *v irreg sep* wash up
abwesend – *adj* absent
Abwesenheit (-en) – *nf* absence
Abzeichen (-) – *nnt* badge
Ach! – *excl* Oh!
acht – *adj* eight
achte – *adj* eighth
Achterbahn (-en) – *nf* rollercoaster
achten (auf + acc) – *v reg* † pay attention (to)
Achtung! – *excl* Look out! Attention!
achtzehn – *adj* eighteen
achtzig – *adj* eighty
ADAC – vehicle breakdown service
addieren – *v reg* † add up
Adjektiv (-e) – *nnt* adjective
adoptieren – *v reg* † adopt
Adoptiv~ – *pref* adopted
Adresse (-n) – *nf* address
Aerobic – *nnt, no pl* aerobics
Affe (-n) – *nm wk* monkey
Afrika – *nnt* Africa
afrikanisch – *adj* African
Agentur (-en) – *nf* agency
aggressiv – *adj* aggressive
ähneln (+ dat) – *v reg* resemble
ähnlich – *adj* similar, like
Ahnung (-en) – *nf* idea, knowledge
    Keine Ahnung! – *excl* No idea!
Aktentasche (-n) – *nf* briefcase
aktiv – *adj* active
aktuell – *adj* current, up to date
Akzent (-e) – *nm* accent
akzeptieren – *v reg* † accept, agree
albern – *adj* foolish
Album (Alben) – *nnt* album
Algebra – *nf* algebra
Alkohol (-e) – *nm* alcohol

alkoholfrei – *adj* alcohol free
    ein alkoholfreies Getränk – *nnt* a soft drink
All – *nnt* space (universe)
alle – all, everybody
    wir alle – all of us
    es ist alle – it's all gone
Allee (-n) – *nf* avenue
allein – *adv* alone
Alleinerziehende – *nmf* ‡ single parent
allergisch gegen (+ acc) – *adj* allergic to
allerlei – all sorts of
alles – everything
    alles in allem – all in all
    Alles Gute – love from, Yours
allgemein – *adj* general
    im allgemeinen – in general
Alltag – *nm* daily routine, weekday
alltäglich – *adj* everyday
Alltagsleben – *nnt* everyday life
Alpen – *npl* Alps
Alphabet (-e) – *nnt* alphabet
Alptraum (-träume) – *nm* nightmare
als – *sub conj* than
als – *sub conj* when (in past)
als ob – *sub conj* as if
also – *adv* so, therefore
Also! – *excl* Right!
alt – *adj* old, elderly
    ich bin 16 (Jahre alt) – I am 16 (years old)
Alter (-) – *nnt* age, old age
    mittleren Alters – middle aged
älter – *adj* elder
älteste – *adj* eldest
altmodisch – *adj* old fashioned
Altpapier – *nnt* paper for recycling
am – (= an dem) on the
    am besten – *adv* best
    am Freitag – *adv* on Friday

---

nm - noun masculine   *nf* - noun feminine   *nnt* - noun neuter   *npl* - noun plural
nom- nominative   *acc* - accusative   *gen* - genitive   *dat* - dative

am liebsten – *adv* best of all
am Rhein – by the Rhine
Amerika – *nnt* America
Amerikaner (-) – *nm* American
Amerikanerin (-nen) – *nf* American
amerikanisch – *adj* American
Ampel (-n) – *nf* traffic lights
Amt (Ämter) – *nnt* office, position
sich amüsieren – *v reg refl* † enjoy oneself, have a good time
an (+ acc/dat) – *prep* at, on (vertical)
an (+ dat)... vorbei – *prep* past
an Bord – on board
an der Themse – by the Thames
Ananas (-) – *nf* pineapple
anbauen – *v reg sep* grow (plants)
anbieten – *v irreg sep* offer
andauernd – *adv* continually
anbinden – *v irreg sep* tie
Andenken (-) – *nnt* souvenir
andere – *adj* other, another
andererseits – *adv* on the other hand
ändern – *v reg* change, alter
anders – *adv* differently
anderthalb – one and a half
Änderung (-en) – *nf* change
andrehen – *v reg sep* turn on (tap)
anfahren – *v irreg sep* knock s.o. over (car)
Anfang (Anfänge) – *nm* beginning
am Anfang – at the beginning
anfangen – *v irreg sep* begin
wieder von vorne anfangen – *v irreg sep* begin again
Anfänger (-) – *nm* beginner
Anfängerin (-nen) – *nf* beginner
Anführungszeichen – *npl* speech marks („...")
angeben – *v irreg sep* boast
Angeber (-) – *nm* show-off
Angeberin (-nen) – *nf* show-off

Angebot (-e) – *nnt* offer
angehen – *v irreg sep* concern
was mich angeht – as for me
Angeln – *nnt* angling
angeln gehen* – *v irreg* go angling
Angelrute (-n) – *nf* fishing rod
angenehm – *adj* pleasant, enjoyable
Angenehm! – *excl* Pleased to meet you!
angestellt sein* – *v irreg* be on the staff
Angestellte – *nmf* ‡ employee
angreifen – *v irreg sep* attack
Angriff (-e) – *nm* attack
Angst haben vor (+ dat) – *v irreg* be frightened of
große Angst haben – *v irreg* be terrified
Keine Angst! – *excl* Don't worry!
ängstlich – *adj* worried, anxious
anhaben – *v irreg sep* have on (clothes)
anhalten* – *v irreg sep* stop, halt
Anhänger (-) – *nm* trailer, pendant
anklagen – *v reg sep* accuse
ankommen* – *v irreg sep* arrive
ankreuzen – *v reg sep* tick (✓)
ankündigen – *v reg sep* announce
Ankunft (-en) – *nf* arrival
anlassen – *v irreg sep* start up (turn key)
anlegen – *v reg sep* dock
Anlieger frei – access only (road sign)
anmachen – *v reg sep* put on, turn on (light)
anmelden – *v reg sep* † register
sich anmelden – *v reg refl sep* † sign in
Anmeldung (-en) – *nf* registration
Anmeldungsformular (-e) – *nnt* registration form
annehmbar – *adj* acceptable
annehmen – *v irreg sep* accept, take
Annonce (-n) – *nf* small ad
Anorak (-s) – *nm* anorak

---

adj - adjective	*v reg* - verb regular	*v sep* - verb separable	† - see verb info
prep - preposition	*v irreg* - verb irregular	*v refl* - verb reflexive	* - takes sein

anprobieren – *v reg sep* † try on (clothes)

Anrichte (-n) – *nf* sideboard

Anruf (-e) – *nm* phone call

Anrufbeantworter (-) – *nm* answering machine

anrufen – *v irreg sep* ring up, phone

Ansager (-) – *nm* announcer

Ansagerin (-nen) – *nf* announcer

anschauen – *v reg sep* look at

sich anschauen – *v reg dat refl sep* take a look at

Anschlagbrett (-er) – *nnt* notice board

anschließen – *v irreg sep* plug in

anschließend – *adv* after that

Anschluß – *nm* connection

sich anschnallen – *v reg refl sep* fasten one's seat-belt

Anschrift (-en) – *nf* address

ansehen – *v irreg sep* look at

Ansichtskarte (-n) – *nf* picture postcard

ansprechen – *v irreg sep* address

anspringen* – *v irreg sep* start (vehicle)

anständig – *adj* decent

anstatt – *conj* instead of

anstellen – *v reg sep* employ

Anstreicher (-) – *nm* painter, decorator

Antenne (-n) – *nf* aerial

Anti~ – *pref* anti~

Antibiotikum (-ka) – *nnt* antibiotic

antibiotisch – *adj* antibiotic

Antiseptikum (-ka) – *nnt* antiseptic

antiseptisch – *adj* antiseptic

Antragsformular (-e) – *nnt* application form

Antwort (-en) – *nf* answer

die richtige Antwort – the right answer

antworten – *v reg* † answer

Anweisung (-en) – *nf* instruction

anwesend – *adj* present, not absent

anwesend sein* – *v irreg* be present, attend

Anwesenheit (-en) – *nf* presence

die Anwesenheit feststellen – *v reg sep* call the register

Anzahlung (-en) – *nf* deposit

Anzeige (-n) – *nf* advertisement

anziehen – *v irreg sep* put on clothes, attract

sich anziehen – *v irreg refl sep* get dressed

Anzug (-züge) – *nm* suit

anzünden – *v reg sep* † switch on, light

AOK – health insurance scheme

Aperitif (-s) – *nm* aperitif

Apfel (Äpfel) – *nm* apple

Apfelbaum (-bäume) – *nm* apple tree

Apfelkuchen (-) – *nm* apple cake

Apfelsaft – *nm* apple juice

Apfelsine (-n) – *nf* orange

Apfelstrudel (-) – *nm* apple strudel

Apfelwein (-e) – *nm* cider

Apotheke (-n) – *nf* chemist's shop

an der Apotheke – at the chemist's

Apotheker (-) – *nm* chemist

Apothekerin (-nen) – *nf* chemist

Apparat (e) – *nm* device, camera, phone

Anne am Apparat – This is Anne speaking

Bleiben Sie am Apparat, bitte! – *excl* Hold the line please!

Appetit (-e) – *nm* appetite

Guten Appetit! – *excl* Enjoy your meal!

Aprikose (-n) – *nf* apricot

April – *nm* April

im April – in April

Arbeit (-en) – *nf* work

---

arbeiten – *v reg* † work
  halbtags arbeiten – *v reg* † work part-time
Arbeiter (-) – *nm* worker
Arbeiterin (-nen) – *nf* worker
Arbeitgeber (-) – *nm* employer
Arbeitgeberin (-nen) – *nf* employer
Arbeitsbogen (-bögen) – *nm* worksheet
Arbeitnehmer (-) – *nm* employee
Arbeitnehmerin (-nen) – *nf* employee
arbeitslos – *adj* out of work
Arbeitslose – *nmf* ‡ unemployed person
Arbeitslosigkeit – *nf* unemployment
Arbeitspraktikum (-en) – *nnt* work experience
Arbeitszimmer (-) – *nnt* study
Architekt (-en) – *nm wk* architect
Architektin (-nen) – *nf* architect
Ärger – *nm* hassle
ärgerlich – *adj* annoying
ärgern – *v reg* annoy
sich ärgern – *v reg refl* be angry
Argument – *nnt* argument, discussion
Arm (-e) – *nm* arm
arm – *adj* poor
Armband (-bänder) – *nnt* bracelet
Armbanduhr (-en) – *nf* wrist watch
Armee (-n) – *nf* army
Ärmel (-) – *nm* sleeve
arrangieren – *v reg* † arrange
Art (-en) – *nf* way, sort of
  auf diese Art und Weise – in this manner
artig – *adj* well-behaved
Artikel (-) – *nm* article
Arzt (Ärzte) – *nm* doctor
Ärztin (-nen) – *nf* doctor
As (-se) – *nnt* ace
Aschenbecher (-) – *nm* ashtray

Aschermittwoch – *nm* Ash Wednesday
asiatisch – *adj* Asian
Asien – *nnt* Asia
aß – *see essen*
Ast (Äste) – *nm* branch
Asthma – *nnt* asthma
asthmatisch – *adj* asthmatic
Atelier (-s) – *nnt* studio, workshop
Atem – *nm* breath
  außer Atem – out of breath
atemlos – *adj* out of breath
Athlet (-en) – *nm wk* athlete
Athletin (-nen) – *nf* athlete
Athletik – *nf* athletics
Atlantik – *nm* Atlantic Ocean
atmen – *v reg* † breathe
Atmosphäre (-n) – *nf* atmosphere
Attest (-e) – *nnt* doctor's certificate
attraktiv – *adj* attractive
ätzend – *adj coll* a pain
auch – *adv* also, too
auch nicht – *adv* neither
auf – up (out of bed)
auf (+ acc/dat) – *prep* on, upon (horizontal)
  auf dem Lande – in the country
  auf deutsch – in German
  auf einmal – *adv* all at once
  auf englisch – in English
  auf links – *adv* inside out
aufbauen – *v reg sep* put up, build up
  das Zelt aufbauen – *v reg sep* pitch the tent
aufblasen – *v irreg sep* blow up, inflate
aufbrechen* – *v irreg sep* break up, set off
aufdrehen – *v reg sep* turn up (radio)
Aufenthalt (-e) – *nm* stay
auffordern – *v reg sep* ask, invite, demand
aufführen – *v reg sep* put on (play)

---

adj - adjective	*v reg* - verb regular	*v sep* - verb separable	† - see verb info
prep - preposition	*v irreg* - verb irregular	*v refl* - verb reflexive	* - takes sein

Aufführung (-en) – *nf* show

auffüllen – *v reg sep* refill

Aufgabe (-n) – *nf* exercise, task (school)

aufgeben – *v irreg sep* give up

aufgehen* – *v irreg sep* rise (sun)

aufgestanden sein* – *v irreg* be up (out of bed)

aufhaben – *v irreg sep* have on (clothes)

aufheben – *v irreg sep* pick up, lift

aufhören – *v reg sep* finish, stop

Aufkleber (-) – *nm* sticker

auflegen – *v reg sep* hang up (phone)

aufmachen – *v reg sep* open

Aufmerksamkeit (-en) – *nf* attention

aufmuntern – *v reg sep* cheer s.o. up

aufnehmen – *v irreg sep* record (on tape)

  auf Video aufnehmen – *v irreg sep* video

aufpassen auf (+ acc) – *v reg sep* be careful, look after

  Paß auf! – *excl* Be careful!

aufpumpen – *v reg sep* pump up tyres

aufräumen – *v reg sep* tidy up

aufregend – *adj* exciting

Aufsatz (-sätze) – *nm* essay

Aufschlag (-schläge) – *nm* service (tennis)

aufschlagen – *v irreg sep* open (book)

Aufschnitt – *nm* mixed cold meats

aufschreiben – *v irreg sep* write down

aufstehen* – *v irreg sep* get up, stand up

aufstellen – *v reg sep* put up

Auftrag (-träge) – *nm* order

  im Auftrag von (+ dat) – on behalf of

aufwachen* – *v reg sep* wake up

aufwachsen* – *v irreg sep* grow up

sich aufwärmen – *v reg refl sep* warm up

Auf Wiederhören! – *excl* Goodbye! (phone)

Auf Wiedersehen! – *excl* Goodbye!

Aufzug (-züge) – *nm* lift

Auge (-n) – *nnt* eye

  unter vier Augen – between you and me, in private

Augenblick (-e) – *nm* moment, instant

  im Augenblick – at this moment

Augenbraue (-n) – *nf* eyebrow

Augenzeuge (-n) – *nm wk* eye witness

Augenzeugin (-nen) – *nf* eye witness

August – *nm* August

  im August – in August

Aula (Aulen) – *nf* hall (school)

aus (+ dat) – *prep* from, out of

  die Schule ist aus – school's finished

aus – *adv* off (electrical)

  aus Backstein – made of brick

  aus Holz – made of wood

  aus Papier – made of paper

  aus Stein – built of stone

  aus zweiter Hand – second-hand

Ausbildung (-en) – *nf* education, training

Ausblick (-e) – *nm* view

Ausdruck (-e) – *nm* expression

Ausfahrt (-en) – *nf* exit, way out

ausfallen* – *v irreg sep* be cancelled

Ausflug (-flüge) – *nm* excursion

ausführen – *v reg sep* lead out

  den Hund ausführen – *v reg sep* walk the dog

Ausführung (-en) – *nf* version

ausfüllen – *v reg sep* fill in

  ein Formular ausfüllen – *v reg sep* fill in a form

Ausgang (-gänge) – *nm* exit, way out

ausgeben – *v irreg sep* spend (money)

ausgebucht – *adj* fully booked

ausgehen* mit (+ dat) – *v irreg sep* go out with

ausgehen* – *v irreg sep* go out (light)

ausgezeichnet – *adj* excellent

aushalten – *v irreg sep* put up with

aushelfen (+ dat) – *v irreg sep* help s.o. out

Aushilfe – *nf* temporary work
  als Aushilfe arbeiten – *v reg* †
  work on a temporary basis

auskommen* mit (+ dat) – *v irreg sep* manage, get on with
  gut auskommen* mit (+ dat) –
  v irreg sep get on well with (friends)

Auskunft (-en) – *nf* information
  um Auskunft bitten – *v irreg* ask
  for information

Auskunftsbüro (-s) – *nnt* information office

Ausland – *nnt* abroad
  im Ausland sein* – *v irreg* to be abroad
  ins Ausland fahren* – *v irreg* to go abroad

Ausländer (-) – *nm* foreigner

Ausländerin (-nen) – *nf* foreigner

ausländisch – *adj* foreign

ausmachen – *v reg sep* put out (light)

Ausnahme (-n) – *nf* exception

auspacken – *v reg sep* unpack

Auspuff (-e) – *nm* exhaust (car)

Ausrede (-n) – *nf* excuse

ausrichten – *v reg sep* † deliver, pass on (message)

ausrufen – *v irreg sep* exclaim

Ausrufezeichen (-) – *nnt* exclamation mark (!)

sich ausruhen – *v reg refl sep* rest

Ausrüstung (-en) – *nf* equipment

ausrutschen* – *v reg sep* slip

Aussage (-n) – *nf* statement

ausschalten – *v reg sep* † switch off

ausschimpfen – *v reg sep* scold

(sich) ausschlafen – *v irreg (refl) sep* have a lie in

Aussehen (-) – *nnt* appearance

aussehen – *v irreg sep* look

aus sein* – *v irreg* be extinguished

Außen (-) – *nm* winger (sport)

Außenseite (-n) – *nf* outside

außer (+ dat) – *prep* apart from, except
  außer Atem – out of breath
  außer Betrieb – out of order, not working
  außer Sicht – out of sight

außerdem – *adv* besides

außergewöhnlich – *adj* extraordinary

außerhalb von (+ dat) – *prep* outside

Aussicht (-en) – *nf* view

aussprechen – *v irreg sep* pronounce

ausstehen – *v irreg sep* put up with
  Ich kann sie nicht ausstehen –
  I can't stand her

aussteigen* aus (+ dat) – *v irreg sep* get off (bus, etc)

Ausstellung (-en) – *nf* exhibition

Ausstieg (-e) – *nm* exit (bus, tram)

Austausch – *nm* school exchange
  einen Austausch machen –
  v reg go on an exchange

austauschen – *v reg sep* exchange

Austauschpartner (-) – *nm* exchange partner

Austauschpartnerin (-nen) – *nf* exchange partner

austragen – *v irreg sep* deliver

Australien – *nnt* Australia

Ausverkauf – *nm* sale

Auswahl – *nf* choice

---

auswählen – *v reg sep* choose, pick (out)
Auswärtsspiel (-e) – *nnt* away game
Ausweis (-e) – *nm* identity card
auswendig – *adj* by heart
ausziehen – *v irreg sep* take off (clothes)
sich ausziehen – *v irreg refl sep* get undressed
Auto (-s) – *nnt* car
Autobahn (-en) – *nf* motorway
Autofahrer (-) – *nm* motorist
Autofahrerin (-nen) – *nf* motorist

Automat (-en) – *nm wk* slot machine
automatisch – *adj* automatic
Autor (-en) – *nm* author
Autorin (-nen) – *nf* authoress
Autoschlüssel (-) – *nm* car key
Autositz (-e) – *nm* car seat
Autotelefon (-e) – *nnt* car phone
Autoverleih – *nm* car hire
Autowaschstraße (-n) – *nf* car wash
Autsch! – *excl* Ouch! Ow!
Avocado(-s) – *nf* avocado pear

B

Baby (-s) – *nnt* baby
babysitten gehen* – *v irreg* go babysitting
Babysitter (-) – *nm* babysitter
Bach (Bäche) – *nm* stream
Backe (-n) – *nf* cheek (face, bottom)
backen – *v irreg* bake
Bäcker (-) – *nm* baker
Bäckerei (-en) – *nf* baker's shop
Bäckerin (-nen) – *nf* baker
Backofen (-öfen) – *nm* oven
Backstein (-e) – *nm* brick
Bad (Bäder) – *nnt* bath
Badeanzug (-züge) – *nm* swimsuit
Badehose (-n) – *nf* bathing trunks
Badekappe (-n) – *nf* bathing cap
Baden – *nnt* bathing
baden – *v reg* † bathe, bath
sich baden – *v reg refl* † have a bath
Badeort (-e) – *nm* seaside resort, spa
Badetuch (-tücher) – *nnt* bath towel
Badewanne (-n) – *nf* bath (tub)
Badezimmer (-) – *nnt* bathroom
Badminton – *nnt* badminton

Bahn (-en) – *nf* railway
Bahnhof (-höfe) – *nm* railway station
Bahnsteig (-e) – *nm* platform
Bahnübergang (-gänge) – *nm* level crossing
bald – *adv* soon
Bis bald! – See you soon!
so bald wie möglich – as soon as possible
Balkon (-s) – *nm* balcony
Ball (Bälle) – *nm* ball
Ballett (-e) – *nnt* ballet
Ballon (-s) – *nm* balloon
Banane (-n) – *nf* banana
Band (-s) – *nf* band (group)
Bangladesch – *nnt* Bangladesh
Bank (-en) – *nf* bank
Bank (Bänke) – *nf* bench
Bankkonto (-konten) – *nnt* bank account
Banknote (-n) – *nf* bank-note
Bankraub (-räube) – *nm* bank robbery
Bar (-s) – *nf* bar (drinks)

---

nm - noun masculine   *nf* - noun feminine   *nnt* - noun neuter   *npl* - noun plural
nom- nominative   *acc* - accusative   *gen* - genitive   *dat* - dative

bar bezahlen – *v reg* † pay cash
Bär (-en) – *nm wk* bear
Bardame (-n) – *nf* barmaid
barfuß – *adj* barefoot
Bargeld – *nnt* cash (not a cheque)
Barmann (-männer) – *nm* barman
Bart (Bärte) – *nm* beard
 mit Bart – bearded
Basel – Basle
basiert auf (+ dat) – *adj* based on
Basis (Basen) – *nf* basis
Basketball – *nm* basketball
basteln – *v reg* do DIY
Batterie (-n) – *nf* battery
Bauarbeiter (-) – *nm* construction worker
Bauarbeiterin (-nen) – *nf* construction worker
Bauch (Bäuche) – *nm* stomach
Bauchschmerzen – *npl* stomach ache
Bauchweh – *nnt coll* stomach ache
bauen – *v reg* build
Bauer (-n) – *nm wk* farmer
Bäuerin (-nen) – *nf* female farmer
Bauernhaus (-häuser) – *nnt* farmhouse
Bauernhof (-höfe) – *nm* farm
Baum (Bäume) – *nm* tree
Baumwolle – *nf* cotton
 aus Baumwolle – made of cotton
Baustelle (-n) – *nf* roadworks, building site
Bauunternehmer (-) – *nm* builder
bayerisch – *adj* Bavarian
Bayern – *nnt* Bavaria
beachten – *v reg* † respect
Beamte – *nm* ‡ official
Beamtin (-nen) – *nf* official
beängstigend – *adj* scary
beantworten – *v reg* † reply to s.o
Becher (-) – *nm* mug (cup)

sich bedanken bei jdm – *v reg refl* † thank s.o.
bedauern – *v reg* † regret
bedeckt mit (+ dat) – *adj* covered with
bedeuten – *v reg* † mean
 Was bedeutet...? – What does...mean?
bedienen – *v reg* † serve
sich bedienen – *v reg refl* † serve oneself
Bedienung – *nf* service (restaurant)
Bedienung inbegriffen – service included
Bedienung (nicht) inklusive – service (not) included
Bedingung (-en) – *nf* condition (of agreement)
bedrohen – *v reg* † threaten
sich beeilen – *v reg refl* † hurry, be quick
 Beeil dich! – *excl* Hurry up!
beenden – *v reg* † finish, end
Befehl (-e) – *nm* order
befehlen – *v irreg* order
sich befinden – *v irreg refl* be situated
beflecken – *v reg* † stain
befragen – *v reg* † question s.o.
befreundet sein* mit (+ dat) – *v irreg* be good friends with
befriedigen – *v reg* † satisfy
befriedigend – *adj* satisfactory
begabt – *adj* gifted
Begabung (-en) – *nf* talent, flair
begegnen* (+ dat) – *v reg* † meet (by chance)
begehen – *v irreg* commit
 ein Verbrechen begehen – *v irreg* commit an offence
begeistert von (+ dat) – *adj* enthusiastic about
Begeisterung – *nf* enthusiasm
begießen – *v irreg* water (plants)

---

adj - adjective   *v reg* - verb regular   *v sep* - verb separable   † - see verb info
prep - preposition   *v irreg* - verb irregular   *v refl* - verb reflexive   * - takes sein

Beginn – *nm* start, beginning
beginnen – *v irreg* begin
begleiten – *v reg* † accompany
begleitet von (+ dat) – *adj* accompanied by
begonnen – *see beginnen*
im Begriff sein* – *v irreg* be about to
begrüßen – *v reg* † greet
behalten – *v irreg* keep
behandeln – *v reg* † treat (medical)
Behandlung (-en) – *nf* treatment
behilflich – *adj* helpful
behindert – *adj* handicapped
Behörde (-n) – *nf* authorities
bei (+ dat) – *prep* at the home of
  bei mir – at my house
beide – *adj* both
Beifall – *nm* applause
beilegen – *v reg sep* enclose
Bein (-e) – *nnt* leg
  sich das Bein brechen – *v irreg dat refl* break one's leg
beinahe – *adv* almost
beißen – *v irreg* bite
Beispiel (-e) – *nnt* example
  zum Beispiel – for example
beitreten* (+ dat) – *v irreg sep* join (club)
bekam – *see bekommen*
bekannt – *adj* known
Bekannte – *nmf* ‡ acquaintance
Bekanntmachung (-en) – *nf* notice, information
sich beklagen über (+ acc) – *v reg refl* † complain about
bekommen – *v irreg* receive, get
beladen – *adj* loaded (goods)
belasten – *v reg* † burden
belegt – *adj* no vacancies
beleidigen – *v reg* † offend, insult
beleidigt – *adj* offended
Belgien – *nnt* Belgium

Belgier (-) – *nm* Belgian person
Belgierin (-nen) – *nf* Belgian person
belgisch – *adj* Belgian
beliebt – *adj* popular
bellen – *v reg* bark
Belohnung (-en) – *nf* reward
bemerkbar – *adj* noticeable
bemerken – *v reg* † notice
benachbart – *adj* neighbouring
sich benehmen – *v irreg refl* behave
beneiden – *v reg* † envy
benutzen – *v reg* † use, make use of
Benutzer (-) – *nm* user
Benutzerin (-nen) – *nf* user
Benutzung – *nf* use
Benzin – *nnt* petrol
  bleifreies Benzin – *nnt* unleaded petrol
  eine Benzinpanne haben – *v irreg* run out of petrol
beobachten – *v reg* † keep an eye on
bequem – *adj* comfortable
beraten – *v irreg* advise
Berater (-) – *nm* advisor
Beraterin (-nen) – *nf* advisor
bereit – *adj* ready, willing
Berg (-e) – *nm* mountain
  in den Bergen – in the mountains
bergab fahren* – *v irreg* go downhill
Bergarbeiter (-) – *nm* miner
bergauf – *adv* uphill
Bergrad (-räder) – *nnt* mountain bike
Bergsteigen – *nnt* mountain climbing
Bergsteiger (-) – *nm* mountaineer
Bergsteigerin (-nen) – *nf* mountaineer
Bericht (-e) – *nm* report
Berliner (-) – *nm* doughnut, Berliner
die Berliner Mauer – the Berlin Wall
bersten* – *v irreg* burst
Beruf (-e) – *nm* occupation

Was sind Sie von Beruf? –
What is your occupation?
beruflich – *adj* professional
Berufs~ – *pref* occupational
Berufsberatung – *nf* careers advice
Berufsfachschulreife – *nf* GNVQ
level 2
Berufspläne – *npl* career plans
Berufspraktikum (-praktika) –
nnt work experience
Berufsschule (-n) – *nf* college (FE)
Berufswunsch (-wünsche) – *nm*
preferred choice of career
sich beruhigen – *v reg refl* † calm
o.s. down
berühmt – *adj* famous
berühren – *v reg* † touch
beschädigt – *adj* damaged
sich beschäftigen – *v reg refl* †
busy o.s.
beschäftigt – *adj* busy
beschäftigt sein* – *v irreg* be busy
beschämend – *adj* shameful
beschämt – *adj* ashamed
Bescherung (-en) – *nf* giving out of
Christmas presents
beschließen – *v irreg* decide to
Beschränkung (-en) – *nf* limit,
restriction
beschreiben – *v irreg* describe
Beschreibung (-en) – *nf* description
sich beschweren über (+ acc) –
v reg refl † complain about
Besen (-) – *nm* broom
besetzt – *adj* occupied (table, seat),
engaged (toilet)
besichtigen – *v reg* † visit (tourist
attraction)
besitzen – *v irreg* own
Besitzer (-) – *nm* owner
Besitzerin (-nen) – *nf* owner
besondere – *adj* particular, special
besonders – *adv* especially

besser – *adj* better
Gute Besserung! – Get well soon!
bestätigen – *v reg* † confirm
beste – *adj* best
mit besten Wünschen – best
wishes
Beste – *nmf* ‡ best
sein Bestes tun – do one's best
Besteck – *nnt* cutlery
bestehen – *v irreg* pass an exam
eine Prüfung nicht bestehen –
v irreg fail an exam
bestehen aus (+ dat) – *v irreg*
consist of
bestellen – *v reg* † order (restaurant)
Bestellung (-en) – *nf* order
(restaurant)
bestimmt – *adj* definite
bestrafen – *v reg* † punish
Besuch (-e) – *nm* visit
Wir haben Besuch – We have
visitors
besuchen – *v reg* † visit, attend school
Ich besuche eine Gesamtschule –
I go to a comprehensive school
Besucher (-) – *nm* visitor, tourist
Besucherin (-nen) – *nf* visitor,
tourist
Besuchszeit (-en) – *nf* visiting time
Beton – *nm* concrete
aus Beton – made of concrete
betreffen – *v irreg* concern
betreten – *v irreg* enter on foot
Betrieb (-e) – *nm* business
außer Betrieb – out of order, not
working
in Betrieb – working
betrunken – *adj* drunk
Bett (-en) – *nnt* bed
ins Bett gehen* – *v irreg* go to
bed
betteln – *v reg* beg
Bettwäsche – *nf, no pl* bedding

Bettzeug – *nnt, no pl* bedclothes
sich beugen – *v reg refl* bow
Beutel (-) – *nm* purse, pouch, bag
  Teebeutel (-) – *nm* tea bag
bevor – *sub conj* before
bewegen – *v reg* † move
Bewegung (-en) – *nf* movement
  körperliche Bewegung (-en) –
  nf exercise (sport)
Beweis (-e) – *nm* evidence
beweisen – *v irreg* prove
sich bewerben um (+ acc) –
  v irreg refl apply for
Bewerber (-) – *nm* applicant
Bewerberin (-nen) – *nf* applicant
Bewerbung (-en) – *nf* job
  application
Bewohner (-) – *nm* occupant
Bewohnerin (-nen) – *nf* occupant
bewölkt – *adj* cloudy
bewundern – *v reg* † admire
bewußtlos – *adj* unconscious
bezahlen – *v reg* † pay (for)
bezahlt – *adj* paid
  gut bezahlt – *adj* well-paid
Bezahlung (-en) – *nf* payment
in bezug auf (+ acc) – *prep*
  concerning
BH (Büstenhalter) – *nm* bra
Bibel – *nf* Bible
Bibliothek (-en) – *nf* library
Bibliothekar (-e) – *nm* librarian
Bibliothekarin (-nen) – *nf* librarian
Bidet (-s) – *nnt* bidet
biegen – *v irreg* bend
Biene (-n) – *nf* bee
Bier (-e) – *nnt* beer
  Bier vom Faß – draught beer
Bierdeckel (-) – *nm* beermat
Bierkrug (-krüge) – *nm* beer mug
bieten – *v irreg* offer
Bikini (-s) – *nm* bikini

Bild (-er) – *nnt* picture
Bildschirm (-e) – *nm* screen (TV)
billig – *adj* cheap
billigen – *v reg* approve of
bin – *see sein**
binden – *v irreg* bind, fasten
Bindestrich (-e) – *nm* hyphen, dash
Biologie – *nf* biology
Birne (-n) – *nf* pear; light bulb
bis (+ acc) – *prep* till, until
Bis bald! – See you soon!
Bis heute abend! – See you this
  evening!
Bis morgen! – See you tomorrow!
Bis Samstag! – See you on Saturday!
Bis später! – See you later!
bis zu (+ dat) – *prep* as far as
  bis zur Ampel – as far as the
  traffic lights
Biß (Bisse) – *nm* bite
ein bißchen – a little
bist – *see sein**
bitte – please
  bitte sehr – it's a pleasure
  bitte wenden (b.w.) – see over
Bitte (-n) – *nf* request
bitten um (+ acc) – *v irreg* ask for
  um Auskunft bitten – *v irreg* ask
  for information
bitter – *adj* bitter
Blase (-n) – *nf* blister, bladder
blasen – *v irreg* blow
Blaskapelle (-n) – *nf* brass band
blaß – *adj* pale (complexion)
Blatt (Blätter) – *nnt* leaf
Blatt Papier – *nnt* sheet of paper
blau – *adj* blue
blechen – *v reg coll* fork out, cough up
Blei – *nnt* lead (metal)
bleiben* – *v irreg* stay
  Bleiben Sie am Apparat, bitte!
  – *excl* Hold the line please!

---

nm - noun masculine   *nf* - noun feminine   *nnt* - noun neuter   *npl* - noun plural
nom- nominative   *acc* - accusative   *gen* - genitive   *dat* - dative

sitzen bleiben* – *v irreg* repeat a year (at school)

bleifrei – *adj* unleaded (petrol)

Bleistift (-e) – *nm* pencil

Bleistiftspitzer (-) – *nm* pencil sharpener

Blick (-e) – *nm* view

blicken (auf + acc) – *v reg* look (at)

blieb – *see bleiben*

blind – *adj* blind

Blinddarmentzündung (-en) – *nf* appendicitis

Blinker (-) – *nm* indicator (car)

Blitz (-e) – *nm* flash of lightning

blitzen – *v reg* flash (lightning)

es blitzt – *v reg* it's lightning

blitzsauber – *adj* spotless

Block (Blöcke) – *nm* block

Blockflöte (-n) – *nf* recorder, flute

blockieren – *v reg* † block

blöd – *adj* stupid

Blödsinn – *nm, no pl* nonsense

blond – *adj* fair-haired, blonde

bloß – *adv* merely

Blouson (-s) – *nm* blouson jacket

Blume (-n) – *nf* flower

Blumenbeet (-e) – *nnt* flower bed

Blumenkohl – *nm* cauliflower

Blumenstrauß (-sträuße) – *nm* bunch of flowers

Bluse (-n) – *nf* blouse

Blut – *nnt* blood

Blutdruck – *nm, no pl* blood pressure

Bluttat (-en) – *nf* violent deed

bluten – *v reg* † bleed

Bockwurst (-würste) – *nf* frankfurter

Boden (Böden) – *nm* ground, floor

auf dem Boden – on the ground

Bodensee – *nm* Lake Constance

Bogenschießen (-) – *nnt* archery

Bohne (-n) – *nf* bean

grüne Bohne (-n) – *nf* French bean

Bombe (-n) – *nf* bomb

Bombenalarm (-e) – *nm* bomb scare

Bon (-s) – *nm* coupon

Bonbon (-s) – *nnt* sweet

Boot (-e) – *nnt* boat

Boot fahren* – *v irreg* go boating

Bootsfahrt (-en) – *nf* boat trip

an Bord – *adv* on board

an Bord gehen* – *v irreg* board a ship

böse – *adj* angry, wicked

böse mit (+ dat) – *adj* angry, cross with

Böse – *nnt* evil

böse werden* – *v irreg* get angry

böswillig – *adj* malicious

Boxsport – *nm* boxing

brach – *see brechen*

brachte – *see bringen*

Brand (Brände) – *nm* fire (accidental or malicious)

Brandung – *nf* surf

Brandwunde (-n) – *nf* burn

braten – *v irreg* fry, roast

Braten – *nm* joint of meat

Brathähnchen (-) – *nnt* roast chicken

Bratkartoffeln – *npl* fried potatoes

Bratsche (-n) – *nf* viola

Bratwurst (-würste) – *nf* fried sausage

Brauch (Bräuche) – *nm* use, custom

brauchen – *v reg* need, use

braun – *adj* brown

Braut (Bräute) – *nf* bride

Bräutigam (-e) – *nm* bridegroom

Brautjungfer (-n) – *nf* bridesmaid

brav – *adj* good, well-behaved

BRD – Federal Republic of Germany

brechen – *v irreg* break

sich das Bein brechen – *v irreg dat refl* break one's leg

breit – *adj* wide, broad

Breite (-n) – *nf* width

Bremse (-n) – *nf* brake

bremsen – *v reg* brake

brennen – *v irreg* burn, go up in flames

es brennt – there is a fire

Brett (-er) – *nnt* board, plank

Brettspiel (-e) – *nnt* board game

Brezel (-n) – *nf* pretzel

Brief (-e) – *nm* letter (post)

Brieffreund (-e) – *nm* pen-friend

Brieffreundin (-nen) – *nf* pen-friend

Briefkasten (-kästen) – *nm* letter box

Briefmarke (-n) – *nf* stamp

Briefpapier (-e) – *nnt* note paper

Brieftasche (-n) – *nf* wallet

Briefträger (-) – *nm* postman

Briefträgerin (-nen) – *nf* postwoman

Briefumschlag (-schläge) – *nm* envelope

Briefwechsel (-) – *nm* correspondence

Brille (-n) – *nf* glasses

bringen – *v irreg* bring, take

Brite (-n) – *nm wk* British person

Britin (-nen) – *nf* British person

britisch – *adj* British

die Britischen Inseln – *npl* the British Isles

Brombeere (-n) – *nf* blackberry

Bronzemedaille – *nf* bronze medal

Broschüre (-n) – *nf* leaflet

Brot (-e) – *nnt* bread

belegtes Brot – *nnt* open sandwich

Brötchen (-) – *nnt* roll (bread)

Brotdose (-n) – *nf* lunch box

Brücke (-n) – *nf* bridge

Bruder (Brüder) – *nm* brother

Brunnen (-) – *nm* well (water)

Brüssel – Brussels

Brust (Brüste) – *nf* chest (body)

Bube (-n) – *nm wk* jack (cards)

Buch (Bücher) – *nnt* book

buchen – *v reg* book

Bücherei (-en) – *nf* bookshop

Bücherregal (-e) – *nnt* bookshelf

Bücherschrank (-schränke) – *nm* book case

Buchhandlung (-en) – *nf* bookshop

Buchstabe (-n) – *nm wk* letter (alphabet)

buchstabieren – *v reg* † spell

Bucht (-en) – *nf* bay (on coast)

sich bücken – *v reg refl* bend over

Bude (-n) – *nf* kiosk

büffeln – *v reg coll* swot

Büffet (-s) – *nnt* buffet

Bügeleisen (-) – *nnt* iron (clothes)

bügeln – *v reg* do ironing, iron

Bühne (-n) – *nf* stage

auf der Bühne sein* – *v irreg* be on the stage

bummeln* – *v reg* stroll

Bummelzug (-züge) – *nm coll* slow train

Bundes~ – *pref* federal, national

Bundesland (-länder) – *nnt* federal state

Bundesliga (-en) – *nf* German football league

Bundesrepublik – *nf* Federal Republic of Germany

Bundesstraße (-n) – *nf* major road

Bungalow (-s) – *nm* bungalow

bunt – *adj* multi-coloured

Burg (-en) – *nf* castle (fortified)

Bürgermeister (-) – *nm* mayor

Bürgermeisterin (-nen) – *nf* mayoress

Bürgersteig (-e) – *nm* pavement

Büro (-s) – *nnt* office

Büroklammer (-n) – *nf* paperclip
Bürste (-n) – *nf* brush
bürsten – *v reg* † brush
  sich die Haare bürsten – *v reg*
  dat refl † brush one's hair
Bus (-se) – *nm* bus
  in den Bus einsteigen* – *v irreg*
  sep get on the bus
Busbahnhof (-höfe) – *nm* bus
  station
Busfahrer (-) – *nm* bus driver

Busfahrerin (-nen) – *nf* bus driver
Bushaltestelle (-n) – *nf* bus stop
Buslinie (-n) – *nf* bus route
Butter – *nf* butter
Butterbrot (-e) – *nnt* sandwich
buttern – *v reg* spread (with butter,
  etc)
b.w. – (bitte wenden) turn over
bzw. – (beziehungsweise) or, that is

C

Café (-s) – *nnt* café
campen – *v reg* camp
Camper (-) – *nm* camper
Campingbus (-se) – *nm* motor home
Camping Carnet (-s) – *nnt* camping
  carnet
Campinggaz® – *nnt* camping gaz®
Campingkocher (-) – *nm* camping
  stove
Campingplatz (-plätze) – *nm*
  campsite
CD (-s) – *nf* CD
CD-ROM (-s) – *nm* CD ROM
CD-Spieler (-) – *nm* CD player
CD-Wechsler (-) – *nm* CD changer
Cello (-s) – *nnt* cello
Celsius – Celsius
Chance (-n) – *nf* chance, opportunity
Charakter (-e) – *nm* character
Chef (-s) – *nm* boss
Chefin (-nen) – *nf* boss
Chemie – *nf* chemistry (subject)
China – *nnt* China

Chinese – *nmf* ‡ Chinese person
chinesisch – *adj* Chinese
Chip (-s) – *nf* chip (micro)
Chipkarte (-n) – *nf* smart card
Chips – *npl* crisps
Chor (Chöre) – *nm* choir
Christ (-en) – *nm wk* Christian
Christin (-nen) – *nf* Christian
Clown (-s) – *nm* clown
Cola – *nf* Coca cola®, cola
Comic (-s) – *nm* cartoon, comic
Comic-Strip (-s) – *nm* cartoon strip
Computer (-) – *nm* computer
Computerspiel (-e) – *nnt* computer
  game
Couchtisch (-e) – *nm* coffee table
Cousine (-n) – *nf* cousin
Cousin (-s) – *nm* cousin
Creme (n) – *nf* cream (medical)
Cursor – *nm* cursor
Currywurst (-würste) – *nf* curried
  sausage

D

da – *adv* there
  da drüben – *adv* over there
da – *sub conj* since
dabei – *adv* with that, etc
Dach (Dächer) – *nnt* roof
Dachboden (-böden) – *nm* attic, loft
dachte – *see denken*
Dackel (-) – *nm* dachshund
dagegen – *adv* on the other hand
dahin – *adv* there (motion)
damals – *adv* at that time
Dame – *nf* draughts
Dame (-n) – *nf* lady
Damen – Ladies' toilets
Damenbinde (-n) – *nf* sanitary towel
Damenkonfektion – *nf* ladies'
  clothes department
damit – *adv* with that
Dampf – *nm* steam
Damfper (-) – *nm* steamer (ship)
danach – *adv* then
Däne (-n) – *nm wk* Dane
Dänemark – *nnt* Denmark
Dänin (-nen) – *nf* Dane
dänisch – *adj* Danish
dank (+ gen/dat) – *prep* thanks to
dankbar (+ dat) – *adj* grateful (to)
danke – *adv* thank you
  danke sehr – thank you very much
  danke schön – thank you very much
  (nein) danke – no thank you
  Nichts zu danken! – You're
    welcome!
  Vielen Dank – Thank you very
    much
danken (+ dat) – *v reg* thank
dann – *adv* then
dann und wann – *adv* from time to
  time
darauf – *adv* then

darf – *see dürfen*
das – *pron nt* the, *rel pron nt* who, which
  Das geht – That's OK
  Das macht.... – That'll be (+ price)
  Das stimmt – That's right
daß – *sub conj* that
Datei (-en) – *nf* file (computer)
Daten – *npl* data
Datenautobahn (-en) – *nf*
  information super highway
Datenbank (-en) – *nf* database
Datum (Daten) – *nnt* date
Dauer – *nf* length (time)
Dauerkarte (-n) – *nf* season ticket
dauern – *v reg* last
Daumen (-) – *nm* thumb
dazu – *adv* with that
DB (Deutsche Bundesbahn) – *nf*
  German railways
DDR – *nf* East Germany
  in der ehemaligen DDR – in the
    former East Germany
Debatte (-n) – *nf* debate
Decke (-n) – *nf* blanket, ceiling
Deckel (-) – *nm* lid (top)
decken – *v reg* cover
  den Tisch decken – *v reg* set the
    table
Defekt (-) – *nm* fault (defect)
dein – *poss adj sing* your (informal)
Dein – *poss adj* With best wishes from
  (male, informal)
Deine – *poss adj* With best wishes
  from (female, informal)
dekorieren – *v reg* † decorate (shop
  window)
Delikatessengeschäft (-e) – *nnt*
  delicatessen
Demonstration (-en) – *nf*
  demonstration
demonstrieren – *v reg* † demonstrate

---

nm - noun masculine   *nf* - noun feminine   *nnt* - noun neuter   *npl* - noun plural
nom- nominative   *acc* - accusative   *gen* - genitive   *dat* - dative

den 12. November – 12th of November (letter heading)

denken – *v irreg* think

denken an (+ acc) – *v irreg* think of
Ich denke nicht daran! – Not likely!

Denkmal (-mäler) – *nnt* monument

denn – *co-ord conj* for

deprimierend – *adj* depressing

deprimiert – *adj* depressed

der – *pron m* the, *rel pron m* who, which, that

derselbe – *dem pron* the same

deshalb – *adv* therefore

Designer (-) – *nm* designer

Designerin (-nen) – *nf* designer

deswegen – *adv* consequently

Detektiv (-e) – *nm* detective

Detektivfilm (-e) – *nm* detective film

deutlich – *adv* clearly

deutsch – *adj* German
    auf deutsch – in German
    Wie sagt man ... auf deutsch?
    – How do you say ... in German?

Deutsch – *nnt* German (language)
    Seit wann lernst du Deutsch? – How long have you been learning German?

Deutsch sprechen – *v irreg* speak German

Deutsche Bundesbahn (DB) – *nf* German railways

Deutsche – *nmf* ‡ German person
    Er ist kein Deutscher – He's not German

Deutschland – *nnt* Germany

Dezember – *nm* December
    im Dezember – in December

d.h. (das heißt) – i.e. (that is)

Dia (-s) – *nnt* slide (transparency)

Diät (-en) – *nf* diet

dich – *pron acc sing* you (informal)

dick – *adj* fat, thick

die – *def art f, pl* the; *rel pron f, pl* who, which, that

Dieb (-e) – *nm* thief

Diebin (-nen) – *nf* thief

Diebstahl – *nm* theft

Diele (-n) – *nf* hallway

dienen – *v reg* serve

Dienst (-e) – *nm* service (maintenance)

Dienstag – *nm* Tuesday
    am Dienstag – on Tuesday

diese – *dem pron* these, this

Diesel – *nm* diesel

dieser – *dem pron* this

diesig – *adj* hazy

diesmal – *adv* this time

Ding (-e) – *nnt* thing

Dingsbums – *nnt coll* whatsit

Dinosaurier (-) – *nm* dinosaur

Diplom (-e) – *nnt* diploma, university degree

dir – *pron dat sing* you, to you, yourself (singular, informal)

direkt – *adj* direct, straight

direkt – *adv* directly

Direktor (-en) – *nm* head teacher

Direktorin (-nen) – *nf* head teacher

Dirndl (-) – *nnt* dirndl dress

Disco (-s) – *nf* disco

Diskette (-n) – *nf* floppy disk

Diskettenlaufwerk (-e) – *nnt* disk drive

Disko (-s) – *nf coll* disco

Diskothek (-en) – *nf* discotheque

Diskussion (-en) – *nf* discussion

diskutieren über (+ acc) – *v reg* † discuss

DJH – *nf* German Youth Hostel

DM – *nf* Deutschmark, German currency

doch – *adv* yes, really

Doktor (-en) – *nm* academic doctor, PhD

Dokumentarfilm (-e) – *nm*
documentary

Dokumentarsendung (-en) – *nf*
documentary programme

dolmetschen – *v reg* interpret

Dolmetscher (-) – *nm* interpreter

Dolmetscherin (-nen) – *nf*
interpreter

Dom (-e) – *nm* cathedral

Donau – *nf* River Danube

Donner – *nm* thunder

donnern – *v reg* thunder

Donnerstag – *nm* Thursday
  am Donnerstag – on Thursday

doof – *adj coll* stupid

Doppel- – *pref* double

Doppelbett (-en) – *nnt* double bed

Doppeldecker (-) – *nm* double
decker

Doppelhaus (-häuser) – *nnt* semi-
detached house

Doppelpunkt (-e) – *nm* colon (:)

doppelt – *adv* doubly

Doppelzimmer (-) – *nnt* double
room

Dorf (Dörfer) – *nnt* village

dort – *adv* there (position towards)

dort drüben – *adv* over there

dort oben – *adv* up there

Dose (-n) – *nf* tin, can

Dosenöffner (-) – *nm* tin opener

Dosis (Dosen) – *nf* dose

Drachen (-) – *nm* kite

Drachenfliegen – *nnt* hang gliding

Drama (Dramen) – *nnt* drama

Drama machen – *v reg* do drama

dransein* – *v irreg sep* have your
turn
  Wer ist dran? – Who's next?

draußen – *adv* outdoors, outside

Dreck – *nm* dirt

dreckig – *adj* dirty

drehen – *v reg* turn

drei – three

Dreieck (-e) – *nnt* triangle

dreimal – *adv* three times

dreißig – *adj* thirty

dreißigste – *adj* thirtieth

Dreiviertel (-) – *nnt* three quarters

Dreiviertelstunde (-n) – *nf* three
quarters of an hour

dreizehn – *adj* thirteen

dressieren – *v reg* † train (animal)

dringend – *adj* urgent

Dringlichkeit – *nf* urgency

drinnen – *adv* indoors, inside

Drittel (-) – *nnt* third (fraction)

dritte – *adj* third (in order)

Droge (-n) – *nf* drug (narcotic)

drogenabhängig – *adj* drug-
dependent

Drogenabhängige – *nmf* ‡ drug
addict

Drogenopfer (-) – *nnt* drugs victim

drogensüchtig – *adj* addicted to
drugs

Drogenszene (-n) – *nf* drugs scene

Drogerie (-n) – *nf* chemist, drug store

Drogist (-en) – *nm wk* chemist

Drogistin (-nen) – *nf* chemist

Druckbuchstabe (-n) – *nm wk*
block letter

drucken – *v reg* print

drücken – *v reg* push, press

Drucker (-) – *nm* printer

Dschungel (-) – *nm* jungle

du – *pron nom sing* you (informal)

dumm – *adj* stupid

Dummheit (-en) – *nf* silly mistake
  eine Dummheit begehen –
  v irreg do something stupid

dunkel – *adj* dark

dunkelblau – *adj* navy blue

dünn – *adj* thin

durch (+ acc) – *prep* through

Durcheinander – *nnt* mess
durcheinander – *adv* in a mess
durchfahren* – *v irreg sep* go direct (train)
Durchfahrt (-en) – *nf* through way
Durchfahrt verboten – no entry
Durchfall – *nm* diarrhoea
durchfallen* – *v irreg sep* fail
   in einer Prüfung durchfallen* – *v irreg sep* fail an exam
Durchgang (-gänge) – *nm* way through
Durchgangszug (-züge) – *nm* express train, through train
gut durchgebraten – *adj* well-cooked (steak)
durchgefallen – *adj* failed
durchnäßt – *adj* soaked
   völlig durchnäßt – *adj* soaked to the skin
durchnehmen – *v irreg sep* do, learn at school

sich durchschlagen – *v irreg refl sep* cope
sich gut durchschlagen – *v irreg refl sep* do well
Durchschnitt (-e) – *nm* average
durchschnittlich – *adj* average
durchstreichen – *v irreg sep* cross out
durchsuchen – *v reg insep* search
dürfen – *v irreg* be allowed, may
durfte – *see dürfen*
Durst – *nm* thirst
Durst haben – *v irreg* be thirsty
   Ich habe Durst – I am thirsty
durstig – *adj* thirsty
Dusche (-n) – *nf* shower
sich duschen – *v reg refl* have a shower
Düsenflugzeug (-e) – *nnt* jet
düster – *adj* gloomy
Dutzend (-e) – *nnt* dozen
D-Zug (D-Züge) – *nm* express train, through train

E

E111-Schein (-e) – *nm* E111 form
Ebbe (-n) – *nf* tide (low)
eben – *adv* just
ebenso – *adv* just as
ebenso ... wie – *adv* just as ... as
echt – *adj* real, genuine
Ecke (-n) – *nf* corner
   an der Ecke – at the corner of
   um die Ecke gehen* – *v irreg* go round a corner
eckig – *adj* square, angular, awkward
Edel~ – high quality
Edelstein (-e) – *nm* jewel
Edinburg – Edinburgh
EDV-Bearbeiter (-) – *nm* computer operator

EG – *nf* EC (European Community)
egal – *adj* equal
   Es ist mir egal – I don't mind
egoistisch – *adj* selfish
ehe – *sub conj* before
Ehe (-n) – *nf* marriage
Ehefrau (-en) – *nf* wife
ehemalig – *adj* ex-, former, previous
Ehemann (-männer) – *nm* husband
Ehepaar (-e) – *nnt* married couple
eher – rather, sooner *adv*
Ehre (-n) – *nf* honour
ehrlich – *adj* honest
Ei (-er) – *nnt* egg

---

adj - adjective	*v reg* - verb regular	*v sep* - verb separable	† - see verb info
prep - preposition	*v irreg* - verb irregular	*v refl* - verb reflexive	* - takes sein

ein gekochtes Ei – a boiled egg
ein hartgekochtes Ei – a hard
boiled egg
Eiche (-n) – *nf* oak tree
eifersüchtig auf (+ acc) – *adj*
jealous of
eigen – *adj* own
Eigenname (-n) – *nm wk* proper
noun
Eigentum – *nnt, no pl* belongings
Eile – *nf* hurry
eilen* – *v reg* hurry
eilig – *adj* hurried
es eilig haben – *v irreg* be in a hurry
Ich habe es eilig – I am in a hurry
Eilzug (-züge) – *nm* local train
Eimer (-) – *nm* bucket
ein – *indef art m, nt* a, an
ein bißchen – *pron inv* a little
ein paar – *pron inv* some
einander – *pron* each other
Einbahnstraße (-n) – *nf* one way
street
Einbildung (-en) – *nf* imagination
einbrechen* – *v irreg sep* break in,
burgle
Einbrecher (-) – *nm* burglar
Eindruck (-e) – *nm* impression
eindrucksvoll – *adj* impressive
eine – *indef art f* a, an
einem – *pron dat sing* you (persons
unspecified)
einen – *pron acc sing* you (persons
unspecified)
einerseits – *adv* on the one hand
eines Tages – one day
einfach – *adj* easy
einmal einfach nach Hamburg
– a single to Hamburg
einfache Fahrkarte (-n) – *nf* single
ticket
Einfahrt (-en) – *nf* entrance, drive
(road in)

Einfahrt freihalten! – Keep
entrance clear!
einfallen* – *v irreg sep* occur to
es fällt mir ein, daß ... – it
occurs to me that ...
Einfamilienhaus (-häuser) – *nnt*
detached house
Einführungsbrief (-e) – *nm* letter of
introduction
Eingang (-gänge) – *nm* entrance,
way in
eingebildet – *adj* snobbish
eingeschlafen – *adj* asleep
Einheit (-en) – *nf* unit, unity
der Tag der deutschen Einheit
– *nm* Day of German Unity
(3rd October)
einige – *adj* some
Einkäufe machen – *v reg* do the
shopping
einkaufen – *v reg sep* shop
einkaufen gehen* – *v irreg* do the
shopping
Einkaufen – *nnt* shopping
einen Einkaufsbummel machen
– *v reg* go round the shops
Einkaufsliste (-n) – *nf* shopping list
Einkaufspassage (-n) – *nf* arcade
(shops)
Einkaufstasche (-n) – *nf* shopping bag
Einkaufswagen (-) – *nm* trolley
(supermarket)
Einkaufszentrum (-zentren) – *nnt*
shopping centre
einladen – *v irreg sep* invite, ask s.o.
for dinner, etc
Freunde einladen – *v irreg sep*
have friends round
Einladung (-en) – *nf* invitation
sich einleben – *v reg refl sep* settle
down
einlösen – *v reg sep* cash in

---

nm - noun masculine   *nf* - noun feminine   *nnt* - noun neuter   *npl* - noun plural
nom- nominative   *acc* - accusative   *gen* - genitive   *dat* - dative

einen Scheck einlösen – *v reg sep* cash a cheque
einmal – *adv* once
einmal nach Dresden, hin und zurück – a return ticket to Dresden
einmalig – *adj* one off, unique
einordnen – *v reg sep* † sort, file
bitte einordnen – get in lane
einpacken – *v reg sep* wrap up (present)
als Geschenk einpacken – *v reg sep* gift wrap
einreiben – *v irreg sep* rub in (cream, fat)
Einrichtung (-en) – *nf* establishment
einsam – *adj* lonely
einschalten – *v reg sep* † switch on (light, radio)
einschenken – *v reg sep* pour a drink
einschl. – including
einschlafen* – *v irreg sep* fall asleep
einschließen – *v irreg sep* shut in
einschließlich – *adv* including
einschränken – *v reg sep* restrict
Einschreibebrief (-e) – *nm* registered letter
einsehen – *v irreg sep* understand, realise
einsteigen* in (+ acc) – *v irreg sep* get into (bus, etc)
in den Zug einsteigen* – *v irreg sep* get on the train
Einstieg (-e) – *nm* entry route
Eintopf – *nm* stew
eintreten* – *v irreg sep* enter
Eintritt (-e) – *nm* entrance (price)
Eintrittsgeld (-er) – *nnt* entrance fee
Eintrittskarte (-n) – *nf* entrance ticket
Eintrittsprüfung (-en) – *nf* entrance examination
einundzwanzig – *adj* twenty-one

einundzwanzigste – *adj* twenty-first
einverstanden – *adj* agreed
einwerfen – *v irreg sep* post
einen Brief einwerfen – *v irreg sep* post a letter
Einwohner (-) – *nm* inhabitant
Einwohnerin (-nen) – *nf* resident
Einwurf – *nm* post letters here
Einzel~ – *pref* single
Einzelbett (-en) – *nnt* single bed
Einzelheit (-en) – *nf* detail
Einzelkind (-er) – *nnt* only child
einzeln – *adj* individual
Einzelzimmer (-) – *nnt* single room
einziehen* – *v irreg sep* move in
einzig – *adj* single, only
Eis~ – *pref* ice
Eis – *nnt* ice, ice-cream
Schokoladeneis – *nnt* chocolate ice-cream
Vanilleeis – *nnt* vanilla ice-cream
Eisbahn (-en) – *nf* ice-rink
Eisbecher (-) – *nm* mixed ice cream
Eisen~ – *pref* iron (metal)
Eisenbahn (-en) – *nf* railway
Eisenwarengeschäft (-e) – *nnt* hardware shop
eisig – *adj* icy
eitel – *adj* vain (conceited)
Eitelkeit (-en) – *nf* vanity
ekelhaft – *adj* disgusting
eklig – *adj* revolting
Elefant (-en) – *nm wk* elephant
elegant – *adj* elegant
Elektriker (-) – *nm* electrician
elektrisch – *adj* electric(al)
Elektrizität – *nf* electricity
Elektro~ – *pref* electric(al)
Elektroherd (-e) – *nm* electric cooker
Elektronik – *nf* electronics
elf – *adj* eleven

---

elfte – *adj* eleventh
Elbe – *nf* River Elbe
Ellenbogen (-) – *nm* elbow
Eltern – *npl* parents
Empfang (Empfänge) – *nm* reception
Empfänger (-) – *nm* receiver
Empfangsdame (-n) – *nf* receptionist
empfehlen – *v irreg* recommend
empfindlich – *adj* sensitive
empfohlen – *adj* recommended
Ende (-n) – *nnt* end
  am Ende – at the end
  am Ende des Ganges – at the end of the corridor
  zu Ende – over, out (finished)
enden – *v reg* † end
endlich – *adv* at last
endlos – *adj* endless
Endspiel (-e) – *nnt* final (sport)
Endstation (-en) – *nf* terminus, end of line
Endsumme (-n) – *nf* total
Energie – *nf* energy
eng – *adj* narrow, tight
engagiert – *adj* committed, keen on
England – *nnt* England
Engländer (-) – *nm* Englishman
Engländerin (-nen) – *nf* Englishwoman
Englisch – *nnt* English (language)
  auf englisch – in English
englisch – *adj* English
englischsprachig – *adj* English speaking
Englischstunde (-n) – *nf* English lesson
Enkel (-) – *nm* grandson
Enkelin (-nen) – *nf* granddaughter
Enkelkind (-er) – *nnt* grandchild
enorm – *adj* immense
entdecken – *v reg* † discover

Ente (-n) – *nf* duck
entfalten – *v reg* † unfold
entfernen – *v reg* † remove
entfernt – away (distance)
  weit entfernt – *adv* far away
  zehn Kilometer von ... entfernt – 10 kilometres from...
Entfernung (-en) – *nf* distance
entfliehen* – *v irreg* flee
entführen – *v reg* † kidnap
Entführer (-) – *nm* kidnapper
Entführerin (-nen) – *nf* kidnapper
entgegen – *adv* towards
enthalten – *v irreg* contain
entkommen* – *v irreg* escape
entlang (+ acc) – *prep* along
  hier entlang – *adv* this way
  die Straße entlang – along the street
entmutigt – *adj* discouraged
(sich) entscheiden – *v irreg (refl)* decide
sich entscheiden für (+ acc) – *v irreg refl* opt for
Entscheidung (-en) – *nf* decision
sich entschließen – *v irreg refl* to make up one's mind
sich entschuldigen bei (+ dat) – *v reg refl* † to apologise to, to make excuses
Entschuldigen Sie, bitte! – Excuse me!
Entschuldigung (-en) – *nf* apology
Entschuldigung! – sorry!
entsetzlich – *adj* horrifying
entsetzt – *adj* horrified
sich entspannen – *v reg refl* † relax
entspannt – *adj* relaxed
Entspannung – *nf* relaxation
enttäuschend – *adj* disappointing·
enttäuscht – *adj* disappointed
entweder ... oder ... – *conj* either ... or...

---

nm - noun masculine   *nf* - noun feminine   *nnt* - noun neuter   *npl* - noun plural
nom- nominative   *acc* - accusative   *gen* - genitive   *dat* - dative

entwerten – *v reg* † cancel ticket
Entwerter (-) – *nm* ticket cancelling machine
entwickeln – *v reg* † develop
Entwicklung (-en) – *nf* development
Entwurf (Entwürfe) – *nm* rough draft
entzückend – *adj* delightful
entzückt – *adj* delighted
er – *pron nom* he, it
erbärmlich – *adj* pathetic
erbeuten – *v reg* † escape with
sich erbrechen – *v irreg refl* vomit
Erbse (-n) – *nf* pea
Erdbeben (-) – *nnt* earthquake
Erdbeere (-n) – *nf* strawberry
Erde (-n) – *nf* earth, ground
Erdgas – *nnt* natural gas
Erdgeschoß – *nnt* ground floor
   im Erdgeschoß – on the ground floor
Erdkunde – *nf* geography
Erdnuß (nüsse) – *nf* peanut
erdrosseln – *v reg* † strangle
Ereignis (-se) – *nnt* event
erfahren – *v irreg* experience
erfahren – *adj* experienced
Erfahrung (-en) – *nf* experience
erfinden – *v irreg* invent
Erfolg (-e) – *nm* success
erfolgreich – *adj* successful
erforschen – *v reg* † explore
erfreut – *adj* pleased
Erfrischung (-en) – *nf* refreshment
ergänzen – *v reg* † complete
Ergebnis (-se) – *nnt* result
ergreifen – *v irreg* grip, seize
erhalten – *v irreg* receive
erhältlich – *adj* obtainable
sich erheben – *v irreg refl* rise (mountain)

sich erholen – *v reg refl* † get better, recover
erinnern an (+ acc) – *v reg* † remind of
sich erinnern an (+ acc) – *v reg refl* † remember
sich erkälten – *v reg refl* † catch cold
erkältet sein* – *v irreg* have a cold
Erkältung (-en) – *nf* cold (illness)
erkennen – *v irreg* recognise
erklären – *v reg* † explain
Erklärung (-en) – *nf* explanation
sich erkundigen (nach + dat) – *v reg refl* † enquire (about)
erlauben – *v reg* † allow, let
Erlaubnis (-se) – *nf* permission
erlaubt – *adj* permitted
   nicht erlaubt – not allowed
Ermäßigung (-en) – *nf* reduction (price)
   10% Ermäßigung – 10% off
   Schülerermäßigung (-en) – *nf* student reduction
ermüdend – *adj* tiring
ermutigen – *v reg* † encourage
erneuern – *v reg* † renew
ernst – *adj* serious
Ernte (-n) – *nf* harvest
ernten – *v reg* † harvest
erreichen – *v reg* † reach
Ersatz – *nm* substitute
Ersatzrad (-räder) – *nnt* spare wheel
Ersatzteil (-e) – *nnt* spare part
erscheinen* – *v irreg* appear
erschießen – *v irreg* shoot dead
erschöpft – *adj* exhausted
erschrecken – *v irreg* terrify
erschreckend – *adj* startling
erschrocken – *adj* frightened
erschüttern – *v reg* † shock
erschüttert – *adj* distressed
ersetzen – *v reg* † replace

---

adj - adjective	*v reg* - verb regular	*v sep* - verb separable	† - see verb info
prep - preposition	*v irreg* - verb irregular	*v refl* - verb reflexive	* - takes sein

Ersparnisse – *npl* savings
erstaunen – *v reg* † astonish
erstaunt – *adj* amazed
erst – *adv* not until, only (+ time)
erste – *adj* first
  einmal erster Klasse, bitte – a first class ticket, please
erste Hilfe – *nf* first aid
erstens – *adv* firstly
ertragen – *v irreg* stand (put up with)
ertrinken* – *v irreg* drown
erwachsen – *adj* adult, grown up
Erwachsene – *nmf* ‡ adult
erwähnen – *v reg* † bring up (mention)
erwarten – *v reg* † expect
erwidern – *v reg* † reply
erzählen – *v reg* † recount
Erzähler (-) – *nm* storyteller
Erzählerin (-nen) – *nf* storyteller
erzeugt – *adj* produced
es (nom/acc) – *pron nt* it
  Es grüßt Dich herzlich – Greetings from
  Es hat geklappt – It worked
  Es kommt darauf an – It depends
  Es macht nichts – It doesn't matter
  Es tut mir leid – I'm sorry
Esel (-) – *nm* donkey
eßbar – *adj* edible

essen – *v irreg* eat
Essen – *nnt* food
  zu Abend essen – *v irreg* have dinner
Essig – *nm* vinegar
Eßzimmer (-) – *nnt* dining room
Etage (-n) – *nf* storey
  auf der Etage – upstairs
etwa – *adv* approximately
etwas – *adj inv* some (uncountable)
etwas – something, anything
  etwas anderes – something else
  etwas Schlechtes – something bad
  Sonst noch etwas? – Anything else?
EU – *nf* European Union
euch – *pron acc/dat pl* you (informal)
euer – *poss adj pl* your (informal)
Europa – *nnt* Europe
Europäer (-) – *nm* European person
Europäerin (-nen) – *nf* European person
europäisch – *adj* European
die Europäische Union – *nf* the European Union
Euroscheck (-s) – *nm* Eurocheque
evangelisch – *adj* Protestant
existieren – *v reg* † exist
Experiment – *nnt* experiment
extrem – *adj* extreme

F

fabelhaft – *adj* fabulous
Fabrik (-en) – *nf* factory
Fabrikarbeiter (-) – *nm* factory worker
Fabrikarbeiterin (-nen) – *nf* factory worker
Fach (Fächer) – *nnt* subject (school)
Facharzt (-ärzte) – *nm* specialist (doctor)
Fachärztin (-nen) – *nf* specialist (doctor)
Fachhochschulreife – *nf* GNVQ Level 3
Fachmann (-männer) – *nm* expert
Fachwerk~ – *pref* half-timbered
fähig – *adj* capable
Fahne (-n) – *nf* flag
Fahrausweis (-e) – *nm* ticket
Fähre (-n) – *nf* ferry
fahren – *v irreg* drive (a car, etc)
fahren* – *v irreg* travel, go
  mit dem Bus fahren* – *v irreg* get the bus
Fahrer (-) – *nm* driver
Fahrerin (-nen) – *nf* driver
Fahrgast (-gäste) – *nm* passenger
Fahrgeld (-er) – *nnt* fare
Fährhafen (-häfen) – *nm* ferry terminal
Fahrkarte (-n) – *nf* ticket (bus, train)
  Fahrkarte erster Klasse – *nf* first class ticket
  einfache Fahrkarte – *nf* single ticket
Fahrkartenautomat (-en) – *nm wk* ticket machine
Fahrkartenschalter (-) – *nm* ticket office
Fahrplan (-pläne) – *nm* timetable (transport)
Fahrpreis (-e) – *nm* full fare

  zum vollen Fahrpreis (-e) – at full fare
fahrplanmäßig – *adj* according to timetable
Fahrprüfung (-en) – *nf* driving test
Fahrrad (-räder) – *nnt* bicycle
Fahrschein (-e) – *nm* ticket
Fahrstuhl (-stühle) – *nm* lift
Fahrt – *nf* journey
  Gute Fahrt! – *excl* Have a good journey!
Fahrzeit (-en) – *nf* journey time
Fahrzeug (-e) – *nnt* vehicle
fair – *adj* fair (just)
Fall (Fälle) – *nm* case, situation
  auf keinen Fall – on no account
  in diesem Fall – in this case
fallen* – *v irreg* fall
fallen lassen – *v irreg* drop
falls – *sub conj* in case
falsch – *adj* wrong
falsch 'rum – wrong way round
falsch verbunden – wrong number
falten – *v reg* † fold
Familie (-n) – *nf* family
Familienname (-n) – *nm wk* surname
Familienzimmer (-) – *nnt* family room (hotel)
Fan (-s) – *nm* fan (supporter)
fand – *see finden*
fangen – *v irreg* catch (fish)
fantastisch – *adj* fantastic
Farbe (-n) – *nf* colour
Fasching – *nm* Carnival
Faschingsdienstag – *nm* Shrove Tuesday
fassen – *v reg* grasp
fast – *adv* almost
faszinierend – *adj* fascinating

---

faul – *adv* lazy, rotten
faulenzen – *v reg* laze about
Faust (Fäuste) – *nf* fist
Fax (-) – *nnt* fax
faxen – *v reg* fax
Faxgerät (-e) – *nnt* fax machine
Faxnummer (-n) – *nf* fax number
Februar – *nm* February
   im Februar – in February
Feder (-n) – *nf* feather
Federball – *nm* badminton
Federmäppchen (-) – *nnt* pencil case
fehlen – *v reg* lack, be missing, miss
Fehler (-) – *nm* mistake
Feier (-n) – *nf* celebration
Feierabend (-e) – *nm* end of the
   working day
feierlich – *adj* solemn
feiern – *v reg* celebrate
Feiertag (-e) – *nm* public holiday
fein – *adj* fine (delicate)
Feld (-er) – *nnt* field, square
Feldbett (-en) – *nnt* camp bed
feminin – *adj* feminine (grammar)
Fenster (-) – *nnt* window
Ferien – *npl* holiday (school)
   die Ferien verbringen – *v irreg*
   spend one's holiday
Ferienhaus (-häuser) – *nnt* holiday
   cottage
fern – *adj* distant
Fernbedienung – *nf* remote control
   (TV)
Ferne – *nf* distance
   in der Ferne – in the distance
Ferngespräch (-e) – *nnt* phone call
Fernseh~ – *pref* TV
Fernsehapparat (-e) – *nm* TV set
Fernsehen – *nnt* television
   im Fernsehen – on television
fernsehen – *v irreg sep* watch TV
Fernseher (-) – *nm* television set

Fernsprecher (-) – *nm* telephone
Ferse (-n) – *nf* heel (foot)
fertig – *adj* ready
   sich fertig machen – *v reg refl*
   get ready
Fertiggericht (-e) – *nnt* ready-made
   meal
fesseln – *v reg* grip (interest)
fesselnd – *adj* gripping
fest – *adj* firm, steady (job)
Fest (-e) – *nnt* festival, fête
Festland – *nnt* continent (-not island)
festhalten – *v irreg sep* hold tight
festmachen – *v reg sep* fasten
Festplatte (-n) – *nf* hard disk
festsetzen – *v reg sep* arrange (time)
feststellen – *v reg sep* establish,
   determine
Festspiele – *npl* drama festival
fettig – *adj* greasy
feucht – *adj* damp
Feuer (-) – *nnt* fire
   Haben Sie Feuer? – Have you
   got a light?
Feueralarm (-e) – *nm* fire alarm
Feuerleiter (-n) – *nf* fire escape
Feuerwehr (-en) – *nf* fire brigade
Feuerwehrmann (-männer) – *nm*
   fireman
Feuerwehrwagen (-) – fire-engine
Feuerwerk – *nnt, no pl* firework
Fieber (-) – *nnt* fever, high temperature
   Fieber haben – *v irreg* have a
   temperature
Fieberthermometer (-) – *nnt*
   thermometer (medical)
fiel – *see fallen**
Figur (-en) – *nf* figure
Filiale (-n) – *nf* branch (firm)
Film (-e) – *nm* film
Filmstar (-s) – *nm* film star
Filterkaffee – *nm* filter coffee
Filzstift (-e) – *nm* felt tip pen

---

nm - noun masculine   *nf* - noun feminine   *nnt* - noun neuter   *npl* - noun plural
nom- nominative   *acc* - accusative   *gen* - genitive   *dat* - dative

finden – *v irreg* find
Finger (-) – *nm* finger
  Ich habe mir den Finger
  verbrannt – I have burnt my finger
Finne (-n) – *nm wk* Finnish person
Finnin (-nen) – *nf* Finnish person
finnisch – *adj* Finnish
Finnland – *nnt* Finland
Firma (Firmen) – *nf* firm
Fisch (-e) – *nm* fish
Fische – Pisces (horoscope)
fischen – *v reg* fish
Fischer (-) – *nm* fisherman
Fischereihafen (-häfen) – *nm*
  fishing port
Fischerin (-nen) – *nf* fisherwoman
Fischhändler (-) – *nm* fishmonger
Fischhändlerin (-nen) – *nf*
  fishmonger
Fischstäbchen (-) – *nnt* fish finger
fit – *adj* fit
Fitneß – *nf* fitness (condition)
Fitneßzentrum (-zentren) – *nnt*
  fitness centre
flach – *adj* flat, level
Flagge (-n) – *nf* flag
Flamme (-n) – *nf* flame
Flasche (-n) – *nf* bottle
  eine Flasche Wein – a bottle of
  wine
Flaschenöffner (-) – *nm* bottle opener
Fleck (-en) – *nm* stain
  ein blauer Fleck (-e) – *nm* a
  bruise
Fledermaus (-mäuse) – *nf* bat
  (mammal)
Fleisch – *nnt* meat
Fleischer (-) – *nm* butcher
Fleischsorte (-n) – *nf* type of meat
fleißig – *adj* hardworking
Fliege (-n) – *nf* fly (insect), bow tie
Fliegen – *nnt* flying (in plane)

fliegen* – *v irreg* fly
fliehen* – *v irreg* flee
fließen* – *v irreg* flow
fließend – *adj* fluent (speech)
flirten – *v reg* † flirt
flog – *see fliegen**
Floh (Flöhe) – *nm* flea
Flohmarkt (-märkte) – *nm* flea
  market
Flöte (-n) – *nf* flute
Flug (Flüge) – *nm* flight (plane)
Flügel (-) – *nm* piano (grand)
Flughafen(-häfen) – *nm* airport
Flugzeug (-e) – *nnt* aeroplane
  mit dem Flugzeug – by plane
Flur (-e) – *nm* hallway
Fluß (Flüsse) – *nm* river
Flüssigkeit (-en) – *nf* liquid
flüstern – *v reg* whisper
Flut (-en) – *nf* high tide
Föhn (-e) – *nm* warm alpine wind
Folge (-n) – *nf* consequence
folgen* (+ dat) – *v reg* follow
folgend – *adj* following
Fön (-e) – *nm* hair dryer
Forelle (-n) – *nf* trout
Form (-en) – *nf* shape
Formular (-e) – *nnt* form (paper)
  ein Formular ausfüllen – *v reg*
  sep fill in a form
fort – *adv* away
fortfahren* – *v irreg sep* go on
  (continue)
fortgehen* – *v irreg* go away
Fortschritt (-e) – *nm* progress
  Fortschritte machen – *v reg*
  make progress
Foto (-s) – *nnt* photo
  Fotos machen – *v reg* take photos
Fotoapparat (-e) – *nm* camera
Fotograf (-en) – *nm wk* photographer

---

adj - adjective	*v reg* - verb regular	*v sep* - verb separable	† - see verb info
prep - preposition	*v irreg* - verb irregular	*v refl* - verb reflexive	* - takes sein

Fotografie – *nf* photography
fotografieren – *v reg* † take a photo
Fotografin (-nen) – *nf* photographer
Fotokopie (-n) – *nf* photocopy
fotokopieren – *v reg* † photocopy
Fotokopiergerät(-e) – *nnt* photocopier
Frage (-n) – *nf* question
  eine mündliche Frage (-n) – *nf* an oral question
  das kommt nicht in Frage – that's out of the question
fragen – *v reg* ask
sich fragen – *v reg refl* wonder
Fragezeichen – *nnt* question mark (?)
Franc (-s) – *nm* franc (French)
Franken (-) – *nm* franc (Swiss)
Frankreich – *nnt* France
Franzose (-n) – *nm wk* French person
Französin (-nen) – *nf* French person
französisch – *adj* French
Französisch – *nnt* French (language)
  auf französisch – in French
Frau – Mrs, Ms
Frau (-en) – *nf* woman, wife
Frauenarzt (-ärzte) – *nm* gynaecologist
Frauenärztin (-nen) – *nf* gynaecologist
Frauenzeitschrift (-en) – *nf* women's magazine
Fräulein (-) – *nnt* Miss
Fräulein! – *excl* Waitress!
frech – *adj* cheeky
frei – *adj* free
  im Freien – in the open air
Freibad (-bäder) – *nnt* open air swimming pool
freihalten – *v irreg sep* keep free, keep clear
Freiheit (-en) – *nf* freedom
Freitag (-e) – *nm* Friday
  am Freitag – on Friday

freitags – *adv* on Fridays
freiwillig – *adj* voluntary
Freiwillige – *nmf* ‡ volunteer
Freizeit – *nf* free time
Freizeitsbeschäftigung (-en) – *nf* hobby
Freizeitszentrum (-zentren) – *nnt* leisure centre
fremd – *adj* foreign, not local
  ich bin hier fremd – I'm a stranger
Fremde – *nmf* ‡ stranger
Fremdenzimmer (-) – *nnt* room to let, B & B
Fremdsprache (-n) – *nf* foreign language
fressen – *v irreg* eat (of animal)
Frettchen (-) – *nnt* ferret
Freude (-n) – *nf* joy
Freudenfeuer – *nnt* bonfire
sich freuen auf (+ acc) – *v reg refl* look forward to
sich freuen über (+ acc) – *v reg refl* be pleased about
Freund (-e) – *nm* friend, boyfriend
  ein Freund/eine Freundin von mir – a friend of mine
Freundin (-nen) – *nf* friend, girlfriend
freundlich – *adj* friendly
mit freundlichen Grüßen – Kind regards, Yours sincerely
Freundlichkeit (-en) – *nf* kindness
Freundschaft (-en) – *nf* friendship
Frieden (-) – *nm* peace
friedlich – *adj* peaceful
frieren – *v irreg* freeze
  Es friert – It is freezing (ice)
  Mir friert's – I'm freezing
Frikadelle (-n) – *nf* rissole
frisch – *adj* fresh
frisch gestrichen – wet paint
Friseur (-) – *nm* hairdresser
Friseuse (-n) – *nf* hairdresser
Frisur (-en) – *nf* hairstyle

---

nm - noun masculine	*nf* - noun feminine	*nnt* - noun neuter	*npl* - noun plural
nom- nominative	*acc* - accusative	*gen* - genitive	*dat* - dative

froh – *adj* happy, merry
Frohe Weihnachten! – Happy Christmas!
fröhlich – *adj* merry
Fröhliche Weihnachten! – Merry Christmas!
Frosch (Frösche) – *nm* frog
Frost – *nm* frost
frostig – *adj* frosty
Frucht~ – *pref* fruit
Fruchtsaft (-säfte) – *nm* fruit juice
früh – *adj* early
  morgen früh – tomorrow morning
früher – *adv* in the past, formerly
Frühjahr – *nnt* spring
Frühling – *nm* spring
  im Frühling – in spring
Frühstück (-e) – *nnt* breakfast
frühmorgens – *adv* in the early morning
frühstücken – *v reg* have breakfast
fühlen – *v reg* feel
sich fühlen – *v reg refl* feel (person)
  ich fühle mich wohl – I feel well, I feel at ease
  ich fühle mich unwohl – I feel ill
fuhr – *see fahren**
führen – *v reg* lead
Führer (-) – *nm* guide, leader
Führerin (-nen) – *nf* guide, leader
Führerschein (-e) – *nm* driving licence
  den Führerschein machen – *v reg* take a driving test
Führung (-en) – *nf* guided tour
  in Führung – in the lead
füllen – *v reg* fill
Füller (-) – *nm* fountain pen
Fundbüro (-s) – *nnt* lost property office
Fundsachen – *npl* lost property

fünf – *adj* five
fünfte – *adj* fifth
fünfzehn – *adj* fifteen
fünfzig – *adj* fifty
Fünfzigmarkschein (-e) – *nm* 50 mark note
funktionieren – *v reg* † work
für (+ acc) – *prep* for
Furcht – *nf* fear
furchtbar – *adj* awful, terrible
furchtbar – *adv* tremendously
fürchterlich – *adj* horrible
Fuß (Füße) – *nm* foot
  zu Fuß gehen* – *v irreg* go on foot
  sich den Fuß verrenken – *v reg dat refl* † to sprain one's ankle
Fußball (-bälle) – *nm* football
Fußballplatz (-plätze) – *nm* football field
Fußballschuh (-e) – *nm* football boot
Fußballspiel (-e) – *nnt* football match
Fußballspieler (-) – *nm* footballer
Fußboden (-böden) – *nm* floor (ground)
Fußgänger (-) – *nm* pedestrian
Fußgängerin (-nen) – *nf* pedestrian
Fußgängerüberweg (-e) – *nm* pedestrian crossing
Fußgängerzone (-n) – *nf* pedestrian zone
Fußgelenk (-e) – *nnt* ankle
  sich das Fußgelenk verstauchen – *v reg dat refl* † sprain one's ankle
  sich das Fußgelenk verrenken – *v reg dat refl* † twist an ankle
Fußweg (-e) – *nm* footpath
füttern – *v reg* feed (animal)

G

g – gramme
gab – *see geben*
  es gab – there was, there were
  es gäbe – there would be
Gabel (-n) – *nf* fork
gähnen – *v reg* yawn
Galerie (-n) – *nf* gallery
Gang (Gänge) – *nm* corridor,
  gear (car)
  (den Gang) schalten – *v reg* †
  change gear
Gans (Gänse) – *nf* goose
ganz – *adv* quite (totally)
  ganz allein – all alone
  ganz viel – quite a lot
ganz – *adj* whole
  das ganze Jahr – all year round
  den ganzen Tag – all day
  die ganze Zeit – the whole time
  im großen und ganzen – on the
  whole
ganztägig – *adj* full time (job)
Ganztagsschule (-n) – *nf* all-day
  school
gar – *adj* cooked
gar – *adv* even
  gar nicht – not at all
  gar nichts – nothing at all
Garage (-n) – *nf* garage (house)
Garantie (-n) – *nf* guarantee
Garderobe (-n) – *nf* cloak-room
Gardine (-n) – *nf* curtain (net)
Garten (Gärten) – *nm* garden
  im Garten arbeiten – *v reg* †
  do (the) gardening
Gartenarbeit – *nf* gardening
Gartenhäuschen (-) – *nnt* shed
Gärtner (-) – *nm* gardener
Gas (-e) – *nnt* gas
Gasflasche (-n) – *nf* gas cylinder

Gasherd (-e) – *nm* gas cooker
Gasse (-n) – *nf* lane, alley
Gast (Gäste) – *nm* guest
Gastarbeiter (-) – *nm* guest worker
Gastfreundschaft – *nf* hospitality
Gastgeber (-) – *nm* host
Gastgeberin (-nen) – *nf* hostess
Gasthaus (-häuser) – *nnt* pub, inn
Gasthof (-höfe) – *nm* pub, inn
Gaststätte (-n) – *nf* pub
geb. – born
Gebäck – *nnt* biscuits, pastries
Gebäude (-) – *nnt* building
geben – *v irreg* give
  Geben Sie mir... – Give me...
  (formal)
  Es wird...geben – There will be
Gebiet (-e) – *nnt* area
Gebirge (-) – *nnt* mountain range,
  range of hills
geblieben – *see bleiben**
geboren – *adj* born
  am 6. Januar geboren – born on
  6th January
geboren sein * – *v irreg* be born
gebracht – *see bringen*
Gebrauch (Gebräuche) – *nm*
  custom
Gebrauch – *nm, no pl* use
gebrauchen – *v reg* † use
Gebrauchsanweisung (-en) – *nf*
  user instructions
gebraucht – *adj* second-hand
gebräunt – *adj* sun-tanned
gebrochen – *adj* broken
Gebühr (-en) – *nf* fee
Geburt (-en) – *nf* birth
gebürtig – *adj* native
Geburtsdatum (-daten) – *nnt* date
  of birth

Geburtsort (-e) – *nm* place of birth

Geburtstag (-e) – *nm* birthday
Herzlichen Glückwunsch zum Geburtstag! – *excl* Happy Birthday!

Geburtstagsgeschenk (-e) – *nnt* birthday present

Geburtstagskarte (-n) – *nf* birthday card

Geburtstagskuchen (-) – *nm* birthday cake

Geburtsurkunde (-n) – *nf* birth certificate

gedacht – *see denken*

Gedächtnis (-se) – *nnt* memory

Gedanke (-n) – *nm wk* thought

Gedränge – *nnt* scrum

gedruckt – *adj* printed

Geduld – *nf* patience

geduldig – *adj* patient

geehrt – *adj* honoured
Sehr geehrter Herr! – Dear Sir

geeignet – *adj* fit (suitable)

Gefahr (-en) – *nf* danger

gefahren – *see fahren**

gefährlich – *adj* dangerous

gefallen (+ dat) – *v irreg* be pleasing
Die Hose gefällt mir – I like the trousers

Gefängnis (se) – *nnt* prison

geflogen – *see fliegen**

Geflügel – *nnt* poultry

gefolgt von (+ dat) – *adj* followed by

gefroren – *adj* frozen
tiefgefroren – *adj* deep-frozen

Gefühl (-e) – *nnt* feeling

gefunden – *see finden*

gegangen – *see gehen**

gegeben – *see geben*

gegen (+ acc) – *prep* against, towards
gegen Mittag – towards midday

Gegend – *nf* area, district
hier in der Gegend – round here

Gegenstand (-stände) – *nm* item

Gegenstück (-e) – *nnt* equivalent

Gegenteil (-e) – *nnt* opposite

gegenüber (+ dat) – *prep* opposite

gegenwärtig – *adj* present (current)

gegessen – *see essen*

gehabt – *see haben*

gehacktes Rindfleisch – minced beef

Gehalt (Gehälter) – *nnt* salary

Gehaltserhöhung (-en) – *nf* pay rise

gehäßig – *adj* spiteful

geheim – *adj* secret

Geheimnis (-se) – *nnt* secret

geheimnisvoll – *adj* mysterious

gehen* – *v irreg* walk, go
Meine Uhr geht vor – My watch is fast
Mir geht es gut – I am well
mit jdm gehen* – *v irreg* go out with s.o.
nach Hause gehen* – *v irreg* go home
nach oben gehen* – *v irreg* go upstairs

Gehirn (-e) – *nnt* brain

geholfen – *see helfen*

gehorchen (+ dat) – *v reg* † obey

gehören (+ dat) – *v reg* † belong to
Das gehört ihnen – It's theirs
Es gehört mir – It's mine

gehorsam – *adj* obedient

Geige (-n) – *nf* violin

Geige spielen – *v reg* play the violin

geil – *adj coll* excellent; randy

Geisteswissenschaften – *npl* humanities

geizig – *adj* mean

gekannt – *see kennen*

gekommen – *see kommen**

gel? – *adv* isn't it?, etc

---

adj - adjective
prep - preposition
v reg - verb regular
v irreg - verb irregular
v sep - verb separable
v refl - verb reflexive
† - see verb info
* - takes sein

Gel – *nnt* hair gel
gelaufen – *see laufen**
gelaunt – *adj* mood
  schlecht gelaunt – in a bad mood
  gut gelaunt – in a good mood
gelb – *adj* yellow
Geld – *nnt* money, cash
  Geld verdienen – *v reg* † make
  money
  Geld wechseln – *v reg* change
  money
Geldautomat (-en) – *nm wk* cash
machine (dispenser)
Geldbeutel (-) – *nm* purse
Geldbörse (-n) – *nf* purse
Geldrückgabe (-n) – *nf* refund,
return coins
Geldschein (-e) – *nm* bank-note
Geldstrafe (-n) – *nf* fine
(punishment)
Geldwechsel – *nm* currency
exchange, bureau de change
Gelee – *nnt* jelly, aspic
gelegen – *adj* situated
Gelegenheit (-en) – *nf* opportunity
  die Gelegenheit haben – *v irreg*
  have the opportunity to
Gelegenheitsarbeiten – *npl* odd
jobs
Gelegenheitsarbeiten verrichten
– *v reg* † do odd jobs
gelegentlich – *adj* occasional
gelesen – *see lesen*
gelingen* – *v irreg* succeed
  Es ist mir gelungen – I've
  succeeded
Gemäldegalerie (-n) – *nf* art gallery
gemein – *adj* mean (nasty)
Gemeinde (-n) – *nf* parish, district
Gemeinderat – *nm* local council
der Gemeinsame Markt – *nm* the
Common Market

Gemeinschaftskunde – *nf* social
studies
gemischt – *adj* mixed, coeducational
Gemüse – *nnt no pl* vegetables, greens
Gemüsehändler (-) – *nm*
greengrocer
Gemüsehändlerin (-nen) – *nf*
greengrocer
gemütlich – *adj* snug, cosy, sociable,
pleasant
genau – *adj* exact
  genau so – *adv* in the same way as
genauso – *adv* just as
Genehmigung (-en) – *nf* licence
Generalprobe (-n) – *nf* dress
rehearsal
Genf – Geneva
geniert – *adj* embarrassed
genießen – *v irreg* enjoy
Genitiv – *nnt* genitive
genommen – *see nehmen*
genug – *adj* enough
geöffnet – *adj* open
Geographie – *nf* geography
Geologie – *nf* geology
Gepäck – *nnt, no pl* luggage
Gepäckaufbewahrung (-en) – *nf*
left luggage office
Gepäckausgabe (-n) – *nf* luggage
carousel
Gepäcknetz (-e) – *nnt* train luggage
rack
Gepäckschließfach (-fächer) – *nnt*
left luggage locker
Gepäckstück (-e) – *nnt* piece of
luggage
Gepäckträger (-) – *nm* porter;
carrier on bicycle
Gepäckzettel (-) – *nm* left luggage
ticket
geparkt – *adj* parked
gepunktet – *adj* spotty (fabric)
gerade – *adj* even, just, straight

---

nm - noun masculine	*nf* - noun feminine	*nnt* - noun neuter	*npl* - noun plural
nom- nominative	*acc* - accusative	*gen* - genitive	*dat* - dative

Ich bin gerade angekommen –
I have just arrived
Er wollte gerade anrufen – He
was on the point of phoning
geradeaus – *adv* straight on
Gehen Sie geradeaus! – Go
straight on!
Gerät (-e) – *nnt* appliance
ins Schleudern geraten* – *v irreg*
skid
Geräusch (-e) – *nnt* noise (quiet)
geräuschlos – *adj* silent
gerecht – *adj* fair, just
Das ist nicht gerecht – It's not
fair!
gereizt – *adj* irritated
Gericht (-e) – *nnt* dish (recipe)
gern – *adv* gladly
gern haben – *v irreg* like
gern machen – *v reg* be keen on
Ich tanze gern – I like dancing
Geruch (Gerüche) – *nm* smell
gesagt – *see sagen* told
Gesamtschule (-n) – *nf*
comprehensive school
Geschäft (-e) – *nnt* shop, business
Geschäftsfrau (-en) – *nf* business
woman
Geschäftsführer (-) – *nm* manager
Geschäftsführerin (-nen) – *nf*
manageress
Geschäftsmann (-männer) – *nm*
business man
Geschäftszeiten – *npl* opening hours
geschehen* – *v irreg* happen
Gern geschehen! – *excl* It's a
pleasure!
Geschenk (-e) – *nnt* gift
als Geschenk einpacken – *v reg*
sep gift wrap
Geschichte – *nf* history, story
geschickt – *adv* skilfully
geschickt – *adj* skilled

geschieden – *adj* divorced
Geschirr – *nnt, no pl* crockery
Geschirrspülautomat (-en) – *nm*
wk dishwasher
Geschirrspülmaschine (-n) – *nf*
dishwasher
Geschirrtuch (-tücher) – *nnt* tea
towel
geschlafen – *see schlafen*
geschlagen – *adj* defeated
Geschlecht (-er) – *nnt* gender
geschlossen – *adj* closed
Geschmack (Geschmäcke) – *nm*
taste, flavour
mit Zitronengeschmack –
lemon flavoured
geschnitten – *see schneiden*
Geschoß (Geschosse) – *nnt* floor
im obersten Geschoß – on the
top floor
geschrieben – *see schreiben*
geschützt von (+ dat) – *adj*
sheltered from
Geschwindigkeit (-en) – *nf* speed
mit hoher Geschwindigkeit –
at high speed
**Geschwindigkeitsbegrenzung
(-en)** – *nf* speed limit
**Geschwindigkeitsbeschränkung
(-en)** – *nf* speed limit
Geschwister – *npl* brothers and
sisters
geschwollen – *adj* swollen
geschwommen – *see schwimmen* (*)
gesehen – *see sehen*
Gesellschaft (-en) – *nf* society,
company
Gesellschaftsspiel (-e) – *nnt* board
game
gesessen – *see sitzen*
Gesetz (-e) – *nnt* law
Gesicht (-er) – *nnt* face
ein Gesicht ziehen – *v irreg* pull
a face

---

gespannt – *adj* eager
Gespenst (-er) – *nnt* ghost
gesperrt – *adj* closed (road)
Gespräch (-e) – *nnt* conversation
gesprächig – *adj* talkative
gesprochen – *see sprechen*
gestattet – *adj* permitted
Gestell (-e) – *nnt* frame (spectacles)
gestern – *adv* yesterday
  gestern abend – *adv* last night,
  yesterday evening
gestochen werden* – *v irreg* get
  stung
gestorben – *adj* dead
gestreift – *adj* striped
gestreßt – *adj* stressed out
gesund – *adj* healthy, well
Gesundheit! – *excl* Bless you!
Gesundheit – *nf* health
getestet – *adj* checked
getragen – *see tragen*
Getränk (-e) – *nnt* drink
  ein alkoholfreies Getränk – *nnt*
  a soft drink
Getränkekarte (-n) – *nf* wine list
getrennt – *adj* separated
getrennt – *adv* separately
  Geht das getrennt oder
  zusammen? – Do you want to
  pay separately or all together?
getrunken – *see trinken*
Gewächshaus (-häuser) – *nnt*
  greenhouse
Gewalt – *nf* violence
gewaltig – *adj* violent (storm)
gewalttätig – *adj* violent (person)
gewaschen – *see waschen*
Gewehr (-e) – *nnt* gun (rifle)
gewesen – *see sein* been
Gewicht (-e) – *nnt* weight
gewinnen – *v irreg* win

einen Punkt gewinnen – *v irreg*
  score a point
gewiß – *adj* certain
Gewitter (-) – *nnt* thunderstorm
  Es wird Gewitter geben – There
  will be thunderstorms
sich gewöhnen an (+ acc) – *v reg*
  refl † get used to
Gewohnheit (-en) – *nf* habit
  Ich habe die Gewohnheit – I am
  in the habit of
gewöhnlich – *adj* ordinary, usual
  wie gewöhnlich – *adv* as usual
gewonnen – *see gewinnen*
geworden – *see werden**
gewußt – *see wissen*
Gib mir – give me... (informal)
gibt – *see geben*
Es gibt (+ acc) – There are, There is
  Es gibt keinen/keine/kein ... –
  There is no ...
  Es gibt keine ... – There are no ...
gierig – *adj* greedy
Gift (-e) – *nnt* poison
giftig – *adj* poisonous
ging – *see gehen**
Gipfel (-) – *nm* summit
Gips (-e) – *nm* plaster (broken arm)
Gitarre (-n) – *nf* guitar
Gitarre spielen – *v reg* play the
  guitar
Glück – *nnt* happiness
glänzend – *adj* shiny
Glas (Gläser) – *nnt* glass, jar
  ein Glas Marmelade – *nnt* a jar
  of jam
Glasscheibe (-n) – *nf* (pane of) glass
glatt – *adj* smooth, straight (hair)
Glatteis – *nnt* black ice
Glatze (-n) – *nf* bald patch
  Er hat eine Glatze – He's bald
glauben – *v reg* think

---

nm - noun masculine   *nf* - noun feminine   *nnt* - noun neuter   *npl* - noun plural
nom- nominative   *acc* - accusative   *gen* - genitive   *dat* - dative

glauben (an + acc) – *v reg* believe (in)

gleich – *adj* same, equal

gleich – *adv* immediately, in a moment

   Ich esse gleich – I am about to eat

gleichaltrig – *adj* of the same age

Gleichfalls! – *excl* I wish you the same!

Gleichheit (-en) – *nf* equality

gleichmäßig – *adj* evenly

gleichzeitig – *adv* at the same time

Gleis – *nnt* track, rails

   auf Gleis 8 – from platform 8

Gletscher (-) – *nm* glacier

glitschig – *adj* slippery

global – *adj* global

Glocke (-n) – *nf* bell (church)

Glotze – *nf coll* telly

Glück – *nnt* luck

   Viel Glück! – *excl* Good luck!

Glück haben – *v irreg* to be lucky

glücklich – *adj* happy, fortunate

   Ein glückliches neues Jahr! –
   excl Happy New Year!

   Herzlichen Glückwunsch zum
   Geburtstag! – *excl* Happy
   Birthday!

glücklicherweise – *adv* fortunately

Glückwunschkarte (-n) – *nf*
   greetings card

Glühbirne (-e) – *nf* light bulb

glühen – *v reg* glow

Go-kart (-s) – *nm* go-kart

Go-kart fahren* – *v irreg* to go go-
   karting

Go-kart-Fahren – *nnt* go-karting

Gold – *nnt* gold

   aus Gold – made of gold

golden – *adj* golden

Goldfisch (-e) – *nm* goldfish

Goldmedaille – *nf* gold medal

Golf – *nm* golf

Golfplatz (-plätze) – *nm* golf course

Gott (Götter) – *nm* God

Gottesdienst (-e) – *nm* church
   service

Grad – *nm* degree (temperature)

Gramm – *nnt* gram

Grammatik – *nf* grammar

Gras (Gräser) – *nnt* grass

gratis – *adj* free

gratulieren (+ dat) – *v reg* †
   congratulate

   Ich gratuliere – Congratulations!

grau – *adj* grey

Graubrot – *nnt* wholemeal bread

grausam – *adj* cruel

greifen – *v irreg* grab

Grenze (-n) – *nf* border, limit

Grieche (-n) – *nm* wk Greek person

Griechenland – *nnt* Greece

Griechin (-nen) – *nf* Greek person

griechisch – *adj* Greek

Griff (-e) – *nm* handle

grillen – *v reg* grill (food)

   vom Grill – grilled

Grillfest (-e) – *nnt* barbecue

grinsen – *v reg* grin

Grippe – *nf* flu

grölen – *v reg* yell

Groschen (-) – *nm* 10 Pfennig piece

groß – *adj* big, tall

   im großen und ganzen – on the
   whole

   nicht so groß wie – not as big as

Groß~ – *pref* big

großartig – *adj* magnificent

Großbritannien – *nnt* Great Britain

Großbuchstabe (-n) – *nm wk*
   capital letter

Größe (-n) – *nf* size, height

Großeltern – *npl* grandparents

größer als – bigger than

Großmutter (-mütter) – *nf*
   grandmother

Großstadt (-städte) – *nf* city

Großvater (-väter) – *nm* grandfather

großzügig – *adj* generous

grün – *adj* green

grüner Salat – *nm* green salad

Grund (Gründe) – *nm* reason

im Grunde – *adv* basically

Grund- – *pref* basic

Grundschule (-n) – *nf* primary school

Grundschullehrer (-) – *nm* primary school teacher

Grundschullehrerin (-nen) – *nf* primary school teacher

Grundstück (-stücke) – *nnt* plot of land

Gruppe (-n) – *nf* group, band

gruselig – *adj* gory

Gruselroman (-e) – *nm* horror story

Gruß (Grüße) – *nm* greeting

Grüß dich! – *excl* Hello!

Grüß Gott! – *excl* Hello!

mit freundlichen Grüßen – Yours sincerely, Kind regards

grüßen – *v reg* greet

gucken – *v reg coll* watch

Gulasch – *nm* stew

gültig – *adj* valid

Gummiband (-bänder) – *nnt* rubber band

günstig – *adj* good value, favourable

Gurke (-n) – *nf* cucumber

Gürtel (-) – *nm* belt

Gürteltasche (-n) – *nf* bumbag

gut – *adj* good

Alles Gute – love from

Gute Besserung! – *excl* Get well soon!

Gute Fahrt! – *excl* Have a good journey!

Gute Heimreise! – *excl* Have a good journey home!

Gute Idee! – *excl* Good idea!

Gute Nacht! – *excl* Good night!

Gute Reise! – *excl* Have a good trip!

Guten Abend! – *excl* Good evening!

Guten Appetit! – *excl* Enjoy your meal!

Guten Morgen! – *excl* Good morning!

Guten Tag! – *excl* Hello, Good afternoon!

guter Laune – in a good mood

gut zu Tieren – kind to animals

gut – *adv* well

Es geht mir gut – I'm fine

gut gelaunt – *adj* good-tempered

Gut gemacht! – *excl* Well done!

gutaussehend – *adj* good looking

Güte – *nf* goodness

guterzogen – *adj* well brought up

gut in .... sein* – *v irreg* be good at

Gymnasium (-ien) – *nnt* grammar school

Gymnastik machen – *v reg* do gymnastics

H

h – o'clock
Haar (-e) – *nnt* hair
  sich die Haare bürsten – *v reg*
  dat refl † brush one's hair
  sich die Haare schneiden
  lassen – *v irreg dat refl* have a
  haircut
  sich die Haare wachsen lassen
  – *v irreg dat refl* grow one's hair
  sich die Haare trocknen – *v reg*
  dat refl † dry one's hair
  sich die Haare waschen –
  v irreg dat refl wash one's hair
Haarbürste (-n) – *nf* hairbrush
Haarschnitt (-e) – *nm* haircut
haben – *v irreg* have, get
  recht haben – *v irreg* be right
  Urlaub haben – *v irreg* have a
  holiday
Hackfleisch – *nnt* mince (meat)
Hafen (Häfen) – *nm* harbour, port
Hafenstadt (-städte) – *nf* port
Hagel – *nm* hail
hageln – *v reg* hail
  Es hagelt – It is hailing
Hähnchen (-) – *nnt* chicken
Haken (-) – *nm* hook, tick, snag
halb – *adj* half
  eine halbe Stunde – half an hour
  zum halben Preis – half-price
halb – half past
  um halb vier – at half past three
Halb~ – *pref* half
Halbbruder (-brüder) – *nm* half-
  brother
Halbfinale (-n) – *nnt* semi-final
Halbjahresferien – *npl* February
  half-term holiday
Halbjahreszeugnis (se) – *nnt* mid-
  year report

Halbpension – *nf* half board
Halbschwester (-n) – *nf* half-sister
halbtags – *adv* part-time
halbwegs – *adv* half way
half – *see helfen*
Hälfte (-n) – *nf* half
Halle (-n) – *nf* hall (public, sport)
Hallenbad (-bäder) – *nnt* pool,
  indoor pool
Hallo! – *excl* Hello! Hi!
Hals (Hälse) – *nm* neck, throat
Halskette (-n) – *nf* necklace
Halsschmerzen – *npl* sore throat
Halstablette (-n) – *nf* throat pastille
Halt! – *excl* Halt! Stop!
Halt machen – *v reg* halt
Halteverbot – *nnt* no stopping
halten – *v irreg* hold
Haltestelle (-n) – *nf* stop
Hamburger (-) – *nm* beefburger
Hameln – Hamelin
Hammelfleisch – *nnt* mutton
Hammer (-) – *nm* hammer
Hamster (-) – *nm* hamster
Hand (Hände) – *nf* hand
  jdm die Hand geben – *v irreg*
  shake hands with s.o.
Hand~ – *pref* manual
Handarbeit – *nf* needlework
Handball (-bälle) – *nm* handball
Handel – *nm* trade, drugs traffic
handeln – *v reg* trade
  Worum handelt es sich? – What
  is it about?
Handgelenk (-e) – *nnt* wrist
handgemacht – *adj* handmade
Handgepäck – *nnt* hand luggage
handgeschrieben – *adj* handwritten
Händler (-) – *nm* shopkeeper

---

adj - adjective	*v reg* - verb regular	*v sep* - verb separable	† - see verb info
prep - preposition	*v irreg* - verb irregular	*v refl* - verb reflexive	* - takes sein

Handlung (-en) – *nf* shop
Handschrift (-en) – *nf* handwriting
Handschuh (-e) – *nm* glove
Handtasche (-n) – *nf* handbag
Handtuch (-tücher) – *nnt* hand towel
Handwerker (-) – *nm* craftsman
Handwerkerin (-nen) – *nf* craftswoman
Hang (Hänge) – *nm* slope
hängen – *v irreg* hang
   Es hängt vom Wetter ab – It depends upon the weather
Hannover – Hanover
Hansaplast® – *nnt* elastoplast®
hart – *adj* hard
Haselnuß (-nüsse) – *nf* hazelnut
hassen – *v reg* hate
häßlich – *adj* ugly
hast – *see haben*
hat – *see haben*
Hat er welche? – Has he got any?
hatte – *see haben*
Haube (-n) – *nf* bonnet
Haufen – *nm* heap, pile
häufig – *adj* frequent
Haupt- – *pref* main, chief
Hauptbahnhof (-höfe) – *nm* main railway station
Hauptgericht (-e) – *nnt* main course
Hauptschule (-n) – *nf* secondary modern school
Hauptstadt (-städte) – *nf* capital (city)
Hauptstraße (-n) – *nf* high street, major road
Hauptverkehrszeit (-en) – *nf* rush hour
Haus (Häuser) – *nnt* home, house
   ins Haus gehen* – *v irreg* to go inside

Kommen Sie/Komm gut gut nach Hause! – *excl* Have a safe journey home!
nach Hause gehen* – *v irreg* go home
zu Hause bleiben* – *v irreg* stay at home
zu Hause sein* – *v irreg* be at home
Hausarbeit – *nf* housework
Hausarbeit machen – *v reg* do housework
Hausaufgaben – *npl* homework
Hausaufgaben machen – *v reg* do homework
Häuschen (-) – *nnt* cottage
Hausflur (-e) – *nm* hall (domestic)
Hausfrau (-en) – *nf* housewife
Haushalt (-e) – *nm* household
Haushaltslehre – *nf* home economics
häuslich – *adj* domestic
Hausmann (-männer) – *nm* househusband
Hausmeister (-) – *nm* caretaker
Hausmeisterin (-nen) – *nf* caretaker
Hausmutter (-mütter) – *nf* matron
Hausnummer (-n) – *nf* house number
Hausschuh (-e) – *nm* slipper
Haustier (-e) – *nnt* pet
Haustür (-en) – *nf* front door
Hauswirtschaftslehre – *nf* home economics
Haut – *nf* skin
Hbf. – main railway station
heben – *v irreg* lift
   hochheben – *v irreg sep* lift up
Heck – *nnt, no pl* back (of car)
Hecke (-n) – *nf* hedge
Heft (-e) – *nnt* exercise book, jotter
Heftklammer (-n) – *nf* staple
Heftmaschine (-n) – *nf* stapler
heilig – *adj* holy
Heiligabend – *nm* Christmas Eve

---

nm - noun masculine   *nf* - noun feminine   *nnt* - noun neuter   *npl* - noun plural
nom- nominative   *acc* - accusative   *gen* - genitive   *dat* - dative

Heilige – *nmf* ‡ saint
heiliger Abend – *nm* Christmas Eve
Heimat – *nf* home area
Heimatstadt – *nf* native town
  Gute Heimreise! – *excl* Have a
  good journey home!
Heimspiel (-e) – *nnt* home game
Heimweh – *nnt* homesickness
  Ich habe Heimweh – I'm
  homesick
Heimwerker (-) – *nm* handyman
heiraten – *v reg* † marry, get married
heiß – *adj* hot
heiß sein* – *v irreg* be hot (weather)
  Mir ist heiß – I am hot
heißen – *v irreg* be called
  das heißt (d.h.) – that is to say (i.e.)
  Ich heiße... – My name is...
  Wie heißt du?/Wie heißen
  Sie? – What is your name?
  Wie heißt ...? – What does... mean?
heiter – *adj* cheerful, bright (of
  weather)
heizen – *v reg* heat
Heizgerät (-e) – *nnt* heater
Heizkörper (-) – *nm* radiator (in
  building)
Heizung (-en) – *nf* heating
Held (-en) – *nm wk* hero
Heldin (-nen) – *nf* heroine
helfen (+ dat) – *v irreg* help, aid,
  assist
hell – *adj* bright, light
hell~ – *pref* pale
hellblau – *adj* pale blue
Helm (-e) – *nm* helmet
Hemd (-en) – *nnt* shirt
Henne (-n) – *nf* hen
her – *adv* towards (speaker)
heraufkommen* – *v irreg sep* come
  up
herausfinden – *v irreg sep* find out

herauskommen* – *v irreg sep* come
  out
herausnehmen – *v irreg sep* take
  out, remove
Herberge (-n) – *nf* hostel
Herbergsmutter (-mütter) – *nf*
  youth hostel warden
Herbergsvater (-väter) – *nm* youth
  hostel warden
Herbst – *nm* autumn
  im Herbst – in autumn
Herbstferien – *npl* autumn half-term
  holiday
Herd (-e) – *nm* cooker, oven, stove
Herde (-n) – *nf* flock, herd
Herein! – *excl* Come in!
hereinkommen* – *v irreg sep* come in
hereinplatzen* – *v reg sep coll* gate-
  crash
Hering (-e) – *nm* herring
Heroin – *nnt* heroin (drug)
Herr (-en) – *nm wk* gentleman,
  master
Herr – Mr, Sir
  Herr Ober! – *excl* Waiter!
  mein Herr – Sir
Herren – Men's toilets
Herrenhaus (-häuser) – *nnt*
  mansion
Herrenkonfektion – *nf* men's
  clothes department
herrlich – *adj* gorgeous
herrschsüchtig – *adj* bossy
herstellen – *v reg sep* manufacture
herüber – *adv* over (across, towards
  speaker)
herum – *adv* about, around (place)
herumalbern – *v reg sep* mess about
herunterkommen* – *v irreg sep*
  come down
hervorragend – *adj* outstanding,
  very good
Herz (-en) – *nnt wk* heart
herzlich – *adj* sincere

Herzlichen Glückwunsch! – *excl* Congratulations!

heulen – *v reg* cry, weep, howl

Heuschnupfen – *nm* hay fever

heute – *adv* today

heute abend – tonight (evening)

heute nacht – tonight (night-time)

heutzutage – *adv* nowadays, today

hielt – *see halten*

hier – *adv* here

hier in der Nähe – nearby

hieß – *see heißen*

Hilfe – *nf* aid, assistance, help

  Erste Hilfe – *nf* first aid

Hilfe! – *excl* Help!

hilflos – *adj* helpless

hilfsbereit – *adj* helpful

Hilfspolizist (-en) – *nm wk* traffic warden

Himbeere (-n) – *nf* raspberry

Himbeertorte (-n) – *nf* raspberry tart

Himmel (-) – *nm* sky

himmelblau – *adj* sky blue

hin – *adv* away (from speaker)

hin und wieder – *adv* occasionally

hin und her laufen* – *v irreg* run backwards and forwards

hin und zurück – *adv* return, there and back

hinauflaufen* – *v irreg sep* run up

hinausgehen* – *v irreg sep* go out

hinauslaufen* aus (+ dat) – *v irreg sep* run out of (building)

sich hinauslehnen – *v reg refl sep* lean out

  Nicht hinauslehnen! – *excl* Do not lean out!

Hindernis (-se) – *nnt* obstacle

hindu – *adj* Hindu

Hindu (-s) – *nm* Hindu person

hineingehen* – *v irreg sep* go in (to)

hinfallen* – *v irreg sep* trip over, fall

hinlegen – *v reg sep* deposit; lay down

sich hinlegen – *v reg refl sep* lie down

sich hinsetzen – *v reg refl sep* sit down

hinstellen – *v reg sep* put down (vertical)

hinten – *adv* back

hinter (+ acc/dat) – *prep* behind, past (beyond)

Hintern (-) – *nm* behind

hinüber – *adv* over (across, away from speaker)

sich hinüberbeugen – *v reg refl sep* lean over

hinunterkommen* – *v irreg sep* come down, go down

hinunterlaufen* – *v irreg sep* run down

  Sie ist die Straße hinuntergelaufen – She ran down the street

Hinweis (-e) – *nm* tip, clue

hinzufügen – *v reg sep* add

historisch – *adj* historic

Hit (-s) – *nm* hit song (in English)

Hitze – *nf* heat

hitzefrei – *adj* school closure due to hot weather

Hitzewelle (-n) – *nf* heatwave

Hobby (-s) – *nnt* hobby

hoch – *adj* high

Hochachtungsvoll – *adv* Yours faithfully (very formal)

Hochhaus (-häuser) – *nnt* block of flats

Hochschule (-n) – *nf* university

höchst – *adj* highest

Höchst~ – *pref* maximum

Höchstgeschwindigkeit (-en) – *nf* maximum speed

  mit Höchstgeschwindigkeit – at full speed

Höchsttemperatur (-en) – *nf* maximum temperature

---

höchstwahrscheinlich – *adv* very probably

Hochwasser – *nnt* high tide

  bei Hochwasser – at high tide

Hochzeit (-en) – *nf* marriage (ceremony), wedding

Hochzeitskleid (-er) – *nnt* wedding dress

Hocker (-) – *nm* stool

Hockey – *nnt* hockey

Hof (Höfe) – *nm* yard (place)

hoffen – *v reg* hope

hoffentlich – *adv* hopefully

Hoffnung (-en) – *nf* hope

höflich – *adj* polite

Höflichkeit (-en) – *nf* politeness

Höhe – *nf* height (geographical)

höher – *adj* higher

hohl – *adj* hollow

Höhle (-n) – *nf* cave

holen – *v reg* fetch, get

Holland – *nnt* Holland

Holländer (-) – *nm* Dutchman

  Der Fliegende Holländer – The Flying Dutchman

Holländerin (-nen) – *nf* Dutchwoman

holländisch – *adj* Dutch

Holz – *nnt* wood

  aus Holz – wooden

Honig (-e) – *nm* honey

hören – *v reg* hear, listen (to)

  Kassetten hören – *v reg* listen to tapes

  von (+ dat) hören – *v reg* hear from

Hörer (-) – *nm* hand set, receiver (phone)

  den Hörer abnehmen – *v irreg sep* pick up phone

Horizont (-e) – *nm* horizon

  am Horizont – on the horizon

Horn (Hörner) – *nnt* horn (music)

Horror – *nm* horror

Horrorfilm (-e) – *nm* horror film

Horrorgeschichte (-n) – *nf* horror story

Hose (-n) – *nf* trousers

  eine kurze Hose – *nf* a pair of shorts

Hotel (-s) – *nnt* hotel

Hotelverzeichnis (-se) – *nnt* list of hotels

hübsch – *adj* pretty

Hubschrauber (-) – *nm* helicopter

Hubschrauberlandeplatz (-plätze) – *nm* heliport

Hüfte (-n) – *nf* hip

Hügel (-n) – *nf* hill

Huhn (Hühner) – *nnt* chicken, hen

Humor – *nm* humour

Hund (-e) – *nm* dog

  ein junger Hund – *nm* a puppy

  Warnung vor dem Hund – beware of the dog

hundert – *adj* hundred

hundertste – *adj* hundredth

Hündin (-nen) – *nf* dog

Hunger – *nm* hunger

Hunger haben – *v irreg* be hungry

  Ich habe Hunger – I am hungry

hungrig – *adj* hungry

hungrig sein* – *v irreg* be hungry

Hupe (-n) – *nf* horn (car)

hupen – *v reg* blow the horn (car)

Hürde (-n) – *nf* hurdle

Husten (-) – *nm* cough

husten – *v reg* † cough

Hustensaft (-säfte) – *nm* cough medicine

Hut (Hüte) – *nm* hat

  ohne Hut – bare-headed

Hüttenkäse – *nm* cottage cheese

hygienisch – *adj* hygienic

---

adj - adjective	*v reg* - verb regular	*v sep* - verb separable	† - see verb info
prep - preposition	*v irreg* - verb irregular	*v refl* - verb reflexive	* - takes sein

I

ich – *pron* I
IC-Zug (-Züge) – *nm* Inter-City train
ideal – *adj* ideal
Idee (-n) – *nf* idea
  ein paar Ideen – some ideas
identifizieren – *v reg* † identify
Identität (-en) – *nf* identity
Idiot (-en) – *nm wk* idiot
idiotisch – *adj* idiotic
ihm – *pron dat m, nt* him, it, to him, to it
ihn – *pron acc m* him, it
ihnen – *pron dat* them, to them
Ihnen – *pron dat sing or pl* you (formal)
ihr – *pron dat f* her, it, to her, to it
ihr – *pron nom pl* you (informal)
ihr – *poss adj* her, its, their
Ihr – *poss adj* your (formal)
Ihr – *poss adj* With best wishes from (male, formal)
Ihre – *poss adj* With best wishes from (female, formal)
Illustration (-en) – *nf* illustration
Illustrierte – *nf* ‡ glossy magazine
im – (= in dem) in the
im Bus – on the bus
im Freien – *adv* outdoors
im Frühling – in spring
im Moment – *adv* at present
im Notfall – in an emergency
im Sommer – in summer
im Zug – on the train
Imbiß (Imbisse) – *nm* snack
Imbißstube (-n) – *nf* snack bar
immer – *adv* always
  für immer – *adv* for ever
immer noch – *adv* still
immer schlimmer – *adv* worse and worse
immer wieder – *adv* again and again

Immobilienmakler (-) – *nm* estate agent
Imperfekt – *nnt* imperfect tense
in (+ acc/dat) – *prep* in, into, to, at (place)
  in die Stadt – into town
  in der Stadt – in town
in Ordnung! – *excl* OK!
in – *adj inv* trendy
inbegr./inbegriffen – included
  alles inbegriffen – all included
  Bedienung inbegriffen – service included
  nicht inbegriffen – not included
indem – *sub conj* whilst
Inder (-) – *nm* Indian person (Asia)
Inderin (-nen) – *nf* Indian person (Asia)
Indianer (-) – *nm* Indian (America)
Indianerin (-nen) – *nf* Indian (America)
indianisch – *adj* Indian (America)
Indien – *nnt* India (Asia)
indisch – *adj* Indian (Asia)
individuell – *adj* individual
Individuum (Individuen) – *nnt* individual
Industrie (-n) – *nf* industry
Industriegebiet (-e) – *nnt* industrial area
industriell – *adj* industrial
Infektion (-en) – *nf* infection
Informatik – *nf* IT, information technology, computer studies
Informatiker (-) – *nm* computer scientist
Informatikerin (-nen) – *nf* computer scientist
Information (-en) – *nf* information
Informationsbüro (-s) – *nnt* tourist information office
informatisieren – *v reg* † computerise

---

nm - noun masculine   *nf* - noun feminine   *nnt* - noun neuter   *npl* - noun plural
nom- nominative   *acc* - accusative   *gen* - genitive   *dat* - dative

informieren – *v reg* † inform, let s.o. know

Ingenieur (-e) – *nm* engineer

Ingwer – *nm* ginger

Inhalt – *nm, no pl* contents

Inhaltsverzeichnis (-se) – *nnt* contents (book)

inkl. – included

inklusive – *adv* included

Inland – *nnt* home (not abroad)

Inline Skates – *npl* roller blades

Innenstadt (-städte) – *nf* town centre

Innere – *nnt* ‡ inside

Insekt (-en) – *nnt* insect

Insel (-n) – *nf* island

Inserat (-e) – *nnt* advert (small ad)

insgesamt – *adv* altogether

installieren – *v reg* † install

Instrument (-e) – *nnt* instrument

intelligent – *adj* intelligent, smart

Intelligenz – *nf* intelligence

Inter-City-Zug (-Züge) – *nm* Inter-City train

interessant – *adj* interesting

Interesse (-n) – *nnt* interest

sich interessieren für (+ acc) – *v reg refl* † be interested in

Internat (-e) – *nnt* boarding school

international – *adj* international

Interne – *nmf* ‡ boarder

Internet – *nnt* internet

das Internet benutzen – *v reg* † surf the net

Interview (-s) – *nnt* interview

inzwischen – *adv* meanwhile

Ire (-n) – *nm wk* Irishman

Ich bin Ire – I am Irish

irgend~ – *pref* some (unspecified)

irgendein – *adj* any

irgendwann – *adv* sometime

irgendwie – somehow

irgendwo – *adv* somewhere

irgendwo anders – somewhere else

Irin (-nen) – *nf* Irishwoman

Ich bin Irin – I am Irish

irisch – *adj* Irish

Irland – *nnt* Eire, Ireland

Nordirland – *nnt* Northern Ireland

Die Republik Irland – *nf* Eire

islamisch – *adj* Islamic

Island – *nnt* Iceland

isländisch – *adj* Icelandic

ist – *see sein**

es ist (+ nom) – it is

ißt – *see essen*

Italien – *nnt* Italy

Italiener (-) – *nm* Italian

Italienerin (-nen) – *nf* Italian

italienisch – *adj* Italian

Italienisch – *nnt* Italian (language)

J

ja – *adv* yes

Jacht (-en) – *nf* yacht

Jachthafen (-häfen) – *nm* yacht marina

Jacke (-n) – *nf* jacket

Jagd – *nf* hunt, chase

auf die Jagd gehen* – *v irreg* hunt

jagen – *v reg* chase

Jahr (-e) – *nnt* year

das ganze Jahr – all year round

Ein glückliches neues Jahr! – *excl* Happy New Year!

---

adj - adjective	*v reg* - verb regular	*v sep* - verb separable	† - see verb info
prep - preposition	*v irreg* - verb irregular	*v refl* - verb reflexive	* - takes sein

jedes Jahr – every year
letztes Jahr – last year
nächstes Jahr – next year
X Jahre alt sein* – be X years old
Jahrestag (-e) – *nm* anniversary
Jahreszeit (-en) – *nf* season of the year
Jahrhundert (-e) – *nnt* century
   im 20. Jahrhundert – in the 20th century
jährlich – *adj* annual, yearly
Jahrmarkt (-märkte) – *nm* fun fair
Jahrtausend – *nnt* millennium
Januar – *nm* January
   im Januar – in January
Japan – *nnt* Japan
Japaner (-) – *nm* Japanese person
Japanerin (-nen) – *nf* Japanese person
japanisch – *adj* Japanese
jawohl – *adv* yes, certainly
Jazz – *nm* jazz
Jazzgruppe (-n) – *nf* jazz band
je – *adv* ever
Jeans – *nf* jeans, a pair of jeans
jede – *adj* each, every
jeden Abend – every evening
jeden Tag – every day
jeder/jede – *indef pron* anybody, each one
jeder einzelne – *pron* every one
jedesmal – *adv* every time
jedoch – *adv* however
jemand – *pron nom, acc* somebody
jemand anders – *pron* someone else
jemandem – *pron dat* somebody
jene – *dem pron* those
jener – *dem pron* that
jetzt – *adv* now
jeweils – *adv* respectively, at that time
Job (-s) – *nm* job
Joga – *nm, no pl* yoga

jodeln – *v reg* yodel
joggen – *v reg* go jogging
Jogging – *nnt* jogging
Jogginganzug (-züge) – *nm* track suit
Joghurt (-s) – *nm* yoghurt
rote Johannisbeere (-n) – *nf* redcurrant
schwarze Johannisbeere (-n) – *nf* blackcurrant
Journalist (-en) – *nm wk* journalist
Journalistin (-nen) – *nf* journalist
Joystick (-s) – *nm* joystick (IT)
Jude (-n) – *nm wk* Jew
Jüdin (-nen) – *nf* Jewess
jüdisch – *adj* Jewish
das jüdische Neujahr – *nnt* Rosh Hashanah
Judo – *nnt* judo
Jugend – *nf, no pl* youth, young people
Jugendherberge (-n) – *nf* youth hostel
Jugendklub (-s) – *nm* youth club
Jugendliche – *nmf ‡* teenager, young person
Juli – *nm* July
   im Juli – in July
Julei – *see* Juli
Jumbojet (-s) – *nnt* jumbo jet
jung – *adj* young
Junge (-n) – *nm wk* boy
jünger – *adj* younger
Jungfrau – (horoscope) Virgo
Junggeselle (-n) – *nm wk* bachelor
jüngste – *adj* youngest
Juni – *nm* June
   im Juni – in June
Juno – *see* Juni
Juwelier (-) – *nm* jeweller
Juweliergeschäft (-e) – *nnt* jeweller's shop
Juwelierin (-nen) – *nf* jeweller

---

nm - noun masculine   *nf* - noun feminine   *nnt* - noun neuter   *npl* - noun plural
nom - nominative   *acc* - accusative   *gen* - genitive   *dat* - dative

K

Kabelfernsehen (-) – *nnt* cable TV
Kabine (-n) – *nf* cabin
Käfer (-) – *nm* beetle
Kaffee – *nm* coffee
  Einen schwarzen Kaffee, bitte
  – A black coffee, please
Kaffee Hag ® – *nm* decaffeinated
  coffee
Kaffee mit Milch – coffee with milk
Kaffee mit Sahne – white coffee
Kaffeekanne (-n) – *nf* coffee pot
Kaffeelöffel (-) – *nm* teaspoon
Kaffeesatz – *nm* coffee grounds
Käfig (-e) – *nm* cage
kahl – *adj* bald
Kai (-s) – *nm* quay
Kakao – *nm* cocoa
Kalb (Kälber) – *nnt* calf
Kalbfleisch – *nnt* veal
Kalender (-) – *nm* diary, calendar
kalt sein* – *v irreg* be cold (weather)
  Es ist kalt – It is cold
  Es ist sehr kalt – It is freezing
kalt – *adj* cold
  Mir ist kalt – I am cold
  kaltes Wasser – *nnt* cold water
Kälte – *nf* cold
kam – *see* kommen*
Kamel (-e) – *nnt* camel
Kamera (-s) – *nf* (video) camera
Kamerad (-en) – *nm wk* friend, mate
Kameradin (-nen) – *nf* friend, mate
Kamin (-e) – *nm* fire-place
Kamm (Kämme) – *nm* comb
  sich kämmen – *v reg refl* comb
  one's hair
Kampf (Kämpfe) – *nm* fight
kämpfen – *v reg* fight
Kanada – *nnt* Canada

Kanal (Kanäle) – *nm* canal
Kanal – *nm* English Channel
Kanaltunnel – *nm* Channel Tunnel
Kanarienvogel (-vögel) – *nm* canary
Kandidat (-en) – *nm wk* candidate
Kandidatin (-nen) – *nf* candidate
Kaninchen (-) – *nnt* rabbit
kann – *see* können
Kännchen (-) – *nnt* small pot
  ein Kännchen Kaffee/Tee – an
  individual pot of coffee/tea
Kanne (-n) – *nf* pot
kannte – *see* kennen
Kantine (-n) – *nf* canteen
Kanton (-e) – *nm* canton
Kanu (-s) – *nm* canoe
Kanu fahren* – *v irreg* canoe
Kanzler (-) – *nm* Chancellor
Kapelle (-n) – *nf* chapel
Kapitän (-e) – *nm* captain (ship)
Kapitel (-) – *nnt* chapter
kaputt – *adj* damaged
kaputt machen – *v reg* spoil, ruin
Karambolage (-n) – *nf* multiple crash
Karate – *nnt* karate
Karfreitag – *nm* Good Friday
kariert – *adj* check pattern
Karneval – *nm* Carnival
Karo (-s) – *nnt* square, diamond,
  check pattern
Karotte (-n) – *nf* carrot
Karriere (-n) – *nf* career
Karte (-n) – *nf* card
  Karten spielen – *v reg* play cards
Kartenspiel (-e) – *nnt* card game
Kartoffel (-n) – *nf* potato
Kartoffelpüree – *nnt* mashed potato
Kartoffelsalat – *nm* potato salad
Karton (-s) – *nm* cardboard box

---

adj - adjective	*v reg* - verb regular	*v sep* - verb separable	† - see verb info
prep - preposition	*v irreg* - verb irregular	*v refl* - verb reflexive	* - takes sein

aus Karton – made of cardboard
Karussell (-s) – *nnt* roundabout (fair)
Käse – *nm* cheese
Käsebrot (-e) – *nnt* cheese sandwich
Käsekuchen (-) – *nm* cheesecake
Kasse (-n) – *nf* cash desk, checkout, till
an die Kasse gehen* – *v irreg* go to the cash desk
Kassette (-n) – *nf* cassette, tape
Kassettenrekorder (-) – *nm* tape recorder
Kassierer (-) – *nm* cashier
Kassiererin (-nen) – *nf* cashier
Kasten (Kästen) – *nm* box
Katalysator (-en) – *nm* catalytic converter
mit Kat – with a catalytic converter
katastrophal – *adj* disastrous
Katastrophe (-n) – *nf* disaster
Kater (-) – *nm* tomcat; hangover
Katholik (-en) – *nm wk* Catholic
Katholikin (-nen) – *nf* Catholic
katholisch – *adj* Catholic
Kätzchen (-) – *nnt* kitten
Katze (-n) – *nf* cat
Kauf (Käufe) – *nm* purchase
kaufen – *v reg* buy, purchase
Kauffrau (-en) – *nf* businesswoman
Kaufhaus (-häuser) – *nnt* department store
Kaufmann (-männer) – *nm* businessman
Kaugummi (-s) – *nm* chewing gum
kaum – *adv* hardly, scarcely
Kaution (-en) – *nf* deposit (against damage)
Kegelbahn (-en) – *nf* bowling alley
kegeln – *v reg* play skittles, bowl
kehren – *v reg* sweep
Kehrseite (-n) – *nf* wrong side
kein – *adj* no, not any
keine – *adj* not any

Keks (-e) – *nm* biscuit
Keller (-) – *nm* cellar, basement
Kellner (-) – *nm* waiter
Kellnerin (-nen) – *nf* waitress
kennen – *v irreg* know (person)
kennenlernen – *v reg sep* get to know, meet
Kennzeichen (-) – *nnt* number plate, registration number (car)
Kerl (-e) – *nm* chap
Kern (-e) – *nm* kernel, nucleus
Kernenergie – *nf* nuclear power
Kernkraftwerk (-e) – *nnt* nuclear power station
Kerze (-n) – *nf* candle
Ketchup – *nm* ketchup
Kette (-n) – *nf* chain
kichern – *v reg* giggle
Kilo – *nnt* kilo(gram)
pro Kilo – by the kilo
zwei Kilo Äpfel – two kilos of apples
Kilometer – *nm* kilometre
zehn Kilometer von ... entfernt – 10 kilometres from...
Kind (-er) – *nnt* child (ren)
Kindergarten (-gärten) – *nm* nursery school
Kindergeld – *nnt* child benefit
kinderleicht – *adj* child's play
Kindermädchen (-) – *nnt* nanny
Kindheit (-en) – *nf* childhood
Kinn (-e) – *nnt* chin
Kino (-s) – *nnt* cinema
Kiosk (-e) – *nm* kiosk
Kirche (-n) – *nf* church
Kirsche (-n) – *nf* cherry
Kissen (-) – *nnt* pillow, cushion
Kissenbezug (-züge) – *nm* pillowcase
Kiste (-n) – *nf* box; banger (car)
Kiwi (-s) – *nf* kiwi fruit
Klammer (-n) – *nf* brackets
in Klammern – in brackets

---

nm - noun masculine
nom- nominative
nf - noun feminine
acc - accusative
nnt - noun neuter
gen - genitive
npl - noun plural
dat - dative

klappen – *v reg* work, function
klar – *adj* clear, distinct
Klarinette (-n) – *nf* clarinet
Klarinette spielen – *v reg* play the clarinet
Klasse (-n) – *nf* class, form
  einmal erster Klasse, bitte – a first class ticket, please
Klasse! – *excl* Great!
Klassenarbeit (-en) – *nf* formal class test
Klassenfahrt (-en) – *nf* school trip
Klassenkamerad (-en) – *nm wk* school friend
Klassenkameradin (-nen) – *nf* school friend
Klassenschwächste – *nmf* ‡ bottom of class
Klassenzimmer (-) – *nnt* classroom
klassisch – *adj* classical
klauen – *v reg coll* steal
Klaviatur (-en) – *nf* keyboard (piano)
Klavier – *nnt* upright piano
Klavier spielen – *v reg* play the piano
kleben – *v reg* stick, paste
Klebstoff (-e) – *nm* glue
Kleid (-er) – *nnt* dress
Kleider (-) – *npl* clothes
Kleiderbügel (-) – *nm* coat hanger
Kleiderschrank (schränke) – *nm* wardrobe
Kleidung (-en) – *nf* clothes, outfit
Kleidungsstück (-e) – *nnt* article of clothing
klein – *adj* small, short (not tall)
Kleinanzeige (-n) – *nf* classified (small) ad
Kleinbus (-se) – *nm* minibus
Kleingeld – *nnt* change (coins)
  Haben Sie Kleingeld? – Have you any change?
Klempner (-) – *nm* plumber

Klempnerin (-nen) – *nf* plumber
klettern – *v reg* climb
Klima (-s) – *nnt* climate
Klimaanlage (-n) – *nf* air conditioning
  mit Klimaanlage – air conditioned
Klingel (-n) – *nf* bell (door, school)
klingeln – *v reg* ring the (door)bell
  es klingelte – *v reg* the (door)bell rang
Klinik (-en) – *nf* hospital, clinic
Klippe (-n) – *nf* cliff
Klo (-s) – *nnt coll* toilet
klopfen – *v reg* knock
  Es klopft – There's a knock at the door
  an die Tür klopfen – knock on the door
Klub (-s) – *nm* club
klug – *adj* clever
knackig – *adj* crisp, crunchy
Knall (-e) – *nm* bang
Knallkörper (-) – *nm* firework
knapp – *adj* short of
  Ich bin knapp bei Kasse – I'm broke
Kneipe (-n) – *nf* pub
Knie (-n) – *nnt* knee
knien – *v reg* kneel
Knoblauch – *nm* garlic
Knochen (-) – *nm* bone
Knopf (Knöpfe) – *nm* button
Knüller (-) – *nm* blockbuster
knurren – *v reg* growl
knusprig – *adj* crunchy
Koch (Köche) – *nm* cook
kochen – *v reg* cook, boil, be boiling
Kochen – *nnt* cookery
Köchin (-nen) – *nf* cook
Koffer (-) – *nm* suitcase
  Koffer packen – *v reg* pack cases
Kofferkuli (-s) – *nm* luggage trolley
Kofferradio (-s) – *nnt* transistor radio
Kofferraum (-räume) – *nm* boot (car)

Kohl – *nm* cabbage
Kohle (-n) – *nf* coal
Kollege (-n) – *nm wk* colleague
Kollegin (-nen) – *nf* colleague
Köln – Cologne
Kölnisch Wasser – *nnt* eau de Cologne
Komfort – *nm* comfort
komisch – *adj* funny, amusing
Komma (-s) – *nnt* comma (,)
kommen* – *v irreg* come
 ans Ziel kommen* – *v irreg* finish (sport)
 Es kommt darauf an – It depends
 ums Leben kommen* – *v irreg* lose one's life
Kommode (-n) – *nf* chest of drawers
Kommunismus – *nm* communism
Komödie (-n) – *nf* comic film
Komplize (-n) – *nm wk* accomplice
kompliziert – *adj* complicated
Komplizin (-nen) – *nf* accomplice
Kompott (-e) – *nnt* stewed fruit
Konditorei (-en) – *nf* cake shop
Kondom (-e) – *nnt* condom
Konfektion (-en) – *nf* ready-made clothes
König (-e) – *nm* king
Königin (-nen) – *nf* queen
das Vereinigte Königreich – *nnt* the United Kingdom
königsblau – *adj* royal blue
können – *v irreg* be able to, can
konnte – *see können* could, was able to
Kontaktlinse (-n) – *nf* contact lense
Kontinent (-e) – *nm* continent (geographical)
Konto (Konten) – *nnt* account (bank)
Kontoauszug (-züge) – *nm* bank statement
Kontrabaß (-bässe) – *nm* double bass
Kontrolle (-en) – *nf* check, control

kontrollieren – *v reg* † check tickets
 den Ölstand kontrollieren – *v reg* † check the oil level
 den Reifendruck kontrollieren – *v reg* † check the tyre pressure
 Fahrkarten kontrollieren – *v reg* † check tickets
Konzert (-e) – *nnt* concert; concerto
Kopf (Köpfe) – *nm* head
 auf den Kopf gestellt – *adj* upside down
 Kopf oder Zahl? – Heads or tails?
Kopfhörer (-) – *nm* headphones
Kopfkissen (-) – *nnt* pillow
Kopfsalat – *nm* lettuce
Kopfschmerzen – *npl* headache
Kopfschmerzen haben – *v irreg* have a headache
kopieren – *v reg* † copy, write down
Koppel (-n) – *nf* paddock
Koran – *nm* Koran
Korb (Körbe) – *nm* basket
Korbball – *nm* netball
Korken (-) – *nm* cork
Korkenzieher (-) – *nm* corkscrew
Kornett (-e) – *nnt* cornet (music)
Körper (-) – *nm* body
körperlich – *adj* physical
körperliche Bewegung (-en) – *nf* exercise (sport)
korrigieren – *v reg* † correct, mark
Kosmetikerin (-nen) – *nf* beautician
Kosmetiktäschchen (-) – *nnt* make-up bag
Kosten – *npl* costs
kosten – *v reg* † cost, taste
 Was kostet das? – How much is it?
kostbar – *adj* precious
kostenlos – *adj* free
köstlich – *adj* delicious, yummy
Kostüm (-e) – *nnt* lady's suit
Kotelett (-s) – *nnt* chop, cutlet
kotzen – *v reg coll* vomit

---

nm - noun masculine	*nf* - noun feminine	*nnt* - noun neuter	*npl* - noun plural
nom- nominative	*acc* - accusative	*gen* - genitive	*dat* - dative

Krabbe (-n) – *nf* crab, shrimp
Krach (Kräche) – *nm* din, loud noise, row
Kraft (Kräfte) – *nf* strength
Kragen (-) – *nm* collar
krank – *adj* ill, unwell
krank werden* – *v irreg* fall ill
Kranke – *nmf* ‡ sick person
Krankenhaus (-häuser) – *nnt* hospital
Krankenpfleger (-) – *nm* male nurse
Krankenschwester (-n) – *nf* nurse
Krankenwagen (-) – *nm* ambulance
Krankheit (-en) – *nf* illness
Kräutertee (-s) – *nm* herbal tea
Krawatte (-n) – *nf* tie
Krebs – *nm* cancer
Kreditkarte (-n) – *nf* credit card
Kreide – *nf* chalk
Kreis (-e) – *nm* circle, district (political)
Kreisdiagramm (-e) – *nnt* pie chart
Kreuz (-e) – *nnt* cross; small of back
  Autobahnkreuz – *nnt* motorway junction
Kreuzfahrt (-en) – *nf* cruise
Kreuzung (-en) – *nf* crossroads
Kreuzworträtsel (-) – *nnt* crossword
Kricket – *nnt* cricket
Krieg (-e) – *nm* war
kriegen – *v reg coll* get, obtain
Kriegsmarine (-n) – *nf* navy
Krimi (-s) – *nm* detective story
Kriminalfilm (-e) – *nm* detective film
Krokodil (-e) – *nnt* crocodile
Krug (Krüge) – *nm* jug
Küche (-n) – *nf* kitchen
Kuchen (-) – *nm* cake, tart
Küchenmaschine (-n) – *nf* food processor
Kuckucksuhr (-en) – *nf* cuckoo clock

Kugelschreiber (-) – *nm* ball-point pen, biro®
Kuh (Kühe) – *nf* cow
kühl – *adj* cool
Kühler (-) – *nm* radiator (in car)
Kühlschrank (-schränke) – *nm* fridge
Kuli (-s) – *nm* ball point pen
sich kümmern um (+ acc) – *v reg refl* care for, look after, be concerned with
Kunde (-n) – *nm wk* customer
Kundin (-nen) – *nf* customer
Kündigung (-en) – *nf* notice, dismissal
künftig – *adj* future
Kunst – *nf* art
Kunsterziehung – *nf* art (education)
Kunstgalerie (-n) – *nf* art gallery
Kunsthochschule (-n) – *nf* art school
Künstler (-) – *nm* artist, performer
Künstlerin (-nen) – *nf* artist, performer
Kunststoff (-e) – *nm* plastic
  aus Kunststoff – made of plastic
Kupplung (-en) – *nf* clutch (car)
Kur (-en) – *nf* cure, course of treatment
Kurort (-e) – *nm* spa
Kurs (-e) – *nm* course; rate of exchange
Kursivschrift – *nf* italic
Kurstadt (-städte) – *nf* spa town
Kurzentrum (-zentren) – *nnt* spa centre
Kurve (-n) – *nf* bend
kurvenreich – *adj* twisty
kurz – *adj* short, brief
kurzsichtig – *adj* short-sighted
Kusine (-n) – *nf* cousin
Kuß (Küsse) – *nm* kiss
küssen – *v reg* kiss
Küste (-n) – *nf* coast
  an der Küste – by the sea, at the seaside

---

adj - adjective	*v reg* - verb regular	*v sep* - verb separable	† - see verb info
prep - preposition	*v irreg* - verb irregular	*v refl* - verb reflexive	* - takes sein

L

l – litre
Labor (-s) – *nnt* laboratory
Lächeln (-) – *nnt* smile
lächeln – *v reg* smile
lächelnd – *adj* smiling
lachen – *v reg* laugh
lächerlich – *adj* ridiculous
Lachs (-e) – *nm* salmon
laden – *v irreg* load
Laden (Läden) – *nm* shop
  Tante-Emma-Laden (-Läden)
  – *nm* small shop
Ladendieb (-e) – *nm* shoplifter
Ladentisch (-e) – *nm* counter (shop)
lag – *see liegen*
Lage (-n) – *nf* position
Lagerfeuer (-) – *nnt* camp-fire
Laken (-) – *nnt* sheet (bed)
Lamm (Lämmer) – *nnt* lamb
  (animal)
Lammfleisch – *nnt* lamb (meat)
Lampe (-n) – *nf* light, lamp
Land (Länder) – *nnt* country, land
  auf dem Lande – in the country
Landarbeiter (-) – *nm* farm worker
landen* – *v reg* † land
Landkarte (-n) – *nf* map
ländlich – *adj* rural
Landschaft (-en) – *nf* countryside,
  scenery
landschaftlich – *adj* scenic
Landstraße (-n) – *nf* country road
Landtag (-e) – *nm* regional parliament
Landung (-en) – *nf* landing (plane)
landwirtschaftlich – *adj* agricultural
lang – *adj* long
  vor langer Zeit – long ago
lange – *adv* for a long time, a long while
  Es war schon lange her – It was
  a long time ago

Länge (-n) – *nf* length (measurement)
länger – *adj* longer
  nicht länger – *adv* no longer
Langeweile – *nf* boredom
langsam – *adj* slow
langsamer werden* – *v irreg* slow
down
Langspielplatte (-n) – *nf* LP
langweilen – *v reg* bore
sich langweilen – *v reg refl* to be bored
langweilig – *adj* boring
Laptop (-s) – *nm* laptop
Lärm – *nm* loud noise
las – *see lesen*
Laserdrucker (-) – *nm* laser printer
lassen – *v irreg* let
  den Arzt kommen lassen –
  v irreg send for the doctor
  etwas machen lassen – *v irreg*
  get sthg done
  etwas reinigen lassen – *v irreg*
  have sthg cleaned
  etwas reparieren lassen –
  v irreg have sthg repaired
  fallen lassen – *v irreg* drop
Lastwagen (-) – *nm* lorry, truck
Lastwagenfahrer (-) – *nm* lorry driver
Lastwagenfahrerin (-nen) – *nf*
lorry driver
Latein – *nnt* Latin
lateinisch – *adj* Latin
Laterne (-n) – *nf* lantern
Lauf (Läufe) – *nm* run, course
laufen* – *v irreg* run
  Was läuft? – What's on? (cinema)
Läufer (-) – *nm* half back
Laune (-n) – *nf* mood
  schlechter Laune – in a bad
  mood

---

nm - noun masculine	*nf* - noun feminine	*nnt* - noun neuter	*npl* - noun plural
nom- nominative	*acc* - accusative	*gen* - genitive	*dat* - dative

guter Laune – in a good mood
laut – *adj* loud, noisy, aloud
läuten – *v reg* † ring (bell)
Lautsprecher (-) – *nm* loudspeaker
Lazarett (-e) – *nnt* sick bay (school)
Leben – *nnt* life
  im täglichen Leben – in daily life
  ums Leben kommen* – *v irreg*
  lose one's life
leben – *v reg* live (be alive)
lebend – *adj* alive, living
lebendig – *adj* lively, alive
Lebenskunde – *nf* PSE
lebenslänglich – *adj* lifelong
Lebenslauf (-läufe) – *nm* CV,
  curriculum vitae
Lebensmittel (-) – *nnt* groceries
Lebensmittelgeschäft (-e) – *nnt*
  grocer's shop
Lebensmittelhändler (-) – *nm* grocer
Lebensmittelhändlerin (-nen) –
  nf grocer
Lebensstandard – *nm* standard of
  living
Leber (-n) – *nf* liver
Leberwurst – *nf* liver sausage
lebhaft – *adj* lively
Lebkuchen – *nm* ginger bread
lecken – *v reg* lick
lecker – *adj* delicious, appetizing
Leder (-) – *nnt* leather
  aus Leder – made of leather
Lederhose – *nf* leather shorts
Lederwaren – *npl* leather goods
ledig – *adj* unmarried
Ledige – *nf* ‡ single person
leer – *adj* empty
leeren – *v reg* empty
legen – *v reg* place, lay sthg down
Leggings – *npl* leggings
lehnen – *v reg* lean
Lehnstuhl (-stühle) – *nm* armchair

Lehre (-n) – *nf* apprenticeship
lehren – *v reg* teach
Lehrer (-) – *nm* teacher, instructor
Lehrerin (-nen) – *nf* teacher, instructor
Lehrerzimmer (-) – *nnt* staff room
Lehrling (-e) – *nm* apprentice
leicht – *adj* light (not heavy)
Leichtathletik – *nf* athletics
Leichtathletik treiben – *v irreg* do
  athletics
Es tut mir leid! – I'm sorry!
leiden – *v irreg* suffer
leider – *adv* unfortunately, sadly
leihen – *v irreg* lend
Leine (-n) – *nf* lead (dog)
Leinwand (-wände) – *nf* screen
  (cinema)
leise – *adj* quiet (without noise)
leise – *adv* silently
leisten – *v reg* † achieve
sich leisten – *v reg dat refl* † afford
Leistung (-en) – *nf* achievement,
  performance
Leistungsfach (-fächer) – *nnt* A
  Level subject
Leistungsgruppe (-n) – *nf* set (school)
Leiter (-n) – *nf* ladder
Leitung (-en) – *nf* leadership,
  management
  eine elektrische Leitung – an
  electrical lead
Leitungswasser – *nnt* tap water
Lektüre – *nf* reading matter
Lenkrad (-räder) – *nnt* steering wheel
lernen – *v reg* learn, study
  Seit wann lernst du Deutsch? –
  How long have you been learning
  German?
Lernprogramm (-e) – *nnt*
  curriculum
lesen – *v irreg* read
Lesen – *nnt* reading
Leser (-) – *nm* reader

adj - adjective	*v reg* - verb regular	*v sep* - verb separable	† - see verb info
prep - preposition	*v irreg* - verb irregular	*v refl* - verb reflexive	* - takes sein

Leserin (-nen) – *nf* reader
letzte – *adj* last, final
  letzte Woche – last week
  letztes Jahr – last year
Leuchtturm (-türme) – *nm* lighthouse
Leute – *npl* people
Licht (-er) – *nnt* light
  das Licht anmachen – *v reg sep*
  put on light
Lichtstift (-e) – *nm* light pen
Lidschatten – *nm* eye shadow
lieb – *adj* likeable, loveable, sweet
  Ich habe dich lieb – I am fond of
  you
Liebe – Dear (in letter to female)
Liebe (-n) – *nf* love
lieben – *v reg* love, adore
liebenswürdig – *adj* agreeable (nice)
Lieber – Dear (in letter to male)
lieber – *adv* preferably
  Ich trinke lieber Tee als
  Kaffee – I prefer tea to coffee
lieber haben – *v irreg* prefer
Liebesroman (-e) – *nm* love story
liebevoll – *adj* affectionate
Liebling – *nm* favourite
Lieblings~ – *pref* favourite
am liebsten – *adv* most of all
Lied (-er) – *nnt* song
lief – *see laufen**
liefern – *v reg* deliver
Lieferung (-en) – *nf* delivery
Lieferwagen (-) – *nm* van
liegen – *v irreg* lie (be situated)
liegenlassen – *v irreg (sep)* leave
  lying around
Liegesitz (-e) – *nm* couchette
Liegestuhl (-stühle) – *nm* deckchair
liest – *see lesen*
Lift – *nm* lift
Liga (Ligen) – *nf* league
lila – *adj inv* mauve

Limo – *nf coll* lemonade
Limonade (-n) – *nf* lemonade
Lineal (-e) – *nnt* ruler
Linie (-n) – *nf* line, route (tram, bus)
  Nehmen Sie den Bus Linie 3! –
  Catch the number three bus!
linke – *adj* left
  auf der linken Seite – on the left
  hand side
links – *adv* on the left
  nach links gehen – to go left
Linksaußen (-) – *nm* left wing (sport)
linkshändig – *adj* left-handed
  Ich bin Linkshänder – (male) I
  am left-handed
  Ich bin Linkshänderin –
  (female) I am left-handed
Linse (-n) – *nf* lens; lentil
Lippe (-n) – *nf* lip
  von den Lippen ablesen –
  v irreg sep lip-read
Lippenstift (-e) – *nm* lipstick
Liste (-n) – *nf* list
Liter – *nm* litre
Literatur – *nf* literature
Litfaßsäule (-n) – *nf* advertising pillar
live – *adj* live (radio, TV)
Live-Sendung (-en) – *nf* live broadcast
LKW (-s) – *nm* lorry (HGV)
loben – *v reg* praise
Loch (Löcher) – *nnt* hole
lockig – *adj* curly
Löffel (-) – *nm* spoon, spoonful
Lohn (Löhne) – *nm* wages, pay
sich lohnen – *v reg refl* be worthwhile
  Es lohnt sich nicht – It's not
  worth it
Lokal (-e) – *nnt* pub
Los! – *excl* Go on! Go ahead!
  Was ist los? – What's wrong?
löschen – *v reg* extinguish
lösen – *v reg* solve

---

nm - noun masculine	*nf* - noun feminine	*nnt* - noun neuter	*npl* - noun plural
nom- nominative	*acc* - accusative	*gen* - genitive	*dat* - dative

losfahren* – *v irreg sep* set off
Lösung (-en) – *nf* solution
loswerden* – *v irreg sep* get rid of
Lotterie (-n) – *nf* lottery, draw
Lotto (-s) – *nnt* bingo
Löwe (-n) – *nm wk* lion; Leo
  (horoscope)
Luft – *nf, no pl* air
Luftdruck – *nm* air pressure
Luftkissenboot (-e) – *nnt* hovercraft
Luftkrankheit – *nf* air sickness
Luftmatratze (-n) – *nf* air-bed
Luftpost – *nf* air mail
  per Luftpost – by air mail
Luftwaffe – *nf, no pl* air force

lügen – *v irreg* lie, tell lies (untruth)
Lügner (-) – *nm* liar
Lügnerin (-nen) – *nf* liar
Lunchpaket (-e) – *nnt* packed lunch
Lust haben zu – *v irreg* wish to
lustig – *adj* amusing
  sich lustig machen über
  (+ acc) – *v reg refl* make fun of
Lutscher (-) – *nm* lollipop
Lüttich – *nnt* Liège
Luxemburg – *nnt* Luxembourg
Luxemburger (-) – *nm* Luxembourger
Luxemburgerin (-nen) – *nf*
  Luxembourger
luxuriös – *adj* luxurious

M

m – metre
machen – *v reg* make, do
  Mach schnell! – *excl* Get a move on!
  Das macht zehn Mark – That
    comes to ten marks
  Es macht nichts – Never mind
  Das macht mir nichts aus –
    I don't mind
  eine Prüfung machen – *v reg* go
    in for an exam
  einen Einkaufsbummel machen
    – *v reg* go round the shops
  einen Schaufensterbummel
    machen – *v reg* go window
    shopping
  einen Spaziergang machen –
    v reg have a walk
  einen Stadtbummel machen –
    v reg go round town
  Notizen machen – *v reg* take notes
  Pause machen – *v reg* have a rest
mächtig – *adj* powerful
Mädchen (-) – *nnt* girl

Mädchenname (-n) – *nm wk*
  maiden name
mag – *see* mögen
Magazin (-e) – *nnt* magazine
Magen (-) – *nm* stomach
Magenschmerzen – *npl* stomach ache
den Rasen mähen – *v reg* mow the
  lawn
Mahlzeit (-en) – *nf* meal
Mahlzeit! – *excl* Enjoy your meal!
Mai – *nm* May
  im Mai – in May
Mailand – Milan
Main – *nm* River Main
majestätisch – *adj* majestic
Make-Up – *nnt* make-up
Mal (-e) – *nnt* occasion, time
  zum ersten Mal – for the first time
  zum letzten Mal – for the last time
malen – *v reg* paint (art)
Maler (-) – *nm* painter
Malerin (-nen) – *nf* painter

---

adj - adjective   *v reg* - verb regular   *v sep* - verb separable   † - see verb info
prep - preposition   *v irreg* - verb irregular   *v refl* - verb reflexive   * - takes sein

malerisch – *adj* picturesque
Mallorca – *nnt* Majorca
man – *pron nom sing* they, you (people in general), one
mangelhaft – *adj* poor; below pass mark
manchmal – *adv* sometimes
Manieren – *npl* manners
Mann (Männer) – *nm* man, husband
Mannequin (-s) – *nnt* model (fashion)
männlich – *adj* male, masculine
Mannschaft (-en) – *nf* team
Mantel (Mäntel) – *nm* coat, overcoat
Mappe (-n) – *nf* briefcase
Märchen (-) – *nnt* fairy tale, myth
Margarine (-n) – *nf* margarine
marineblau – *adj* navy blue
Mark (-) – *nf* mark (money)
Marke (-n) – *nf* make, brand name
Markstück (-) – *nnt* mark piece, mark coin
Markt (Märkte) – *nm* market
der Gemeinsame Markt – *nm* the Common Market
Markthalle (-n) – *nf* market hall
Marktplatz(-plätze) – *nm* market place
Marmelade (-n) – *nf* jam
    ein Glas Marmelade – *nnt* a jar of jam
März – *nm* March
    im März – in March
Maschine (-n) – *nf* machine
maschinengeschrieben – *adj* typewritten
Maschinenschreiben – *nnt* typewriting
mäßig – *adj* moderate
Maskenkostüm (-e) – *nnt* fancy dress
Materialien – *npl* materials
Mathe – *nf* maths
Mathematik – *nf* mathematics
Matratze (-n) – *nf* mattress

Matrose (-n) – *nm wk* sailor (navy)
Matura – *nf* Swiss and Austrian A Level/GNVQ Level 3 equivalent
Mauer (-n) – *nf* wall; The Berlin Wall
Maurer (-) – *nm* bricklayer
Maus (Mäuse) – *nf* mouse
Mayonnaise – *nf* mayonnaise
Mechaniker (-) – *nm* mechanic
Mechanikerin (-nen) – *nf* mechanic
Medaille (-n) – *nf* medal
Medien – *npl* media
Medikament (-e) – *nnt* medicine (remedy)
Medizin – *nf* medicine (science)
Meer (-e) – *nnt* sea
Meeresfrüchte – *npl* seafood
Meerschweinchen (-) – *nnt* guinea-pig
Mehl – *nnt* flour
mehr – *adv* more
    ein bißchen mehr – a little more
    mehr als – more than
    immer mehr – *adv* more and more
    mehr oder weniger – *adv* more or less
    Es ist nichts mehr da – There is no more
mehrere – *adj* several
Mehrwertsteuer (MwSt) – *nf* VAT
Meile (-n) – *nf* mile
mein – *poss adj* my, mine
meinen – *v reg* think, feel (have opinion)
Meinung (-en) – *nf* opinion
    meiner Meinung nach – in my opinion
Meinungsumfrage (-n) – *nf* survey, opinion poll
die meisten – most (people)
am meisten – *adv* most
meistens – *adv* for the most part
Meister (-) – *nm* champion
Meisterin (-nen) – *nf* champion
Meisterschaft (-en) – *nf* championship

Meldeschein (-e) – *nm* residence registration document

Melodie (-n) – *nf* tune (music)

Melone (-n) – *nf* melon

Menge (-n) – *nf* crowd, quantity, amount

   eine Menge – lots of

Mensch (-en) – *nm wk* man (person)

Menü (-s) – *nnt* set price menu

merken – *v reg* realise

merkwürdig – *adj* remarkable

messen – *v irreg* measure

Messer (-) – *nnt* knife

Metall (-) – *nnt* metal

Meter – *nm* metre

Methode (-n) – *nf* method

Metzger (-) – *nm* butcher

Metzgerei (-en) – *nm* butcher's shop

mich – *pron acc* me, myself

mies – *adj* lousy, awful

Miete (-n) – *nf* hire, rent

mieten – *v reg* † hire, rent

Mieter (-) – *nm* tenant

Mieterin (-nen) – *nf* tenant

Mietwohnung (-en) – *nf* lodging

Mikrochip (-s) – *nm* microchip

Mikrocomputer (-) – *nm* microcomputer

Mikrophon (-e) – *nnt* microphone

Mikroskop (-e) – *nnt* microscope

Mikrowelle (-n) – *nf* microwave

Mikrowellenherd (-e) – *nm* microwave oven

Milch – *nf* milk

Milchmann (-männer) – *nm* milkman

mild – *adj* mild

Militär – *nnt* armed forces

   beim Militär – in the services

Milkshake – *nm* milk shake

Million (-en) – *nf* million

minderjährig – *adj* minor

Minderjährige – *nmf* ‡ minor (under 18)

Mindest~ – *pref* minimum

Mindesttemperatur (-en) – *nf* minimum temperature

Mineralwasser – *nnt* mineral water

Minimum (Minima) – *nnt* minimum

minus – *prep* minus (maths)

Minute (-n) – *nf* minute

   alle zehn Minuten – every ten minutes

mir – *pron dat* me, to me, myself

mischen – *v reg* mix

Mißverständnis (-se) – *nnt* misunderstanding

mit (+ dat) – *prep* with

   mit dem Auto – by car

   mit dem Bus – by bus

   mit der Bahn – by train

   mit dem Reisebus fahren* – *v irreg* travel by coach

   mit dem Wagen fahren* – *v irreg* travel by car

   mit freundlichen Grüßen – *adv* Yours sincerely

   mit Höchstgeschwindigkeit – at top speed

mitbringen – *v irreg sep* bring

Mitglied (-er) – *nnt* member

Mitgliedskarte (-n) – *nf* membership card

mitmachen – *v reg sep* participate, take part

mitnehmen – *v irreg sep* take away

   Kannst du mich mitnehmen? – Can I have a lift?

   zum Mitnehmen – take away (food); please take one

Mittag – *nm* midday

   um Mittag – at midday

   zu Mittag essen – *v irreg* have lunch

Mittagessen (-) – *nnt* lunch, midday meal

Mittagspause (-n) – *nf* lunch hour
Mitte (-n) – *nf* middle, centre
  in der Mitte von (+ dat) – in the
  middle of
Mitteilung (-en) – *nf* message
Mittel gegen (+ acc) – *nnt* remedy for
Mittel~ – *pref* medium
mittelalterlich – *adj* medieval
Mittelengland – *nnt* Midlands
mittelgroß – *adj* medium size
Mittellandkanal – *nm* canal between
  the rivers Ems and Elbe
mittellang – *adj* medium length
mittelmäßig – *adj* fair (average)
Mittelmeer – *nnt* Mediterranean
Mitternacht – *nf* midnight
  um Mitternacht – at midnight
Mittwoch – *nm* Wednesday
  am Mittwoch – on Wednesday
Möbel – *npl* furniture
Möbelstück (-e) – *nnt* piece of
  furniture
Möbelwagen (-) – *nm* removal van
möbliert – *adj* furnished
mochte – *see mögen*
ich möchte – I would like
  ich möchte gern – I'd love to
Mode (-n) – *nf* fashion
Modell (-e) – *nnt* design, model
  ein maßstabgerechtes Modell
  – *nnt* a scale model
Modem (-s) – *nnt* modem
Moderator (-en) – *nm wk* presenter
  (TV)
Moderatorin (-nen) – *nf* presenter
  (TV)
moderieren – *v reg* † present (radio,
  TV)
modern – *adj* modern
Modezeichner (-) – *nm* fashion
  designer
Modezeichnerin (-nen) – *nf* fashion
  designer

modisch – *adj* fashionable, smart
mogeln – *v reg* cheat
mögen – *v irreg* like
möglich – *adj* possible
  so bald wie möglich – as soon as
  possible
möglicherweise – *adv* possibly
Möglichkeit (-en) – *nf* possibility,
  opportunity
Mohammedaner (-) – *nm* Muslim
Mohammedanerin (-nen) – *nf* Muslim
mohammedanisch – *adj* Muslim
mollig – *adj* plump
Moment (-e) – *nm* moment
  im Moment – at the moment
momentan – *adj* current, present
Monat (-e) – *nm* month
  im Monat – per month
  pro Monat – per month
monatelang – *adj* for months on end
monatlich – *adj* monthly
Mond (-e) – *nm* moon
Montag (-e) – *nm* Monday
  am Montag – on Monday
Moped (-s) – *nnt* moped
Morgen (-) – *nm* morning
  am nächsten Morgen – next
  morning
  Guten Morgen! – *excl* Good
  morning!
morgen – *adv* tomorrow
  Bis morgen! – See you tomorrow!
  morgen abend – tomorrow evening
  morgen früh – tomorrow morning
Morgenrock (-röcke) – *nm*
  dressing gown
morgens – *adv* in the morning
Moschee (-n) – *nf* mosque
Mosel – *nf* Moselle
Moselwein (-e) – *nm* Moselle wine
Moskau – Moscow
Moskito (-s) – *nm* mosquito
Motor (-en) – *nm* engine, motor

Motorboot (-e) – *nnt* motor boat
Motorrad (-räder) – *nnt* motorbike
Motorradfahrer (-) – *nm* motorcyclist
Motorradfahrerin (-nen) – *nf* motorcyclist
Mountainbike (-s) – *nnt* mountain bike
Möwe (-n) – *nf* seagull
müde – *adj* tired
Mühe (-n) – *nf* effort
sich die Mühe geben – *v irreg dat refl* take trouble to, bother
Müll – *nm* rubbish
Müllabfuhr – *nf* refuse collection
Mülleimer (-) – *nm* rubbish bin
Müllhalde (-n) – *nf* tip (rubbish)
Mülltonne (-n) – *nf* dustbin
München – Munich
Mund (Münder) – *nm* mouth
Mundharmonika (-harmoniken) – *nf* mouth organ
mündlich – *adj* oral
   mündliche Frage (-n) – *nf* oral question
   mündliche Prüfung (-en) – *nf* speaking test
Mundvoll (-) – *nm* mouthful
Münster – Munster
munter – *adj* cheerful

Münzautomat (-en) – *nm wk* slot machine
Münze (-n) – *nf* coin
Münzfernsprecher (-) – *nm* pay phone
Münzwäscherei (-en) – *nf* laundrette
murren – *v reg* grumble
Museum (Museen) – *nnt* museum
Musik – *nf* music
   klassische Musik – *nf* classical music
Musikabteilung (-en) – *nf* music department
Musiker (-) – *nm* musician
Musikerin (-nen) – *nf* musician
Musikraum (räume) – *nm* music room
muß – *see müssen*
müssen – *v irreg* have to, got to (must)
mußte – *see müssen*
Mut – *nm* courage
mutig – *adj* bold
Mutter (Mütter) – *nf* mother
mütterlich – *adj* motherly
Muttersprache (-n) – *nf* mother tongue
Mutti (-s) – *nf* mum(my)
Mütze (-n) – *nf* cap, hat
MwSt (Mehrwertsteuer) – *nf* VAT

N

na und? – so what?
nach (+ dat) – *prep* after, to, past (time), according to
   fünf nach vier – five past four
   meiner Meinung nach – in my opinion
   nach Berlin – to Berlin
   nach unten gehen* – *v irreg* go downstairs
Nachbar (-en) – *nm wk* neighbour

Nachbarin (-nen) – *nf* neighbour
Nachbarschaft (-en) – *nf* neighbourhood
nachdem – *sub conj* after
nachdenken über (+ acc) – *v irreg sep* think about
nachgeben – *v irreg sep* give in
nachher – *adv* afterwards
nachholen – *v reg sep* catch up with

---

adj - adjective	*v reg* - verb regular	*v sep* - verb separable	† - see verb info
prep - preposition	*v irreg* - verb irregular	*v refl* - verb reflexive	* - takes sein

nachmachen – *v reg sep* copy (imitate)

Nachmittag (-e) – *nm* afternoon

am Nachmittag – in the afternoon

nachmittags – *adv* p.m.

Nachname (-n) – *nm wk* surname

Nachrichten – *npl* news (radio, TV)

eine gute Nachricht – good news

nachschauen – *v reg sep* check

nachsehen – *v irreg sep* check

das Wasser nachsehen – *v irreg sep* check the water level

Nachsitzen – *nnt* detention

nachsitzen müssen – *v irreg* be in detention

Nachspeise (-n) – *nf* dessert

nächst – *adj* next, nearest

am nächsten Tag – next day

nächstes Jahr – next year

nächste Woche – next week

Nacht (Nächte) – *nf* night

Gute Nacht! – *excl* Good night!

Nachteil (-e) – *nm* disadvantage

Nachthemd (-en) – *nnt* nightdress

Nachtisch (-e) – *nm* pudding, dessert

Nachtklub (-s) – *nm* night club

nachts – *adv* at night

Nachttisch (-e) – *nm* bedside table

Nachttischlampe (-n) – *nf* bedside light

Nacken (-) – *nm* back of neck

nackt – *adj* bare, naked

Nadel (-n) – *nf* needle

Nagel (Nägel) – *nm* nail

nagelneu – *adj* brand new

nah – *adj* close (-near)

Nähe – *nf* vicinity, surrounding area

hier in der Nähe – around here

in der Nähe – close by

in der Nähe (von + dat) – near (to)

nähen – *v reg* sew

Nähen – *nnt* sewing

näher – *adj* nearer

sich nähern (+ dat) – *v reg refl* go near to, approach

nahm – *see nehmen*

Nähmaschine (-n) – *nf* sewing machine

Nahverkehrszug (-züge) – *nm* local train, slow train

Name (-n) – *nm wk* name

im Namen (+ gen) – in the name (of)

im Namen Smith – in the name of Smith

Narr (-en) – *nm wk* fool

Närrin (-nen) – *nf* fool

Nase (-n) – *nf* nose

sich die Nase putzen – *v reg dat refl* blow one's nose

Ich habe die Nase voll – I've had enough, I'm fed up

Nasenbluten (-) – *nnt* nosebleed

Nashorn (-hörner) – *nnt* rhinoceros

naß – *adj* wet

national – *adj* national

nationalistisch – *adj* nationalist

Natur – *nf* nature

Naturkunde – *nf* natural history

natürlich – *adj* natural

natürlich – *adv* of course, naturally

Naturschutzgebiet (-e) – *nnt* nature reserve

Naturwissenschaft (-en) – *nf* science

Naturwissenschaften – *npl* natural sciences

Nebel – *nm* fog, mist

nebelig – *adj* foggy, misty

neben (+ acc/dat) – *prep* next to, beside

nebenan – *adv* next door

nebeneinander – *adv* side by side

neblig – *adj* foggy, misty

necken – *v reg* tease

Neffe (-n) – *nm wk* nephew
negativ – *adj* negative
nehmen – *v irreg* take, catch
(bus, etc)
   den Bus nehmen – *v irreg* catch
the bus
   Nehmen Sie den Bus Linie 3! –
Catch the number three bus!
   **Nehmen Sie die erste Straße
links!** – Take the first on the left!
nein – *adv* no
Nektarine (-n) – *nf* nectarine
nennen – *v irreg* call, name
nennenswert – *adj* noteworthy
Nerven – *npl* nerves
   Er geht mir auf die Nerven –
He gets on my nerves
nervös – *adj* nervous, tense
nett – *adj* nice, kind, sweet
neu – *adj* new, recent
   Ein glückliches neues Jahr! –
excl Happy New Year!
neuest – *adj* latest
neugierig – *adj* curious, nosy
Neujahr (-e) – *nnt* New Year
Neujahrstag (-e) – *nm* New Year's
Day
neulich – *adv* recently, the other day
neun – *adj* nine
neunte – *adj* ninth
neunzehn – *adj* nineteen
neunzig – *adj* ninety
Neuseeland – *nnt* New Zealand
Neusprache(-n) – *nf* modern
language
Neutrum – *nnt* neuter
nicht – not
   bitte nicht – please do not...
   nicht gut in (+ dat) – no good at
   nicht länger – no longer
   nicht mehr – no more
   nicht wahr? – don't you, doesn't
he?

noch nicht – *adv* not yet
Nichte (-n) – *nf* niece
Nichtraucher (-) – *nm* non-smoker
Nichtraucher~ – *pref* non smoking
nichts – nothing
   nichts anderes – nothing else
   nichts Neues – nothing new
   Nichts zu danken! – You're
welcome!
nichtsdestoweniger – *adv* none the
less
nie – *adv* never
   noch nie – *adv* never before
Niederlande – *npl* Netherlands
Niedersachsen – Lower Saxony
Niederschlag – *nm* precipitation, rain
or snow
niederschlagsfrei – *adj* dry
niedlich – *adj* sweet (cute)
niedrig – *adj* low
niemand – *pron* no-one, nobody
   sonst niemand – no-one else
niesen – *v reg* sneeze
nimmt – *see nehmen*
nirgendwo – *adv* nowhere, anywhere
(negative)
Niveau – *nnt* standard, level (school)
noch – *adv* another (more)
   noch einmal – *adv* once more
   Noch etwas Brot? – Any more
bread?
noch – *adv* still, yet
   noch nicht – *adv* not yet
   noch besser – *adj* even better
   noch nie – *adv* never before
   weder ... noch – *adv* neither...nor
nochmals – *adv* yet again, once more
Nord~ – *pref* north
Nordamerika – *nnt* North America
Norddeutschland – *nnt* North
Germany
Norden – *nm* north

---

adj - adjective   *v reg* - verb regular   *v sep* - verb separable   † - see verb info
prep - preposition   *v irreg* - verb irregular   *v refl* - verb reflexive   * - takes sein

im Norden – in the north
Nordire (-n) – *nm wk* Northern Irishman
Nordirin (-nen) – *nf* Northern Irishwoman
nordirisch – *adj* North Irish
Nordirland – *nnt* Northern Ireland
nördlich von (+ dat) – *adj* north of
nördlich – *adj* northerly
Nordsee – *nf* North Sea
normal – *adj* normal, usual, ordinary
normalerweise – *adv* usually, normally
Norwegen – *nnt* Norway
norwegisch – *adj* Norwegian
Not~ – *pref* emergency
Notarzt (-ärzte) – *nm* emergency doctor
Notausgang (-gänge) – *nm* emergency exit
Notdienst (-e) – *nm* emergency service
Note (-n) – *nf* mark, grade (school)
Notfall (-fälle) – *nm* emergency
Nothilfe (-n) – *nf* emergency aid
notieren – *v reg* † note down
nötig – *adj* necessary
Notiz (-en) – *nf* note (message)
Notizblock (-blöcke) – *nm* notepad

Notizbuch (-bücher) – *nnt* notebook
Notizen machen – *v reg* take notes
Notruf (-e) – *nm* emergency phone number
notwendig – *adj* necessary
Notwendigkeit (-en) – *nf* necessity
November – *nm* November
im November – in November
Nr. – number
Nudeln – *npl* noodles, pasta
null – *adj* nil
zwei zu null – 2:0, two - nil
Null (-en) – *nf* zero, nought
Null zu Null Unentschieden – *nnt* goalless draw
Nummer (-n) – *nf* number (house, etc)
die Nummer wählen – *v reg* dial the number
nun – *adv* now
nur – *adv* only, just
nicht nur – not only
nicht nur...sondern auch – not only...but also
Nuß (Nüsse) – *nf* nut
nützlich – *adj* useful
nutzlos – *adj* useless
Nylon – *nnt* nylon
aus Nylon – made of nylon

O

ob – *sub conj* if, whether
oben – *adv* above, at the top, upstairs
oben auf (+ dat) – *adv* on top of
nach oben gehen* – *v irreg* go upstairs
ober~ – *pref* upper, senior
Herr Ober! – *excl* Waiter!
Obergeschoß (-geschosse) – *nnt* upper floor

im zweiten Obergeschoß – on the second floor
Oberlippenbart (-bärte) – *nm* moustache
Oberstufe (-n) – *nf* sixth form
in der Oberstufe sein* – be in Year 12
Oberstufenkolleg (-kollegien) – *nnt* sixth form college

---

nm - noun masculine	*nf* - noun feminine	*nnt* - noun neuter	*npl* - noun plural
nom- nominative	*acc* - accusative	*gen* - genitive	*dat* - dative

obgleich – *sub conj* although
obligatorisch – *adj* obligatory
Oboe (-n) – *nf* oboe
Obst – *nnt* fruit
Obstbaum (-bäume) – *nm* fruit tree
Obsthändler (-) – *nm* fruit seller
Obstsorten – *npl* fruits
obwohl – *sub conj* although
oder – *coord conj* or
  entweder ... oder ... – *conj*
  either ... or...
Oder – *nf* River Oder
Ofen (Öfen) – *nm* stove (oven)
offen – *adj* open, frank
offensichtlich – *adj* obvious
öffentlich – *adj* public
  öffentliche Verkehrsmittel –
  npl public transport
offiziell – *adj* official
öffnen – *v reg* † open
Öffnung (-en) – *nf* opening
Öffnungszeiten – *npl* opening hours
oft – *adv* often, frequently
  sehr oft – many, many times
ohne (+ acc) – *prep* without
ohnmächtig werden* – *v irreg*
  faint (swoon)
Ohr (-en) – *nnt* ear
Ohrenschmerzen – *npl* earache
Ohrring (-e) – *nm* earring
Öko~ – ecological
Ökologe (-n) – *nm wk* ecologist
Ökologie (-n) – *nf* ecology
Ökologin (-en) – *nf* ecologist
Oktober – *nm* October
  im Oktober – in October
Öl – *nnt* oil
Ölgemälde – *nnt* oil painting
Olivenöl – *nnt* olive oil
die Olympischen Spiele – *npl* the
  Olympic Games
Oma (-s) – *nf* granny

Omelett (-s) – *nnt* omelette
Omi (-s) – *nf* granny
Onkel (-) – *nm* uncle
Opa (-s) – *nm* grandpa
Oper (-n) – *nf* opera
Operation (-en) – *nf* operation
operieren – *v reg* † operate
  sich operieren lassen – *v irreg*
  refl have an operation
Opernhaus (-häuser) – *nnt* opera
  house
Opfer (-) – *nnt* victim
Opi (-s) – *nm* grandpa
Optiker (-) – *nm* optician
Optikerin (-nen) – *nf* optician
Optimist (-en) – *nm wk* optimist
optimistisch – *adj* optimistic
orange – *adj* orange
Orangenmarmelade (-n) – *nf*
  marmalade
Orangensaft – *nm* orange juice
Orchester (-) – *nnt* orchestra
ordentlich – *adj* neat, tidy, orderly
Ordinalzahl (-en) – *nf* ordinal
  number
ordnen – *v reg* † put in the right order
Ordner (-) – *nm* file, ring binder
Ordnung (-en) – *nf* order (tidiness)
  In Ordnung! – *excl* Alright! Fine!
organisieren – *v reg* † organise
organisiert – *adj* organised
original – *adj* original
  im Originalton – in the original
  version (soundtrack)
Ort (-e) – *nm* place (town, etc)
örtlich – *adj* local
Ortschaft (-en) – *nf* town, built up area
Ost~ – *pref* eastern
Osten – *nm* east
  im Osten – in the east
Osterei (-er) – *nnt* Easter egg
Osterferien – *npl* Easter holidays

---

adj - adjective	*v reg* - verb regular	*v sep* - verb separable	† - see verb info
prep - preposition	*v irreg* - verb irregular	*v refl* - verb reflexive	* - takes sein

Osterhase (-n) – *nm wk* Easter bunny
Ostern – *npl* Easter
zu Ostern – at Easter
Österreich – *nnt* Austria
Österreicher (-) – *nm* Austrian
Österreicherin (-nen) – *nf* Austrian
österreichisch – *adj* Austrian

Ostersonntag – *nm* Easter Day
östlich von (+ dat) – *prep* east of
Ostsee – *nf* Baltic Sea
oval – *adj* oval
Overall (-s) – *nm* overalls
Ozean (-e) – *nm* ocean
Ozonschicht (-en) – *nf* ozone layer

P

Paar – *nnt* pair (of)
  ein Paar Schuhe – *nnt* a pair of shoes
ein paar – a few
  Ein paar Leute waren da – A few people were there
Päckchen (-) – *nnt* packet
packen – *v reg* pack (case)
Packung (-en) – *nf* packet
Paket (-e) – *nnt* parcel, package
Pakistan – *nnt* Pakistan
Pakistaner (-) – *nm* Pakistani person
Pakistanerin (-nen) – *nf* Pakistani person
pakistanisch – *adj* Pakistani
Pampelmuse (-n) – *nf* grapefruit
Panne (-n) – *nf* breakdown
  eine Panne haben – *v irreg* break down
Pantoffel (-n) – *nm* slipper
Papagei (-en) – *nm* parrot
Papier (-e) – *nnt* paper
  ein Blatt Papier – *nnt* a sheet of paper
Papierkorb (-körbe) – *nm* waste paper basket
Papiertaschentuch (-tücher) – *nnt* tissue
Pappe – *nf* cardboard
Paprika (-s) – *nm* green pepper

Parfüm – *nnt* perfume
Park (-s) – *nm* park
Parkanlage (-n) – *nf* park
Parken verboten – no parking
parken – *v reg* park
Parken – *nnt* parking
Parkett – *nnt* stalls (theatre)
Parkhaus (-häuser) – *nnt* multi-storey car park
Parkplatz (-plätze) – *nm* car park
Parkuhr (-en) – *nf* parking meter
Parkverbot (-e) – *nnt* parking forbidden
Parlament (-e) – *nnt* parliament (national)
Partei (-en) – *nf* party (political)
Parterre (-s) – *nnt* stalls (theatre)
Partizip(-ien) – *nnt* participle
Partner (-) – *nm* partner
Partnerin (-nen) – *nf* partner
Partnerstadt (-städte) – *nf* twin town
Party (-s) – *nf* party (celebration)
Paß (Pässe) – *nm* passport
Passagier (-e) – *nm* passenger
Passagierin (-nen) – *nf* passenger
Passahfest (-e) – *nnt* Passover
Passant (-en) – *nm wk* passer-by
Passantin (-nen) – *nf* passer-by
passen – *v reg* be convenient, suit

Es paßt mir nicht – It doesn't fit me, It doesn't suit me, It's not convenient

passend – *adj* suitable, convenient

passieren* – *v reg* † happen

Pastete (-n) – *nf* pâté

Pastor (-en) – *nm* protestant vicar

Pastorin (-nen) – *nf* protestant vicar (female)

Patient (-en) – *nm wk* patient

Patientin (-nen) – *nf* patient

pauken – *v reg* swot

pauschal – *adj* all-inclusive

Pauschalreise (-n) – *nf* package tour

Pause (-n) – *nf* break, pause

Pause machen – *v reg* have a rest

PC (-s) – *nm* PC

Pech! – *excl* Too bad! Hard luck!

Pech – *nnt* bad luck

Pech haben – *v irreg* be unlucky

peinlich – *adj* embarrassing, awkward

pendeln* – *v reg* commute

Pension – *nf* guest house, board (food)

per – *prep* by

perfekt – *adj* perfect

Periode (-n) – *nf* period (menstrual)

Person (-en) – *nf* person, character (drama) (male or female)

pro Person – per person

Personalausweis (-e) – *nm* identity card

Personenzug (-züge) – *nm* slow train

persönlich – *adj* personal; *adv* in person

Pf – pfennig

Pfadfinder (-) – *nm* scout

Pfadfinderin (-nen) – *nf* guide

Pfand – *nm* deposit (on empty bottle)

Pfanne (-n) – *nf* frying pan

Pfannkuchen (-) – *nm* pancake

Pfeffer – *nm* pepper (spice)

Pfefferminz – *nm* mint

Pfefferminztee – *nm* mint tea

Pfeife (-n) – *nf* pipe

pfeifen – *v irreg* whistle

Pfeil (-e) – *nm* arrow

Pfennig – *nm* pfennig (100 Pf = 1DM)

Pferd (-e) – *nnt* horse

Pferderennen – *nnt* races

Pferdeschwanz (-schwänze) – *nm* pony tail

Pferdestall (-ställe) – *nm* stable

Pfingsten – *npl* Whitsun

Pfingstferien – *npl* summer half-term holiday (Whitsuntide)

Pfirsich (-e) – *nm* peach

Pflanze (-n) – *nf* plant

pflanzen – *v reg* plant

Pflaster – *nnt* plaster (sticking)

Pflaume (-n) – *nf* plum

pflegen – *v reg* care for

Pflicht – *nf* duty

Pflichtfach (-fächer) – *nnt* compulsory subject

pflücken – *v reg* pick, collect fruit

Pfote (-n) – *nf* paw

Pfund – *nnt* pound

ein Pfund Käse – a pound of cheese

phantastisch – *adj* fantastic

Physik – *nf* physics

Physiotherapeut (-en) – *nm wk* physiotherapist

Physiotherapeutin (-nen) – *nf* physiotherapist

Pickel (-) – *nm* spot, zit

pickelig – *adj* spotty (zits)

Picknick (-s) – *nnt* picnic

picknicken – *v reg* picnic

Pille (-n) – *nf* pill (contraceptive)

Pilot (-en) – *nm wk* pilot (air)

Pils – *nm* lager

Pilsener – *nm* lager

Pilz (-e) – *nm* mushroom

pingelig – *adj coll* fussy

---

adj - adjective   *v reg* - verb regular   *v sep* - verb separable   † - see verb info
prep - preposition   *v irreg* - verb irregular   *v refl* - verb reflexive   * - takes sein

Pinsel (-) – *nm* brush (painting)
Piste (-n) – *nf* ski-run, course (route)
Pistole (-n) – *nf* gun (handgun)
Pizza (-s) – *nf* pizza
PKW (-s) – *nm* car
Plakat (-e) – *nnt* placard
Plan (Pläne) – *nm* plan
planen – *v reg* plan
Plastik – *nnt coll* plastic
Plastiktüte (-n) – *nf* plastic bag
platt – *adj* flat (of tyre, etc)
Platte (-n) – *nf* dish; record
  kalte Platte – *nf* mixed cold meats
Plattenspieler (-) – *nm* record player
Platz (Plätze) – *nm* place, seat,
  square (town), ground, pitch (sport),
  site (camping)
  einen Platz reservieren – *v reg* †
  book a seat
  Platz nehmen – *v irreg* take one's
  place
Platzanweiserin (-nen) – *nf*
  usherette
Platzregen (-) – *nm* downpour
plaudern – *v reg* chat
pleite – *adj inv* broke
  Ich bin pleite – *sl* I'm broke
Plombe (-n) – *nf* filling (teeth)
plötzlich – *adj* sudden, *adv* suddenly
Plural (-e) – *nm* plural
  im Plural – in the plural
plus – *prep* plus
Plusquamperfekt – *nnt* pluperfect
Pokal (-e) – *nm* cup (trophy)
Pokalendspiel (-e) – *nnt* cup final
Polen – Poland
polieren – *v reg* † polish
Politesse (-n) – *nf* female traffic
  warden
Politik – *nf* policy
Politiker (-) – *nm* politician
Politikerin (-nen) – *nf* politician

Polizei – *nf* police
Polizeiwache (-n) – *nf* police station
Polizist (-en) – *nm wk* policeman
Polizistin (-nen) – *nf* police woman
polnisch – *adj* Polish
Pommes – *npl* chips
Pommes frites – *npl* chips
Pony (-s) – *nnt* pony
Pony (-s) – *nm* fringe
Popmusik – *nf* pop music
Portemonnaie (-s) – *nnt* purse
Portion (-en) – *nf* portion
Portugal – *nnt* Portugal
Portugiese (-n) – *nm wk* Portuguese
  person
Portugiesin (-nen) – *nf* Portuguese
  person
portugiesisch – *adj* Portuguese
Posaune (-n) – *nf* trombone
positiv – *adj* positive
Post – *nf* post office, mail
Postamt (-ämter) – *nnt* post office
Poster (-) – *nnt* poster
Postkarte (-n) – *nf* postcard
Postleitzahl (-en) – *nf* post code
Postwertzeichen – *npl* stamps
praktisch – *adj* practical, useful
Praline (-n) – *nf* chocolate (individual)
Präsens – *nnt* present (tense)
Praxis (Praxen) – *nf* clinic (surgery)
Preis (-e) – *nm* cost, price, charge,
  prize
  zum halben Preis – half-price
  zum Preis von (+ dat) – *prep*
  costing
Preisliste (-n) – *nf* price list
Preistafel (-n) – *nf* price list
preiswert – *adj* good value
Presse – *nf* press (media)
Priester (-) – *nm* priest (RC)
prima! – *excl* great!
Prinzip (-ien) – *nnt* principle

---

nm - noun masculine	*nf* - noun feminine	*nnt* - noun neuter	*npl* - noun plural
nom- nominative	*acc* - accusative	*gen* - genitive	*dat* - dative

privat – *adj* private
private Grundschule (-n) – *nf*
prep(aratory) school
Privatschule (-n) – *nf* private
school, public school (UK)
pro (+ acc) – *prep* per
  pro Kilo – by the kilo
  pro Stunde – by the hour
  pro Tag – per day
Probe (-n) – *nf* rehearsal
probieren – *v reg* † taste, try (food)
Problem (-e) – *nnt* problem
  Probleme haben – *v irreg* be in
  trouble
Produkt (-e) – *nnt* product
Programm (-e) – *nnt* programme,
channel (TV)
  im zweiten Programm – on the
  second channel
programmieren – *v reg* † program
Programmierer (-) – *nm* computer
programmer
Programmiererin (-nen) – *nf*
computer programmer
Projekt (-e) – *nnt* project
Pronomen (-) – *nnt* pronoun
Prospekt (-e) – *nm* leaflet
Prost! – *excl* Cheers!
Protestant (-en) – *nm wk* Protestant
Protestantin (-nen) – *nf* Protestant
protestieren – *v reg* † protest
Proviant – *nm* food, provisions
Provinz (-en) – *nf* province
Prozent – *nnt* per cent
Prozeß (Prozesse) – *nm* process
prüfen – *v reg* examine
Prüfung (-en) – *nf* examination
(school)

eine Prüfung bestehen – *v irreg*
pass an exam
eine Prüfung machen – *v reg*
take an exam
eine Prüfung wiederholen –
v reg insep † resit exam
in einer Prüfung durchfallen*
– *v irreg* fail an exam
mündliche Prüfung (-en) – *nf*
speaking test
schriftliche Prüfung – *nf* written
test
Publikum – *nnt* audience
Pudding (-s) – *nm* cold milk dessert
Pudel (-) – *nm* poodle
Puder (-) – *nm* powder (cosmetic)
Pulli (-s) – *nm* pullover
Pullover (-) – *nm* pullover
Pullunder (-) – *nm* sleeveless
pullover
Pulver (-) – *nnt* powder
Pulverkaffee – *nm* instant coffee
Punkt (-e) – *nm* point, full stop (.)
  einen Punkt gewinnen – *v irreg*
  score a point
  zehn Punkte haben – *v irreg* get
  ten out of ten
pünktlich – *adj* on time, punctual
Puppe (-n) – *nf* doll
purpur – *adj inv* purple
putzen – *v reg* clean
  sich die Nase putzen – *v reg dat*
  refl blow one's nose
  sich die Zähne putzen – *v reg*
  dat refl clean one's teeth
Putzfrau (-en) – *nf* cleaning lady

---

adj - adjective	*v reg* - verb regular	*v sep* - verb separable	† - see verb info
prep - preposition	*v irreg* - verb irregular	*v refl* - verb reflexive	* - takes sein

Q

Qualifikation (-en) – *nf*
qualification
Qualität (-en) – *nf* quality
  guter Qualität – good quality
  schlechter Qualität – poor
  quality
Quark – *nm* curd cheese
Quatsch – *nm* nonsense

quatschen – *v reg* chatter
Quelle (-n) – *nf* source, spring
quer – *adv* across, at an angle
quetschen – *v reg* squeeze
Quittung (-en) – *nf* receipt
Quiz (-) – *nnt* quiz

R

Rabatt (-e) – *nm* discount
Rad (Räder) – *nnt* cycle, bike, wheel
radfahren* – *v irreg sep* cycle, go
  for a bike ride
Radfahren – *nnt* cycling
Radfahrer (-) – *nm* cyclist
Radfahrerin (-nen) – *nf* cyclist
Radiergummi (-s) – *nm* rubber (eraser)
Radio (-s) – *nnt* radio
  im Radio sein* – *v irreg* be on the
  radio
Radiokassettenrekorder (-) – *nm*
  radio cassette player
Radiowecker (-) – *nm* clock radio
Radtour (-en) – *nf* bike ride
  eine Radtour machen – *v reg* go
  for a bike ride
Radverleih – *nm* cycle hire
Rahmen (-) – *nm* frame (photo, etc)
Ramadan – *nm* Ramadan
Rand (Ränder) – *nm* edge, outskirts
  am Rand – on the edge
Rang (Ränge) – *nm* row (cinema)
Ranzen (-) – *nm* schoolbag
Rappen (-) – *nm* Swiss coin
  (SF1 = 100 Rappen)
Rasen (-) – *nm* lawn

den Rasen mähen – *v reg* mow
  the lawn
Rasierapparat (-e) – *nm* razor
sich rasieren – *v reg refl* † shave
Rasse (-n) – *nf* race (nationality)
Rastplatz (-plätze) – *nm* picnic area
  (motorway)
Rasthof (-höfe) – *nm* motorway
  service area
Raststätte (-n) – *nf* motorway service
  area
Rat – *nm, no pl* advice
raten – *v irreg* guess
Rathaus (-häuser) – *nnt* town hall
Ratschlag (-schläge) – *nm* piece of
  advice
Rätsel (-) – *nnt* puzzle
Ratte (-n) – *nf* rat
Rattenfänger (-) – *nm* rat catcher,
  the Pied Piper
Rauch – *nm* smoke
rauchen – *v reg* smoke
Rauchen verboten – no smoking
Raucher (-) – *nm* smoker
Raucher- – *pref* smoking (area)
Raucherin (-nen) – *nf* smoker
Rasierapparat (-e) – *nm* electric razor
Raum (Räume) – *nm* room, space

'Raus! – *excl* Get out!

Realschule (-n) – *nf* technical secondary school

Rebstock – *nm* vine

Rechnen – *nnt* arithmetic

rechnen – *v reg* † calculate, reckon

Rechnung (-en) – *nf* bill, account, sum

recht haben – *v irreg* be right

Du hast recht – You are right

rechts – *adv* right, on the right, to the right

rechts fahren* – *v irreg* keep to the right, drive on the right hand side of the road

Rechts halten! – *excl* Keep to the right!

Rechtsanwalt (-anwälte) – *nm* solicitor, lawyer

Rechtsanwältin (-nen) – *nf* solicitor, lawyer

Rechtsaußen (-) – *nm* right wing (sport)

Rechtschreibung – *nf* spelling

rechtshändig – *adj* right-handed

recyceln – *v reg* † recycle

Rede (-n) – *nf* speech (in public)

reduzieren – *v reg* † reduce

reduziert – *adj* reduced

Reflexivverbum (-verben) – *nnt* reflexive verb

Reformkost – *nf* health food

Regal (-e) – *nnt* shelf

Regel (-n) – *nf* rule

in der Regel – as a rule

regelmäßig – *adj* regular

Regen – *nm* rain

der saure Regen – *nm* acid rain

im Regen – in the rain

Regenbogen (-bögen) – *nm* rainbow

Regenjacke (-n) – *nf* cagoule

Regenmantel (-mäntel) – *nm* raincoat

Regenschauer (-) – *nm* shower (rain)

Regenschirm (-e) – *nm* umbrella

Region (-en) – *nf* region

regnen – *v reg* † rain

Es regnet – It is raining

Es regnete – It was raining

Es wird regnen – It will rain

regnerisch – *adj* rainy

reiben – *v irreg* rub

reich – *adj* rich

reichen – *v reg* pass (at table), be enough

Das reicht – That's enough

reif – *adj* ripe

Reife – *nf* maturity

Hochschulreife – *nf* A Level/GNVQ Level 3 equivalent

Reifen (-) – *nm* tyre

Reifendruck – *nm* tyre pressure

den Reifendruck kontrollieren – *v reg* † check the tyre pressure

Reifenpanne (-n) – *nf* puncture, flat tyre

Reihe (-n) – *nf* row

der Reihe nach – in turn

in alphabetischer Reihenfolge – in alphabetical order

Reihenhaus (-häuser) – *nnt* terraced house

rein – *adj* clean

reinigen – *v reg* clean

etwas reinigen lassen – *v irreg* have something cleaned

Reis – *nm* rice

Reise (-n) – *nf* journey, trip

Gute Reise! – *excl* Have a good trip!

Reisebüro (-s) – *nnt* travel agency

Reisebus (-se) – *nm* coach

Reiseführer (-) – *nm* guide book

reisen* – *v reg* travel

Reisende – *nmf* ‡ traveller

Reisescheck (-s) – *nm* travellers' cheque

Reisetasche (-n) – *nf* holdall

Reißverschluß (-verschlüsse) – *nm* zip

---

adj - adjective	*v reg* - verb regular	*v sep* - verb separable	† - see verb info
prep - preposition	*v irreg* - verb irregular	*v refl* - verb reflexive	* - takes sein

reiten (*) – *v irreg* ride (horse)
reiten gehen* – *v irreg* go horse riding
Reiten – *nnt* horse riding
Reitkappe (-n) – *nf* riding hat
reizbar – *adj* irritable
reizen – *v reg* irritate
Reklame (-n) – *nf* advertisement (for products)
Rekord (-e) – *nm* record (sport, etc)
relativ – *adv* relatively
Religion (-en) – *nf* RE, RS, religion
Rennboot (-e) – *nnt* speedboat
Rennen (-) – *nnt* race (sport)
Rentner (-) – *nm* retired person, senior citizen, pensioner
Rentnerin (-nen) – *nf* retired person, senior citizen, pensioner
Reparatur (-en) – *nf* repair
Reparaturwerkstatt (-werkstätten) – *nf* repair workshop, garage
reparieren – *v reg* † repair, mend, fix
   etwas reparieren lassen – *v irreg* have something repaired
Reporter (-) – *nm* reporter
Reporterin (-nen) – *nf* reporter
Republik (-en) – *nf* republic
   die Republik Irland – the Irish Republic, Eire
reservieren – *v reg* † reserve
reserviert – *adj* reserved, booked
Reservierung (-en) – *nf* reservation
Respekt – *nm* respect
Rest – *nm* remainder, the rest
Restaurant (-s) – *nnt* restaurant
retten – *v reg* † save, rescue
Rettungsring (-e) – *nm* lifebelt
Rettungsschwimmer (-) – *nm* lifeguard
Revolver (-) – *nm* revolver
Rezept (-e) – *nnt* recipe, prescription
Rezeption – *nf* reception desk (hotel)

Rhein – *nm* River Rhine
Rhein-Main-Donau-Kanal – *nm* Rhine-Main-Danube Canal
Rheinwein (-e) – *nm* Rhine wine, hock
Richter (-) – *nm* judge
Richterin (-nen) – *nf* judge
richtig – *adj* right, true, correct
Richtlinien – *npl* code (guidelines)
Richtung (-en) – *nf* direction
   Gehen Sie in diese Richtung! – Go that way!
   in alle Richtungen – in all directions
   in entgegengesetzter Richtung – in the opposite direction
   in Richtung – towards, in the direction of
riechen (nach + dat) – *v irreg* smell (of)
rief – *see* **rufen**
rief an – *see* **anrufen**
Riese (-n) – *nm wk* giant
riesengroß – *adj* enormous
riesig – *adj* gigantic, huge
Rinderbraten (-) – *nm* roast beef
Rindfleisch – *nnt* beef
   gehacktes Rindfleisch – minced beef
Ring (-e) – *nm* ring
Rippe (-n) – *nf* rib
Risiko (Risiken) – *nnt* risk
Rock (Röcke) – *nm* skirt
Rockmusik – *nf* rock music
roh – *adj* raw
Rolladen (Rolläden) – *nm* blind, shutter
Rollbrett (-er) – *nnt* skateboard
   Rollbrett fahren* – *v irreg* skateboard
Rolle (-n) – *nf* role, part, reel
Rollenspiel (-e) – *nnt* role play
Roller (-) – *nm* scooter

---

nm - noun masculine	*nf* - noun feminine	*nnt* - noun neuter	*npl* - noun plural
nom- nominative	*acc* - accusative	*gen* - genitive	*dat* - dative

Rollschuh fahren* – *v irreg* roller skate
Rollschuhe – *npl* roller skates
Rollstuhl (-stühle) – *nm* wheelchair
Rolltreppe (-n) – *nf* escalator
Rom – Rome
Roman (-e) – *nm* novel
romantisch – *adj* romantic
röntgen – *v reg* X-ray
  sich röntgen lassen – *v irreg refl* to be X-rayed
Röntgenbild – *nnt* X-ray
rosa – *adj inv* pink
Rose (-n) – *nf* rose
Rosenkohl – *nm, no pl* Brussels sprout
Roséwein (-e) – *nm* rosé wine
rot – *adj* red
  rot werden* – *v irreg* go red
rotbraun – *adj* auburn
Rotkäppchen – Little Red Riding Hood
rothaarig – *adj* red haired, ginger
Rotwein (-e) – *nm* red wine
Routine (-n) – *nf* routine
Rowdy (-s) – *nm* hooligan
Rücken (-) – *nm* back
Rückfahrkarte (-n) – *nf* return ticket
Rückfahrt (-en) – *nf* return journey
Rucksack (-säcke) – *nm* rucksack
rücksichtslos – *adj* careless
Rückspiegel (-) – *nm* driving mirror
rückwärts – *adv* backwards
  rückwärts fahren* – *v irreg* reverse, back (car)

rudern – *v reg* row (boat)
Ruf (-e) – *nm* reputation
rufen – *v irreg* shout, call, cry
Rugby – *nnt* rugby
Ruhe – *nf* peace, tranquillity
  Laß mich in Ruhe! – *excl* Leave me in peace!
Ruhestand – *nm* retirement
  in den Ruhestand treten* – *v irreg* retire
  im Ruhestand – retired
Ruhetag (-e) – *nm* rest day (hotel, etc)
ruhig – *adj* calm, quiet
  Sei ruhig! – *excl* Be quiet! (informal)
Rührei (-er) – *nnt* scrambled egg
rülpsen – *v reg* belch
Rumänien – *nnt* Romania
Rumpelkammer (-n) – *nf* junk room
rund – *adj* round
rund – *adv* approximately
Runde (n) – *nf* round of drinks
  eine Runde drehen – *v reg* go for a short walk
Rundfahrt (-en) – *nf* guided tour (by coach, etc)
runzeln – *v reg* wrinkle
  die Stirn runzeln – *v reg* frown
Russe (-n) – *nm wk* Russian person
Rüssel (-) – *nm* elephant's trunk
Russin (-nen) – *nf* Russian person
russisch – *adj* Russian
Rußland – *nnt* Russia
Rutschbahn (-en) – *nf* slide (playground)

---

adj - adjective	*v reg* - verb regular	*v sep* - verb separable	† - see verb info
prep - preposition	*v irreg* - verb irregular	*v refl* - verb reflexive	* - takes sein

S

Saal (Säle) – *nm* hall (public, smart)
Sache (-n) – *nf* thing
Sachen – *npl* belongings
Sachsen – Saxony
Sack (Säcke) – *nm* sack
Sackgasse (-n) – *nf* cul de sac
Saft (Säfte) – *nm* juice, syrup
  Fruchtsaft – *nm* fruit juice
  Orangensaft – *nm* orange juice
sagen – *v reg* say
  Wie sagt man ... auf deutsch?
  – How do you say ... in German?
  jdm sagen – *v reg* tell
sah – *see sehen*
Sahne – *nf* cream (milk)
Saison (-s) – *nf* season (football, etc)
  außerhalb der Saison – out of
  season
Saite (-n) – *nf* string (violin, racket)
Salami – *nf* salami
Salat (-e) – *nm* lettuce
  gemischter Salat – *nm* mixed
  salad
  grüner Salat – *nm* green salad
Salbe (-n) – *nf* cream (medicine)
Salz – *nnt* salt
salzig – *adj* salty
Salzkartoffeln – *npl* boiled potatoes
sammeln – *v reg* collect (stamps, etc)
  Briefmarken sammeln – *v reg*
  collect stamps
Sammelstelle (-n) – *nf* collection
point
Sammlung (-en) – *nf* collection
Samstag (-e) – *nm* Saturday
  am Samstag – on Saturday
  Bis Samstag! – See you on
  Saturday!
Samt – *nm* velvet
Sand – *nm* sand

Sandale (-n) – *nf* sandal
Sandburg (-en) – *nf* sand castle
sanft – *adj* gentle
Sänger (-) – *nm* singer
Sängerin (-nen) – *nf* singer
Sanitäranlage (-n) – *nf* toilet block
Sankt – *adj inv* saint
Sardine (-n) – *nf* sardine
saß – *see sitzen*
Satellit (-en) – *nm wk* satellite
Satellitenschüssel (-n) – *nf* satellite
dish
satt – *adj* fed up
Sattel (Sättel) – *nm* saddle
Satz (Sätze) – *nm* sentence
sauber – *adj* clean
saubermachen – *v reg sep* clean
Saubermachen – *nnt* cleaning
sauer – *adj* sour
Sauerkraut – *nnt* sauerkraut, hot
pickled cabbage
Sauerstoff – *nm* oxygen
saufen – *v irreg coll* booze
der saure Regen – *nm* acid rain
Saxophon (-e) – *nnt* saxophone
SB (Selbstbedienung) – *nf* self-
service
S-Bahn (-en) – *nf* city and suburban
railway
Schach – *nnt* chess
Schachtel (-n) – *nf* box (cardboard)
schade – *adj* pity
schade! – it is a pity!
  Wie schade! – *excl* What a pity!
Schaden (Schäden) – *nm* damage
Schadstoffe – *npl* harmful substances
Schaf (-e) – *nnt* sheep
etwas schaffen – *v reg* manage to do
sthg
Schaffner (-) – *nm* ticket inspector

---

nm - noun masculine   *nf* - noun feminine   *nnt* - noun neuter   *npl* - noun plural
nom- nominative   *acc* - accusative   *gen* - genitive   *dat* - dative

Schaffnerin (-nen) – *nf* ticket inspector

Schal (-s) – *nm* scarf (long)

schälen – *v reg* peel

Schallplatte (-n) – *nf* record (pop, etc)

(den Gang) schalten – *v reg* † change gear

Schalter (-) – *nm* ticket office; counter; switch
   am Schalter – at the ticket office

sich schämen vor (+ dat) – *v reg refl* be ashamed of

schändlich – *adj* disgraceful

scharf – *adj* sharp; spicy

Schatten (-) – *nm* shade
   im Schatten – in the shade

Schatz (Schätze) – *nm* treasure

schätzen – *v reg* appreciate

schauen – *v reg* look

Schauer (-) – *nm* shower (rain)
   es wird Schauer geben – there will be showers

Schaufenster (-) – *nnt* shop window
   einen Schaufensterbummel machen – *v reg* go window shopping

Schaukel (-n) – *nf* swing (child's)

schaukeln – *v reg* swing

Schaukelstuhl (-stühle) – *nm* rocking chair

Schaumwein (-e) – *nm* sparkling wine

Schauspieler (-) – *nm* actor

Schauspielerin (-nen) – *nf* actress

Scheck (-s) – *nm* cheque
   einen Scheck einlösen – *v reg sep* cash a cheque

Scheckheft (-e) – *nnt* cheque book

Scheckkarte (-n) – *nf* cheque card

Scheibe (-n) – *nf* slice

Scheibenwischer (-) – *nm* windscreen wiper

sich scheiden lassen – *v irreg refl* get a divorce

Schein (-e) – *nm* banknote; certificate

E-111-Schein (-e) – *nm* E111 certificate

scheinen – *v irreg* seem, shine

Scheinwerfer (-) – *nm* headlight

Schenkel (-) – *nm* thigh

schenken – *v reg* give as a present

Schere (-n) – *nf* scissors (pair of)

scheu – *adj* shy, timid

Scheune (-n) – *nf* barn

scheußlich – *adj* vile

schick – *adj* smart, chic

schicken – *v reg* send

schieben – *v irreg* push (a car)

Schiedsrichter (-) – *nm* referee

Schiedsrichterin (-nen) – *nf* referee

schiefgehen* – *v irreg sep* go wrong

schießen – *v irreg* shoot

Schießen – *nnt* shooting

Schiff (-e) – *nnt* ship

schikanieren – *v reg* † hassle

Schild (-er) – *nnt* sign

Schildkröte (-n) – *nf* tortoise

Schilling – *nm* schilling (Austrian currency)

Schinken (-) – *nm* ham

Schinkenbrot (-e) – *nnt* ham sandwich

Schirm (-e) – *nm* umbrella

Schlacht (-en) – *nf* battle

Schlaf – *nm* sleep

Schlafanzug (-züge) – *nm* pyjamas

schlafen – *v irreg* sleep

Schlafenszeit (-en) – *nf* bedtime

Schlafraum (-räume) – *nm* dormitory

schläfrig – *adj* sleepy

Schlafsack (-säcke) – *nm* sleeping bag

Schlafwagen (-) – *nm* sleeper car

Schlafzimmer (-) – *nnt* bedroom

Schlag (Schläge) – *nm* blow (hit)

schlagen – *v irreg* hit, strike

Schlager (-) – *nm* hit song (in German)

Schläger (-) – *nm* racket, bat

Schlagsahne – *nf* whipped cream

Schlagzeile (-n) – *nf* headline

Schlagzeug – *nnt* drum kit

Schlamm – *nm* mud

schlammig – *adj* muddy

Schlange (-n) – *nf* queue, snake

Schlange stehen – *v irreg* queue

schlank – *adj* slim

eine Schlankheitskur machen – *v reg* be on a diet

schlau – *adj* crafty

Schlauchboot (-e) – *nnt* dinghy (inflatable)

schlecht – *adj* bad

schlecht gelaunt – bad-tempered

Schleier (-) – *nm* veil

schlendern* – *v reg* stroll

schleppen – *v reg* tow

ins Schleudern geraten* – *v irreg* skid

schlief – *see schlafen*

schließen – *v irreg* shut

Schließfach (-fächer) – *nnt* locker

schließlich – *adv* finally

schlimm – *adj* bad

schlimmer – *adj* worse

Schlips (-e) – *nm* tie

Schlitten (-) – *nm* sledge

Schlittschuh (-e) – *nm* skate

Schlittschuh laufen* – *v irreg* skate

Schlittschuhlaufen – *nnt* ice-skating

Schloß (Schlösser) – *nnt* castle; lock (door)

Schlüssel (-) – *nm* key

Schlüsselbund (-e) – *nm* bunch of keys

Schlüsselloch (-löcher) – *nnt* keyhole

Schlüsselring (-e) – *nm* key ring

Schluß (Schlüsse) – *nm* end, conclusion

Schluß machen mit jdm – *v reg* to finish with s.o.

Schlußverkauf (-verkäufe) – *nm* sale

im Schlußverkauf – in the sales

schmal – *adj* narrow

schmecken – *v reg* taste

Es schmeckt – It tastes good

Schmerz (-en) – *nm* pain

Schmerzen haben – *v irreg* be in pain

schmerzhaft – *adj* painful

Schmetterling (-e) – *nm* butterfly

schmieren – *v reg* spread (with butter, etc)

Schmierheft (-e) – *nnt* rough book

sich schminken – *v reg refl* put on make-up

schmollen – *v reg* sulk

Schmuck – *nm* jewellery

Schnaps (Schnäpse) – *nm* spirits, schnaps

Schnapsidee (-n) – *nf coll* daft idea

Schmutz – *nm* dirt

schmutzig – *adj* dirty

schnarchen – *v reg* snore

Schnecke (-n) – *nf* snail

Schnee – *nm* snow

Schneeball (-bälle) – *nm* snowball

Schneefall (-fälle) – *nm* snowfall

Schneemann (-männer) – *nm* snowman

Schneesturm (-stürme) – *nm* snowstorm

schneiden – *v irreg* cut, slice

Ich habe mich in den Finger geschnitten – I have cut my finger

sich die Haare schneiden lassen – *v irreg dat refl* have a haircut

Schneider (-) – *nm* tailor
Schneiderin (-nen) – *nf* tailor
schneien – *v reg* snow
schnell – *adj* quick
Schnellimbiß (-imbisse) – *nm* snack
Schnellhefter (-) – *nm* folder (file)
Schnellzug (-züge) – *nm* express train
schnitt – *see schneiden*
Schnitzel (-) – *nnt* escalope
schnuggeln – *v reg* snuggle
Schnupfen (-) – *nm* cold
Schnur (Schnüre) – *nf* string
Schnurrbart (-bärte) – *nm* moustache
schnurren – *v reg* purr
Schokolade – *nf* chocolate (bar)
Schokoladen~ – *pref* chocolate
schon – *adv* already
schön – *adj* beautiful, fine
   Einen schönen Tag! – *excl* Have a nice day!
   Einen schönen Abend! – *excl* Have a nice evening!
   Schönes Wochenende! – *excl* Have a good weekend!
Schönheit (-en) – *nf* beauty
Schornstein (-e) – *nm* chimney
Schotte (-n) – *nm wk* Scotsman
Schottenmuster – *nnt* tartan
Schottin (-nen) – *nf* Scotswoman
schottisch – *adj* Scottish
Schottland – *nnt* Scotland
schräg – *adj* sloping
Schrank (Schränke) – *nm* cupboard
Schraubenzieher (-) – *nm* screwdriver
Schrebergarten (-gärten) – *nm* allotment
Schreck (-e) – *nm* fright
schrecklich – *adj* terrible
Schrei (-e) – *nm* shout

Schreibblock (-blöcke) – *nm* pad (writing)
schreiben – *v irreg* write
   eine Prüfung schreiben – *v irreg* take an exam
   Wie schreibt man das? – How do you spell that?
schreiben an (+ acc) – *v irreg* write to
Schreibmaterial – *nnt* writing materials
Schreibmaschine (-n) – *nf* typewriter
Schreibpapier – *nnt* writing paper
Schreibtisch (-e) – *nm* desk
Schreibwarengeschäft (-e) – *nnt* stationer's shop
Schreibwarenhandlung (-en) – *nf* stationer's shop
schreien – *v irreg* shout (scream)
schrieb – *see schreiben*
Schrift (-en) – *nf* writing, handwriting
schriftlich – *adj* in writing
schriftliche Prüfung (-en) – *nf* written test
Schriftsteller (-) – *nm* writer
Schriftstellerin (-nen) – *nf* writer
Schritt (-e) – *nm* footstep
Schubkarre (-n) – *nf* wheelbarrow
Schublade (-n) – *nf* drawer
schüchtern – *adj* shy
Schuh (-e) – *nm* shoe
   ein Paar Schuhe – *nnt* a pair of shoes
   schmutzige Schuhe – *npl* muddy shoes
Schuhgeschäft (-e) – *nnt* shoe shop
Schuhgröße (-n) – *nf* shoe size
Schul~ – *pref* educational
Schulbuch (-bücher) – *nnt* text book
Schulbus (-busse) – *nm* school bus
Schuld – *nf* blame, fault
   jdm die Schuld geben – *v irreg* blame s.o.

Es ist meine Schuld – It's my fault

schulden – *v reg* † owe (money)

schuldig – *adj* guilty

Schuldirektor (-en) – *nm* headmaster

Schuldirektorin (-nen) – *nf* headmistress

Schule (-n) – *nf* school, academy
Die Schule ist aus – School is finished
in der Schule – in school
Ich gehe zu Fuß zur Schule – I walk to school

Schüler (-) – *nm* schoolboy

Schülerin (-nen) – *nf* schoolgirl

Schulferien – *npl* school holidays

schulfrei – *adj* off school

Schulhof (-höfe) – *nm* school playground

Schuljahr (-e) – *nnt* school year
im sechsten Schuljahr – in Year 7
im siebten Schuljahr – in Year 8
im achten Schuljahr – in Year 9
im neunten Schuljahr – in Year 10
im zehnten Schuljahr – in Year 11

Schuljahresanfang (-anfänge) – *nm* start of school year

Schulleiter (-) – *nm* headmaster

Schulleiterin (-nen) – *nf* headmistress

Schulregel (-n) – *nf* school rule

Schultasche (-n) – *nf* school bag

Schulter (-n) – *nf* shoulder

Schuluniform (-en) – *nf* school uniform

Schulweg (-e) – *nm* way to school
auf dem Schulweg – on the way to school

Schürze (-n) – *nf* apron

Schüssel (-n) – *nf* bowl (dish)

Schutz (-e) – *nm* protection

Schutzbrille (-n) – *nf* goggles

Schütze – (horoscope) Sagittarius

schützen vor (+ dat) – *v reg* protect from

schwach – *adj* weak

Schwager (Schwäger) – *nm* brother-in-law

Schwägerin (-nen) – *nf* sister-in-law

Schwalbe (-n) – *nf* swallow (bird)

Schwamm (Schwämme) – *nm* sponge

schwanger – *adj* pregnant

Schwanz (Schwänze) – *nm* tail

schwänzen – *v reg* truant

schwärmen für (+ acc) – *v reg* be keen on

schwarz – *adj* black

Schwarzbrot (-e) – *nnt* black bread

Schwarzfahrer (-) – *nm* fare dodger

Schwarzfahrerin (-nen) – *nf* fare dodger

Schwarzwälderkirschtorte (-n) – *nf* Black Forest Gateau

Schwede (-n) – *nm wk* Swedish person

Schweden – *nnt* Sweden

Schwedin (-nen) – *nf* Swedish person

schwedisch – *adj* Swedish

schweigen – *v irreg* be silent

Schwein (-e) – *nnt* pig

Schwein haben – *v irreg coll* be lucky

Schweinebraten – *nm* roast pork

Schweinefleisch – *nnt* pork

Schweinekotelett (-s) – *nnt* pork chop

die Schweiz – *nf* Switzerland
in der Schweiz – in Switzerland

Schweizer (-) – *nm* Swiss person '

Schweizerin (-nen) – *nf* Swiss person

schweizerisch – *adj* Swiss

---

schwer – *adj* difficult, heavy, severe
schwerhörig – *adj* hard of hearing
Schwester (-n) – *nf* sister
Schwiegermutter (-mütter) – *nf* mother-in-law
Schwiegersohn (-söhne) – *nm* son-in-law
Schwiegertochter (-töchter) – *nf* daughter-in-law
Schwiegervater (-väter) – *nm* father-in-law
schwierig – *adj* difficult
Schwierigkeit (-en) – *nf* difficulty
Schwierigkeiten haben – *v irreg* have difficulty
Schwimmbad (-bäder) – *nnt* swimming pool
schwimmen (*) – *v irreg* swim, float
Schwimmen – *nnt* swimming
Schwimmweste (-n) – *nf* lifejacket
schwindlig – *adj* dizzy
Mir ist schwindlig – I'm dizzy
schwül – *adj* sultry
Science Fiction – *nf* science fiction
Science-Fiction-Film (-e) – *nm* science fiction film
Science-Fiction-Roman (-e) – *nm* science fiction story, book
sechs – *adj* six
sechste – *adj* sixth
sechzehn – *adj* sixteen
sechzehnte – *adj* sixteenth
sechzig – *adj* sixty
See (-n) – *nm* lake
See (-n) – *nf* sea
Seebad (-bäder) – *nnt* seaside resort
seekrank – *adj* seasick
Seemann (-männer) – *nm* sailor (civilian)
Segel (-) – *nnt* sail
Segelboot (-e) – *nnt* dinghy (sailing)
segeln – *v reg* sail
segeln gehen* – *v irreg* go sailing

Segelschiff (-e) – *nnt* sailing ship
sehen – *v irreg* see
sehenswert – *adj* worth seeing
Sehenswürdigkeit (-en) – *nf* sight (tourist)
sehr – *adv* very
Sehr geehrte Herren – Dear Sirs
seid – *see sein**
Seide (-n) – *nf* silk
aus Seide – made of silk
Seife (-n) – *nf* soap
Seifenoper (-n) – *nf* soap opera
Seilbahn (-en) – *nf* cable car
sein – *poss adj* his, its
sein* – *v irreg* be
seit (+ dat) – *prep* since, for (since)
Seit wann lernst du Deutsch? – How long have you been learning German?
seit wann? – how long?
seitdem – *sub conj* since
Seite (-n) – *nf* page, side
auf der anderen Seite – on the other side
auf der linken Seite – on the left hand side
auf Seite 51 – on page 51
unten auf der Seite – at the bottom of the page
oben auf der Seite – at the top of the page
Sekretär (-e) – *nm* secretary
Sekretärin (-nen) – *nf* secretary
Sekt – *nm* German champagne
Sekunde (-n) – *nf* second (time)
selbst – *pron* itself, oneself, yourself
selbständig – *adj* independent
Selbstbedienung – *nf* self-service
Selbstbedienungsrestaurant (-s) – *nnt* self-service restaurant
selbstbewußt – *adj* self-confident
selbstgemacht – *adj* home-made
selbstverständlich – *adv* of course

---

adj - adjective	*v reg* - verb regular	*v sep* - verb separable	† - see verb info
prep - preposition	*v irreg* - verb irregular	*v refl* - verb reflexive	* - takes sein

selten – *adj* rare
selten – *adv* seldom
seltsam – *adj* strange, odd
Semester (-) – *nnt* term (university)
Semikolon (-s) – *nnt* semi-colon (;)
Semmel (-n) – *nf* bread roll
senden – *v reg* † broadcast
Sendung (-en) – *nf* programme (TV)
Senf – *nm* mustard
sensationell – *adj* sensational
sensibel – *adj* sensitive
September – *nm* September
  im September – in September
Serie (-n) – *nf* serial
Serviette (-n) – *nf* serviette
Servus! – *excl* Hi!; Goodbye!
Sessel (-) – *nm* armchair
Sesselbahn (-en) – *nf* chair lift
setzen – *v reg* set (put)
setzen auf (+ acc) – *v reg* place on
sich setzen – *v reg refl* sit down
  Setz dich! – Sit down! (informal)
  Setzen Sie sich! – Sit down!
  (formal)
sexistisch – *adj* sexist
Shampoo (-s) – *nm* shampoo
Sherry (-s) – *nm* sherry
Shorts – *npl* shorts
Show (-s) – *nf* show (variety)
sich – *pron refl* herself, himself,
  oneself,
sicher – *adj* certain, safe
Sicherheit – *nf* safety
Sicherheitsgurt (-e) – *nm* seat belt
Sicht – *nf, no pl* visibility, sight
sicherlich – *adv* surely
in Sicht – in sight
sichtbar – *adj* visible
sie – *pron nom/acc* she, her, it, they,
  them
Sie – *pron nom/acc sing or pl* you
  (singular or plural polite)

sieben – *adj* seven
siebte – *adj* seventh
siebzehn – *adj* seventeen
siebzig – *adj* seventy
Siedlung (-en) – *nf* housing estate
Sieg (-e) – *nm* victory
siegen – *v reg* win
Sieger (-) – *nm* winner
Siegerin (-nen) – *nf* winner
siegreich – *adj* victorious
sieht – *see sehen*
Signal (-e) – *nnt* signal, tone (on
  phone)
Silber – *nnt* silver
Silbermedaille – *nf* silver medal
silbern – *adj* silver
Silvester – *nnt* New Year's Eve
sind – *see sein**
singen – *v irreg* sing
Singular – *nm* singular (grammar)
  im Singular – in the singular
sinken* – *v irreg* sink
Sinn (-e) – *nm* sense
  Es hat keinen Sinn – There's no
  point
sinnvoll – *adj* sensible
Situation (-en) – *nf* situation
sitzen – *v irreg* sit
sitzen bleiben* – *v irreg* repeat a
  year (at school)
Skifahren – *nnt* skiing
Ski (-er) – *nm* ski
Ski fahren* – *v irreg* go skiing
Skilaufen – *nnt* skiing
Skilift (-s) – *nm* ski lift
Skischuh (-e) – *nm* ski boots
Skistiefel (-) – *nm* ski boot
Skorpion – Scorpio (horoscope)
Slip (-s) – *nm* knickers
die Slowakei – *nf* Slovakia
Snooker – *nnt* snooker
so – so

---

sobald – *sub conj* as soon as
sobald wie möglich – *adv* as soon as possible
so viel – *adv* so much
so viele – so many
so ... wie – *adv* as ... as
 Sie ist so groß wie ich – She is as big as me
Socke (-n) – *nf* sock
Sofa (-s) – *nnt* settee
sofort – *adv* immediately, at once
sofortig – *adj* immediate (instant)
Software – *nf* software
sogar – *adv* even
sogleich – *adv* at once
Sohn (Söhne) – *nm* son
Soja~ – *pref* soya
solche – such
 ein solcher – such a
Soldat (-en) – *nm wk* soldier
solide – *adj* solid
sollen – *v irreg* ought
 Ich sollte es tun – I ought to do it
sollte – *see sollen*
Sommer – *nm* summer
 im Sommer – in summer
Sommerferien – *npl* summer holidays
sommerlich – *adj* summery
Sommerschlußverkauf (-verkäufe) – *nm* summer sales
Sonderangebot (-e) – *nnt* special offer
Sonderpreis (-e) – *nm* special price
Sonnabend (-e) – *nm* Saturday
 am Sonnabend – on Saturday
Sonne (-n) – *nf* sun
sich sonnen – *v reg refl* sunbathe
Sonnenaufgang (-gänge) – *nm* sunrise
Sonnenbrand – *nm* sunburn
Sonnenbrille (-n) – *nf* sun-glasses
Sonnencreme – *nf* sun cream

Sonnenmilch – *nf* sun milk
Sonnenöl – *nnt* sun-tan oil
Sonnenschein – *nm* sunshine
Sonnenschirm (-e) – *nm* sunshade
Sonnenstich – *nm* sun-stroke
Sonnenstrahl (-en) – *nm* sunbeam
Sonnenuntergang (-gänge) – *nm* sunset
sonnig – *adj* sunny
Sonntag – *nm* Sunday
 am Sonntag – on Sunday
 Bis Sonntag! – See you on Sunday!
sonst – *adv* otherwise
Sonst noch etwas? – Anything else?
Sorge (-n) – *nf* worry
sich Sorgen machen über (+ acc) – *v reg dat refl* worry
sorgen für (+ acc) – *v reg* look after
sorgfältig – *adv* carefully
Sorte (-n) – *nf* sort, kind
Soße (-n) – *nf* sauce, gravy
Souvenir (-s) – *nnt* souvenir
soviel – so much
soviel wie möglich – *adv* as much as possible
sowieso – *adv* anyway
sozial – *adj* social
Sozialkunde – *nf* social studies
Sozialwohnung (-en) – *nf* council flat
Spaghetti – *nf* spaghetti
Spanien – *nnt* Spain
Spanier (-) – *nm* Spaniard
Spanierin (-nen) – *nf* Spaniard
spanisch – *adj* Spanish
Spanisch – *nnt* Spanish (language)
spannend – *adj* exciting
Sparbuch (-bücher) – *nnt* savings pass book
sparen für (+ acc) – *v reg* save up for
 Geld sparen – *v reg* save money
Spargel – *nm* asparagus

---

adj - adjective	*v reg* - verb regular	*v sep* - verb separable	† - see verb info
prep - preposition	*v irreg* - verb irregular	*v refl* - verb reflexive	* - takes sein

Sparkasse (-n) – *nf* bank
sparsam – *adj* economical
Sparschwein (-e) – *nnt* piggy bank
Spaß (Späße) – *nm* fun
　Es macht (mir) Spaß – It's fun
Spaß haben – *v irreg* to have fun
　Viel Spaß! – *excl* Have a good time!
spät – *adj* late
　Wie spät ist es? – What time is it?
Spaten (-) – *nm* spade
später – *adj* later
　Bis später! – See you later!
spazieren gehen* – *v irreg* go for a walk
　mit dem Hund spazieren gehen* – *v irreg* take the dog for a walk
Spaziergang (-gänge) – *nm* walk (stroll)
　einen Spaziergang machen – *v reg* go for a walk
Speck – *nm* bacon
Speicher (-) – *nm* memory (computer)
speichern – *v reg* save (computer)
Speisekarte (-n) – *nf* menu
Speisesaal (-säle) – *nm* dining hall
Speisewagen (-) – *nm* dining car
Sperre (-n) – *nf* barrier
Spezialität (-en) – *nf* speciality
Spiegel (-) – *nm* mirror
Spiegelei (-er) – *nnt* fried egg
Spiel (-e) – *nnt* game, match, pack of cards
　ein Spiel verlieren – *v irreg* lose a match
Spielautomat (-en) – *nm wk* fruit machine
spielen – *v reg* play, act (drama)
　Fußball spielen – *v reg* play football

Gitarre spielen – *v reg* play the guitar
Spieler (-) – *nm* player
Spielerin (-nen) – *nf* player
Spielfilm (-e) – *nm* feature film
Spielhalle (-n) – *nf* amusement arcade
Spielkarte (-n) – *nf* playing card
Spielplatz (-plätze) – *nm* playground
Spielraum (-räume) – *nm* games room
Spielwaren – *npl* toys
Spielwarengeschäft (-e) – *nnt* toy shop
Spielzeug (-e) – *nnt* toy
Spinat – *nm* spinach
Spinne (-n) – *nf* spider
Spion (-e) – *nm* spy
Spionage – *nf* spying
Spionagefilm (-e) – *nm* spy film
Spionagegeschichte (-n) – *nf* spy story
Spionin (-nen) – *nf* spy
Spirituosen – *npl* spirits (alcohol)
spitz – *adj* pointed
spitze – *adj inv coll* excellent
Spitzenpolitiker (-) – *nm* top politician
Spitzname (-n) – *nm wk* nickname
Sport (Sportarten) – *nm* PE, games, sport
Sport treiben – *v irreg* do games
　gern Sport treiben – *v irreg* be keen on sport
Sportart (-en) – *nf* type of sport
sportlich – *adj* athletic
Sportmöglichkeit (-en) – *nf* sporting facility
Sportplatz (-plätze) – *nm* sports ground
Sportverein (-e) – *nm* sports club
Sportwagen (-) – *nm* sports car; push chair

---

nm - noun masculine　　*nf* - noun feminine　　*nnt* - noun neuter　　*npl* - noun plural
nom - nominative　　*acc* - accusative　　*gen* - genitive　　*dat* - dative

Sportzentrum (-zentren) – *nnt*
sports centre

sprach – *see sprechen*

Sprache (-n) – *nf* language

Sprachlabor (-s) – *nnt* language
laboratory

sprachlos – *adj* speechless

sprechen (mit + dat) – *v irreg*
speak (to)

    Deutsch sprechen – *v irreg* speak
    German

    jdm sprechen – *v irreg* speak to
    s.o.

    laut sprechen – *v irreg* speak
    loudly

Sprechstunde (-n) – *nf* surgery
(time)

spricht – *see sprechen*

springen* – *v irreg* jump

    Trampolin springen* – *v irreg*
    trampoline

Spritze (-n) – *nf* injection

spritzen – *v reg* spray

Sprudel (-) – *nm* sparkling water

sprudelnd – *adj* fizzy

Sprühdose (-n) – *nf* aerosol

Sprungbrett (-er) – *nnt* springboard

Spülbecken (-) – *nnt* sink

spülen – *v reg* do washing up

Spülmaschine (-n) – *nf* dishwasher

Spülmittel (-) – *nnt* washing up
liquid

Squash – *nnt* squash (sport)

Stöpsel (-) – *nm* plug (bath)

Staat (-en) – *nm* state (nation)

Staatsangehörigkeit (-en) – *nf*
nationality

Staatsexamen (-) – *nnt* degree
(university exam)

Stachelbeere (-n) – *nf* gooseberry

Stadion (Stadien) – *nnt* stadium

Stadt (Städte) – *nf* town

    in der Stadt – in town

    Sam fährt in die Stadt – Sam
    goes into town

Stadtbummel – *nm* stroll around
town

    einen Stadtbummel machen –
    v reg go round town

Stadtführung (-en) – *nf* guided tour
of town

städtisch – *adj* urban, municipal

Stadtmitte (-n) – *nf* town centre

    in der Stadtmitte – in the town
    centre

Stadtplan (-pläne) – *nm* town plan

Stadtrand (-ränder) – *nm* edge of
town, outskirts

    am Stadtrand – on the edge of
    town

Stadtrundfahrt (-en) – *nf* tour of
town (coach, boat, etc)

Stadtteil (-e) – *nm* part of town

Stadtviertel (-) – *nnt* district of city

Stadtzentrum (-zentren) – *nnt*
town centre

stahl – *see stehlen*

stammeln – *v reg* stutter

Stammtisch (-e) – *nm* table reserved
for regular customers

stand – *see stehen*

Stand (Stände) – *nm* stall

Star (-s) – *nm* celebrity

starb – *see sterben**

stark – *adj* strong

    Es regnet stark – It's raining
    heavily

    stark gebaut – *adj* well-built
    (person)

Startbahn (-en) – *nf* runway

starten* – *v reg* † take off (aircraft)

Station (-en) – *nf* station
(underground)

statt – *conj* instead of

statt (+ gen) – *prep* instead of

stattfinden – *v irreg sep* take place

---

adj - adjective	*v reg* - verb regular	*v sep* - verb separable	† - see verb info
prep - preposition	*v irreg* - verb irregular	*v refl* - verb reflexive	* - takes sein

Stau (-s) – *nm* traffic jam
Staub – *nm* dust
staubsaugen – *v reg* vacuum
Staubsauger (-) – *nm* vacuum cleaner
Steak (-s) – *nnt* steak
stechen – *v irreg* sting
Stechpalme (-n) – *nf* holly
Steckdose (-n) – *nf* socket, power point
stecken – *v reg* put, place (insert)
Stecker (-) – *nm* plug (electric)
stehen (*) – *v irreg* stand (on feet)
stehen – *v irreg* suit
  Es steht mir – It suits me
Stehlampe (-n) – *nf* standard lamp
stehlen – *v irreg* steal
steif – *adj* stiff
steigen* – *v irreg* climb
steil – *adj* steep (hill)
Stein (-e) – *nm* stone
Steinbock – Capricorn (horoscope)
Steinbruch (-brüche) – *nm* quarry
Stelle (-n) – *nf* place, job, passage (in book)
stellen – *v reg* place (vertical)
  den Wecker stellen – *v reg* set the alarm
  eine Frage stellen – *v reg* ask a question
Stellenangebot (-e) – *nnt* job offer
Stenographie – *nf* shorthand
Stenotypist (-en) – *nm wk* typist
Stenotypistin (-nen) – *nf* typist
Steppdecke (-n) – *nf* duvet, quilt
Steppdeckenbezug (-bezüge) – *nm* duvet cover
sterben* – *v irreg* die
Stereoanlage (-n) – *nf* stereo, Hi-Fi system
Stern (-e) – *nm* star (sky)
Steuer (-n) – *nf* tax

Steuerberater (-) – *nm* accountant
Steuerberaterin (-nen) – *nf* accountant
Steward (-s) – *nm* steward
Stewardeß (-essen) – *nf* air hostess, stewardess
Stich (-e) – *nm* bite, sting (insect)
Stiefbruder (-brüder) – *nm* stepbrother
Stiefel (-) – *nm* boot (shoe)
Stiefmutter (-mütter) – *nf* stepmother
Stiefschwester (-n) – *nf* stepsister
Stiefsohn (-söhne) – *nm* stepson
Stieftochter (-töchter) – *nf* stepdaughter
Stiefvater (-väter) – *nm* stepfather
Stier (-e) – *nm* bull; Taurus (horoscope)
Stift (-e) – *nm* pen
Stil (-e) – *nm* style
still – *adj* still, quiet, peaceful
Stille (-n) – *nf* silence
stillstehen – *v irreg sep* stand still
Stimme (-n) – *nf* voice
stimmen – *v reg* tune (instrument)
  Das stimmt – That's right
  Das stimmt so – Keep the change
stinken – *v irreg* smell (stink)
stinkig – *adj* smelly
Stock (Stöcke) – *nm* stick
Stock (Stockwerke) – *nm* floor
  im ersten Stock – on the first floor
  im nächsten Stock – on the next floor
  im obersten Stock – on the top floor
Stockung (-en) – *nf* blockage
Stockwerk (-e) – *nnt* storey
Stoff (-e) – *nm* cloth
stöhnen – *v reg* moan
stolz (auf + acc) – *adj* proud (of)

---

nm - noun masculine *nf* - noun feminine *nnt* - noun neuter *npl* - noun plural
nom- nominative *acc* - accusative *gen* - genitive *dat* - dative

stören – *v reg* bother, disturb
Stoßstange (-n) – *nf* bumper
Str. (Straße) – Rd.; St.
Strafe (-n) – *nf* punishment
Straftat (-en) – *nf* offence
Strafzettel (-) – *nm* parking ticket
Strand (Strände) – *nm* beach
  am Strand – on the beach
Strandbad (-bäder) – *nnt* bathing
  beach
Strandburg (-en) – *nf* windbreak
Strandkorb (-körbe) – *nm* wicker
  beach seat
Straßburg – Strasbourg
Straße (-n) – *nf* street, road
  auf der Straße – in the street
Straßenbahn (-en) – *nf* tram
Straßenkarte (-n) – *nf* road map
Straßenschild (-er) – *nnt* road sign
Straßenverkehrsordnung
  (StVO) – *nf* highway code
Strauch (Sträuche) – *nm* bush
Streber (-) – *nm coll* swot
Streberin (-nen) – *nf coll* swot
streichen – *v irreg* cancel; cross out
streichen – *v irreg* decorate (paint)
Streichholz (-hölzer) – *nnt* match
Streichholzschachtel (-n) – *nf*
  matchbox
Streichinstrument (-e) – *nnt*
  stringed instrument (with bow)
Streichorchester (-) – *nnt* string
  orchestra
Streifenkarte (-n) – *nf* book of
  tickets
Streik (-s) – *nm* strike (walk-out)
streiken – *v reg* go on strike
Streikende – *nmf* ‡ striker
  (on strike)
Streit (-e) – *nm* row (argument)
sich streiten – *v irreg refl* argue,
  quarrel
Streitkräfte – *npl* armed forces

streng – *adj* strict, harsh
Streß – *nm* stress
stressig – *adj coll* stressful
stricken – *v reg* knit
Strickjacke (-n) – *nf* cardigan
Strohdach (-dächer) – *nnt* thatched
  roof
Strohhalm (-e) – *nm* drinking straw
Strom – *nm* current (electricity)
Strumpf (Strümpfe) – *nm* stocking
Strumpfhose (-n) – *nf* pair of tights
Stube (-n) – *nf* room
Stück (-) – *nnt* piece (of), coin
  ein Stück Schokolade – a piece
    of chocolate
  ein Zweimarkstück – a 2 DM
    coin
Student (-en) – *nm wk* student
Studentin (-nen) – *nf* student
studieren – *v reg* † study (at
  university)
Studio (-s) – *nnt* studio (TV)
Studium (Studien) – *nnt* studies
Stufe (-n) – *nf* step (on stairs)
  Vorsicht Stufe! – *excl* Mind the
    step!
Stuhl (Stühle) – *nm* chair
stumm – *adj* dumb
stumpf – *adj* dull, blunt
stumpfsinnig – *adj* apathetic, tedious
Stunde (-n) – *nf* hour, lesson
  eine halbe Stunde – half an hour
  pro Stunde – per hour
stundenlang – *adv* for hours on end
Stundenplan (-pläne) – *nm*
  timetable (school)
stündlich – *adj* hourly
stur – *adj* stubborn, obstinate
Sturm (Stürme) – *nm* storm, gale
Stürmer (-) – *nm* striker, forward
  (football)
stürmisch – *adj* stormy

---

adj - adjective   *v reg* - verb regular   *v sep* - verb separable   † - see verb info
prep - preposition   *v irreg* - verb irregular   *v refl* - verb reflexive   * - takes sein

Sturzhelm (-e) – *nm* crash helmet
StVO – *nf* highway code
Substantiv (-e) – *nnt* noun
suchen – *v reg* hunt for, look for
Südafrika – *nnt* South Africa
Südamerika – *nnt* South America
Süden – *nm* south
  im Süden – in the south
  in Süddeutschland – in South
  Germany
südlich – *adj* southern
südlich von (+ dat) – *prep* south of
super – *adj inv* super
Super bleifrei – *nm* super unleaded
petrol
Super verbleit – *nnt* 4-star leaded
petrol

Supermarkt (-märkte) – *nm*
supermarket
Suppe (-n) – *nf* soup
Surfbrett (-er) – *nnt* surfboard,
sailboard
Surfen (-) – *nnt* surfing
  das Internet surfen – *v reg* surf
  the net
süß – *adj* sweet (tasting)
Süßigkeit (-en) – *nf* sweet
Sweatshirt (-s) – *nnt* sweatshirt
sympathisch – *adj* likeable
Synagoge (-n) – *nf* synagogue
Synchronisierung – *nf* dubbing
System (-e) – *nnt* system
Szene (-n) – *nf* scene (play)

T

T-Shirt (-s) – *nnt* T-shirt
Tabak – *nm* tobacco
Tabakhändler (-) – *nm* tobacconist
Tabakhändlerin (-nen) – *nf*
tobacconist
Tabakhandlung (-en) – *nf*
tobacconist's shop
Tablett (-s) – *nnt* tray
Tablette (-n) – *nf* tablet
Tafel (-n) – *nf* blackboard, bar of
chocolate
Tafelwein (-e) – *nm* table wine
Tag (-e) – *nm* day
  am nächsten Tag – next day
  am Tag – by day
  den ganzen Tag – all day long
  Einen schönen Tag! – *excl* Have
  a nice day!
  eines Tages – some day
  Guten Tag! – *excl* Hello! Good
  afternoon!

  jeden Tag – every day
  pro Tag – per day
  der Tag der deutschen Einheit
  – *nm* German Unity Day (3rd
  October)
  vierzehn Tage – fortnight
  vor ein paar Tagen – the other
  day, a few days ago
Tage – *npl* period (menstrual)
  Ich habe meine Tage – I've got
  my period
Tagebuch (-bücher) – *nnt* diary
(reminiscences)
Tagesablauf – *nm* daily routine
Tagesgericht (-e) – *nnt* dish of the
day
Tageskarte (-n) – *nf* menu of the day
Tageslichtprojektor (-en) – *nm*
overhead projector
Tagesmutter (-mütter) – *nf* child-
minder

---

nm - noun masculine   *nf* - noun feminine   *nnt* - noun neuter   *npl* - noun plural
nom- nominative   *acc* - accusative   *gen* - genitive   *dat* - dative

Tagesrückfahrkarte (-n) – *nf* day return

Tagesschüler (-) – *nm* day boy

Tagesschülerin (-nen) – *nf* day girl

Tageszeitung (-en) – *nf* daily paper

täglich – *adj* daily
    im täglichen Leben – in daily life

tagsüber – by day

Taille (-n) – *nf* waist(line)

taktlos – *adj* tactless

taktvoll – *adj* tactful

Tal (Täler) – *nnt* valley

talentiert – *adj* talented

Tampon (-s) – *nm* tampon

tanken – *v reg* fill up with petrol

Tankstelle (-n) – *nf* petrol station

Tankstellenbesitzer (-) – *nm* garage owner

Tankwart (-e) – *nm* petrol-pump attendant

Tannenbaum (-bäume) – *nm* fir tree

Tante (-n) – *nf* aunt

Tanz~ – *pref* dance

Tanz (Tänze) – *nm* dance

tanzen – *v reg* dance

Tänzer (-) – *nm* dancer

Tänzerin (-nen) – *nf* dancer

Tapete (-n) – *nf* wallpaper

tapezieren – *v reg* † wallpaper

tapfer – *adj* brave

Tarif (-e) – *nm* charge, rate, fare

Tasche (-n) – *nf* bag, pocket

Taschenbuch (-bücher) – *nnt* paperback

Taschendieb (-e) – *nm* pickpocket

Taschengeld – *nnt* pocket money

Taschenlampe (-n) – *nf* torch

Taschenmesser (-) – *nnt* penknife

Taschenrechner (-) – *nm* calculator

Taschentuch (-tücher) – *nnt* handkerchief

Tasse (-n) – *nf* cup
    eine Tasse Tee – cup of tea

Tastatur (-en) – *nf* keyboard (IT)

Taste (-n) – *nf* key (keyboard)

Tat (-en) – *nf* action (deed)
    in der Tat – *adv* in fact

tat – *see* tun

Tätigkeit (-en) – *nf* activity

Tatort (-e) – *nm* scene (crime)

Tatsache (-n) – *nf* fact

tatsächlich – *adv* in fact

taub – *adj* deaf

taubstumm – *adj* deaf and dumb

tauchen* – *v reg* dive

Taufe (-n) – *nf* christening

tauschen – *v reg* swap

täuschen – *v reg* deceive

tausend – *adj* thousand

Tausende von (+ dat) – thousands of

Taxi (-s) – *nnt* taxi

Taxifahrer (-) – *nm* taxi driver

Taxifahrerin (-nen) – *nf* taxi driver

Taxistand (-stände) – *nm* taxi rank

Technik – *nf* technology

Techniker (-) – *nm* technician

Technikerin (-nen) – *nf* technician

technisch – *adj* technical

technisches Zeichnen – *nnt* engineering drawing

Technologie (-n) – *nf* technology

Teddybär (-en) – *nm wk* teddy bear

Tee – *nm* tea

Teebeutel (-) – *nm* teabag

Teekanne (-n) – *nf* teapot

Teetasse (-n) – *nf* tea cup

TEE-Zug (-Züge) – *nm* Trans-European express train

Teich (-e) – *nm* pond

Teig (-e) – *nm* pastry

Teil (-e) – *nm* part

---

teilen – *v reg* share, separate
teilnehmen an (+ dat) – *v irreg sep* take part in
　am Austausch teilnehmen – *v irreg sep* go on an exchange
Teilnehmer (-) – *nm* competitor
Teilnehmerin (-nen) – *nf* competitor
Teilzeit~ – *pref* part-time
Teilzeitarbeit (-en) – *nf* part-time work
Telefon (-e) – *nnt* phone
　am Telefon – on the phone
Telefonbuch (-bücher) – *nnt* telephone directory
telefonieren mit (+ dat) – *v reg* † telephone s.o
telefonisch – *adv* by phone
Telefonkabine (-n) – *nf* phone box
Telefonkarte (-n) – *nf* phone card
Telefonnummer (-n) – *nf* phone number
Telefonzelle (-n) – *nf* phone box
Telegramm (-e) – *nnt* telegram
Teller (-) – *nm* plate
Temperatur (-en) – *nf* temperature
Tendenz (-en) – *nf* trend
Tennis – *nnt* tennis
Tennisball (-bälle) – *nm* tennis ball
Tennisplatz (-plätze) – *nm* tennis court
Tennisschläger (-) – *nm* tennis racket
Tennisschuh (-e) – *nm* tennis shoe
Tennisspiel (-e) – *nnt* game of tennis
Teppich (-e) – *nm* carpet, rug
Teppichboden (-böden) – *nm* fitted carpet
Termin (-e) – *nm* appointment
　einen Termin ausmachen – *v reg sep* make an appointment
Terrasse (-n) – *nf* terrace, patio
Tesafilm® – *nm* sellotape®

Test (-s) – *nm* test
Testbogen (-bögen) – *nm* paper (exam)
teuer – *adj* expensive
Textverarbeitung – *nf* word processing
Textverarbeitungsprogramm (-e) – *nnt* word processing program
Theater – *nnt* theatre; *coll* fuss
Theater machen über (+ acc) – *v reg coll* make a fuss about sthg
Theaterkunde – *nf* performing arts (school)
Theaterstück (-e) – *nnt* play
Thema (Themen) – *nnt* topic
Themse – *nf* River Thames
Thermometer (-) – *nnt* thermometer
• **Thunfisch (-e)** – *nm* tuna
Ticket (-s) – *nnt* ticket (plane)
tief – *adj* deep, low
tiefgefroren – *adj* deep frozen
Tiefkühltruhe (-n) – *nf* deep freeze
Tiefseetauchen – *nnt* scuba diving
Tiefsttemperatur (-en) – *nf* minimum temperature
　bei Tiefwasser – at low tide
Tier (-e) – *nnt* animal
Tierarzt (-ärzte) – *nm* vet
Tierärztin (-nen) – *nf* vet
Tiergarten (-gärten) – *nm* zoo
Tiger (-) – *nm* tiger
Tinte (-n) – *nf* ink
Tintenfisch (-e) – *nm* squid; octopus; cuttlefish
Tintenlöscher (-) – *nm* ink eraser pen
Tintenstrahldrucker (-) – *nm* ink jet printer
Tip (-s) – *nm* tip (hint)
tippen – *v reg* type
Tisch (-e) – *nm* table
　den Tisch decken – *v reg* set the table

---

nm - noun masculine	*nf* - noun feminine	*nnt* - noun neuter	*npl* - noun plural
nom- nominative	*acc* - accusative	*gen* - genitive	*dat* - dative

den Tisch verlassen – *v irreg* leave the table

zu Tisch kommen* – *v irreg* sit down at table

Tischdecke (-n) – *nf* table-cloth

Tischtennis – *nnt* table tennis

Titel (-) – *nm* title, heading

Toast – *nm* toast (bread)

Tochter (Töchter) – *nf* daughter

Tod (-e) – *nm* death

Toilette (-n) – *nf* toilet

Toilettenpapier – *nnt* toilet paper

Toilettentisch (-e) – *nm* dressing table

tolerieren – *v reg* † tolerate

toll – *adj* great; mad

Tollwut – *nf* rabies

Tomate (-n) – *nf* tomato

Tomatensalat – *nm* salad (tomato)

Ton (Töne) – *nm* tone

Tonband (-bänder) – *nnt* tape

Tonbandgerät (-e) – *nnt* tape recorder

Tonne (-n) – *nf* ton

Topf (Töpfe) – *nm* saucepan

Töpferei (-en) – *nf* pottery (workshop)

Topfpflanze (-n) – *nf* pot plant

Tor (-e) – *nnt* gate, goal (sport)

ein Tor schießen – *v irreg* score a goal

Torpfosten (-) – *nm* goalpost

Torte (-n) – *nf* flan

Torwart (-e) – *nm* goalkeeper

tot – *adj* dead

total – *adv* totally

töten – *v reg* † kill

Toto – *nnt* National Lottery

Tour (-en) – *nf* tour

Tourismus – *nm* tourism

Tourist (-en) – *nm wk* tourist

Touristenstadt (-städte) – *nf* tourist centre

Touristin (-nen) – *nf* tourist

Tournier (-e) – *nnt* tournament

Tradition (-en) – *nf* tradition

Tracht (-en) – *nf* national costume

traditionell – *adj* traditional

tragen – *v irreg* carry, wear

Tragflügelboot (-e) – *nnt* hydrofoil

Trainer (-) – *nm* trainer (person)

trainieren – *v reg* † train (sport)

Trainingsanzug (-anzüge) – *nm* tracksuit

Trainingsschuhe – *npl* trainers

Traktor (-en) – *nm* tractor

Trampolin (-e) – *nnt* trampoline

trank – *see trinken*

Transportmittel (-) – *nnt* transport

Traube (-n) – *nf* grapes

Traubensaft (-säfte) – *nm* grape juice

trauen – *v reg* trust

Traum (Träume) – *nm* dream

träumen – *v reg* dream

traurig – *adj* sad

Traurigkeit – *nf* sadness

Treffen (-) – *nnt* meeting

treffen – *v irreg* meet; hit target

sich treffen – *v irreg refl* meet by arrangement

treiben – *v irreg* do (sport)

gern Sport treiben – *v irreg* be keen on sport

Treibhauseffekt – *nm* greenhouse effect

Trend (-s) – *nm* trend

trennbares Verb – *nnt* separable verb

trennen – *v reg* separate

sich trennen – *v reg refl* separate by agreement

Trennung (-en) – *nf* separation

Treppe (-n) – *nf* flight of stairs

Er ist die Treppe hinaufgelaufen – He ran up the stairs

---

adj - adjective   *v reg* - verb regular   *v sep* - verb separable   † - see verb info
prep - preposition   *v irreg* - verb irregular   *v refl* - verb reflexive   * - takes sein

Treppenflur (-e) – *nm* landing (house)

Tresor (-e) – *nnt* safe

treten – *v irreg* kick (ball, etc)

treten* – step, tread

in den Ruhestand treten* – *v irreg* retire

Trickfilm (-e) – *nm* cartoon film

Trimester (-) – *nnt* term (school)

trimmen – *v reg* keep fit

trinkbar – *adj* drinkable

trinken – *v irreg* drink

Trinkgeld (-er) – *nnt* tip (money)

Trinkwasser – *nnt* drinking water

kein Trinkwasser – non-drinking water

trocken – *adj* dry

Trockenreinigung (-en) – *nf* dry cleaner's

trocknen – *v reg* † dry

sich die Haare trocknen – *v reg* *dat refl* † dry one's hair

Trompete (-n) – *nf* trumpet

trotz (+ gen) – *prep* in spite of

trotzdem – *adv* nevertheless

trug – *see tragen*

Truthahn (-hähne) – *nm* turkey

die Tschechische Republik – *nf* the Czech Republic

Tschüs! – *excl coll* Goodbye!

T-Shirt (-s) – *nnt* T-shirt

Tube (-n) – *nf* tube (toothpaste, etc)

Tuch (Tücher) – *nnt* scarf (square)

Tulpe (-n) – *nf* tulip

tun – *v irreg* do

tun so, als ob – *v irreg* pretend

Tunnel (-) – *nm* tunnel

Tür (-en) – *nf* door

an die Tür klopfen – knock on the door

Türke (-n) – *nm wk* Turk

die Türkei – *nf* Turkey

Türkin (-nen) – *nf* Turk

türkis – *adj inv* turquoise

türkisch – *adj* Turkish

Turm (Türme) – *nm* tower

Turnen – *nnt* gym(nastics)

turnen – *v reg* do gymnastics

Turnhalle (-n) – *nf* gym(nasium)

Turnschuh (-e) – *nm* trainer (shoe)

tut – *see tun*

Tütchen (-) – *nnt* cornet (ice cream)

Tüte (-n) – *nf* bag (paper, plastic)

TÜV – *nm* MOT; technical approval agency

Typ (-en) – *nm* type, bloke

typisch – *adj* typical

U

U-Bahn (-en) – *nf* underground

U-Bahnfahrkarte (-n) – *nf* underground ticket

U-Bahnstation (-en) – *nf* underground station

übel – *adj* bad

Mir ist übel – I feel sick

sich übel fühlen – *v reg refl* feel sick

üben – *v reg* practise

über (+ acc/dat) – *prep* above, over, across, about

Überdosis – *nf* overdose

Überfahrt (-en) – *nf* crossing (channel)

überall – *adv* everywhere

übereinstimmen mit (+ dat) – *v reg sep* agree with

n - noun masculine	*nf* - noun feminine	*nnt* - noun neuter	*npl* - noun plural
nm- nominative	*acc* - accusative	*gen* - genitive	*dat* - dative

überfahren – *v irreg insep* run over (accident)

Überfall (-fälle) – *nm* holdup (robbery)

überfallen – *v irreg insep* attack, mug

Übergang (-gänge) – *nm* crossing

sich übergeben – *v irreg refl insep* vomit

überhaupt – *adv* at all

überhaupt nicht – *adv* not at all

überholen – *v reg insep* overtake

überlegen – *adj* superior

sich etwas anders überlegen – *v reg dat refl insep* change one's mind

Ich habe mir das anders überlegt – I've changed my mind

übermorgen – *adv* day after tomorrow

übernachten – *v reg insep* † stay the night

in einem Hotel übernachten – *v reg insep* † stay at a hotel

Übernachtung (-en) – *nf* overnight stay

überqueren – *v reg insep* go across

überraschen – *v reg insep* surprise

überraschend – *adj* surprising

überrascht – *adj* surprised

Überraschung (-en) – *nf* surprise

überreden – *v reg insep* † persuade

sich überschlagen – *v irreg refl insep* overturn (car)

Überschrift (-en) – *nf* title (homework)

Überschwemmung (-en) – *nf* flood

Übersee~ – *pref* overseas

übersetzen – *v reg insep* translate (in writing)

Übersetzung (-en) – *nf* translation

überwachen – *v reg insep* supervise

überzeugt – *adj* convinced

übrig – *adv* over (left)

übrigbleiben* – *v irreg sep* remain (left over)

übrigens – by the way

Übung (-en) – *nf* practice

Übung macht den Meister – practice makes perfect

Ufer (-) – *nnt* bank (river)

Uhr (-en) – *nf* clock, time

Meine Uhr geht vor/nach – My watch is fast/slow

um sechs Uhr – at six o'clock

um wieviel Uhr? – at what time?

Uhrzeit (-en) – *nf* time

um (+ acc) – *prep* around, about, at (time)

um ... zu – *conj* in order to

um ... herum (+ acc) – *prep* round about

sich umdrehen – *v reg refl sep* turn round

Umfrage (-n) – *nf* survey

umgangssprachlich – *adj* colloquial

umgeben von (+ dat) – *adj* surrounded by

Umgebung (-en) – *nf* area (surrounding)

Umgehungstraße (-n) – *nf* bypass

umkippen* – *v reg sep* overturn (boat)

Umkleidekabine (-n) – *nf* fitting room

Umkleideraum (-räume) – *nm* changing-room (sport)

Umleitung (-en) – *nf* diversion

Umschlag (Umschläge) – *nm* envelope

sich umsehen – *v irreg refl sep* look round

umsonst – *adv* free; in vain

umsteigen* – *v irreg sep* change (trains)

Umtausch (-e) – *nm* exchange

umtauschen – *v reg sep* change (exchange)

Umwelt – *nf* environment

---

adj - adjective   *v reg* - verb regular   *v sep* - verb separable   † - see verb info
prep - preposition   *v irreg* - verb irregular   *v refl* - verb reflexive   * - takes sein

umweltbelastend – *adj*
environmentally undesirable
umweltbewußt – *adj*
environmentally aware
umweltfeindlich – *adj*
environmentally damaging
umweltfreundlich – *adj*
environmentally friendly
umweltschonend – *adj*
environmentally friendly
Umweltschmutz – *nm* pollution
Umweltschutz – *nm* protection of the
environment
umziehen* – *v irreg sep* move house
sich umziehen – *v irreg refl sep* get
changed
un~ – *pref* un~
unangenehm – *adj* unpleasant
unartig – *adj* naughty
unbedingt – *adv* absolutely
unbedingt notwendig – *adj* vital
unbekannt – *adj* unknown
unbequem – *adj* uncomfortable
und – *co-ord conj* and
undankbar – *adj* ungrateful
unehrlich – *adj* untruthful
unentbehrlich – *adj* essential
unentschieden – *adj* drawn (score)
unentschieden spielen – *v reg* draw
(match)
unerträglich – *adj* unbearable
unerwartet – *adj* unexpected
unfair – *adj* unfair
Unfall (Unfälle) – *nm* accident
Unfallstation (-en) – *nf* emergency
dept (hospital)
unfit – *adj inv* unfit
unfreundlich – *adj* unfriendly, nasty
Ungarn – *nnt* Hungary
ungarisch – *adj* Hungarian
Ungeduld – *nf* impatience
ungeduldig – *adj* impatient
ungefähr – *adv* approximately

Ungeheuer (-) – *nnt* monster
ungenau – *adj* vague
ungerade – odd (number)
ungerecht – *adj* unjust
ungern – *adv* reluctantly
ungeschickt – *adj* awkward (clumsy)
ungewiß – *adj* uncertain
ungewöhnlich – *adj* unusual
ungewohnt – *adj* unaccustomed
ungezogen – *adj* rude (very)
unglaublich – *adj* incredible
ungleich – *adj* uneven
Unglück – *nnt* accident, misfortune
unglücklich – *adj* unhappy, unlucky
unglücklicherweise – *adv*
unfortunately
ungünstig – *adj* unfavourable
unhöflich – *adj* rude (impolite)
uni – *adj inv* plain (no pattern)
Uni (-s) – *nf coll* university
Uniform (-en) – *nf* uniform
Union – *nf* union
    die Europäische Union – *nf*
    the European Union
Universal~ – *pref* universal
Universität (-en) – *nf* university
Universum (Universen) – *nnt*
universe
Unkraut – *nnt, no pl* weeds
unmöglich – *adj* impossible
Unmöglichkeit (-en) – *nf*
impossibility
unnötig – *adj* unnecessary
unordentlich – *adj* untidy
unpraktisch – *adj* impractical
unrecht haben – *v irreg* be wrong
    Ich habe unrecht – I am wrong
uns – *pron refl* ourselves
uns – *pers pron acc/dat* us
unser – *poss adj* our
Unsinn – *nm* nonsense, rubbish
unten – *adv* downstairs, down

---

nm - noun masculine   *nf* - noun feminine   *nnt* - noun neuter   *npl* - noun plural
nom - nominative   *acc* - accusative   *gen* - genitive   *dat* - dative

nach unten gehen* – *v irreg* go
downstairs
weiter unten – *adv* lower down
unter (+ acc/dat) – *prep* under,
below, among
unter Freunden – among friends
unter~ – *pref* sub~
unterbringen – *v irreg sep* put up
(guest)
Unterführung (-en) – *nf* subway
(under road)
Untergeschoß (-geschosse) – *nnt*
basement
unterhalb von (+ dat) – *prep*
beneath
sich unterhalten mit (+ dat) –
v irreg refl insep talk to s.o.
Unterhaltung (-en) – *nf*
entertainment
Unterhemd (-er) – *nnt* vest
Unterhose (-n) – *nf* underpants (pair
of)
Unterkunft – *nf* accommodation
Untermieter (-) – *nm* lodger
Untermieterin (-nen) – *nf* lodger
Unternehmen (-) – *nnt* firm,
company
unternehmen – *v irreg insep*
undertake
Unternehmer (-) – *nm* entrepreneur
Unternehmerin (-nen) – *nf*
entrepreneur
Unterricht – *nm* teaching (lesson)
unterrichten – *v reg insep* † teach
Unterschied (-e) – *nm* difference
unterschiedlich – *adj* different
(varied)
unterschreiben – *v irreg insep* sign
Unterschrift (-en) – *nf* signature

untersetzt – *adj* stocky
unterstreichen – *v irreg insep*
underline
unterstützen – *v reg insep* support
untersuchen – *v reg insep*
investigate, examine (medical)
Untersuchung (-en) – *nf*
examination (medical)
Untertasse (-n) – *nf* saucer
mit Untertiteln – subtitled
Unterwäsche – *nf, no pl* underwear
unterwegs – *adv* on the way
ununterbrochen – *adj* uninterrupted
unvergeßlich – *adj* unforgettable
unverheiratet – *adj* unmarried
unverletzt – *adj* unhurt
unvermeidlich – *adj* unavoidable
unwichtig – *adj* unimportant
unwohl – *adj* unwell
Mir ist unwohl – I am unwell
unzufrieden – *adj* dissatisfied
Urgroßmutter (-mütter) – *nf*
great-grandmother
Urgroßvater (-väter) – *nm* great-
grandfather
Urlaub – *nm* holiday
auf Urlaub – on holiday
in Urlaub fahren* – *v irreg* go
on holiday
Ich habe Urlaub–I'm on holiday
Urlauber (-) – *nm* holiday maker
Urlauberin (-nen) – *nf* holiday
maker
Urlaubspläne – *npl* holiday plans
Ursache (-n) – *nf* cause
USA – *npl* USA
usw. (und so weiter) – etc

V

Vanille – *nf* vanilla
Vanilleeis – *nnt, no pl* vanilla ice cream
Vanillesoße – *nf* custard
Vase (-n) – *nf* flower vase
Vater (Väter) – *nm* father, dad(dy)
Vati – *nm* daddy
vegan – *adj* vegan
Veganer (-) – *nm* vegan
Veganerin (-nen) – *nf* vegan
Vegetarier (-) – *nm* vegetarian
Vegetarierin (-nen) – *nf* vegetarian
vegetarisch – *adj* vegetarian
sich verabschieden – *v reg refl* †
say goodbye to s.o.
veränderlich – *adj* changeable
veranstalten – *v reg* † organise (event)
verantwortlich – *adj* responsible
Verantwortung – *nf* responsibility
veräppeln – *v reg* † *coll* make fun of, play a trick on
Verb (-en) – *nnt* verb
ein trennbares Verb – *nnt*
separable verb
Verband (-bände) – *nm* bandage, dressing
Verbandkasten (-kästen) – *nm*
first aid kit
verbessern – *v reg* † correct, improve
Verbesserungen – *npl* corrections
verbieten – *v irreg* forbid
verbinden – *v irreg* join (together)
Verbindung (-en) – *nf* connection
verbleit – *adj* leaded
verblüfft – *adj* dumbfounded
verboten – *adj* forbidden
Parken verboten – no parking
Rauchen verboten – no smoking
verbracht – *see verbringen*
verbrachte – *see verbringen*

Verbrechen(-) – *nnt* crime, offence
ein Verbrechen begehen –
v irreg commit an offence
Verbrecher (-) – *nm* criminal
Verbrecherin (-nen) – *nf* criminal
sich verbrennen – *v irreg refl* burn o.s.
verbringen – *v irreg* spend (time)
Verbum – *nnt see* verb
verbunden – *adj* connected
falsch verbunden – wrong number (phone)
Verdacht – *nm* suspicion
verdächtigen – *v reg* † suspect
Verdammt! – *excl* Blast!
jdm etwas verdanken – *v reg* †
owe s.o. sthg (eg thanks)
verdienen – *v reg* † earn, deserve
**(sich) seinen Lebensunterhalt
verdienen** – *v reg (dat refl)* † earn one's living
verdrießlich – *adj* grumpy
Verein (-e) – *nm* club
wie vereinbart – *adj* as agreed
vereinigen – *v reg* † unify
das Vereinigte Königreich – *nnt*
UK
Vereinigte Staaten – *npl* USA
Vereinigung – *nf* unification
vereist – *adj* icy (road)
verekelt – *adj* disgusted
verfügbar – *adj* available
zur Verfügung haben – *v irreg* to
have at one's disposal
sich verfahren – *v irreg refl* lose one's way (by car, etc)
verfaulen* – *v reg* † go bad (food)
Verflucht! – *excl* Blow!
vergangen – *adj* previous
Vergangenheit (-en) – *nf* past tense
vergaß – *see vergessen*

---

nm - noun masculine   *nf* - noun feminine   *nnt* - noun neuter   *npl* - noun plural
nom - nominative   *acc* - accusative   *gen* - genitive   *dat* - dative

vergeben – *v irreg* forgive
vergebens – *adv* in vain
vergessen – *v irreg* forget
vergißt – *see* **vergessen**
Vergleich (-e) – *nm* comparison
vergleichen – *v irreg* compare
Vergnügen (-) – *nnt* pleasure
  mit Vergnügen – with pleasure
Vergnügungspark (-s) – *nm*
  amusement park
verhaften – *v reg* † arrest
sich verhalten – *v irreg refl* act
  (behave)
Verhältnis (se) – *nnt* relationship
verheiratet – *adj* married
verhindern – *v reg* † prevent
verhüten – *v reg* † stop (prevent)
Verkauf (Verkäufe) – *nm* sale
verkaufen – *v reg* † sell
  zu verkaufen – for sale
Verkäufer (-) – *nm* shop assistant
Verkäuferin (-nen) – *nf* shop
  assistant
verkauft – *adj* sold
Verkehr – *nnt* traffic (vehicles)
Verkehrsamt (-ämter) – *nnt* tourist
  office
Verkehrskreisel (-) – *nm*
  roundabout (traffic)
öffentliche Verkehrsmittel – *npl*
  public transport
Verkehrsteilnehmer (-) – *nm* road
  user
Verkehrsteilnehmerin (-nen) – *nf*
  road-user
verlangen – *v reg* † demand
verlassen – *v irreg* leave (house, etc)
sich verlaufen – *v irreg refl* get lost
  (on foot)
verlegen – *adj* embarrassed
Verlegenheit – *nf* embarrassment
verletzen – *v reg* † injure

sich verletzen – *v reg refl* † hurt
  oneself
verletzt – *adj* injured
verletzt werden* – *v irreg* get hurt
Verletzung (-en) – *nf* injury
verleugnen – *v reg* † deny
in jdn verliebt sein* – *v irreg* be in
  love with s.o.
  Ich bin in dich verliebt – I'm in
  love with you
verlieren – *v irreg* lose
  ein Spiel verlieren – *v irreg* lose
  a match
verließ – *see* **verlassen**
verlobt – *adj* engaged (to marry)
Verlobte – *nm* ‡ fiancé
Verlobte – *nf* ‡ fiancée
verlor – *see* **verlieren**
verloren – *adj* lost
vermeiden – *v irreg* avoid
vermeintlich – *adj* imaginary
vermieten – *v reg* † let (rent out)
  zu vermieten – to let, for hire
Vermietung (-en) – *nf* renting out
vermissen – *v reg* † miss (person)
vermutlich – *adj* probable
vernachlässigen – *v reg* † neglect
vernachlässigt – *adj* neglected
vernünftig – *adj* sensible (wise)
verpassen – *v reg* † miss (train, etc)
Verpflegung – *nf* provisions, picnic
verpflichtet – *adj* obliged
verreisen* – *v reg* † go away on
  holiday
sich das Fußgelenk verrenken –
  v reg dat refl † twist an ankle
verrückt – *adj* crazy, mad
Versammlung (-en) – *nf* assembly
versäumen – *v reg* † miss (lesson)
verschieben – *v irreg* postpone
verschieden – *adj* different
verschieden sein* – *v irreg* vary

---

adj - adjective	*v reg* - verb regular	*v sep* - verb separable	† - see verb info
prep - preposition	*v irreg* - verb irregular	*v refl* - verb reflexive	* - takes sein

verschleißen – v irreg wear out
verschlissen – adj worn out
verschlucken – v reg † swallow
Verschmutzung – nf pollution
verschmutzt – adj polluted
verschnupft sein* – v irreg have a cold
verschreiben – v irreg prescribe
verschwand – see verschwinden
verschwenden – v reg † waste
verschwenderisch – adj wasteful
verschwinden* – v irreg disappear
verschwunden – see verschwinden
versichern – v reg † assure, insure
Versicherung (-en) – nf insurance
verspäten – v reg † delay
Verspätung (-en) – nf delay
Versprechen (-) – nnt promise
jdm versprechen – v irreg promise s.o.
verstanden – adj understood
Verständnis – nnt understanding
sich das Fußgelenk verstauchen – v reg dat refl † sprain one's ankle
verstecken – v reg † hide
sich verstecken – v reg refl † hide o.s.
versteckt – adj hidden
verstehen – v irreg get (understand)
sich verstehen mit (+ dat) – v irreg refl get on with (person)
verstopft – adj constipated, blocked
Versuch (-e) – nm experiment
versuchen – v reg † try
Verteidiger (-) – nm back (sport)
vertreten – v irreg represent
Vertreter (-) – nm representative, agent
Vertreterin (-nen) – nf representative, agent
sich vertun – v irreg refl be mistaken
verursachen – v reg † cause

einen Unfall verursachen – v reg † cause an accident
verwandeln – v reg † transform
Verwandte – nmf ‡ relative, relation
verweigern – v reg † refuse (permission)
von der Schule verweisen – v irreg expel
verwitwet – adj widowed
verwöhnen – v reg † spoil (child)
verwöhnt – adj spoilt (child)
Verzeihung! – excl Sorry!
Verzeihung – nf forgiveness
verzollen – v reg † declare to customs
verzweifelt – adj desperate
Vetter (-) – nm male cousin
Video~ – pref video
Videokamera (-s) – nf video camera
Videokassette (-n) – nf video cassette
Videokassettenrekorder (-) – nm video recorder
Videorecorder (-) – nm camcorder
Videospiel (-e) – nnt video game
viel – adv much, lot
nicht viel – not much, nothing much
vielen Dank – thank you very much
Viel Glück! – excl Good luck!
Viel Spaß! – excl Have a good time!
viele – adj many
vielleicht – adv perhaps, maybe
vier – adj four
viereckig – adj rectangular, square
vierte – adj fourth
Viertel (-) – nnt quarter, district
Viertel nach eins – quarter past one
Viertel vor zwei – quarter to two
um Viertel vor vier – at quarter to four
Viertelstunde – nf quarter of an hour
vierzehn – adj fourteen

vierzig – *adj* forty
einundvierzig – *adj* forty-one
Violine (-n) – *nf* violin
Visum (Visen) – *nnt* visa
Vogel (Vögel) – *nm* bird
Vokabel (-n) – *nf* vocabulary
(individual items)
Volk (Völker) – *nnt* nation
Volkslied (-er) – *nnt* folk song
Volksmusik – *nf* folk music
Volkswirtschaft – *nf* economics
voll – *adj* full, full of
Ich habe die Nase voll – I'm fed
up (annoyed)
vollenden – *v reg* † complete
Volleyball – *nm* volleyball
völlig – *adj* complete
völlig – *adv* entirely
vollkommen – *adj* absolute
Vollkornbrot (-e) – *nnt* wholemeal
bread
Vollpension – *nf* full board
volltanken – *v reg sep* fill up (petrol,
diesel)
von (+ dat) – *prep* from, of
sechs von zehn – six out of ten
vor (+ dat) – *prep* before, in front of,
ago, to (clock time)
Es ist Viertel vor vier – It's
quarter to four
vor 8 Tagen – a week ago
vor 14 Tagen – a fortnight ago
vor vielen Jahren – a long time
ago
vor allem – above all
vor kurzem – recently
Vor~ – *pref* preparatory
vorangehen* – *v irreg sep* go
forward
vorankommen* – *v irreg sep* get on
(succeed)
im voraus – *adv* beforehand
vorbei – *adv* over (finished)

an (+ dat) vorbei – *prep* past
(travelling)
vorbeifahren* an (+ dat) – *v irreg*
sep pass (in car)
vorbeigehen* an (+ dat) – *v irreg*
sep pass (on foot)
Ich gehe an der Schule vorbei
– I'm walking past the school
vorbeikommen* – *v irreg sep* call
on s.o.
vorbereiten – *v reg sep* † prepare
Vorbereitung (-en) – *nf* preparation
Vorderrad (-räder) – *nnt* front
wheel
Vorderseite (-n) – *nf* front
Vorfahrt – *nf* priority (traffic)
Vorführung (-en) – *nf* showing
(film)
vorgehen* – *v irreg sep* happen
vorgestern – *adv* the day before
yesterday
etwas vorhaben – *v irreg sep* plan
sthg, intend to do sthg
vorhanden – *adj* available
Vorhang (-hänge) – *nm* curtain
(opaque)
vorig – *adj* previous
am vorigen Tag – the day before
vorkommen* – *v irreg sep* happen
vorlesen – *v irreg sep* read aloud
Vormittag (-e) – *nm* morning
am Vormittag – in the morning
vormittags – *adv* a.m., in the mornings
vorn – *adv* at the front
Vorname (-n) – *nm wk* first name
vornehm – *adj* posh
Vorort (-e) – *nm* suburb
in einem Vorort – in a suburb
in den Vororten – in the suburbs
vorschlagen – *v irreg sep* suggest,
propose
Vorsicht! – *excl* Beware! Be careful!
vorsichtig – *adj* careful

Vorsichtsmaßnahme (-n) – *nf* precaution

Vorspeise (-n) – *nf* starter (food)

vorstellen – *v reg sep* introduce, present

sich vorstellen – *v reg refl sep* introduce o.s.

sich vorstellen – *v reg dat refl sep* imagine

Vorstellung (-en) – *nf* performance (drama)

Vorteil (-e) – *nm* advantage

vorteilhaft – *adj* advantageous

Vorwahl (-en) – *nf* dialling code

Vorwahlnummer (-n) – *nf* dialling code

vorwärts – *adv* forwards, onwards

vorziehen – *v irreg sep* prefer

W

Waage – Libra (horoscope)

wach – *adj* awake

Warschau – Warsaw

Wache (-n) – *nf* police station

wachsen* – *v irreg* grow (get bigger)

sich die Haare wachsen lassen – *v irreg dat refl* grow one's hair

Wackelpudding – *nm* jelly (dessert)

Waffel (-n) – *nf* waffle (edible)

Wahl (-en) – *nf* choice; election

Wagen (-) – *nm* car

wagen – *v reg* dare

Wagenheber (-) – *nm* jack (car)

Wagon (-s) – *nm* railway carriage

wählen – *v reg* choose, dial

Wahlfach (-fächer) – *nnt* optional subject

wahr – *adj* true

nicht wahr? – isn't it, don't you, doesn't he?

während – *sub conj* as, while

während (+ gen) – *prep* during

Wahrheit (-en) – *nf* truth

wahrscheinlich – *adj* probably, likely

Währung (-en) – *nf* currency

Waise (-n) – *nf* orphan

Wald (Wälder) – *nm* forest

Waldlauf (-läufe) – *nm* cross country (run)

Wales – *nnt* Wales

Waliser (-) – *nm* Welshman

Waliserin (-nen) – *nf* Welsh woman

walisisch – *adj* Welsh

Walisisch – *nnt* Welsh (language)

Walkman® (Walkmen) – *nm* walkman®

Wand (Wände) – *nf* wall (interior)

Wanderer (-) – *nm* hiker

Wanderin (-nen) – *nf* hiker

Wanderkarte (-n) – *nf* hiker's map

wandern* – *v reg* go for a hike

Wanderschuh (-e) – *nm* walking boot

Wanderung (-en) – *nf* hike, long walk

Wange (-n) – *nf* cheek (face)

wann – *adv* when? (question)

seit wann? – how long?

war – *see* sein*

es war – it was

Das wär's – That's all

Ware (-n) – *nf* merchandise

Warenhaus (-häuser) – *nnt* department store

warf – *see* werfen

---

nm - noun masculine   *nf* - noun feminine   *nnt* - noun neuter   *npl* - noun plural

nom- nominative   *acc* - accusative   *gen* - genitive   *dat* - dative

warm – *adj* warm
   Es ist warm – It is warm/hot
   (weather)
   Mir ist warm – I am warm/hot
   warmes Wasser – hot water
Warnblinkanlage – *nf* hazard
warning lights
warnen vor (+ dat) – *v reg* warn
about
Warnung (-en) – *nf* warning
   Warnung vor dem Hund! –
   Beware of the dog!
warten – *v reg* † wait
warten auf (+ acc) – *v reg* † wait
(for)
Warteraum (-räume) – *nm* waiting
room
Wartesaal (-säle) – *nm* waiting
room
Wartezimmer (-) – *nnt* waiting
room
warum? – *adv* why?
was – *sub conj* what
   Was ist das? – What is that?
   Was für (+ acc) – What sort of...?
   Was für einen Wagen? – What
   kind of car?
   Was gibt's neues? – What's new?
   Was hast du gesagt? – What did
   you say?
   Was ist los? – What's going on?
   Was macht das? – How much is
   that altogether?
   Was sonst? – What else?
was? – *excl* eh?
Waschbecken (-) – *nnt* wash basin,
basin
Wäsche – *nf, no pl* washing, linen
   die Wäsche machen – *v reg* do
   (the) washing
   schmutzige Wäsche – *nf* dirty
   linen
waschen – *v irreg* wash (clothes etc)

sich waschen – *v irreg refl* have a
wash.
sich die Haare waschen –
   v irreg dat refl shampoo one's hair
Ich habe mich gewaschen –
   I have washed
Wäscherei (-en) – *nf* laundry
(building)
Wäschetrockner (-) – *nm* dryer,
tumble drier (clothes)
Waschlappen (-) – *nm* flannel
Waschmaschine (-n) – *nf* washing
machine
Waschpulver – *nnt* washing powder
Wasser – *nnt, no pl* water
   kaltes Wasser – *nnt* cold water
   warmes Wasser – hot water
Wasser kochen – *v reg* boil water
wasserdicht – *adj* waterproof
Wasserhahn (-hähne) – *nm* tap
Wassermann – Aquarius
(horoscope)
Wasserskifahren – *nnt* water skiing
Wasserski laufen* – *v irreg* water-
ski
Wassersport – *nm* water sports
   Wassersport treiben – *v irreg* do
   water sports
Watte – *nf* cotton wool
WC (-s) – *nnt* WC, toilet
Wechsel (-) – *nm* exchange (money)
wechselhaft – *adj* changeable
Wechselkurs (-e) – *nm* rate of
exchange
wechseln – *v reg* change
   Geld wechseln – *v reg* change
   money
Wechselstube (-n) – *nf* currency
exchange office
wecken – *v reg* wake s.o.
Wecker (-) – *nm* alarm clock
   den Wecker stellen – *v reg* set
   the alarm clock
weder ... noch – *adv* neither...nor

Ich habe weder Paß noch Personalausweis – I have neither a passport nor an identity card

weg – *adv* away, off

Weg (-e) – *nm* path, way (route)

sich auf den Weg machen – *v reg refl* set out

wegen (+ gen) – *prep* because of, on account of

weggehen* – *v irreg sep* go away, depart

weglaufen* – *v irreg sep* run away

weglegen – *v reg sep* put away

Wegweiser (-) – *nm* signpost

Weh (-e) – *nm* pain

weh tun – *v irreg* hurt

sich weh tun – *v irreg dat refl* hurt o.s.

wehen – *v reg* blow (wind)

Wehrdienst – *nm* military service

Wehrpflicht – *nf* compulsory military service

wehrpflichtig – *adj* liable for military service

Weibchen (-) – *nnt* female (animals)

weiblich – *adj* female

weich – *adj* soft

sich weigern – *v reg refl* refuse (to do sthg)

Weihnachten – *npl* Christmas

zu Weihnachten – at Christmas

Frohe/Fröhliche Weihnachten! – *excl* Happy Christmas!

Weihnachtsbaum (-bäume) – *nm* Christmas tree

Weihnachtsferien – *npl* Christmas holidays

Weihnachtsgeschenk (-e) – *nnt* Christmas present

Weihnachtslied (-er) – *nnt* carol

Weihnachtsmann (-männer) – *nm* Father Christmas

der 1. Weihnachtstag – *nm* Christmas Day

der 2. Weihnachtstag – *nm* Boxing Day

weil – *sub conj* as, because, for

Weile (-n) – *nf* while

Wein (-e) – *nm* wine

Weinbauer (-n) – *nm wk* vine grower

Weinbäuerin (-nen) – *nf* vine grower

Weinberg (-e) – *nm* vineyard

weinen – *v reg* cry, weep

Weinkarte (-n) – *nf* wine list

Weinstube (-n) – *nf* wine bar

Weintraube (-n) – *nf* grape

Weise (-n) – *nf* manner

auf diese Weise – in this way

weise – *adj* wise

weiß – *adj* white

weiß – *see* wissen

Ich weiß es nicht – I don't know

Weißwein (-e) – *nm* white wine

weit – *adj* far away

Ist es weit? – Is it far?

nicht weit von hier – not far from here

weit entfernt – *adv* far away

weit verbreitet – *adj* widely known

weit weg – a long way off

weiter – *adv* further

und so weiter (usw.) – and so on (etc)

Weiterbildung – *nf* further education

weiterfahren* – *v irreg sep* travel on

weitermachen – *v reg sep* continue, carry on

weiterstudieren – *v reg sep* † continue to study

weitsichtig – *adj* long-sighted

welche – *pron* any

welche – *adj* which? what?

Welche Farbe? – What colour?

Welle (-n) – *nf* wave (sea)

Wellensittich (-e) – *nm* budgerigar

Welt (-en) – *nf* world

auf der Welt – in the world
Weltmeisterschaft (-en) – *nf* world championship
weltweit – *adj* worldwide
wem? – to whom?
   Wem hast du das Buch gegeben? – Who did you give the book to?
wen? – who(m)?
   Wen hast du gesehen? – Who(m) did you see?
Wende (-n) – *nf* reunification, change
sich wenden an (+ acc) – *v reg refl* † contact
bitte wenden (b.w.) – PTO
wenige – *adj* a few (not many)
weniger – *adv* less
weniger als – fewer than
weniger ... als – less ... than
weniger als zwei Kilo – less than two kilos
wenigste – *adj* least
wenn – *sub conj* if, when (whenever)
wer? – who?
   Wer kommt mit? – Who is coming with us?
Werbung (-en) – *nf* advertising, publicity
werden* – *v irreg* become, get, go, grow
werfen – *v irreg* fling, throw, bowl
Werken – *nnt* CDT, woodwork
Werkstatt (-stätten) – *nf* garage, workshop (repair)
Werktag (-e) – *nm* working day
werktags – *adv* on working days
Werkzeug (-e) – *nnt* tool
Wert (-e) – *nm* value ,worth
   Es ist DM 2 000 wert – It's worth DM 2,000
wertlos – *adj* worthless
Wertsachen – *npl* valuables
wertvoll *adj* precious, valuable

Weser – *nf* River Weser
Wespe (-n) – *nf* wasp
wessen – *rel pron* whose
Weste (-n) – *nf* waistcoat
Westen – *nm* west
   im Westen – in the west
Western (-) – *nm* western (film)
Westinder (-) – *nm* West Indian (male)
Westinderin (-nen) – *nf* West Indian (female)
westindisch – *adj* West Indian
Die Westindischen Inseln – *npl* The West Indies
westlich – *adj* western
westlich von (+ dat) – *prep* to the west of
Wettbewerb (-e) – *nm* competition, contest
wetten – *v reg* † bet
Wetter – *nnt, no pl* weather
   bei schlechtem Wetter – in bad weather
   bei gutem Wetter – in good weather
Wetteraussichten – *npl* weather prospects
Wetterbericht (-e) – *nm* weather report
Wettervorhersage (-n) – *nf* weather forecast
Whisky – *nm, no pl* whisky
wichtig – *adj* important
Widder – Aries (horoscope)
widerstandsfähig – *adj* tough (resilient)
widerwärtig – *adj* vile
wie – *adv* how, what; like
   Wie bitte? – What (did you say)?
   Wie geht's? – How are you?
   Wie geht es dir? – How are you? (informal)

Wie geht es Ihnen? – How are you? (formal)

wie geplant – as planned

Wie heißt das auf deutsch? – What is it in German?

Wie heißt du? – What is your name?

Wie ist ...? – What is ...like?

Wie kommt man am besten zum/zur? – What is the best way to ...? (+ building)

Wie kommt man nach ...? – What is the way to...? (+ town name)

wie oft? – how often?

Wie schreibt man das? – How do you spell that?

Wie sieht er aus? – What does he look like?

Wie spät ist es? – What is the time?

wieder – *adv* again

immer wieder – *adv* over and over (again)

wiederholen – *v reg insep* † repeat

wiedersehen – *v irreg sep* see again

Auf Wiedersehen! – *excl* Goodbye!

Wiedervereinigung – *nf* reunification

wiederverwerten – *v reg insep* † recycle

Wiederverwertung – *nf* recycling

wiegen – *v irreg* weigh

Wien – Vienna

Wiener Schnitzel – Wiener schnitzel, veal escalope

Wiese (-n) – *nf* meadow

wieso? – *adv* why?

wieviel? – how much?

Wieviel Uhr ist es? – What time is it?

Den wievielten haben wir heute? – What is the date today?

wieviele? – how many?

wild – *adj* fierce, wild

Wildleder – *nnt* suede

will – *see wollen*

willkommen – *adj* welcome

willkommen heißen – *v irreg* welcome

Herzlich willkommen! – Welcome!

Wind (-e) – *nm* wind

windig – *adj* windy

Windschutzscheibe (-n) – *nf* windscreen

windsurfen – *v reg* windsurf

windsurfen gehen* – *v irreg* go windsurfing

winken – *v reg* wave (hand)

Winter – *nm* winter

im Winter – in winter

Wintergarten (-gärten) – *nm* conservatory

Wintersport – *nm, no pl* winter sports

winzig – *adj* tiny

wir – *pers pron* we

wird – *see werden**

wirft – *see werfen*

wirklich – *adj* real (true)

wirklich – *adv* really

Wirklichkeit (-en) – *nf* reality

wirksam – *adj* effective

Wirtshaus (-häuser) – *nnt* pub, inn

wischen – *v reg* wipe

wissen – *v irreg* know (fact)

wissen, daß – *v irreg* be aware that

Wissenschaftler (-) – *nm* scientist

Wissenschaftlerin (-nen) – *nf* scientist

wissenschaftlich – *adj* scientific

Witwe (-n) – *nf* widow

Witwer (-) – *nm* widower

---

nm - noun masculine	*nf* - noun feminine	*nnt* - noun neuter	*npl* - noun plural
nom- nominative	*acc* - accusative	*gen* - genitive	*dat* - dative

Witz (-e) – *nm* joke

wo – *sub conj* where

wo – *adv* where?

Woche (-n) – *nf* week
  in der Woche – during the week
  jede Woche – every week
  letzte Woche – last week
  nächste Woche – next week
  pro Woche – per week

Wochenende (-n) – *nnt* weekend
  Schönes Wochenende! – *excl*
  Have a good weekend!

Wochenkarte (-n) – *nf* weekly ticket

Wochentag (-e) – *nm* weekday

wochentags – *adv* on weekdays

wöchentlich – *adj* weekly

woher – *adv* where (from)?
  Woher kommst du? – Where do
  you come from?

wohin – *adv* (to) where?
  Wohin gehst du? – Where are
  you going (to)?

wohl – *adj* all right
  Zum Wohl! – *excl* Cheers!

wohlriechend – *adj* sweet-smelling

Wohnblock (-s) – *nm* block of flats,
tower block

wohnen – *v reg* live (inhabit)
  Wo wohnst du? – Where do you
  live?

wohnen bei (+ dat) – *v reg* lodge
with, stay with

Wohnort (-e) – *nm* town of residence

Wohnschlafzimmer (-) – *nnt* bed-
sit

Wohnsitz (-e) – *nm* place of
residence

Wohnung (-en) – *nf* apartment, flat

Wohnwagen (-) – *nm* caravan

Wohnzimmer (-) – *nnt* living room,
lounge, sitting room

Wolke (-n) – *nf* cloud

Wolkenkratzer (-) – *nm* skyscraper

wolkenlos – *adj* cloudless

wolkig – *adj* cloudy

Wolle (-n) – *nf* wool
  aus Wolle – woollen

wollen – *v irreg* want (to), wish (to)

wollte – *see wollen*

Wort (Worte) – *nnt* word

Wörterbuch (-bücher) – *nnt*
dictionary

Wortschatz – *nm* vocabulary
(complete list)

Wortspiel (-e) – *nnt* pun

Wunde (-n) – *nf* wound

wunderbar! – *excl* great!

wunderbar – *adj* marvellous, terrific,
wonderful

wunderschön – *adj* wonderful

Wunsch (Wünsche) – *nm* desire,
wish
  auf Wunsch – optional
  mit besten Wünschen – Best
  wishes

wünschen – *v reg* desire, wish

wurde – *see werden**

würde – *see werden**

Würfel (-) – *nm* dice

würfeln – *v reg* throw dice

Wurm (Würmer) – *nm* worm

Wurst (Würste) – *nf* sausage
  Leberwurst – *nf* liver sausage
  Bockwurst – *nf* frankfurter
  Bratwurst – *nf* fried sausage

Würstchen – *nnt* small sausage

wußte – *see wissen*

Wüste (-n) – *nf* desert

Wüstenspringmaus (-mäuse) – *nf*
gerbil

wütend – *adj* furious

Z

zäh – *adj* tough (meat)
Zahl (-en) – *nf* number (numeral)
Kopf oder Zahl? – Heads or
  tails?
zahlen – *v reg* pay (bill)
zählen – *v reg* count
Zahlkarte (-n) – *nf* postal order
zahlreich – *adj* numerous
zahm – *adj* tame
Zahn (Zähne) – *nm* tooth
  sich die Zähne putzen – *v reg*
  dat refl clean one's teeth
Zahnarzt (-ärzte) – *nm* dentist
Zahnärztin (-nen) – *nf* dentist
Zahnbürste (-n) – *nf* toothbrush
Zahnpasta – *nf* toothpaste
Zahnschmerzen – *npl* toothache
Zapfsäule (-n) – *nf* petrol pump
zart – *adj* gentle, tender
Zauber – *nm* magic
  Die Zauberflöte – *nf*
  The Magic Flute
Zauberer (-) – *nm* magician
Zaun (Zäune) – *nm* fence
z.B. (zum Beispiel) – e.g.
  (for example)
Zebra (-s) – *nnt* zebra
Zebrastreifen – *nm* zebra crossing
Zeh (-en) – *nm* toe
zehn – *adj* ten
  zehn Kilometer entfernt –
  10 kilometres away
zehnte – *adj* tenth
Zeichensetzung (-en) – *nf*
  punctuation
Zeichentrickfilm (-e) – *nm* cartoon
  film
zeichnen – *v reg* draw (picture)
  technisches Zeichnen – *nnt*
  engineering drawing

Zeichnung (-en) – *nf* drawing
zeigen – *v reg* show
Zeile (-n) – *nf* line (writing)
Zeit (-en) – *nf* time, period
  die ganze Zeit – all the time
  für eine lange Zeit – for a long
  time
  Ich habe keine Zeit mehr –
  I have run out of time
  vor langer Zeit – long ago
  zu derselben Zeit – at the same
  time as
Zeitpunkt (-e) – *nm* period (in time)
Zeitschrift (-en) – *nf* magazine
Zeitung (-en) – *nf* newspaper
  die Zeitungen austragen –
  v irreg sep deliver the papers
Zeitungshändler (-) – *nm*
  newsagent
Zeitungshändlerin (-nen) – *nf*
  newsagent
Zeitungsstand (-stände) – *nm*
  newspaper stand
Zeitverschwendung – *nf, no pl*
  a waste of time
Zeitvertreib (-e) – *nm* pastime,
  amusement
Zelt (-e) – *nnt* tent
  ein Zelt aufbauen – *v reg sep*
  pitch a tent
  ein Zelt abbauen – *v reg sep* take
  down a tent
zelten – *v reg* † go camping
zelten gehen* – *v irreg* go camping
Zentimeter (-) – *nm* centimetre
Zentralheizung – *nf* central heating
Zentrum (Zentren) – *nnt* centre
zerbrechlich – *adj* fragile
zerquetschen – *v reg* † crush, squash

---

nm - noun masculine	*nf* - noun feminine	*nnt* - noun neuter	*npl* - noun plural
nom- nominative	*acc* - accusative	*gen* - genitive	*dat* - dative

zerreißen – *v irreg* tear, rip
zerrissen – *adj* torn
zerstören – *v reg* † destroy
zerstreut – *adj* absent-minded
Zettel (-) – *nm* note, slip of paper
Zeuge (-n) – *nm wk* witness
Zeugin (-nen) – *nf* witness
Zeugnis(-se) – *nnt* certificate, school
report
Ziege (-n) – *nf* goat
ziehen – *v irreg* draw, pull
Ziel (-e) – *nnt* destination, goal
  ans Ziel kommen* – *v irreg*
  finish (sport)
ziemlich – *adv* fairly, quite, rather
zierlich – *adj* delicate
Zigarette (-n) – *nf* cigarette
Zimmer (-) – *nnt* room
Zimmer frei – vacancies, B & B
Zirkus (-se) – *nm* circus
Zitat (-e) – *nnt* quotation
Zither (-n) – *nf* zither
zitieren – *v reg* † quote
Zitrone (-n) – *nf* lemon
Zitronentee – *nm* lemon tea
zittern – *v reg* shake, shiver, tremble
zitternd – *adj* trembling
Zivildienst – *nm* community service
instead of military service
zog – *see ziehen*
zögern – *v reg* hesitate
Zoll – *nm* customs, toll
Zollbeamte – *nm* ‡ customs officer
Zollbeamtin (-nen) – *nf* customs
officer
zollfrei – *adj* duty-free
Zone (-n) – *nf* zone
Zoo (-s) – *nm* zoo
Zopf (Zöpfe) – *nm* plait
Zorn – *nm* anger
zu – *adv* off (tap)
zu – *adv* too

zu haben – available
zu viel – too much
zu viele – too many
  zu viele Leute – too many people
um ... zu – *conj* in order to
zu (+ dat) – *prep* to
  zu den Gleisen – to the trains
  zu Ostern – at Easter
  zu Weihnachten – at Christmas
züchten – *v reg* † breed
Zucker – *nm* sugar
zuckerkrank – *adj* diabetic
Zuckerkrankheit – *nf* diabetes
Zuckerwatte – *nf* candy floss
zudecken – *v reg sep* cover
zudrehen – *v reg sep* turn off (tap)
zuerst – *adv* at first, first of all
Zufahrt (-en) – *nf* approach (road)
Zufahrtsstraße (-n) – *nf* access road
Zufall (Zufälle) – *nm* chance (fate)
zufällig – *adj* by accident
zufälligerweise – *adv* by chance
zufrieden – *adj* pleased, satisfied,
glad
zufrieden mit (+ dat) – *adj* happy
with
Zug (Züge) – *nm* train, procession
Zugang (Zugänge) – *nm* access
zugänglich – *adj* accessible
zugreifen – *v irreg sep* help o.s.
zugestiegen – *adj* got on train
  Noch jemand zugestiegen? –
  Any more tickets?
zuhören – *v reg sep* listen to
Zukunft – *nf* future
  in Zukunft – *adv* in future
Zukunftspläne – *npl* future plans
zuletzt – *adv* most recently
zum Mitnehmen – take away (food)
zumachen – *v reg sep* close (shut)
zunächst – *adv* first of all
Zunge (-n) – *nf* tongue

---

adj - adjective	*v reg* - verb regular	*v sep* - verb separable	† - see verb info
prep - preposition	*v irreg* - verb irregular	*v refl* - verb reflexive	* - takes sein

zur Post – to the post office
zur Schule – to the school
zur Zeit – at the present moment
zurechtkommen* – *v irreg sep* get along, manage
zurück – *adv* back
zurückbekommen – *v irreg sep* recover (get back)
zurückbringen – *v irreg sep* bring back
zurückgeben – *v irreg sep* give back
zurückgehen* – *v irreg sep* go back
zurückhalten – *v irreg sep* hold back
zurückkehren* – *v reg sep* return
zurückkommen* – *v irreg sep* return, come back, get back
zurücklassen – *v irreg sep* leave behind
zurücklegen – *v reg sep* put back
zurücknehmen – *v irreg sep* take back
zurückstellen – *v reg sep* put back
zusammen – *adv* together
Geht das getrennt oder zusammen? – Do you want to pay separately or all together?
Zusammenstoß (-stöße) – *nm* collision, crash, bump
zusammenstoßen* mit (+ dat) – *v irreg sep* collide with, bump into
zusätzlich – *adj* extra
zuschauen – *v reg sep* watch
Zuschauer – *npl* audience
Zuschauer (-) – *nm* spectator, viewer
Zuschauerin (-nen) – *nf* spectator, viewer
Zuschlag (-schläge) – *nm* extra charge
zusehen – *v irreg sep* watch
Zustand (Zustände) – *nm* condition (state)
in gutem Zustand – in good condition

in schlechtem Zustand – in poor condition
Zutaten – *npl* ingredients
kein Zutritt – no entry (on foot)
zuverlässig – *adj* reliable
zwanzig – *adj* twenty
zwanzigste – *adj* twentieth
zwar – *adv* admittedly; to be more precise
Zweck (-e) – *nm* purpose
Es hat keinen Zweck – There's no point
zwecklos – *adj* pointless
zwei – *adj* two
Zweibettzimmer (-) – *nnt* room with twin beds
Zweifamilienhaus (-häuser) – *nnt* semi-detached house
zweifelhaft – *adj* doubtful
zweifellos – *adv* without doubt
zweimal – *adv* twice
zweisprachig – *adj* bilingual
zweit~ – *pref* second
Zweite – *nmf* ‡ runner up (sport)
zweite – *adj* second
zweiter Klasse – second class (ticket)
Zwiebel (-n) – *nf* onion
Zwillinge – *npl* twins, Gemini (horoscope)
Zwillingsbruder (-brüder) – *nm* twin brother
Zwillingsschwester (-n) – *nf* twin sister
zwingen – *v irreg* force
zwischen (+ acc/dat) – *prep* between
Zwischenzeugnis (-se) – *nnt* mid-year report
zwo – *see* zwei
zwölf – *adj* twelve
zwölfte – *adj* twelfth

---

nm - noun masculine   nf - noun feminine   nnt - noun neuter   npl - noun plural
nom- nominative   acc - accusative   gen - genitive   dat - dative

A

a – ein *indef art m, n*
a – eine *indef art f*
abandon – (desert) verlassen *v irreg*
abbey – Abtei (-en) *nf*
abbreviation – Abkürzung (-en) *nf*
able – fähig *adj*
  be able to – können *v irreg*
aboard – an Bord *adv*
about – (approx) etwa, ungefähr *adv*
about – (place) herum *adv*
about – (relating to) über (+ acc/dat) *prep*
about – (place) um (+ acc) *prep*
  I am about to eat – Ich esse gleich
above – oben *adv*
above – über (+ acc/dat) *prep*
above all – vor allem *adv*
abroad – Ausland *nnt*
  be abroad – im Ausland sein* *v irreg*
  go abroad – ins Ausland fahren* *v irreg*
absence – Abwesenheit (-en) *nf*
absent – abwesend *adj*
absent-minded – zerstreut *adj*
absolute – vollkommen *adj*
absurd – absurd *adj*
academy – Schule (-n) *nf*
accent – Akzent (-e) *nm*
accept – (take) annehmen *v irreg sep*
accept – (agree) akzeptieren *v reg* †
acceptable – annehmbar *adj*
access – Zugang (Zugänge) *nm*
accessible – zugänglich *adj*
access road – Zufahrtsstraße (-n) *nf*
access only – Anlieger frei
accident – Unfall (Unfälle) *nm*
  by accident – zufällig *adj*

acclaim – Beifall *nm*
accommodation – Unterkunft *nf*
accompany – begleiten *v reg* †
accompanied by – begleitet von (+ dat) *adj*
accomplice – (male) Komplize (-n) *nm wk*
accomplice – (female) Komplizin (-nen) *nf*
according to – nach (+ dat) *prep*
account – (bank) Konto (-s) *nnt*
account – (bill) Rechnung (-en) *nf*
account – (report) Bericht (-e) *nm*
  on account of – wegen (+ gen) *prep*
  on no account – auf keinen Fall
accountant – (male) Steuerberater (-) *nm*
accountant – (female) Steuerberaterin (-nen) *nf*
accurate – genau *adj*
accuse – anklagen *v reg sep*
ace – As (-se) *nnt*
ache – Schmerz (-en) *nm*
  I have a headache – Ich habe Kopfschmerzen
achieve – leisten *v reg* †
achievement – Leistung (-en) *nf*
acid rain – der saure Regen *nm*
acquaintance – Bekannte *nmf* ‡
across – über (+ acc/dat) *prep*
go across – überqueren *v reg insep*
act – (behave) sich verhalten *v irreg refl*
act – (drama) spielen *v reg*
action – (deed) Tat (-en) *nf*
active – aktiv *adj*
activity – Tätigkeit (-en) *nf*
actor – Schauspieler (-) *nm*
actress – Schauspielerin (-nen) *nf*
add – hinzufügen *v reg sep*

---

add up – addieren *v reg* †
address – Adresse (-n) *nf*
address – ansprechen *v irreg sep*
adjective – Adjektiv (-e) *nnt*
admire – bewundern *v reg* †
adolescent – Jugendliche *nmf* ‡
adopt – adoptieren *v reg* †
adopted – Adoptiv~ *pref*
adore – lieben *v reg*
adult – Erwachsene *nmf* ‡
adult – erwachsen *adj*
advance – Fortschritt (-e) *nm*
advantage – Vorteil (-e) *nm*
advantageous – vorteilhaft *adj*
adventure – Abenteuer (-) *nnt*
adventure film – Abenteuerfilm (-e) *nm*
adventure story – Abenteuerroman (-e) *nm*
advert – (small ad) Inserat (-e) *nnt*
advertisement – (for products) Reklame (-n) *nf*, Anzeige (-n) *nf*
advertising – Werbung *nf*
advice – Rat *nm, no pl*
  piece of advice – Ratschlag (-schläge) *nm*
advise – beraten *v irreg*
advisor – (male) Berater (-) *nm*
advisor – (female) Beraterin (-nen) *nf*
aerial – Antenne (-n) *nf*
aerobics – Aerobic *nnt, no pl*
aeroplane – Flugzeug (-e) *nnt*
aerosol – Sprühdose (-n) *nf*
affectionate – liebevoll *adj*
afford – sich leisten *v reg dat refl* †
(be) afraid (of) – Angst haben vor (+ dat) *v irreg*
Africa – Afrika *nnt*
African – afrikanisch *adj*
after – nach (+ dat) *prep*
after all – (finally) schließlich *adv*
afternoon – Nachmittag (-e) *nm*

afterwards – nachher *adv*
again – wieder *adv*
again and again – immer wieder *adv*
against – gegen (+ acc) *prep*
age – Alter (-) *nnt*
  I am 15 years of age – Ich bin 15 Jahre alt
  of the same age – gleichaltrig *adj*
agency – Agentur (-en) *nf*
agent – (male) Vertreter (-) *nm*
agent – (female) Vertreterin (-nen) *nf*
aggressive – aggressiv *adj*
ago – vor (+ dat) *prep*
  It was a long time ago – Es war schon lange her
  a fortnight ago – vor 14 Tagen
  a week ago – vor 8 Tagen
agree with – übereinstimmen mit (+ dat) *v reg sep*
agreeable – (nice) liebenswürdig *adj*
agreed – einverstanden *adj*
Agreed! – Abgemacht! *excl*
agricultural – landwirtschaftlich *adj*
aid – Hilfe *nf*
  first aid – erste Hilfe *nf*
aid – helfen (+ dat) *v irreg*
air – Luft *nf, no pl*
  by air mail – per Luftpost
  in the open air – im Freien
airbed – Luftmatratze (-n) *nf*
air conditioned – mit Klimaanlage
air conditioning – Klimaanlage (-n) *nf*
aircraft – Flugzeug (-e) *nnt*
air force – Luftwaffe *nf, no pl*
air hostess – Stewardeß (-essen) *nf*
airport – Flughafen(-häfen) *nm*
air sickness – Luftkrankheit *nf*
alarm clock – Wecker (-) *nm*
  set the alarm – den Wecker stellen *v reg*
Alas! – Ach! *excl*
alcohol – Alkohol (-e) *nm*

---

alcohol free – alkoholfrei *adj*
A level – Abitur *nnt*
algebra – Algebra *nf*
alive – lebend *adj*
all – alle
  all alone – ganz allein
  all included – alles inbegriffen
  all in all – alles in allem
  all of us – wir alle
  all over – (everywhere) überall *adv*
  all over – (finished) zu Ende
  all sorts of – allerlei
  all the same – (however) trotzdem *adv*
  all the time – die ganze Zeit
  all year round – das ganze Jahr
  not at all – überhaupt nicht
allergic to – allergisch gegen (+ acc) *adj*
allow – erlauben *v reg* †
  be allowed – dürfen *v irreg*
allowance – (money) Geld *nnt*
almost – fast *adv*
alone – allein *adv*
along – entlang (+ acc) *prep*
aloud – laut *adj*
  read aloud – vorlesen *v irreg sep*
alphabet – Alphabet (-e) *nnt*
Alps – Alpen *npl*
already – schon *adv*
alright! – in Ordnung! *excl*
also – auch *adv*
alter – ändern *v reg*
although – obwohl, obgleich *sub conj*
altogether – zusammen *adv*, insgesamt *adv*
always – immer *adv*
am – bin *see sein**
a.m. – vormittags *adv*
amazed – erstaunt *adj*
  be amazed – erstaunt sein* *v irreg*
ambulance – Krankenwagen (-) *nm*

America – Amerika *nnt*
American – amerikanisch *adj*
American – (male) Amerikaner (-) *nm*
American – (female) Amerikanerin (-nen) *nf*
among – unter (+ acc/dat) *prep*
among friends – unter Freunden
amount – Menge (-n) *nf*
amusement – (pastime) Zeitvertreib (-e) *nm*
amusement park – Vergnügungspark (-s) *nm*
amusement arcade – Spielhalle (-n) *nf*
amusing – lustig *adj*
an – ein *indef art m, nt*
an – eine *indef art f*
ancient – alt *adj*
and – und *co-ord conj*
anger – Zorn *nm*
angling – Angeln *nnt*
  go angling – angeln gehen* *v irreg*
angry – böse *adj*
  get angry – böse werden* *v irreg*
animal – Tier (-e) *nnt*
ankle – Fußgelenk (-e) *nnt*
  sprain one's ankle – sich den Fuß verrenken *v reg dat refl* †
anniversary – Jahrestag (-e) *nm*
announce – ankündigen *v reg sep*
announcer – (male) Ansager (-) *nm*
announcer – (female) Ansagerin (-nen) *nf*
annoy – ärgern *v reg*
  get annoyed – sich ärgern *v reg*
annoying – ärgerlich *adj*
annual – jährlich *adj*
anorak – Anorak (-s) *nm*
another – (more) noch *adv*
another – (different) andere *pron*
answer – Antwort (-en) *nf*
answer – antworten *v reg* †

---

adj - adjective	*v reg* - verb regular	*v sep* - verb separable	† - see verb info
prep - preposition	*v irreg* - verb irregular	*v refl* - verb reflexive	* - takes sein

answering machine –
Anrufbeantworter (-) *nm*
anti~ – Anti~ *pref*
antibiotic – Antibiotikum (-ka) *nnt*
antibiotic – antibiotisch *adj*
antiseptic – Antiseptikum (-ka) *nnt*
antiseptic – antiseptisch *adj*
anxious – ängstlich *adj*
any – irgendein *adj*
  not any – keine *adj*
any – welche *pron*
  Has he got any? – Hat er welche?
  Any more bread? – Noch etwas
  Brot?
anybody – jeder/jede, jemand *pron*
anybody – (negative) niemand *pron*
  I can't hear anyone – Ich kann
  niemand hören
anything – etwas *pron*
Anything else? – Sonst noch etwas?
anyway – sowieso *adv*
anywhere – irgendwo *adv*
  not anywhere –nirgendwo *adv*
apartment – Wohnung (-en) *nf*
apart from – außer (+ dat) *prep*
aperitif – Aperitif (-s) *nm*
apologise – sich entschuldigen *v reg*
  refl †
apology – Entschuldigung (-en) *nf*
appalling – schrecklich *adj*
appear – (seem) scheinen *v irreg*
appear – erscheinen* *v irreg*
appearance – Aussehen (-) *nnt*
appendicitis – Blinddarmentzündung
  (-en) *nf*
appetite – Appetit (-e) *nm*
appetizing – lecker *adj*
applause – Beifall *nm*
apple – Apfel (Äpfel) *nm*
apple cake – Apfelkuchen (-) *nm*
apple strudel – Apfelstrudel (-) *nm*
apple tree – Apfelbaum (-bäume) *nm*

appliance – Gerät (-e) *nnt*
applicant – (male) Bewerber (-) *nm*
applicant – (female) Bewerberin
  (-nen) *nf*
application – (for job) Bewerbung
  (-en) *nf*
apply for – sich bewerben um
  (+ acc) *v irreg refl*
appointment – Termin (-e) *nm*
  make an appointment – einen
  Termin ausmachen *v reg sep*
appreciate – schätzen *v reg*
apprentice – Lehrling (-e) *nm*
apprenticeship – Lehre (-n) *nf*
approach – (road) Zufahrt (-en) *nf*
approach – sich nähern (+ dat) *v reg*
  refl
approve of – billigen *v reg*
approximately – ungefähr, etwa *adv*
apricot – Aprikose (-n) *nf*
April – April *nm*
  in April – im April
apron – Schürze (-n) *nf*
Aquarius – Wassermann
arcade – (shops) Einkaufspassage (-n)
  nf
archery – Bogenschießen (-) *nnt*
architect – (male) Architekt (-en)
  nm wk
architect – (female) Architektin
  (-nen) *nf*
are – *see sein**
area – Gebiet (-e) *nnt*
area – (surrounding) Umgebung (-en)
  nf
  parking area – Parkplatz (-plätze)
  nm
  picnic area – (motorway)
  Rastplatz (-plätze) *nm*
  rest area – Raststätte (-n) *nf*
aren't – *see sein**
argue – sich streiten *v irreg refl*
argument – (discussion) Argument
  nnt

---

argument – (quarrel) Streit (-e) *nm*
Aries – Widder
arithmetic – Rechnen *nnt*
arm – Arm (-e) *nm*
armchair – Sessel (-) *nm*
army – Armee (-n) *nf*
around – herum *adv*
around – um (+ acc) *prep*
around here – hier in der Nähe
arrange – arrangieren *v reg* †
arrange – (time) festsetzen *v reg sep*
arrest – verhaften *v reg* †
arrival – Ankunft (-en) *nf*
arrive – ankommen* *v irreg sep*
arrow – Pfeil (-e) *nm*
art – Kunst *nf*
art gallery – Kunstgalerie (-n) *nf*
art school – Kunsthochschule (-n) *nf*
article – Artikel (-) *nm*
article of clothing – Kleidungsstück
(-e) *nnt*
artist – (male) Künstler (-) *nm*
artist – (female) Künstlerin (-nen) *nf*
as – (while) während *sub conj*
as – (because) weil *sub conj*
as agreed – wie vereinbart *adj*
as ... as – so ... wie *adv*
   She is as big as me – Sie ist so
   groß wie ich
as far as – bis zu (+ dat) *prep*
as far as the traffic lights – bis
zur Ampel
as for me – was mich angeht
as if – als ob *sub conj*
as much as possible – soviel wie
möglich *adv*
as soon as – sobald *sub conj*
   as soon as possible – sobald wie
   möglich *adv*
as well – auch *adv*
ashamed – beschämt *adj*

be ashamed of – sich schämen vor
(+ dat) *v reg refl*
ashtray – Aschenbecher (-) *nm*
Ash Wednesday – Aschermittwoch
nm
Asia – Asien *nnt*
Asian – asiatisch *adj*
ask a question – eine Frage stellen
v reg
ask – fragen *v reg*
ask for – (information) bitten um
(+ acc) *v irreg*
ask – (s.o. for dinner, etc) einladen
v irreg sep
asleep – eingeschlafen *adj*
   fall asleep – einschlafen* *v irreg*
   sep
asparagus – Spargel *nm*
assembly – Versammlung (-en) *nf*
assignment – Aufgabe (-n) *nf*
assist – helfen (+ dat) *v irreg*
assistance – Hilfe *nf*
assistant – (male) Verkäufer (-) *nm*
assistant – (female) Verkäuferin
(-nen) *nf*
assure – versichern *v reg* †
asthma – Asthma *nnt*
asthmatic – asthmatisch *adj*
astonish – erstaunen *v reg* †
at – (position) an (+ dat) *prep*
at – (time) um (+ acc) *prep*
   at all – überhaupt *adv*
   at last – endlich *adv*
   at my house – bei mir
   at once – sofort *adv*
   at times – ab und zu *adv*
   at the (house of) – bei (+ dat)
   prep
   at the bottom of the page –
   unten auf der Seite
   at the end of – am Ende von
   (+ dat)

---

at the same time as – zu
derselben Zeit
at top speed – mit
Höchstgeschwindigkeit
ate – *see essen*
athlete – (male) Athlet (-en) *nm wk*
athlete – (female) Athletin (-nen) *nf*
athletic – sportlich *adj*
athletics – Leichtathletik *nf*
Atlantic Ocean – Atlantik *nm*
atmosphere – Atmosphäre (-n) *nf*
attach – festmachen *v reg sep*
attack – Angriff (-e) *nm*
attack – angreifen *v irreg sep*
attempt – versuchen *v reg* †
attend – (school) besuchen *v reg* †
attend – (be present) anwesend sein*
v irreg
attention – Aufmerksamkeit (-en) *nf*
Attention! – Achtung!
attic – Dachboden (-böden) *nm*
attract – anziehen *v irreg sep*
attractive – attraktiv *adj*
auburn – rotbraun *adj*
audience – Zuschauer *npl*,
(theatre) Puklikum *nnt*
August – August *nm*
  in August – im August
aunt – Tante (-n) *nf*
Australia – Australien *nnt*
Austria – Österreich *nnt*

Austrian – österreichisch *adj*
Austrian – (male) Österreicher (-) *nm*
Austrian – (female) Österreicherin
(-nen) *nf*
author – (male) Schriftsteller (-) *nm*
author – (female) Schriftstellerin
(-nen) *nf*
authorities – Behörde (-n) *nf*
automatic – automatisch *adj*
autumn – Herbst *nm*
  in autumn – im Herbst
available – verfügbar *adj*
avenue – Allee (-n) *nf*
average – durchschnittlich *adj*
average – Durchschnitt (-e) *nm*
avocado pear – Avocado (-s) *nf*
avoid – vermeiden *v irreg*
awake – wach *adj*
away – weg, fort *adv*
away – (distance) entfernt
  10 kilometres away – zehn
Kilometer entfernt
go away – weggehen* *v irreg sep*
away game – Auswärtsspiel (-e) *nnt*
awful – furchtbar *adj*
awkward – (clumsy) ungeschickt *adj*
awkward – (difficult) schwierig *adj*
awkward – (embarrassing) peinlich
adj

B

B & B – Zimmer frei
baby – Baby (-s) *nnt*
babysitter – Babysitter (-) *nm*
go babysitting – babysitten gehen*
  v irreg
back – zurück *adv*
back – (reverse car, etc) rückwärts
  fahren* *v irreg*
  come back – (come)
  zurückkommen* *v irreg sep*
back – hinten *adv*
  at the back of – hinter (+ dat) *prep*
back – (of car) Heck *nnt, no pl*
back – (sport) Verteidiger (-) *nm*
  left back – (sport) linker
  Verteidiger (-) *nm*
  right back – (sport) rechter
  Verteidiger (-) *nm*
back – (body) Rücken (-) *nm*
back pack – Rucksack (-säcke) *nm*
backwards – rückwärts *adv*
  run backwards and forwards
  – hin und her laufen* *v irreg*
bacon – Speck *nm*
bad – schlecht, schlimm *adj*
bad – (ill) krank *adj*
bad – (serious) ernst *adj*
bad – (wicked) böse *adj*
bad-tempered – schlecht gelaunt
  Too bad! – Pech! *excl*
badge – Abzeichen (-) *nnt*
badly – schlecht *adv*
badminton – Badminton *nnt*,
  Federball *nm*
bag – Tasche (-n) *nf*
  school bag – Schultasche (-n) *nf*
bag – (paper, plastic) Tüte (-n) *nf*
baggage – Gepäck *nnt, no pl*
bake – backen *v irreg*
baker – (male) Bäcker (-) *nm*

baker – (female) Bäckerin (-nen) *nf*
baker's shop – Bäckerei (-en) *nf*
balcony – Balkon (-s) *nm*
bald – kahl *adj*
bald patch – Glatze (-n) *nf*
ball – Ball (Bälle) *nm*
ballet – Ballett *nnt*
ball-point pen – Kugelschreiber (-)
  nm
balloon – Ballon (-s) *nm*
Baltic Sea – Ostsee *nf*
banana – Banane (-n) *nf*
band – (group) Band (-s) *nf*,
  Gruppe (-n) *nf*
bandage – Verband (Verbände) *nm*
bang – Knall (-e) *nm*
banger – (car) Kiste (-n) *nf coll*
banger – (firework) Knallkörper (-)
  nm
banger – (sausage) Bratwurst
  (-würste) *nf*
Bangladesh – Bangladesch *nnt*
Bangladeshi – bangladeschisch *adj*
Bangladeshi person – (male)
  Bangladescher (-) *nm*
Bangladeshi person – (female)
  Bangladeschin (-nen) *nf*
bank – (river) Ufer (-) *nnt*
bank – Bank (-en) *nf*, Sparkasse (-n) *nf*
bank account – Bankkonto (-konten)
  nnt
banker's card – Scheckkarte (-n) *nf*
Bank holiday – Feiertag (-e) *nm*
banknote – Geldschein (-e) *nm*
bank robbery – Bankraub (-räube) *nm*
bar – (drinks) Bar (s) *nf*
bar – (chocolate) Tafel (-n) *nf*
barbecue – Grillfest (-e) *nnt*
barber – Friseur (-e) *nm*
bare – (room) leer *adj*

| adj - adjective | v reg - verb regular | v sep - verb separable | † - see verb info |
| prep - preposition | v irreg - verb irregular | v refl - verb reflexive | * - takes sein |

bare – (naked) nackt *adj*
barefoot – barfuß *adj*
bare-headed – ohne Hut
bargain – Sonderangebot (-e) *nnt*
bark – bellen *v reg*
barmaid – Bardame (-n) *nf*
barman – Barmann (-männer) *nm*
barn – Scheune (-n) *nf*
based on – basiert auf (+ dat) *adj*
basement – Keller (-) *nm*
basic – Grund~ *pref*
basically – im Grunde *adv*
basin – Waschbecken (-) *nnt*
basis – Basis (Basen) *nf*
basket – Korb (Körbe) *nm*
basketball – Basketball *nm*
Basle – Basel
bat – (table tennis, etc) Schläger (-) *nm*
bat – (mammal) Fledermaus (-mäuse) *nf*
bath – (tub) Badewanne (-n) *nf*
bath – (wash) Bad (Bäder) *nnt*
  have a bath – sich baden *v reg refl* †
bathe – baden *v reg* †
bathing – Baden *nnt*
bathing cap – Badekappe (-n) *nf*
bathing trunks – Badehose (-n) *nf*
bathroom – Badezimmer (-) *nnt*
bath towel – Badetuch (-tücher) *nnt*
battery – Batterie (-n) *nf*
battle – Schlacht (-en) *nf*
Bavaria – Bayern *nnt*
Bavarian – bayerisch *adj*
bay – (on coast) Bucht (-en) *nf*
be – sein* *v irreg*
be able to – können *v irreg*
be afraid – Angst haben *v irreg*
be amazed – erstaunt sein* *v irreg*
be ashamed of – sich schämen vor (+ dat) *v reg refl*
be at – anwesend sein* *v irreg*
be aware that – wissen, daß *v irreg*

be bored – sich langweilen *v reg refl*
be born – geboren sein* *v irreg*
be busy – beschäftigt sein* *v irreg*
be careful – vorsichtig sein* *v irreg*
Be careful! – Vorsicht! Paß auf! *excl*
be cold – (weather) kalt sein* *v irreg*
  I am cold – Mir ist kalt
be fine – (weather) schön sein* *v irreg*
be fit – fit sein* *v irreg*
be good at – gut in .... sein* *v irreg*
be hot – (weather) heiß sein* *v irreg*
  I am hot – Mir ist heiß
be hungry – Hunger haben *v irreg*, hungrig sein* *v irreg*
be ill – krank sein* *v irreg*
be in a hurry – es eilig haben *v irreg*
be in detention – nachsitzen müssen *v irreg*
be interested in – sich interessieren für (+ acc) *v reg refl* †
be keen on – schwärmen für (+ acc) *v reg*
be lucky – Glück haben *v irreg*, Schwein haben *v irreg coll*
be mistaken – sich vertun *v irreg refl*
be obliged to – müssen *v irreg*
be on stage – auf der Bühne sein* *v irreg*
be on television – im Fernsehen sein* *v irreg*
be on the radio – im Radio sein* *v irreg*
be on the staff – angestellt sein* *v irreg*
be out of breath – außer Atem sein* *v irreg*
Be quiet! – (informal) Sei ruhig! *excl*
be right – recht haben *v irreg*
be situated – sich befinden *v irreg refl*
be sleepy – schläfrig sein* *v irreg*
be sorry – bedauern *v reg* †
be thirsty – durstig sein* *v irreg*, Durst haben *v irreg*

---

nm - noun masculine   *nf* - noun feminine   *nnt* - noun neuter   *npl* - noun plural
nom- nominative   *acc* - accusative   *gen* - genitive   *dat* - dative

be up – (out of bed) auf sein* *v irreg*
be well – gesund sein* *v irreg*
be warm – (weather) warm sein*
   v irreg
I am warm – Mir ist warm
be worried – sich Sorgen machen
   v reg dat refl
be wrong – unrecht haben *v irreg*
beach – Strand (Strände) *nm*
   on the beach – am Strand
bean – Bohne (-n) *nf*
bear – Bär (-en) *nm wk*
beard – Bart (Bärte) *nm*
bearded – mit Bart
beastly – scheußlich *adj*
beat – schlagen *v irreg*
beaten – geschlagen *adj*
beautician – Kosmetikerin (-nen) *nf*
beautiful – schön *adj*
beauty – Schönheit (-en) *nf*
because – weil *sub conj*
because of – wegen (+ gen) *prep*
become – werden* *v irreg*
bed – Bett (-en) *nnt*
   air bed – Luftmatratze (-n) *nf*
   camp bed – Feldbett (-en) *nnt*
   double bed – Doppelbett (-en) *nnt*
   flower bed – Blumenbeet (-e) *nnt*
   go to bed – ins Bett gehen* *v irreg*
   make the bed – das Bett machen
   v reg
   single bed – Einzelbett (-en) *nnt*
bedding – Bettwäsche *nf, no pl*
bedroom – Schlafzimmer (-) *nnt*
bedside table – Nachttisch (-e) *nm*
bedside light – Nachttischlampe (-n)
   nf
bed-sit – Wohnschlafzimmer (-) *nnt*
bedtime – Schlafenszeit (-en) *nf*
bee – Biene (-n) *nf*
beef – Rindfleisch *nnt*
beefburger – Hamburger (-) *nm*

beefsteak – Steak (-s) *nnt*
minced beef – gehacktes
   Rindfleisch
beer – Bier (-e) *nnt*
beer mug – Bierkrug (-krüge) *nm*
beermat – Bierdeckel (-) *nm*
beetle – Käfer (-) *nm*
before – bevor *sub conj*
before – ehe *sub conj*
before – vor (+ dat) *prep*
before long – bald *adv*
   never before – noch nie *adv*
beforehand – im voraus *adv*
before leaving – vor der Abfahrt
   the day before – am vorigen Tag
   the day before yesterday –
   vorgestern *adv*
beg – betteln *v reg*
begin – anfangen *v irreg sep*, beginnen
   v irreg
beginner – (male) Anfänger (-) *nm*
beginner – (female) Anfängerin
   (-nen) *nf*
begin again – wieder von vorne
   anfangen *v irreg sep*
beginning – Anfang (Anfänge) *nm*
   at the beginning – am Anfang
behave – sich benehmen *v irreg refl*
behind – Hintern (-) *nm*
behind – hinter (+ acc/dat) *prep*
   leave behind – zurücklassen
   v irreg sep
belch – rülpsen *v reg*
Belgian – belgisch *adj*
Belgian person – (male) Belgier (-)
   nm
Belgian person – (female) Belgierin
   (-nen) *nf*
Belgium – Belgien *nnt*
believe (in) – glauben (an + acc) *v reg*
bell – (church) Glocke (-n) *nf*
bell – (door, school) Klingel (-n) *nf*
belong to – gehören (+ dat) *v reg* †

---

adj - adjective	*v reg* - verb regular	*v sep* - verb separable	† - see verb info
prep - preposition	*v irreg* - verb irregular	*v refl* - verb reflexive	* - takes sein

belongings – Sachen *npl*, Eigentum *nnt, no pl*
below – unter (+ acc/dat) *prep*
belt – Gürtel (-) *nm*
   seat belt – Sicherheitsgurt (-e) *nm*
bench – Bank (Bänke) *nf*
bend – Kurve (-n) *nf*
bend – biegen *v irreg*
bend over – sich bücken *v reg refl*
beneath – unterhalb von (+ dat) *prep*
benefit – Geld (-er) *nnt*
   child benefit – Kindergeld *nnt*
beside – neben (+ acc/dat) *prep*
besides – außerdem *adv*
best – Beste *nmf* ‡
best – am besten *adv*
   do one's best – sein Bestes tun
   Best Wishes – mit besten Wünschen
bet – Wette (-n) *nf*
bet – wetten *v reg* †
better – besser *adj*
   get better – sich erholen *v reg refl* †
between – zwischen (+ acc/dat) *prep*
   between you and me – unter vier Augen
Beware! – Vorsicht! *excl*
Bible – Bibel *nf*
bicycle – Fahrrad (-räder) *nnt*
bidet – Bidet (s) *nnt*
big – groß *adj*
   bigger than – größer als
bike – Rad (Räder) *nnt*
   go for a bike ride – radfahren* *v irreg sep*
biker – (motorbike, male) Motorradfahrer (-) *nm*
biker – (motorbike, female) Motorradfahrerin (-nen) *nf*
bikini – Bikini (s) *nm*
bilingual – zweisprachig *adj*
bill – Rechnung (-en) *nf*
bin – (rubbish) Abfalleimer (-) *nm*

bind – (fasten) binden *v irreg*
bingo – Lotto (-s) *nnt*
biology – Biologie *nf*
bird – Vogel (Vögel) *nm*
biro® – Kugelschreiber (-) *nm*
birth – Geburt (-en) *nf*
   date of birth – Geburtsdatum (-daten) *nnt*
   birth certificate – Geburtsurkunde (-n) *nf*
birthday – Geburtstag (-e) *nm*
   birthday cake – Geburtstagskuchen (-) *nm*
   birthday card – Geburtstagskarte (-n) *nf*
   birthday present – Geburtstagsgeschenk (-e) *nnt*
birth place – Geburtsort (-e) *nm*
biscuit – Keks (-e) *nm*
bite – Biß (Bisse) *nm*
bite – (insect) Stich (-e) *nm*
bite – beißen *v irreg*
bitter – bitter *adj*
black – schwarz *adj*
   A black coffee, please – Einen schwarzen Kaffee, bitte
black ice – Glatteis *nnt*
blackberry – Brombeere (-n) *nf*
blackboard – Tafel (-n) *nf*
black bread – Schwarzbrot *nnt*
blackcurrant – schwarze Johannisbeere (-n) *nf*
Black Forest – der Schwarzwald *nm*
Black Forest gateau – Schwarzwälderkirschtorte (-n) *nf*
blame – Schuld *nf*
blame s.o. – jdm die Schuld geben *v irreg*
blanket – Decke (-n) *nf*
Blast! – Verdammt! *excl*
bleed – bluten *v reg* †
Bless you! – Gesundheit! *excl*
blind – blind *adj*

---

blind – Rolladen (Rolläden) *nm*
blister – Blase (-n) *nf*
block – Block (Blöcke) *nm*
block of flats – Wohnblock (-s) *nm*
block – blockieren *v reg* †
blockbuster – Knüller (-) *nm*
bloke – Typ (-en) *nm*
blonde – blond *adj*
blood – Blut *nnt*
blouse – Bluse (-n) *nf*
blouson jacket – Blouson (-s) *nm*
blow – (hit) Schlag (Schläge) *nm*
blow – blasen *v irreg*
blow – (wind) wehen *v reg*
blow one's nose – sich die Nase putzen *v reg dat refl*
blow the horn – (car) hupen *v reg*
blow up – (inflate) aufblasen *v irreg sep*
Blow! – Verflucht! *excl*
blue – blau *adj*
  light blue – hellblau *adj*
  navy blue – dunkelblau *adj*
blunt – stumpf *adj*
board – (plank) Brett (-er) *nnt*
board – (food) Pension *nf*
  full board – Vollpension *nf*
  half board – Halbpension *nf*
board – (at school) Interne sein* *v irreg*
boarder – Interne *nmf* ‡
board a ship – an Bord gehen* *v irreg*
  on board – an Bord
board game – Gesellschaftsspiel (-e) *nnt*
boarding school – Internat (-e) *nnt*
boast – angeben *v irreg sep*
boat – Boot (-e) *nnt*
boat trip – Bootsfahrt (-en) *nf*
body – Körper (-) *nm*
boil, be boiling – kochen *v reg*

boiled egg – ein gekochtes Ei *nnt*
boiled potatoes – Salzkartoffeln *npl*
boil water – Wasser kochen *v reg*
bold – mutig *adj*
bomb – Bombe (-n) *nf*
bomb scare – Bombenalarm (-e) *nm*
bone – Knochen (-) *nm*
bonfire – Freudenfeuer *nnt*
bonnet – Haube (-n) *nf*
book – Buch (Bücher) *nnt*
  sci-fi book – Science-Fiction Buch (Bücher) *nnt*
book – Heft (-e) *nnt*
book – buchen *v reg*
book of tickets – Streifenkarte (-n) *nf*
book a seat – einen Platz reservieren *v reg* †
book case – Bücherschrank (-schränke) *nm*
booked – reserviert *adj*
  fully booked – ausgebucht *adj*
booking office – Schalter (-) *nm*
booklet – Broschüre (-n) *nf*
bookshelf – Bücherregal (-e) *nnt*
bookshop – Buchhandlung (-en) *nf*
boot (of car) – Kofferraum (-räume) *nm*
boot – Stiefel (-) *nm*
  football boot – Fußballschuh (-e) *nm*
  ski boot – Skischuh (-e) *nm*
  walking boot – Wanderschuh (-e) *nm*
booze – Alkohol *nm*
booze – saufen *v irreg coll*
border – Grenze (-n) *nf*
border – (flower) Blumenbeet (-e) *nnt*
bore – langweilen *v reg*
  to be bored – sich langweilen *v reg refl*
boredom – Langeweile *nf*
boring – langweilig *adj*
born – geboren *adj*

born on 6th January – am
6. Januar geboren
be born – geboren sein* *v irreg*
borrow (from) – leihen *v irreg*
boss – (male) Chef (-s) *nm*
boss – (female) Chefin (-nen) *nf*
bossy – herrschsüchtig *adj*
both – beide *adj*
bother – sich die Mühe geben *v irreg*
dat refl
bother – stören *v reg*
bottle – Flasche (-n) *nf*
bottle opener – Flaschenöffner (-)
nm
bottom of class – Klassenschwächste
nmf ‡
bottom – unten *adv*
at the bottom of the page –
unten auf der Seite
bow – sich beugen *v reg refl*
bow tie – Fliege (-n) *nf*
bowl – (dish) Schüssel (-n) *nf*
bowl – (skittles) kegeln *v reg*
bowl – (throw) werfen *v irreg*
bowling alley – Kegelbahn (-en) *nf*
box – Kasten (Kästen) *nm*
boxing – Boxsport *nm*
box – (wooden) Kiste (-n) *nf*
box – (cardboard) Karton (-s) *nm*
box – Schachtel (-n) *nf*
Boxing Day – zweiter
Weihnachtsfeiertag *nm*
boy – Junge (-n) *nm wk*
boyfriend – Freund (-e) *nm*
bra – BH (Büstenhalter) *nm*
bracelet – Armband (-bänder) *nnt*
bracket – Klammer (-n) *nf*
in brackets – in Klammern
brain – Gehirn (-e) *nnt*
brake – Bremse (-n) *nf*
brake – bremsen *v reg*
branch – (tree) Ast (Äste) *nm*

branch – (firm) Filiale (-n) *nf*
brand name – Marke (-n) *nf*
brand new – nagelneu *adj*
brass band – Blaskapelle (-n) *nf*
brave – tapfer *adj*
bread – Brot (-e) *nnt*
break – Pause (-n) *nf*
break – brechen *v irreg*
break one's leg – sich das Bein
brechen *v irreg dat refl*
breakdown – Panne (-n) *nf*
breakdown lorry –
Abschleppwagen (-) *nm*
break down – eine Panne haben
v irreg
breakfast – Frühstück (-e) *nnt*
have breakfast – frühstücken
v reg
break in – einbrechen* *v irreg sep*
break up – aufbrechen *v irreg sep*
breath – Atem *nm*
out of breath – außer Atem
breathe – atmen *v reg* †
breed – züchten *v reg* †
brick – Backstein (-e) *nm*
made of brick – aus Backstein
bricklayer – Maurer (-) *nm*
bride – Braut (Bräute) *nf*
bridegroom – Bräutigam (-e) *nm*
bridesmaid – Brautjungfer (-n) *nf*
bridge – Brücke (-n) *nf*
brief – kurz *adj*
briefcase – Mappe (-n) *nf,*
Aktentasche (-n) *nf*
briefs – (pants) Unterhose (-n) *nf*
bright – (clever) intelligent *adj*
bright – (not dark) hell *adj*
bright – (weather) heiter
bring – bringen *v irreg*
bring – mitbringen *v irreg sep*
bring back – zurückbringen *v irreg*
sep

---

nm - noun masculine	*nf* - noun feminine	*nnt* - noun neuter	*npl* - noun plural
nom- nominative	*acc* - accusative	*gen* - genitive	*dat* - dative

bring up – (be sick) sich übergeben
v irreg refl insep
bring up – (mention) erwähnen *v reg* †
British – britisch *adj*
the British Isles – die Britischen
Inseln *npl*
British person – (male) Brite (-n) *nm*
wk
British person – (female) Britin
(-nen) *nf*
broad – breit *adj*
broadcast – senden *v reg* †
broadcast – Sendung (-en) *nf*
brochure – Broschüre (-n) *nf*
broke – pleite *adj inv*
I'm broke – Ich bin pleite *coll*
broken – gebrochen *adj*
broom – Besen (-) *nm*
brother – Bruder (Brüder) *nm*
brother-in-law – Schwager
(Schwäger) *nm*
brother and sisters – Geschwister
nnt, no pl
brown – braun *adj*
bruise – blauer Fleck (-e) *nm*
brush – Bürste (-n) *nf*
brush – (broom) Besen (-) *nm*
brush – (painting) Pinsel (-) *nm*
brush – bürsten *v reg* †
brush one's hair – sich die Haare
bürsten *v reg dat refl* †
Brussels – Brüssel
Brussels sprout – Rosenkohl *nm,*
no pl
bucket – Eimer (-) *nm*
budgerigar – Wellensittich (-e) *nm*
buffet – Büffet (-s) *nnt*
build – bauen *v reg*
builder – Bauunternehmer (-) *nm*
building – Gebäude (-) *nnt*
bull – Stier (-e) *nm*
bumbag – Gürteltasche (-n) *nf*
bump – Zusammenstoß (-stöße) *nm*

bumper – Stoßstange (-n) *nf*
bump into – zusammenstoßen* mit
(+ dat) *v irreg sep*
bump into – (meet) begegnen* (+
dat) *v reg* †
bunch of flowers – Blumenstrauß
(-sträuße) *nm*
bunch of grapes – Trauben *npl*
bungalow – Bungalow (-s) *nm /*
bureau de change – Geldwechsel *nm*
burglar – Einbrecher (-) *nm*
burgle – einbrechen* *v irreg sep*
burn – Brandwunde (-n) *nf*
burn – brennen *v irreg*
burn o.s. – sich verbrennen *v irreg*
refl
I have burnt my finger –
Ich habe mir den Finger verbrannt
burst – bersten* *v irreg*
bus – Bus (-se) *nm*
bus driver – (male) Busfahrer (-) *nm*
bus driver – (female) Busfahrerin
(-nen) *nf*
bus route – Buslinie (-n) *nf*
bus stop – Bushaltestelle (-n) *nf*
catch the bus – den Bus nehmen
v irreg
bush – Strauch (Sträuche) *nm*
business – Geschäft (-e) *nnt*
business man – Geschäftsmann
(-männer) *nm*
business woman – Geschäftsfrau
(-en) *nf*
busy – beschäftigt *adj*
busy o.s. – sich beschäftigen *v reg* †
but – aber *co-ord conj*
butcher – Metzger (-) *nm*
butcher's shop – Metzgerei (-en) *nm*
butter – Butter *nf*
butterfly – Schmetterling (-e) *nm*
button – Knopf (Knöpfe) *nm*
buy – kaufen *v reg*
by – per *prep*

---

by bus – mit dem Bus
by car – mit dem Auto
by coach – mit dem Reisebus
by day – am Tag, tagsüber
by the day – pro Tag

by the hour – pro Stunde
by the kilo – pro Kilo
Bye! – Tschüs *excl*
bypass – Umgehungsstraße (-n) *nf*

C

cabbage – Kohl *nm*
cable car – Seilbahn (-en) *nf*
cable TV – Kabelfernsehen (-) *nnt*
café – Café (-s) *nnt*
café terrace – Terrasse (-n) *nf*
cage – Käfig (-e) *nm*
cagoule – Regenjacke (-n) *nf*
cake – Kuchen (-) *nm*
  birthday cake –
  Geburtstagskuchen (-) *nm*
cake shop – Konditorei (-en) *nf*
calculate – rechnen *v reg* †
calculator – Taschenrechner (-) *nm*
calendar – Kalender (-) *nm*
calf – Kalb (Kälber) *nnt*
call – (phone) Anruf (-e) *nm*
call – (phone) anrufen *v irreg sep*
call – (shout) rufen *v irreg*
  be called – heißen *v irreg*
call box – Telefonzelle (-n) *nf*
call for – (friend) abholen *v reg sep*
call in on – vorbeikommen* *v irreg
sep*
call the register – die Anwesenheit
feststellen *v reg sep*
calm – ruhig *adj*
calm o.s. down – sich beruhigen
  v reg refl †
camcorder – Videorecorder (-) *nm*
came – *see kommen**
camel – Kamel (-e) *nnt*
camera – Fotoapparat (-e) *nm*

camp – campen *v reg*
camper – Camper (-) *nm*
camp-fire – Lagerfeuer (-) *nnt*
camping carnet – Camping Carnet
(-s) *nnt*
camping cooker – Campingkocher
(-) *nm*
camping gas – Campinggaz® *nnt*
campsite – Campingplatz (-plätze) *nm*
  go camping – zelten gehen*
  v irreg
can – (tin) Dose (-n) *nf*
can-opener – Dosenöffner (-) *nm*
can – (be able to) können *v irreg*
  Can I? – Kann ich?
  I can't – Ich kann nicht
Canada – Kanada *nnt*
canal – Kanal (Kanäle) *nm*
canary – Kanarienvogel (-vögel) *nm*
cancel – streichen *v irreg*
cancer – Krebs *nm*
candidate – (male) Kandidat (-en)
nm wk
candidate – (female) Kandidatin
(-nen) *nf*
candle – Kerze (-n) *nf*
candy floss – Zuckerwatte *nf*
canoe – Kanu (-s) *nm*
canoe – Kanu fahren* *v irreg*
canteen – Kantine (-n) *nf*
cap – (hat) Mütze (-n) *nf*
capable – fähig *adj*
capital – (city) Hauptstadt (-städte) *nf*

---

nm - noun masculine   *nf* - noun feminine   *nnt* - noun neuter   *npl* - noun plural
nom- nominative   *acc* - accusative   *gen* - genitive   *dat* - dative

capital letter – Großbuchstabe (-n) *nm wk*
Capricorn – (horoscope) Steinbock
captain – (ship) Kapitän (-e) *nm*
car – Auto (-s) *nnt,* Wagen (-) *nm*
  by car – mit dem Auto
  car ferry – Fähre (-n) *nf*
  car hire – Autoverleih *nm*
  car key – Autoschlüssel (-) *nm*
  car park – Parkplatz (-plätze) *nm*
  car phone – Autotelefon (-e) *nnt*
  car seat – Autositz (-e) *nm*
  car wash – Autowaschstraße (-n) *nf*
caravan – Wohnwagen (-) *nm*
card – Karte (-n) *nf*
  credit card – Kreditkarte (-n) *nf*
  identity card – Ausweis (-e) *nm*
  post card – Postkarte (-n) *nf*
  play cards – Karten spielen *v reg*
  card game – Kartenspiel (-e) *nnt*
cardboard – Pappe *nf*
cardigan – Strickjacke (-n) *nf*
care – sich kümmern um (+ acc) *v reg refl*
care for – pflegen *v reg*
career – Karriere (-n) *nf*
careers advice – Berufsberatung *nf*
careful – vorsichtig *adj*
careful with money – geizig *adj*
  be careful – aufpassen *v reg sep*
  Be careful! – Paß auf! *excl*
carefully – sorgfältig *adv*
careless – rücksichtslos *adj*
caretaker – (male) Hausmeister (-) *nm*
caretaker – (female) Hausmeisterin (-nen) *nf*
Carnival – Karneval *nm,* Fasching *nm*
carol – Weihnachtslied (-er) *nnt*
carpet – Teppich (-e) *nm*
carpet – (fitted) Teppichboden (-böden) *nm*
carrot – Karotte (-n) *nf*

carry – tragen *v irreg*
carry on – weitermachen *v reg sep*
cartoon – (cinema) Zeichentrickfilm (-e) *nm*
cartoon – Comic (-s) *nm*
cartoon strip – Comic-Strip (-s) *nm*
case – (suitcase) Koffer (-) *nm*
  pack cases – Koffer packen *v reg*
case – (example) Fall (Fälle) *nm*
cash – (money) Geld *nnt*
cash – (not a cheque) Bargeld *nnt*
  pay cash – bar bezahlen *v reg* †
cash a cheque – einen Scheck einlösen *v reg sep*
cash desk – Kasse (-n) *nf*
  go to the cash desk – an die Kasse gehen* *v irreg*
cashier – (male) Kassierer (-) *nm*
cashier – (female) Kassiererin (-nen) *nf*
cash machine – (dispenser) Geldautomat (-en) *nm wk*
cassette – Kassette (-n) *nf*
  video cassette – Videokassette (-n) *nf*
cassette recorder – Kassettenrekorder (-) *nm*
castle – (fortified) Burg (-en) *nf*
castle – (palace) Schloß (Schlösser) *nnt*
cat – Katze (-n) *nf*
  tomcat – Kater (-) *nm*
catalytic converter – Katalysator (-en) *nm*
catch – (bus, etc) nehmen *v irreg*
  Catch the number three bus! – Nehmen Sie den Bus Linie 3!
catch – (fish) fangen *v irreg*
catch cold – sich erkälten *v reg refl* †
catch up with – nachholen *v reg sep*
cathedral – Dom (-e) *nm*
Catholic – katholisch *adj*
Catholic – Katholiker (-) *nm*

---

adj - adjective	*v reg* - verb regular	*v sep* - verb separable	† - see verb info
prep - preposition	*v irreg* - verb irregular	*v refl* - verb reflexive	* - takes sein

Catholic – Katholikerin (-nen) *nf*
cauliflower – Blumenkohl *nm*
cause – Ursache (-n) *nf*
cause an accident – einen Unfall verursachen *v reg* †
cause stress – Streß verursachen *v reg* †
cave – Höhle (-n) *nf*
CD – CD (-s) *nf*
CD player – CD-Spieler (-) *nm*
CD ROM – CD-ROM (-s) *nm*
CDT – Werken *nnt*
ceiling – Decke (-n) *nf*
celebrate – feiern *v reg*
celebration – Feier (-) *nf*
celebrity – Star (-s) *nm*
cellar – Keller (-) *nm*
cello – Cello (-s) *nnt*
centimetre – Zentimeter (-) *nm*
central heating – Zentralheizung *nf*
centre – Mitte (-n) *nf*
   in the centre of – in der Mitte von (+ dat)
   in the town centre – in der Stadtmitte
century – Jahrhundert (-e) *nnt*
certain – gewiß *adj*, sicher *adj*
certificate – Zeugnis(-se) *nnt*
chain – Kette (-n) *nf*
chair – Stuhl (Stühle) *nm*
chair lift – Sesselbahn (-en) *nf*
chalk – Kreide *nf*
champagne – (German) Sekt *nm*
champion – (male) Meister (-) *nm*
champion – (female) Meisterin (-nen) *nf*
championship – Meisterschaft (-en) *nf*
chance – (opportunity) Gelegenheit (-en) *nf*
chance – (fate) Zufall (Zufälle) *nm*
   by chance – zufälligerweise *adv*

Chancellor – Kanzler (-) *nm*
change – Änderung (-en) *nf*
change – (coins) Kleingeld *nnt*
   Have you any change? – Haben Sie Kleingeld?
   Keep the change! – Das stimmt so!
change – (alter) ändern *v reg*
change – (exchange) umtauschen *v reg sep*
change – (trains) umsteigen* *v irreg sep*
change – (reunification) Wende (-n) *nf*
change clothes – sich umziehen *v irreg refl sep*
change gear – (den Gang) schalten *v reg* †
change money – Geld wechseln *v reg*
change one's mind – sich etwas anders überlegen *v reg dat refl insep*
   I've changed my mind – Ich habe mir das anders überlegt
changeable – veränderlich *adj*
changing-room – (shop) Umkleidekabine (-n) *nf*
changing-room – (sport) Umkleideraum (-räume) *nm*
channel – (TV) Programm (-e) *nnt*
   on Channel Two – im zweiten Programm
Channel Tunnel – Kanaltunnel *nm*
English Channel – Kanal *nm*
chap – Kerl (-e) *nm*
chapel – Kapelle (-n) *nf*
chapter – Kapitel (-) *nnt*
character – Charakter (-e) *nm*
character – (drama) Person (-en) *nf*
charge – Preis (-e) *nm*
charge card – Kreditkarte (-n) *nf*
charming – entzückend *adj*
chase – jagen *v reg*
chat – plaudern *v reg*

---

cheap – billig *adj*
cheat – mogeln *v reg*
check – Kontrolle (-n) *nf*
check – kontrollieren *v reg* †
  check the oil level – den Ölstand
  kontrollieren *v reg* †
  check the tyres –
  die Reifen kontrollieren *v reg* †
  check the water level – das
  Wasser nachsehen *v irreg sep*
checked – getestet *adj*
checked – (pattern) kariert *adj*
checkout – Kasse (-n) *nf*
check tickets – Fahrkarten
  kontrollieren *v reg* †
cheek – (face) Wange (-n) *nf*
cheek – (face, bottom) Backe (-n) *nf*
cheeky – frech *adj*
cheerful – munter *adj*, heiter *adj*
Cheers! – Prost! Zum Wohl! *excl*
cheese – Käse *nm*
cheese sandwich – Käsebrot (-e) *nnt*
chemist – (male) Apotheker (-) *nm*
chemist – (female) Apothekerin (-nen)
  nf
chemist's shop – Apotheke (-n) *nf*
  at the chemist's –
  an der Apotheke
chemistry – (subject) Chemie *nf*
cheque – Scheck (-s) *nm*
cheque book – Scheckheft (-e) *nnt*
cheque card – Scheckkarte (-n) *nf*
  cash a cheque – einen Scheck
  einlösen *v reg sep*
cherry – Kirsche (-n) *nf*
chess – Schach *nnt*
  play chess – Schach spielen *v reg*
chest – (body) Brust (Brüste) *nf*
chest – (box) Kiste (-n) *nf*
chest of drawers – Kommode (-n) *nf*
chew – kauen *v reg*
chewing gum – Kaugummi (-s) *nm*

chic – schick *adj*
chicken – Hähnchen (-) *nnt*
chief – Haupt~ *pref*
child (ren) – Kind (-er) *nnt*
  only child – Einzelkind (-er) *nnt*
childhood – Kindheit (-en) *nf*
child-minder – Tagesmutter
  (-mütter) *nf*
chimney – Schornstein (-e) *nm*
chin – Kinn (-e) *nnt*
China – China *nnt*
Chinese – chinesisch *adj*
Chinese person – Chinese *nmf* ‡
chip – (micro) Chip (-s) *nf*
chips – Pommes frites *npl*
chocolate – (bar) Schokolade *nf*
chocolate – (individual) Praline (-n)
  nf
chocolate – Schokoladen~ *pref*
choice – Auswahl *nf*
choir – Chor (Chöre) *nm*
choose – wählen *v reg*
chop – Kotelett (-s) *nnt*
Christian – (male) Christ (-en) *nm wk*
Christian – (female) Christin (-nen)
  nf
Christian name – Vorname (-n)
  nm wk
Christmas – Weihnachten *npl*
  at Christmas – zu Weihnachten
  Father Christmas –
  Weihnachtsmann (-männer) *nm*
  Happy Christmas! – Frohe
  Weihnachten!
Christmas Eve – Heiliger Abend *nm*
Christmas holidays –
  Weihnachtsferien *npl*
Christmas present –
  Weihnachtsgeschenk (-e) *nnt*
Christmas tree – Weihnachtsbaum
  (-bäume) *nm*
church – Kirche (-n) *nf*
church service – Gottesdienst (-e) *nm*

cider – Apfelwein (-e) *nm*
cigarette – Zigarette (-n) *nf*
cinema – Kino (-s) *nnt*
circle – Kreis (-e) *nm*
circus – Zirkus (-se) *nm*
city – Großstadt (-städte) *nf*
civil servant – Beamte *nm* ‡
civil servant – Beamtin (-nen) *nf*
clarinet – Klarinette (-n) *nf*
 play the clarinet – Klarinette
 spielen *v reg*
class – Klasse (-n) *nf*
classical – klassisch *adj*
classical music – klassische Musik *nf*
classified (small) ad – Kleinanzeige
 (-n) *nf*
classroom – Klassenzimmer (-) *nnt*
clean – sauber *adj*
clean – saubermachen *v reg sep*
clean one's teeth – sich die Zähne
 putzen *v reg dat refl*
 I cleaned my teeth – ich habe mir
 die Zähne geputzt
cleaning – Saubermachen *nnt*
cleaning lady – Putzfrau (-en) *nf*
clear – klar *adj*
clear away – abräumen *v reg sep*
clearly – deutlich *adv*
clear up – (tidy) aufräumen *v reg sep*
clever – klug *adj*
cliff – Klippe (-n) *nf*
climate – Klima (-s) *nnt*
climb – klettern *v reg*
clinic – (surgery) Praxis (Praxen) *nf*
cloak-room – Garderobe (-n) *nf*
clock – Uhr (-en) *nf*
clock radio – Radiowecker (-) *nm*
close – (near) nah *adj*
 close by – in der Nähe
close – (shut) zumachen *v reg sep*
closed – geschlossen *adj*
cloth – Stoff (-e) *nm*

clothes – Kleider (-) *npl*
clothes department – (men's)
 Herrenkonfektion *nf*
clothes department – (ladies')
 Damenkonfektion *nf*
cloud – Wolke (-n) *nf*
cloudless – wolkenlos *adj*
cloudy – wolkig *adj*
club – Verein (-e) *nm*, Klub (-s) *nm*
clutch – (car) Kupplung (-en) *nf*
clutch – (seize) greifen *v irreg*
coach – trainieren *v reg* †
coach – Reisebus (-se) *nm*
coach station – Busbahnhof (-höfe)
 nm
coal – Kohle (-n) *nf*
coast – Küste (-n) *nf*
coat – Mantel (Mäntel) *nm*
coat hanger – Kleiderbügel (-) *nm*
Coca cola® – Cola *nf*
cocoa – Kakao *nm*
code – (guidelines) Richtlinien *npl*
co-educational – gemischt *adj*
coffee – Kaffee *nm*
 a cup of coffee – eine Tasse
 Kaffee
 an individual pot of coffee –
 ein Kännchen Kaffee
 decaffeinated coffee – Kaffee
 Hag® *nm*
 filter coffee – Filterkaffee *nm*
coffee with milk – Kaffee mit Milch
coffee pot – Kaffeekanne (-n) *nf*
coffee table – Couchtisch (-e) *nm*
coin – Münze (-n) *nf*
 2 DM coin – Zweimarkstück *nnt*
coke – Cola (-s) *nf*
cold – kalt *adj*
 I am cold – Mir ist kalt
cold water – kaltes Wasser *nnt*
cold – (illness) Erkältung (-en) *nf*
 catch cold – sich erkälten *v reg refl* †
 I have a cold – Ich bin verschnupft

cold – (temperature) Kälte *nf*
collar – Kragen (-) *nm*
colleague – (male) Kollege (-n) *nm wk*
colleague – (female) Kollegin (-nen) *nf*
collect – (stamps, etc) sammeln *v reg*
collect – (pick up) abholen *v reg sep*
collection – Sammlung (-en) *nf*
college – (sixth form) Oberstufenkolleg (-ien) *nnt*
college – (FE) Berufsschule (-n) *nf*
collide with – zusammenstoßen* mit (+ dat) *v irreg sep*
collision – Zusammenstoß (-stösse) *nm*
colloquial – umgangssprachlich *adj*
Cologne – Köln
eau de Cologne – Kölnisch Wasser
colon (:) – Doppelpunkt (-e) *nm*
colour – Farbe (-n) *nf*
comb – Kamm (Kämme) *nm*
comb one's hair – sich kämmen *v reg refl*
come – kommen* *v irreg*
come back – zurückkommen* *v irreg sep*
come down – herunterkommen* *v irreg sep*
come in – hereinkommen* *v irreg sep*
Come on! – Mach schnell! *excl*
come out – herauskommen* *v irreg sep*
come up – heraufkommen* *v irreg sep*
comfort – Komfort *nm*
comfortable – bequem *adj*
comic – komisch *adj*
comic – Comic (-s) *nm*
comic film – Komödie (-n) *nf*
comic strip – Comic (-s) *nnt*

coming from – (train) aus (+ dat) *prep*
comma (,) – Komma (-s) *nnt*
command – Befehl (-e) *nm*
command – befehlen *v irreg*
common – gewöhnlich *adj*
the Common Market – der Gemeinsame Markt *nm*
communism – Kommunismus *nm*
commute – pendeln* *v reg*
compact disc – CD (-s) *nf*
company – Gesellschaft (-en) *nf*
compare – vergleichen *v irreg*
comparison – Vergleich (-e) *nm*
competition – Wettbewerb (-e) *nm*
competitor – (male) Teilnehmer (-) *nm*
competitor – (female) Teilnehmerin (-nen) *nf*
complain – sich beklagen *v reg* †
complete – völlig *adj*
complete – ergänzen *v reg*, vollenden *v reg* †, beenden *v reg* †
complicated – kompliziert *adj*
compulsory – pflicht *adj inv*
compulsory subject – Pflichtfach (-fächer) *nnt*
computer – Computer (-) *nm*
computer game – Computerspiel (-e) *nnt*
computerise – informatisieren *v reg* †
computer operator – EDV-Bearbeiter (-) *nm*
computer programmer – (male) Programmierer (-) *nm*
computer programmer – (female) Programmiererin (-nen) *nf*
computer scientist – (male) Informatiker (-) *nm*
computer scientist – (female) Informatikerin (-nen) *nf*
computer studies – Informatik *nf*
concern – betreffen *v irreg*

---

be concerned with – (care for) sich kümmern um (+ acc) *v reg refl*

concerning – in bezug auf (+ acc) *prep*

concert – Konzert (-e) *nnt*

conclusion – Schluß (Schlüße) *nm*

concrete – Beton *nm*

made of concrete – aus Beton

condition – (of agreement) Bedingung (-en) *nf*

condition – (state) Zustand (Zustände) *nm*

in good condition – in gutem Zustand

in poor condition – in schlechtem Zustand

condom – Kondom (-e) *nnt*

confirm – bestätigen *v reg* †

congratulate – gratulieren (+ dat) *v reg* †

Congratulations! – Ich gratuliere

connection – (train) Verbindung (-en) *nf*

consequently – deswegen *adv*

conservatory – Wintergarten (-gärten) *nm*

consist (of) – bestehen (aus + dat) *v irreg*

constipated – verstopft *adj*

construct – bauen *v reg*

construction worker – (male) Bauarbeiter (-) *nm*

construction worker – (female) Bauarbeiterin (-nen) *nf*

consult – fragen *v reg*

contact – sich wenden an (+ acc) *v reg refl* †

contact lens – Kontaktlinse (-n) *nf*

contain – enthalten *v irreg*

contents – Inhalt *nm, no pl*

contents – (book) Inhaltsverzeichnis (-se) *nnt*

contest – Wettbewerb (-e) *nm*

continent – (not island) Festland *nnt*

continent – (geographical) Kontinent (-e) *nm*

continue – (doing sthg) weitermachen *v reg sep*

continue – (speaking) fortfahren* *v irreg sep*

continue – (travelling) weiterfahren* *v irreg sep*

continue – (studying) weiterstudieren *v reg sep* †

continuous – ununterbrochen *adj*

convenient – passend *adj*

It's not convenient – Das paßt mir nicht

conversation – Gespräch (-e) *nnt*

convinced – überzeugt *adj*

cook – (male) Koch (Köche) *nm*

cook – (female) Köchin (-nen) *nf*

cook – kochen *v reg*

cooker – Herd (-e) *nm*

cookery – Kochen *nnt*

cool – kühl *adj*

cope – sich durchschlagen *v irreg refl sep*

copy – (imitate) nachmachen *v reg sep*

copy – (write down) kopieren *v reg* †

cork – Korken (-) *nm*

corkscrew – Korkenzieher (-) *nm*

corner – Ecke (-n) *nf*

at the corner of – an der Ecke

cornet – (music) Kornett (-e) *nnt*

cornet – (ice cream) Tütchen (-) *nnt*

correct – richtig *adj*

correct – korrigieren *v reg* †

corrections – Verbesserungen *npl*

correspondence – Briefwechsel *nm*

corridor – Gang (Gänge) *nm*

cost – (price) Preis (-e) *nm*

cost – kosten *v reg* †

costing – zum Preis von (+ dat) *prep*

cottage – Häuschen (-) *nnt*

cottage cheese – Hüttenkäse *nm*

cotton – Baumwolle *nf*

---

made of cotton – aus Baumwolle
cotton wool – Watte *nf*
couchette – Liegesitz (-e) *nm*
cough – Husten (-) *nm*
cough – husten *v reg* †
cough medicine – Hustensaft (-säfte) *nm*
could – (possibly) könnte *see können*
could – (was able to) konnte
see können
council flat – Sozialwohnung (-en) *nf*
count – zählen *v reg*
counter – (PO, bank) Schalter (-) *nm*
counter – (shop) Ladentisch (-e) *nm*
country – Land (Länder) *nnt*
in the country – auf dem Land
countryside – Landschaft (-en) *nf*
coupon – Bon (-s) *nm*
courage – Mut *nm*
course – (school) Kurs (-e) *nm*
course – (route) Piste (-n) *nf*
of course – natürlich *adv*
court – (outdoor sport) Platz (Plätze) *nm*
court – (indoor sport) Halle (-n) *nf*
cousin – (male) Cousin (-s) *nm*
cousin – (female) Kusine (-n) *nf*
cover – zudecken *v reg sep*
covered with – bedeckt mit (+ dat) *adj*
cow – Kuh (Kühe) *nf*
crab – Krabbe (-n) *nf*
craftsman – Handwerker (-) *nm*
craftswoman – Handwerkerin (-nen) *nf*
crafty – schlau *adj*
crash – Zusammenstoß (-stöße) *nm*
crash into – zusammenstoßen* mit (+ dat) *v irreg sep*
crazy – verrückt *adj*
cream – (milk) Sahne *nf*
cream – (medicine) Salbe (-n) *nf*
sun cream – Sonnencreme *nf*
credit card – Kreditkarte (-n) *nf*

cricket – Kricket *nnt*
criminal – (male) Verbrecher (-) *nm*
criminal – (female) Verbrecherin (-nen) *nf*
crisps – Chips *npl*
crockery – Geschirr *nnt, no pl*
crocodile – Krokodil (-e) *nnt*
cross with – (angry) böse mit (+ dat) *adj*
cross – überqueren *v reg insep*
cross country run – Waldlauf (-läufe) *nm*
cross out – durchstreichen *v irreg sep*
crossing – (channel) Überfahrt (-en) *nf*
crossing – (level) Bahnübergang (-gänge) *nm*
crossing – (pedestrian) Fußgängerüberweg (-e) *nm*
crossroads – Kreuzung (-en) *nf*
crossword – Kreuzworträtsel (-) *nnt*
crowd – Menge (-n) *nf*
cruel – grausam *adj*
cruise – Kreuzfahrt (-en) *nf*
crunchy – knusprig *adj*
crush – zerquetschen *v reg* †
cry – (shout) rufen *v irreg*
cry – (weep) weinen *v reg*
cucumber – Gurke (-n) *nf*
cul de sac – Sackgasse (-n) *nf*
cup – Tasse (-n) *nf*
a cup of tea – eine Tasse Tee
cup – (trophy) Pokal (-e) *nm*
cup final – Pokalendspiel (-e) *nnt*
cup tie – Pokalspiel (-e) *nnt*
cupboard – Schrank (Schränke) *nm*
curious – neugierig *adj*
curly – lockig *adj*
currency – Währung (-en) *nf*
currency exchange office – Wechselstube (-n) *nf*
current – aktuell *adj*
current – (electricity) Strom *nm*

---

curriculum – Lernprogramm (-e) *nnt*
curried sausage – Currywurst *nf*
cursor – Cursor *nm*
curtain – (opaque) Vorhang (-hänge) *nm*
curtain – (net) Gardine (-n) *nf*
cushion – Kissen (-) *nnt*
custard – Vanillesoße *nf*
custom – Gebrauch (Gebräuche) *nm*
customer – (male) Kunde (-n) *nm wk*
customer – (female) Kundin (-nen) *nf*
customs – Zoll *nm*
customs officer – (male) Zollbeamte *nm* ‡
customs officer – (female) Zollbeamtin (-nen) *nf*

cut – schneiden *v irreg*
  I have cut my finger – Ich habe mich in den Finger geschnitten
cut lawn – den Rasen mähen *v reg*
cutlery – Besteck *nnt*
cutlet – Kotelett (-s) *nnt*
CV – Lebenslauf (-läufe) *nm*
cycle – Rad (Räder) *nnt*
cycle – radfahren* *v irreg sep*
cycle hire – Radverleih *nm*
cycling – Radfahren *nnt*
cyclist – (male) Radfahrer (-) *nm*
cyclist – (female) Radfahrerin (-nen) *nf*
the Czech Republic – die Tschechische Republik *nf*

D

dad(dy) – Vater (Väter) *nm*
daddy – Vati *nm*
daily – täglich *adj*
daily life – der Alltag *nm*, das tägliche Leben
  in daily life – im täglichen Leben
daily paper – Tageszeitung (-en) *nf*
daily routine – Tagesablauf (-läufe) *nm*
damage – Schaden (Schäden) *nm*
damaged – beschädigt *adj*
damp – feucht *adj*
dance – Tanz (Tänze) *nm*
dance – tanzen *v reg*
dancer – (male) Tänzer (-) *nm*
dancer – (female) Tänzerin (-nen) *nf*
Dane – (male) Däne (-n) *nm wk*
Dane – (female) Dänin (-nen) *nf*
danger – Gefahr (-en) *nf*
dangerous – gefährlich *adj*
Danish – dänisch *adj*

dare – wagen *v reg*
dark – dunkel *adj*
dark – (colour) dunkel~ *pref*
dash (-) – (punctuation) Bindestrich (-e) *nm*
data – Daten *npl*
database – Datenbank (-en) *nf*
date – Datum (Daten) *nnt*
  up to date – aktuell *adj*
date – (meeting) Termin (-e) *nm*
date of birth – Geburtsdatum (-daten) *nnt*
daughter – Tochter (Töchter) *nf*
daughter-in-law – Schwiegertochter (-töchter) *nf*
day – Tag (-e) *nm*
  all day – den ganzen Tag
  closing day – Ruhetag (-e) *nm*
  next day – am nächsten Tag
  one day – eines Tages
  on working days – werktags
  per day – pro Tag

---

the day after tomorrow –
übermorgen *adv*
the day before yesterday –
vorgestern *adv*
the other day – vor ein paar Tagen
day boy – Tagesschüler (-) *nm*
day girl – Tagesschülerin (-nen) *nf*
day off – (public holiday) Feiertag (-e)
nm
a day off – (work) ein freier Tag
day return – Tagesrückfahrkarte (-n)
nf
dead – tot *adj*
dead end – Sackgasse (-n) *nf*
deaf – taub *adj*
deaf and dumb – taubstumm *adj*
dear – (expensive) teuer *adj*
Dear – (a letter to male) Lieber
Dear – (a letter to female) Liebe
Dear Sirs – Sehr geehrte Herren
death – Tod (-e) *nm*
debate – Debatte (-n) *nf*
deceive – täuschen *v reg*
December – Dezember *nm*
in December – im Dezember
decide – (sich) entscheiden *v irreg*
(refl)
decide to – beschließen *v irreg*
decision – Entscheidung (-en) *nf*
deckchair – Liegestuhl (-stühle) *nm*
declare – erklären *v reg* †
declare – (to customs) verzollen *v reg* †
decorate – (paint) streichen *v irreg*
decorate – (wallpaper) tapezieren
v reg †
decorate – (shop window) dekorieren
v reg †
deep – tief *adj*
deep freeze – Tiefkühltruhe (-n) *nf*
deep frozen – tiefgefroren *adj*
defeated – geschlagen *adj*
definite – bestimmt *adj*
definitely – unbedingt *adv*

degree – (temperature) Grad
degree – (university exam)
Staatsexamen (-) *nnt*
delay – Verspätung (-en) *nf*
delay – verspäten *v reg* †
delicate – zierlich *adj*
delicatessen – Delikatessengeschäft
(-e) *nnt*
delicious – lecker *adj*
delighted – entzückt *adj*
delightful – entzückend *adj*
deliver – liefern *v reg*
deliver the papers – die Zeitungen
austragen *v irreg sep*
delivery – Lieferung (-en) *nf*
demand – verlangen *v reg* †
demonstrate – demonstrieren *v reg* †
demonstration – Demonstration
(-en) *nf*
Denmark – Dänemark *nnt*
dentist – (male) Zahnarzt (-ärzte) *nm*
dentist – (female) Zahnärztin (-nen) *nf*
deny – verleugnen *v reg* †
depart – abfahren* *v irreg sep*
depart – (plane) abfliegen* *v irreg sep*
department – Abteilung (-en) *nf*
department store – Kaufhaus
(-häuser) *nnt*
departure – Abfahrt (-en) *nf*
departure – Abflug (Abflüge) *nm*
departure board – Abfahrtsplan
(-pläne) *nm*
depend – abhängen von (+ dat) *v irreg*
sep
It depends – Es kommt darauf an
deposit – (down payment) Anzahlung
(-en) *nf*
deposit – (on empty bottle) Pfand *nm*
deposit – (against damage) Kaution
(-en) *nf*
deposit – hinlegen *v reg sep*
depressed – deprimiert *adj*
depressing – deprimierend *adj*

---

describe – beschreiben *v irreg*
description – Beschreibung (-en) *nf*
desert – Wüste (-n) *nf*
deserve – verdienen *v reg* †
design – Modell (-e) *nnt*
designer – (male) Designer (-) *nm*
designer – (female) Designerin (-nen) *nf*
desire – Wunsch (Wünsche) *nm*
desire – wünschen *v reg*
desk – Schreibtisch (-e) *nm*
desperate – verzweifelt *adj*
dessert – (pudding) Nachtisch (-e) *nm*
dessert spoon – Eßlöffel (-) *nm*
destination – Ziel (-e) *nnt*
destroy – zerstören *v reg* †
detached house – Einfamilienhaus (-häuser) *nnt*
detail – Einzelheit (-en) *nf*
detective – Detektiv (-e) *nm*
detective film – Kriminalfilm (-e) *nm*
detective story – Krimi (-s) *nm*
detention – Nachsitzen *nnt*
  be in detention – nachsitzen müssen *v irreg*
develop – entwickeln *v reg* †
development – Entwicklung (-en) *nf*
diabetes – Zuckerkrankheit *nf*
diabetic – zuckerkrank *adj*
dial – wählen *v reg*
dialling code – Vorwahl (-en) *nf*
dial the number – die Nummer wählen *v reg*
diarrhoea – Durchfall *nm*
diary – (appointment) Kalender (-) *nm*
diary – (reminiscences) Tagebuch (-bücher) *nnt*
dice – Würfel (-) *nm*
  throw dice – würfeln *v reg*
dictionary – Wörterbuch (-bücher) *nnt*
did – *see machen*

die – sterben* *v irreg*
diesel – Diesel *nm*
diet – Diät (-en) *nf*
  be on a diet – eine Schlankheitskur machen *v reg*
difference – Unterschied (-e) *nm*
different – (not the same) verschieden *adj*
different – (varied) unterschiedlich *adj*
differently – anders *adv*
difficult – schwierig *adj*
difficult – schwer *adj*
difficulty – Schwierigkeit (-en) *nf*
  have difficulty – Schwierigkeiten haben *v irreg*
dim – (stupid) dumm *adj*
din – Krach (Kräche) *nm*
dinghy – (inflatable) Schlauchboot (-e) *nnt*
dinghy – (sailing) Segelboot (-e) *nnt*
dining car – Speisewagen (-) *nm*
dining hall – Speisesaal (-säle) *nm*
dining room – Eßzimmer (-) *nnt*
dinner – (evening meal) Abendessen (-) *nnt*
dinner hour – (lunch time) Mittagspause (-n) *nf*
dinosaur – Dinosaurier (-) *nm*
direct – direkt *adj*
direction – Richtung (-en) *nf*
  in the direction of – in Richtung
  in the opposite direction – in entgegengesetzter Richtung
  in all directions – in alle Richtungen
directly – direkt *adv*
dirty – schmutzig, dreckig *adj*
disadvantage – Nachteil (-e) *nm*
disagreeable – unangenehm *adj*
disappear – verschwinden* *v irreg*
disappointed – enttäuscht *adj*
disappointing – enttäuschend *adj*

---

nm - noun masculine	*nf* - noun feminine	*nnt* - noun neuter	*npl* - noun plural
nom- nominative	*acc* - accusative	*gen* - genitive	*dat* - dative

disaster – Katastrophe (-n) *nf*
disastrous – katastrophal *adj*
disc – (record) Schallplatte (-n) *nf*
disco – Disko (-s) *nf coll*
discount – Rabatt (-e) *nm*
discouraged – entmutigt *adj*
discover – entdecken *v reg* †
discuss – diskutieren über (+ acc) *v reg* †
discussion – Diskussion (-en) *nf*
disgraceful – schändlich *adj*
disgusted – verekelt *adj*
disgusting – ekelhaft *adj*
dish – (plate) Schüssel (-n) *nf*
dish – (recipe) Gericht (-e) *nnt*
  dish of the day – Tagesgericht (-e) *nnt*
dishwasher – Spülmaschine (-n) *nf*
disk – (computer) Diskette (-n) *nf*
disk drive – Diskettenlaufwerk (-e) *nnt*
display – Ausstellung (-en) *nf*
dissatisfied – unzufrieden *adj*
distance – Entfernung (-en) *nf*
  in the distance – in der Ferne
distant – fern *adj*
distinct – klar *adj*
distressed – erschüttert *adj*
district – Viertel (-) *nnt*
district of city – Stadtviertel (-) *nnt*
disturb – stören *v reg*
dive – tauchen* *v reg*
diversion – Umleitung (-en) *nf*
divide – teilen *v reg*
divorced – geschieden *adj*
DIY – basteln *v reg*
dizzy – schwindlig *adj*
  I'm dizzy – Mir ist schwindlig
do – machen *v reg*
do athletics – Leichtathletik treiben *v irreg*
do drama – Drama machen *v reg*

do (an) experiment – ein Experiment machen *v reg*
do gardening – im Garten arbeiten *v reg* †
do gymnastics – Gymnastik machen *v reg*
do homework – Hausaufgaben machen *v reg*
do housework – Hausarbeit machen *v reg*
do ironing – bügeln *v reg*
do odd jobs – kleinere Reparaturarbeiten machen *v reg*
do one's hair – sich kämmen *v reg refl*
do shopping – einkaufen *v reg sep*
do sport – Sport treiben *v irreg*
do (the) washing – die Wäsche machen *v reg*
do washing up – spülen *v reg*
do water sports – Wassersport treiben *v irreg*
do well – sich gut durchschlagen *v irreg refl sep*
Do you see? – Siehst du?
dock – (ship) anlegen *v reg sep*
doctor – (male) Arzt (Ärzte) *nm*
doctor – (female) Ärztin (-nen) *nf*
doctor's certificate – Attest (-e) *nnt*
documentary – Dokumentarfilm (-e) *nm*
dog – (male) Hund (-e) *nm*
dog – (female) Hündin (-nen) *nf*
  Beware of the dog! – Warnung vor dem Hund! Bissiger Hund!
dole – (on the) arbeitslos *adj*
doll – Puppe (-n) *nf*
domestic – häuslich *adj*
done – *see machen*
  Well done! – Gut gemacht!
don't you, doesn't he? – nicht wahr?
donkey – Esel (-) *nm*
door – Tür (-en) *nf*

---

knock on the door – an die Tür klopfen
dormitory – Schlafraum (-räume) *nm*
dose – Dosis (Dosen) *nf*
double – doppelt *adj*
double – Doppel- *pref*
double bass – Kontrabaß (-bässe) *nm*
double decker – Doppeldecker (-) *nm*
double room – Doppelzimmer (-) *nnt*
doubtful – zweifelhaft *adj*
doughnut – Berliner (-) *nm*
down – unten *adv*
lower down – weiter unten *adv*
come down, go down – hinunterkommen* *v irreg sep*
go downhill – bergab fahren* *v irreg*
downpour – Platzregen (-) *nm*
downstairs – unten *adv*
go downstairs – nach unten gehen* *v irreg*
dozen – Dutzend (-e) *nnt*
drama – Drama (Dramen) *nnt*
do drama – Drama machen *v reg*
Drat! – Verflucht! *excl*
draughts – Dame *nf*
draw – (score) unentschieden *adj*
draw – (lottery) Lotterie (-n) *nf*
draw – (picture) zeichnen *v reg*
draw – (pull) ziehen *v irreg*
drawback – Nachteil (-e) *nm*
drawer – Schublade (-n) *nf*
drawing – Zeichnung (-en) *nf*
drawn – (match) unentschieden spielen *v reg*
dreadful – furchtbar *adj*
dream – Traum (Träume) *nm*
dream – träumen *v reg*
dress – Kleid (-er) *nnt*
dress o.s. – sich anziehen *v irreg refl sep*

dresser – (sideboard) Anrichte (-n) *nf*
dressing – (medical) Verband (-bände) *nm*
dressing – (sauce) Soße (-n) *nf*
dressing gown – Morgenrock (-röcke) *nm*
dressing table – Toilettentisch (-e) *nm*
dress rehearsal – Generalprobe (-n) *nf*
drink – Getränk (-e) *nnt*
drink – trinken *v irreg*
drinkable – trinkbar *adj*
drinking water – Trinkwasser *nnt*
drive – Einfahrt (-en) *nf*
drive – (travel) fahren* *v irreg*
drive on – weiterfahren* *v irreg sep*
drive – (a car, etc) fahren *v irreg*
driver – (male) Fahrer (-) *nm*
driver – (female) Fahrerin (-nen) *nf*
driving licence – Führerschein (-e) *nm*
take a driving test – den Führerschein machen *v reg*
driving mirror – Rückspiegel (-) *nm*
drop – fallen lassen *v irreg*
drown – ertrinken* *v irreg*
drug – (medical) Medikament (-e) *nnt*
drug – (narcotic) Droge (-n) *nf*
addicted to drugs – drogensüchtig *adj*
drug dependent – drogenabhängig *adj*
drugs scene – Drogenszene (-n) *nf*
drum kit – Schlagzeug *nnt*
drunk – betrunken *adj*
dry – trocken *adj*
dry – trocknen *v reg* †
dry cleaner's – Trockenreinigung (-en) *nf*
dry one's hair – sich die Haare trocknen *v reg dat refl* †

---

nm - noun masculine   *nf* - noun feminine   *nnt* - noun neuter   *npl* - noun plural
nom - nominative   *acc* - accusative   *gen* - genitive   *dat* - dative

dryer – (clothes) Wäschetrockner (-) *nm*
  hair dryer – Fön (-e) *nm*
duck – Ente (-n) *nf*
dumb – stumm *adj*
dumbfounded – verblüfft *adj*
duration – Dauer *nf*
during – während (+ gen) *prep*
dust – Staub *nm*
dust – abstauben *v reg sep*

dustbin – Mülltonne (-n) *nf*
Dutch – holländisch *adj*
Dutchman – Holländer (-) *nm*
  The Flying Dutchman – Der
  Fliegende Holländer
Dutchwoman – Holländerin (-nen) *nf*
duty-free – zollfrei *adj*
duvet – Steppdecke (-n) *nf*
duvet cover – Steppdeckenbezug
  (-bezüge) *nm*

E

E111 certificate – E-111 Schein (-e) *nm*
each – jede *adj*
each one – jede *indef pron*
each other – einander *adv*
each time – jedesmal *adv*
ear – Ohr (-en) *nnt*
earache – Ohrenschmerzen *npl*
earring – Ohrring (-e) *nm*
earlier – früher *adv*
early – früh *adj*
earn – verdienen *v reg* †
earth – Erde (-n) *nf*
earthquake – Erdbeben (-) *nnt*
easily – einfach *adv*
east – Osten *nm*
  in the east – im Osten
  east of – östlich von (+ dat)
Easter – Ostern *npl*
  at Easter – zu Ostern
Easter Bunny – Osterhase (-n) *nm wk*
Easter egg – Osterei (-er) *nnt*
Easter holidays – Osterferien *npl*
Easter Sunday – Ostersonntag *nm*
easy – einfach *adj*
eat – essen *v irreg*

ecologist – (male) Ökologe (-n) *nm wk*
ecologist – (female) Ökologin (-en) *nf*
ecology – Ökologie (-n) *nf*
economical – sparsam *adj*
economics – Volkswirtschaft *nf*
economise – sparen *v reg*
edge – Rand (Ränder) *nm*
  on the edge – am Rand
  on the edge of town – am
  Stadtrand
edible – eßbar *adj*
Edinburgh – Edinburg
education – Ausbildung (-en) *nf*
educational – Schul~ *pref*
effective – wirksam *adj*
effort – Mühe (-n) *nf*
egg – Ei (-er) *nnt*
  a boiled egg – ein gekochtes Ei
  a hard boiled egg – ein
  hartgekochtes Ei
  fried egg – Spiegelei (-er) *nnt*
  scrambled egg – Rührei (-er) *nnt*
eh? – was? *excl*
eight – acht *adj*
eighteen – achtzehn *adj*
eighth – achte *adj*
eighty – achtzig *adj*

---

eighty-one – einundachtzig *adj*

Eire – Irland *nnt*

either ... or... – entweder ... oder ... *conj*

elastoplast® – Hansaplast® *nnt*

elbow – Ellenbogen (-) *nm*

elder – älter *adj*

elderly – alt *adj*

eldest – ältest *adj*

election – Wahl (-en) *nf*

electric(al) – Elektro- *pref*

electric(al) – elektrisch *adj*

electric cooker – Elektroherd (-e) *nm*

electrician – Elektriker (-) *nm*

electricity – Elektrizität *nf*

electric razor – Rasierapparat (-e) *nm*

electronics – Elektronik *nf*

elegant – elegant *adj*

elephant – Elefant (-en) *nm wk*

elephant's trunk – Rüssel (-) *nm*

eleven – elf *adj*

eleventh – elfte *adj*

embarrassed – geniert, verlegen *adj*

embarrassing – peinlich *adj*

embarrassment – Verlegenheit *nf*

emergency – Notfall (-fälle) *nm*
  in an emergency – im Notfall

emergency aid – Nothilfe (-n) *nf*

emergency dept – (hospital) Unfallstation (-en) *nf*

emergency doctor – Notarzt (-ärzte) *nm*

emergency exit – Notausgang (-gänge) *nm*

emergency service – Notdienst (-e) *nm*

employ – anstellen *v reg sep*

employee – (male) Arbeitnehmer (-) *nm*

employee – (female) Arbeitnehmerin (-nen) *nf*

employer – (male) Arbeitgeber (-) *nm*

employer – (female) Arbeitgeberin (-nen) *nf*

empty – leer *adj*

empty – leeren *v reg*

enclose – beilegen *v reg sep*

encourage – ermutigen *v reg* †

end – Ende (-n) *nnt*
  at the end – am Ende
  at the end of the corridor – am Ende des Ganges
  in the end – endlich *adv*

end – beenden *v reg* †, enden *v reg* †

endless – endlos *adj*

energy – Energie *nf*

engaged – (toilet) besetzt *adj*

engaged – (to marry) verlobt *adj*

engine – Motor (-en) *nm*

engineer – Ingenieur (-e) *nm*

engineering drawing – technisches Zeichnen *nnt*

England – England *nnt*

English – englisch *adj*

English – (language) Englisch *nnt*
  in English – auf englisch
  English speaking – englischsprachig *adj*

English Channel – Kanal *nm*

English lesson – Englischstunde (-n) *nf*

Englishman – Engländer (-) *nm*

Englishwoman – Engländerin (-nen) *nf*

enjoy – genießen *v irreg*

Enjoy your meal! – Guten Appetit!, Mahlzeit! *excl*

enjoyable – angenehm *adj*

enormous – riesig, riesengroß *adj*

enough – genug *adj*
  I've had enough – (food) Ich bin satt
  I've had enough – (annoyance) Ich habe die Nase voll *coll*

enquire about – sich erkundigen nach (+ dat) *v reg refl* †
enter – eintreten* *v irreg sep*
entertainment – Unterhaltung (-en) *nf*
enthusiasm – Begeisterung *nf*
enthusiastic about – begeistert von (+ dat) *adj*
entirely – völlig *adv*
entrance – (way in) Eingang (-gänge) *nm*
entrance – (road in) Einfahrt (-en) *nf*
entrance – (price) Eintritt (-e) *nm*
entrance examination – Eintrittsprüfung (-en) *nf*
entrance fee – Eintrittsgeld (-er) *nnt*
entrance ticket – Eintrittskarte (-n) *nf*
envelope – Umschlag (Umschläge) *nm*
environment – Umwelt *nf*
environmentally aware – umweltbewußt *adj*
environmentally friendly – umweltfreundlich *adj*
environmental protection – Umweltschutz *nm*
envy – beneiden *v reg* †
equal – gleich *adj*
equality – Gleichheit (-en) *nf*
equally – genau so *adv*
equipment – Ausrüstung (-en) *nf*
equivalent – entsprechend *adj*, gleichwertig *adj*
equivalent – Gegenstück (-e) *nnt*
error – Fehler (-) *nm*
escalator – Rolltreppe (-n) *nf*
escape – entkommen* *v irreg*
especially – besonders *adv*
essay – Aufsatz (-sätze) *nm*
essential – unentbehrlich *adj*
establish – feststellen *v reg sep*
establishment – Einrichtung (-en) *nf*

estate agent – Immobilienmakler (-) *nm*
EU – Europäische Union *nf*
Eurocheque – Euroscheck (-s) *nm*
Europe – Europa *nnt*
European – europäisch *adj*
European person – (male) Europäer (-) *nm*
European person – (female) Europäerin (-nen) *nf*
the European Union – die Europäische Union *nf*
even – (not odd) gerade *adj*
even – sogar *adv*
even better – noch besser *adj*
even though – obwohl *sub conj*
evening – Abend (-e) *nm*
    Good Evening! – Guten Abend!
    See you this evening! – Bis heute abend!
evening meal – (cold) Abendbrot (-e) *nnt*
evening meal – (hot) Abendessen (-) *nnt*
evenly – gleichmäßig *adj*
event – Ereignis (-se) *nnt*
eventually – endlich *adv*
ever – je *adv*
ever since – seitdem *sub conj*
every – (all) alle *adj*
every – (each) jede *adj*
everybody – alle *pron*
everyday – alltäglich *adj*
every day – jeden Tag
every evening – jeden Abend
everyone – alle *pron*
every one – jeder einzelne *pron*
every ten minutes – alle zehn Minuten
everything – alles
every time – jedesmal *adv*
every week – jede Woche
everywhere – überall *adv*

---

adj - adjective	*v reg* - verb regular	*v sep* - verb separable	† - see verb info
prep - preposition	*v irreg* - verb irregular	*v refl* - verb reflexive	* - takes sein

every year – jedes Jahr
evidence – Beweis (-e) *nm*
evil – Böse *nnt*
ex- – ehemalig *adj*
exact – genau *adj*
examination – (degree) Staatsexamen (-) *nf*
examination – (medical) Untersuchung (-en) *nf*
examination – (school) Prüfung (-en) *nf*
  fail an exam – in einer Prüfung durchfallen* *v irreg sep*
  pass an exam – eine Prüfung bestehen *v irreg*
  take an exam – eine Prüfung schreiben *v irreg*
examine – prüfen *v reg*
examine – (medical) untersuchen *v reg insep*
example – Beispiel (-e) *nnt*
  for example – zum Beispiel
excellent – ausgezeichnet *adj*
except – außer (+ dat) *prep*
exception – Ausnahme (-n) *nf*
exchange – (money) Wechsel (-) *nm*
exchange – (school) Austausch *nm*
  go on an exchange – einen Austausch machen *v reg*
exchange rate – Wechselkurs (-e) *nm*
exciting – aufregend, spannend *adj*
exclaim – ausrufen *v irreg sep*
exclamation mark (!) – Ausrufezeichen (-) *nnt*
excursion – Ausflug (-flüge) *nm*
excuse – Ausrede (-n) *nf*
  excuse o.s. – sich entschuldigen bei (+ dat) *v reg refl* †
Excuse me! – Entschuldigen Sie, bitte!

exercise – (sport) körperliche Bewegung (-en) *nf*
exercise – (school) Aufgabe (-n) *nf*
exercise book – Heft (-e) *nnt*
exhaust – (car) Auspuff (-e) *nm*
exhausted – erschöpft *adj*
exhaust fumes – Abgase *npl*
exhibition – Ausstellung (-en) *nf*
exist – existieren *v reg* †
exit – (motorway) Ausfahrt (-en) *nf*
exit – (on foot) Ausgang (-gänge) *nm*
  emergency exit – Notausgang (-gänge) *nm*
expect – erwarten *v reg* †
expel – von der Schule verweisen *v irreg*
expensive – teuer *adj*
experience – Erfahrung (-en) *nf*
experience – erfahren *v irreg*
experiment – Versuch (-e) *nm*
explain – erklären *v reg* †
explanation – Erklärung (-en) *nf*
explore – erforschen *v reg* †
express train – D-Zug, Durchgangszug (D-Züge) *nm*
expression – Ausdruck (-e) *nm*
extinguish – löschen *v reg*
extra – zusätzlich *adj*
extra charge – Zuschlag (-schläge) *nm*
extraordinary – außergewöhnlich *adj*
extreme – extrem *adj*
eye – Auge (-n) *nnt*
eyebrow – Augenbraue (-n) *nf*
eye shadow – Lidschatten *nm*
eye witness – Augenzeuge (-n) *nm wk*
eye witness – Augenzeugin (-nen) *nf*

F

fabulous – phantastisch *adj*
face – Gesicht (-er) *nnt*
fact – Tatsache (-n) *nf*
 in fact – tatsächlich *adv*
factory – Fabrik (-en) *nf*
factory worker – (male)
 Fabrikarbeiter (-) *nm*
factory worker – (female)
 Fabrikarbeiterin (-nen) *nf*
fail – durchfallen* *v irreg sep*
 fail an exam – eine Prüfung nicht
 bestehen *v irreg*
failed – durchgefallen *adj*
faint – schwach *adj*
faint – (swoon) ohnmächtig werden*
 v irreg
fair – (colour) blond *adj*
fair – (average) mittelmäßig *adj*
fair – (just) fair *adj*, gerecht *adj*
 It's not fair! – Das ist nicht
 gerecht!
fair – (weather) schön *adj*
fair – (amusement) Jahrmarkt
 (-märkte) *nm*
fairly – ziemlich *adv*
fairy tale – Märchen (-) *nnt*
faithfully, Yours – mit freundlichen
 Grüßen *adv*
fall – fallen* *v irreg*
 fall asleep – einschlafen* *v irreg*
 sep
 fall ill – krank werden* *v irreg*
false – falsch *adj*
familiar – bekannt *adj*
family – Familie (-n) *nf*
family room – (hotel)
 Familienzimmer (-) *nnt*
famous – berühmt *adj*
fan – (supporter) Fan (-s) *nm*
fancy dress – Maskenkostüm (-e) *nnt*

fantastic – phantastisch *adj*
far away – weit *adj*
 Is it far? – Ist es weit?
far away – weit entfernt *adv*
fare – Fahrgeld (-er) *nnt*
fare dodger – (male) Schwarzfahrer (-)
 nm
fare dodger – (female)
 Schwarzfahrerin (-nen) *nf*
farm – Bauernhof (-höfe) *nm*
farmer – (male)Bauer (-n) *nm wk*
farmer – (female) Bäuerin (-nen) *nf*
farmhouse – Bauernhaus (-häuser)
 nnt
farm worker – Landarbeiter(-) *nm*
fascinating – faszinierend *adj*
fashion – Mode (-n) *nf*
fashion designer – (male)
 Modezeichner (-) *nm*
fashion designer – (female)
 Modezeichnerin (-nen) *nf*
fashionable – modisch *adj*
fast – schnell *adj*
 My watch is fast – Meine Uhr
 geht vor
fasten – festmachen *v reg sep*
fasten seat belt – sich anschnallen
 v reg refl sep
fast train – D-Zug (-Züge) *nm*
fat – dick *adj*
father – Vater (Väter) *nm*
Father Christmas –
 Weihnachtsmann (-männer) *nm*
father-in-law – Schwiegervater
 (-väter) *nm*
fault – (defect) Defekt (-) *nm*
fault – (blame) Schuld *nf*
 It's my fault – Es ist meine Schuld
favourable – günstig
favourite – Liebling *nm*
favourite – Lieblings- *pref*

---

adj - adjective	*v reg* - verb regular	*v sep* - verb separable	† - see verb info
prep - preposition	*v irreg* - verb irregular	*v refl* - verb reflexive	* - takes sein

fax – Fax (-) *nnt*
fax – faxen *v reg*
fax machine – Faxgerät (-e) *nnt*
fax number – Faxnummer (-n) *nf*
fear – Furcht *nf*
feather – Feder (-n) *nf*
February – Februar *nm*
  in February – im Februar
I'm fed up – (annoyed) Ich habe die
  Nase voll
fee – Gebühr (-en) *nf*
feed the cat – die Katze füttern *v reg*
feel – (think) meinen *v reg*
feel – (person) sich fühlen *v reg refl*
  I feel awful – Ich fühle mich unwohl
  I feel at ease – Ich fühle mich wohl
  I feel cold – Mir ist kalt
  I feel happy – Ich bin glücklich
  I feel hot – Mir ist warm
  I feel hungry – Ich habe Hunger
  I feel ill – Ich fühle mich unwohl
  I feel like – (want) Ich möchte
  I feel sick – Mir ist übel
  I feel sleepy – Ich bin schläfrig
  I feel thirsty – Ich habe Durst
  I feel tired – Ich bin müde
  I feel well – Ich fühle mich wohl
feeling – Gefühl (-e) *nnt*
feet – *see foot*
fell – *see fall*
felt – *see feel*
felt tip pen – Filzstift (-e) *nm*
female – weiblich *adj*
female – (animals) Weibchen (-) *nnt*
feminine – (grammar) feminin *adj*
fence – Zaun (Zäune) *nm*
ferret – Frettchen (-) *nnt*
ferry – Fähre (-n) *nf*
ferry terminal – Fährhafen (-häfen)
  nm
festival – Fest (-e) *nnt*
fetch – holen *v reg*

fête – Fest (-e) *nnt*
fever – Fieber (-) *nnt*
few – (not many) wenige *adj*
  a few – (some) ein paar, einige *adj*
  A few people were there – Ein
  paar Leute waren da
fewer than – weniger als
fiancé – Verlobte *nm* ‡
fiancée – Verlobte *nf* ‡
fiddle – (violin) Geige (-n) *nf*
field – Feld (-er) *nnt*
fierce – wild *adj*
fifteen – fünfzehn *adj*
fifth – fünfte *adj*
fifty – fünfzig *adj*
fight – kämpfen *v reg*
fight – Kampf (Kämpfe) *nm*
figure – Figur (-en) *nf*
file – (computer) Datei (-en) *nf*
file – (ring binder) Ordner (-) *nm*
fill – füllen *v reg*
fill in a form – ein Formular
  ausfüllen *v reg sep*
filling station – Tankstelle (-n) *nf*
filling – (teeth) Plombe (-n) *nf*
fill up – (petrol, diesel) volltanken
  v reg sep
film – Film (-e) *nm*
  detective film – Detektivfilm (-e)
  nm
  a dubbed film – ein
  synchronisierter Film (-e) *nm*
  sci-fi film – Science-Fiction-Film
  (-e) *nm*
film star – Filmstar (-s) *nm*
filter coffee – Filterkaffee *nm*
filthy – schmutzig *adj*
final – letzte *adj*
final – (sport) Endspiel (-e) *nnt*
finally – schließlich *adv*
find – finden *v irreg*
find out – herausfinden *v irreg sep*

---

nm - noun masculine   *nf* - noun feminine   *nnt* - noun neuter   *npl* - noun plural
nom- nominative   *acc* - accusative   *gen* - genitive   *dat* - dative

fine – (delicate) fein *adj*
fine – (beautiful) schön *adj*
  I'm fine – es geht mir gut
fine – (punishment) Geldstrafe (-n) *nf*
fine! – in Ordnung!
finger – Finger (-) *nm*
finish – beenden *v reg* †
  School is finished – Die Schule
  ist aus
finish – (stop doing) aufhören *v reg*
  sep
finish – (sport) ans Ziel kommen*
  v irreg
Finland – Finnland *nnt*
Finnish – finnisch *adj*
Finnish person – (male) Finne (-n)
  nm wk
Finnish person – (female) Finnin
  (-nen) *nf*
fir (tree) – Tannenbaum (-bäume) *nm*
fire – Feuer (-) *nnt*
fire – (accidental/malicious) Brand
  (Brände) *nm*
  there is a fire – es brennt
fire alarm – Feueralarm (-e) *nm*
fire brigade – Feuerwehr (-en) *nf*
fire engine – Feuerwehrwagen (-) *nm*
fire escape – Feuerleiter (-n) *nf*
fireman – Feuerwehrmann (-männer)
  nm
fire-place – Kamin (e) *nm*
firework – Feuerwerk *nnt, no pl*
firm – fest *adj*
firm – Firma (Firmen) *nf*
first – erste *adj*
  at first – zuerst *adv*
  on the first floor – im ersten Stock
first aid – Erste Hilfe *nf*
first aid kit – Verbandkasten
  (-kästen) *nm*
first class ticket – Fahrkarte erster
  Klasse *nf*

  a first class ticket, please –
  einmal erster Klasse, bitte
firstly – erstens *adv*
first name – Vorname (-n) *nm wk*
first of all – zuerst *adv*
fish – Fisch (-e) *nm*
fish – angeln *v reg*
fish finger – Fischstäbchen (-) *nnt*
fisherman – Fischer (-) *nm*
fisherwoman – Fischerin (-nen) *nf*
fishing – Angeln *nnt*
  go fishing – angeln *v reg*
fishing port – Fischereihafen (-häfen)
  nm
fishing rod – Angelrute (-n) *nf*
fishmonger – (male) Fischhändler (-)
  nm
fishmonger – (female) Fischhändlerin
  (-nen) *nf*
  I'm going to the fish shop – Ich
  gehe ins Fischgeschäft
fist – Faust (Fäuste) *nf*
fit – (healthy) gesund *adj*
fit – (suitable) geeignet *adj*
  It does not fit me – Es paßt mir
  nicht
fitness – (health) Gesundheit *nf*
fitness – (condition) Fitneß *nf*
fitted carpet – Teppichboden
  (-böden) *nm*
fitting room – Umkleidekabine (-n)
  nf
five – fünf *adj*
fix – (repair) reparieren *v reg* †
fixed – fest *adj*
fixture – Spiel (-e) *nnt*
fizzy – sprudelnd *adj*
flag – Fahne (-n) *nf*
flame – Flamme (-n) *nf*
  go up in flames – brennen *v irreg*
flan – Torte (-n) *nf*
flannel – Waschlappen (-) *nm*
flash of lightning – Blitz (-e) *nm*

---

adj - adjective	*v reg* - verb regular	*v sep* - verb separable	† - see verb info
prep - preposition	*v irreg* - verb irregular	*v refl* - verb reflexive	* - takes sein

flat – Wohnung (-en) *nf*
block of flats – Wohnblock (-s) *nm*
flat – (level) flach *adj*
flat – (of tyre, etc) platt *adj*
flat tyre – Reifenpanne (-n) *nf*
flavour – Geschmack (Geschmäcke) *nm*
lemon flavoured – mit Zitronengeschmack
flea – Floh (Flöhe) *nm*
flea market – Flohmarkt (-märkte) *nm*
flee – fliehen* *v irreg*
flight – (plane) Flug (Flüge) *nm*
flight – (departure) Abflug (Abflüge) *nm*
flight of stairs – Treppe (-n) *nf*
fling – werfen *v irreg*
flip-flops – Sandale (-n) *nf*
flirt – flirten *v reg* †
float – schwimmen* *v irreg*
flock – Herde (-n) *nf*
flood – Überschwemmung (-en) *nf*
floor – (ground) Fußboden (-böden) *nm*
floor – Stock (Stockwerke) *nm*
on the first floor – im ersten Stock
on the ground floor – im Erdgeschoß
on the next floor – im nächsten Stock
on the top floor – im obersten Stock
floppy disk – Diskette (-n) *nf*
flour – Mehl *nnt*
flow – fließen* *v irreg*
flower – Blume (-n) *nf*
flower bed – Blumenbeet (-n) *nnt*
flower vase – Vase (-n) *nf*
flu – Grippe *nf*
fluent – (speech) fließend *adj*
flute – Flöte (-n) *nf*

fly – (insect) Fliege (-n) *nf*
fly – fliegen* *v irreg*
flying – (in plane) Fliegen *nnt*
fog – Nebel *nm*
foggy – neblig *adj*
fold – falten *v reg* †
folder – (file) Schnellhefter (-) *nm*
folk – Leute *npl*
folk music – Volksmusik *nf*
folk song – Volkslied (-er) *nnt*
follow – folgen* (+ dat) *v reg*
followed by – gefolgt von (+ dat) *adj*
following – folgend *adj*
food – Essen *nnt*
food processor – Küchenmaschine (-n) *nf*
fool – (male) Narr (-en) *nm wk*
fool – (female) Närrin (-nen) *nf*
foolish – albern *adj*
foot – Fuß (Füße) *nm*
on foot – zu Fuß
football – Fußball (-bälle) *nm*
football boots – Fußballschuhe *npl*
footballer – Fußballspieler (-) *nm*
football field – Fußballplatz (-plätze) *nm*
football match – Fußballspiel (-e) *nnt*
footpath – Fußweg (-e) *nm*
footstep – Schritt (-e) *nm*
for – denn *co-ord conj*
for – weil *sub conj*
for – für (+ acc) *prep*
for – (since) seit (+ dat) *prep*
for ever – für immer *adv*
for example – zum Beispiel
for hire – zu vermieten
for sale – zu verkaufen
forbid – verbieten *v irreg*
forbidden – verboten *adj*
force – zwingen *v irreg*

---

nm - noun masculine	*nf* - noun feminine	*nnt* - noun neuter	*npl* - noun plural
nom- nominative	*acc* - accusative	*gen* - genitive	*dat* - dative

forecast – (weather) Wettervorhersage (-n) *nf*

foreign – ausländisch *adj*

foreigner – (male) Ausländer (-) *nm*

foreigner – (female) Ausländerin (-nen) *nf*

forest – Wald (Wälder) *nm*

forget – vergessen *v irreg*

forgive – vergeben *v irreg*

fork – Gabel (-n) *nf*

fork out – blechen *v reg coll*

form – (class) Klasse (-n) *nf*

form – (paper) Formular (-e) *nnt*

former – (previous) früher *adj*, ehemalig *adj*

fortnight – vierzehn Tage

fortunate – glücklich *adj*

fortunately – glücklicherweise *adv*

forty – vierzig *adj*

forty-one – einundvierzig *adj*

forwards – vorwärts *adv*

  go forward – vorangehen* *v irreg sep*

forward – (sport) Stürmer (-) *nm*

found – *see* find

fountain pen – Füller (-) *nm*

four – vier *adj*

fourteen – vierzehn *adj*

fourth – vierte *adj*

fragile – zerbrechlich *adj*

frame – (photo, etc) Rahmen (-) *nm*

frame – (spectacles) Gestell (-e) *nnt*

franc – (Swiss) Franken (-) *nm*

franc – (French) Franc (-s) *nm*

France – Frankreich *nnt*

frank – offen *adj*

frankfurter – Bockwurst (-würste) *nf*

free – frei *adj*, kostenlos *adj*

freedom – Freiheit (-en) *nf*

free time – Freizeit *nf*

freeze – frieren *v irreg*

  It is freezing – (ice) Es friert

  It is freezing – Es ist sehr kalt

  I'm freezing – Mir friert's

freezer – Tiefkühltruhe (-n) *nf*

French – französisch *adj*

  in French – auf französisch

French – (language) Französisch *nnt*

French bean – grüne Bohne (-n) *nf*

French fries – Pommes frites *npl*

French person – (male) Franzose (n) *nm wk*

French person – (female) Französin (-nen) *nf*

frequent – häufig *adj*

frequently – oft *adv*

fresh – frisch *adj*

Friday – Freitag (-e) *nm*

  on Friday – am Freitag

  Good Friday – Karfreitag *nm*

fridge – Kühlschrank (-schränke) *nm*

friend – (male) Freund (-e) *nm*

friend – (female) Freundin (-nen) *nf*

friendly – freundlich *adj*

friendly with – befreundet mit (+ dat) *adj*

friendship – Freundschaft (-en) *nf*

fright – Schreck (-e) *nm*

frightened – erschrocken *adj*

  be frightened of – Angst haben vor (+ dat) *v irreg*

frightening – schrecklich *adj*

fringe – Pony (-s) *nm*

frog – Frosch (Frösche) *nm*

from – von (+ dat) *prep*

from – (out of) aus (+ dat) *prep*

from – (according to) nach (+ dat) *prep*

from – (date, prices) ab (+ dat) *prep*

front – Vorderseite (-n) *nf*

  in front of – vor (+ acc/dat) *prep*

front door – Haustür (-en) *nf*

front wheel – Vorderrad (-räder) *nnt*

frost – Frost *nm*

---

frosty – frostig *adj*
frown – die Stirn runzeln *v reg*
frozen – gefroren *adj*
frozen – (food) tiefgefroren *adj*
fruit – Obst *nnt*
  stewed fruit – Kompott (-e) *nnt*
fruit juice – Fruchtsaft (-säfte) *nm*
fruit machine – Spielautomat (-en)
  nm wk
fruits – Obstsorten *npl*
fruit seller – Obsthändler (-) *nm*
fruit tree – Obstbaum (-bäume) *nm*
fry – braten *v irreg*
frying pan – Pfanne (-n) *nf*
full – voll *adj*
  at full fare – zum vollen Fahrpreis
full – (well fed) satt *adj*
full board – Vollpension *nf*
full of – voll *adj*
full stop (.) – Punkt (-e) *nm*
at full speed – mit
  Höchstgeschwindigkeit
full time – (job) ganztägig *adj*
fun – Spaß (Späße) *nm*

be fun – Spaß machen *v reg*
It's fun – Es macht (mir) Spaß
have fun – Spaß haben *v irreg*
make fun of – veräppeln *v reg* †
  coll
fun fair – Jahrmarkt (-märkte) *nm*
funny – (amusing) komisch *adj*
funny – (strange) seltsam *adj*
furious – wütend *adj*
furnished – möbliert *adj*
furniture – Möbel *npl*
  piece of furniture – Möbelstück
  (-e) *nnt*
further – weiter *adv*
further education – Weiterbildung
  nf
fuss – Theater *nnt coll*
  make a fuss about sthg –
    Theater machen über (+ acc)
    v reg coll
fussy – pingelig *adj coll*
future – Zukunft *nf*
future – künftig *adj*
  in future – in Zukunft *adv*

G

gale – Sturm (Stürme) *nm*
gallery – Galerie (-n) *nf*
  art gallery – Gemäldegalerie (-n)
  nf
game – Spiel (-e) *nnt*
  arcade game – Spielautomat (-en)
  nm wk
  board game – Brettspiel (-e) *nnt*
  computer game – Computerspiel
  (-e) *nnt*
  video game – Videospiel (-e) *nnt*
game of tennis – Tennisspiel (-e) *nnt*

games room – Spielraum (-räume)
  nm
games – Sport *nm*
  do games – Sport treiben *v irreg*
garage – (petrol) Tankstelle (-n) *nf*
garage – (repair) Werkstatt (-stätten)
  nf
garage – (house) Garage (-n) *nf*
garage owner – Tankstellenbesitzer
  (-) *nm*
garden – Garten (Gärten) *nm*
gardener – Gärtner (-) *nm*
gardening – Gartenarbeit *nf*

do the gardening – im Garten arbeiten *v reg* †

garlic – Knoblauch *nm*

garment – Kleidungsstück (-e) *nnt*

gas – Gas (-e) *nnt*

gas cooker – Gasherd (-e) *nm*

gas cylinder – Gasflasche (-n) *nf*

gate – Tor (-e) *nnt*

gate-crash – hereinplatzen* *v reg sep coll*

gather – (collect) sammeln *v reg*

GB – Großbritannien *nnt*

gear – (car) Gang (Gänge) *nm*

gel – (hair) Gel *nnt*

Gemini – Zwillinge

gender – Geschlecht (-er) *nnt*

general – allgemein *adj*
    in general – im allgemeinen *adv*

generous – großzügig *adj*

Geneva – Genf

genitive – Genitiv *nnt*

gentle – zart, sanft *adj*

gentleman – Herr (-en) *nm wk*

Gentlemen – Herren *npl*

genuine – echt *adj*

geography – Erdkunde *nf*, Geographie *nf*

geology – Geologie *nf*

gerbil – Wüstenspringmaus (-mäuse) *nf*

German – deutsch *adj*

German – (language) Deutsch *nnt*
    in German – auf deutsch

German person – Deutsche *nmf* ‡

Germany – Deutschland *nnt*

get – (become) werden* *v irreg*

get – (buy) kaufen *v reg*

get – (fetch) holen *v reg*

get – (receive) bekommen *v irreg*, kriegen *v reg coll*

get – (understand) verstehen *v irreg*

get a divorce – sich scheiden lassen *v irreg refl*

get about – (travel) fahren* *v irreg*

get across – (to the other side) überqueren *v reg insep*

get along – (manage) zurechtkommen* *v irreg sep*

get angry – böse werden* *v irreg*

get annoyed – sich ärgern *v reg refl*

get away – entkommen* *v irreg*

get back – zurückkommen* *v irreg sep*

get better – sich erholen *v reg refl* †

get changed – sich umziehen *v irreg refl sep*

get done – etwas machen lassen *v irreg*

get dressed – sich anziehen *v irreg refl sep*

get hurt – verletzt werden* *v irreg*

get in – (arrive) ankommen* *v irreg sep*

get injured – sich verletzen *v reg refl* †

get into – (bus, etc) einsteigen* in (+ acc) *v irreg sep*

get lost – (on foot) sich verlaufen *v irreg refl*

get lost – (in car) sich verfahren *v irreg refl*

get married – heiraten *v reg*

get off – (bus, etc) aussteigen* aus (+ dat) *v irreg sep*

get on – (succeed) vorankommen* *v irreg sep*

get on the train – in den Zug einsteigen* *v irreg sep*

get on with – (person) sich verstehen mit (+ dat) *v irreg refl*

get over – (illness) sich erholen *v reg refl* †

get ready – sich fertig machen *v reg refl*

get rid of – loswerden* *v irreg sep*

get round – (avoid) vermeiden *v irreg*

get stung – gestochen werden* *v irreg*
get the bus – mit dem Bus fahren*
v irreg
get to – (arrive) ankommen* in (+ dat)
v irreg sep
get to – (reach) erreichen *v reg* †
get to know – kennenlernen *v reg sep*
get used to – sich gewöhnen an
(+ acc) *v reg refl* †
get undressed – sich ausziehen
v irreg refl sep
get up – aufstehen* *v irreg sep*
ghost – Gespenst (-er) *nnt*
giant – Riese (-n) *nm wk*
gift – Geschenk (-e) *nnt*
gift wrap – als Geschenk einpacken
v reg sep
gifted – begabt *adj*
gig – Konzert (-e) *nnt*
gigantic – riesig *adj*
giggle – kichern *v reg*
ginger – (hair) rothaarig *adj*
ginger – Ingwer *nm*
ginger bread – Lebkuchen *nm*
girl – Mädchen (-) *nnt*
girlfriend – Freundin (-nen) *nf*
give – geben *v irreg*
  Give me... – (formal) Geben Sie mir
  Give me... – (informal) Gib mir
give – (gift) schenken *v reg*
give back – zurückgeben *v irreg sep*
give in – nachgeben *v irreg sep*
give up – aufgeben *v irreg sep*
glacier – Gletscher (-) *nm*
glad – zufrieden *adj*
gladly – gern *adv*
glance – Blick (-e) *nm*
glass – (drinking) Glas (Gläser) *nnt*
glass – (mirror) Spiegel (-) *nm*
glass – (pane of) Glasscheibe (-n) *nf*
glasses – (pair of) Brille (-n) *nf*
glen – Tal (Täler) *nnt*

global – global *adj*
gloomy – düster *adj*
glove – Handschuh (-e) *nm*
glow – glühen *v reg*
glue – Klebstoff (-e) *nm*
GNVQ Level 2 –
  Berufsfachschulreife *nf*
GNVQ Level 3 – Fachhochschulreife
nf
go – (on foot) gehen* *v irreg*
go – (travel) fahren* *v irreg*
go – (become) werden* *v irreg*
go – (depart) abfahren* *v irreg sep*
go – (function) funktionieren *v reg* †
go – (leave house, etc) das Haus
  verlassen *v irreg*
go – (vanish) verschwinden* *v irreg*
go and fetch someone – holen *v reg*
go and see – besuchen *v reg* †
go away – weggehen* *v irreg sep*
Go away! – Hau ab! *excl*
go babysitting – babysitten gehen*
v irreg
go back – zurückgehen* *v irreg sep*
go by car – mit dem Auto fahren*
v irreg
go boating – Boot fahren* *v irreg*
go camping – zelten *v reg* †
go down the street – die Straße
  entlang gehen* *v irreg sep*
go downstairs – nach unten gehen*
v irreg
go fishing – angeln gehen* *v irreg*
go for – (fetch) holen *v reg*
go for a bike ride – eine Radtour
  machen *v reg*
go for a walk – einen Spaziergang
  machen *v reg*
go home – nach Hause gehen* *v irreg*
go horse riding – reiten gehen*
v irreg
go in (to) – hineingehen* *v irreg sep*

---

nm - noun masculine	*nf* - noun feminine	*nnt* - noun neuter	*npl* - noun plural
nom- nominative	*acc* - accusative	*gen* - genitive	*dat* - dative

go in for an exam – eine Prüfung machen *v reg*

go jogging – joggen *v reg*

go near to – sich nähern (+ dat) *v reg refl*

go off – (depart) weggehen* *v irreg sep*

go off – (food) verfaulen* *v reg* †

go on – (continue) fortfahren* *v irreg sep*

go on an exchange – am Austausch teilnehmen *v irreg sep*

go on foot – zu Fuß gehen* *v irreg*

go on holiday – in Urlaub fahren* *v irreg*

go out – hinausgehen* *v irreg sep*

go out – (light) ausgehen* *v irreg sep*

go out with – ausgehen* mit (+ dat) *v irreg sep*

go red – rot werden* *v irreg*

go round the shops – einen Einkaufsbummel machen *v reg*

go round town – einen Stadtbummel machen *v reg*

go sailing – segeln gehen* *v irreg*

go shopping – einkaufen gehen* *v irreg*

go skiing – skifahren* *v irreg sep*

Go straight on! – Gehen Sie geradeaus!

Go that way! – Gehen Sie in diese Richtung!

go to bed – ins Bett gehen* *v irreg*

go upstairs – nach oben gehen* *v irreg*

go walking – spazieren gehen* *v irreg*

go window shopping – einen Schaufensterbummel machen *v reg*

go windsurfing – windsurfen gehen* *v irreg*

go-kart – Go-kart (-s) *nm*

go-karting – Go-kart-Fahren *nnt*

to go go-karting – Go-kart fahren* *v irreg*

goal – Ziel (-e) *nnt*

goal – (sport) Tor (-e) *nnt*

goalkeeper – Torwart (-e) *nm*

goalless draw – Null zu Null Unentschieden *nnt*

goalpost – Torpfosten (-) *nm*

goat – Ziege (-n) *nf*

God – Gott (Götter) *nm*

goggles – (pair of) Schutzbrille (-n) *nf*

going to – in Richtung

gold – Gold *nnt*

  made of gold – aus Gold

golden – golden *adj*

goldfish – Goldfisch (-e) *nm*

golf – Golf *nm*

golf course – Golfplatz (-plätze) *nm*

gone – *see fahren*, gehen**

  It's all gone – Es ist alle

good – gut *adj*

  good at – gut in (+ dat)

good – (well-behaved) brav *adj*

good – (well) gut *adv*

Good afternoon! – Guten Tag! *excl*

Goodbye! – Auf Wiedersehen! *excl*

say goodbye – sich verabschieden *v reg refl* †

Good evening! – Guten Abend! *excl*

Good Friday – Karfreitag *nm*

Good idea! – Gute Idee! *excl*

good looking – gutaussehend *adj*

Good luck! – Viel Glück! *excl*

Good morning! – Guten Morgen! *excl*

goodness – Güte *nf*

good news – eine gute Nachricht

Good night! – Gute Nacht! *excl*

good-tempered – gut gelaunt *adj*

good value – günstig *adj*, preiswert *adj*

goose – Gans (Gänse) *nf*

---

gooseberry – Stachelbeere (-n) *nf*
gorgeous – herrlich *adj*
got to – (must) müssen *v irreg*
got – (have) haben *v irreg*
grab – greifen *v irreg*
grade – (mark) Note (-n) *nf*
gram – Gramm *nnt*
grammar – Grammatik *nf*
grammar school – Gymnasium (-ien) *nnt*
grandchild – Enkelkind (-er) *nnt*
grandad – Opa (-s) *nm*
granddaughter – Enkelin (-nen) *nf*
grandfather – Großvater (-väter) *nm*
grandmother – Großmutter (-mütter) *nf*
grandparents – Großeltern *npl*
grandson – Enkel (-) *nm*
granny – Oma (-s) *nf*
grapefruit – Pampelmuse (-n) *nf*
grape – Weintraube (-n) *nf*
grape juice – Traubensaft *nm*
grass – Gras (Gräser) *nnt*
grateful – dankbar *adj*
gravy – Soße (-n) *nf*
greasy – fettig *adj*
Great! – Klasse! Wunderbar! Prima! *excl*
great – (big) groß *adj*
great-grandfather – Urgroßvater (-väter) *nm*
great-grandmother – Urgroßmutter (-mütter) *nf*
Great Britain – Großbritannien *nnt*
Greece – Griechenland *nnt*
Greek – griechisch *adj*
Greek person – (male) Grieche (-n) *nm wk*
Greek person – (female) Griechin (-nen) *nf*
greedy – gierig *adj*
green – grün *adj*
green bean – Bohne (-n) *nf*

green pepper – Paprika (-s) *nm*
green salad – grüner Salat *nm*
greengrocer – (male) Gemüsehändler (-) *nm*
greengrocer – (female) Gemüsehändlerin (-nen) *nf*
greenhouse – Gewächshaus (-häuser) *nnt*
greenhouse effect – Treibhauseffekt *nm*
greens – Gemüse *nnt*
greet – begrüßen *v reg* †
greetings card – Glückwunschkarte (-n) *nf*
grey – grau *adj*
grill – (food) grillen *v reg*
grin – grinsen *v reg*
grip – (grasp) ergreifen *v irreg*
grip – (interest) fesseln *v reg*
gripping – fesselnd *adj*
grocer – (male) Lebensmittelhändler (-) *nm*
grocer – (female) Lebensmittelhändlerin (-nen) *nf*
groceries – Lebensmittel (-) *nnt*
grocer's shop – Lebensmittelgeschäft (-e) *nnt*
ground – (earth) Erde *nf*
  on the ground – auf dem Boden
ground – (sport) Platz (Plätze) *nm*
ground floor – Erdgeschoß *nnt*
  on the ground floor – im Erdgeschoß
group – Gruppe (-n) *nf*
grow – (become) werden* *v irreg*
grow – (plants) anbauen *v reg sep*
grow – (get bigger) wachsen* *v irreg*
grow one's hair – sich die Haare wachsen lassen *v irreg dat refl*
grow up – aufwachsen* *v irreg sep*
grown up – erwachsen *adj*
growl – knurren *v reg*
grumble – murren *v reg*

---

nm - noun masculine	*nf* - noun feminine	*nnt* - noun neuter	*npl* - noun plural
nom- nominative	*acc* - accusative	*gen* - genitive	*dat* - dative

grumpy – verdrießlich *adj*
guarantee – Garantie (-n) *nf*
guess – raten *v irreg*
guest – Gast (Gäste) *nm*
guest house – Pension *nf*
guide – (male) Führer (-) *nm*
guide – (female) Führerin (-nen) *nf*
  girl guide – Pfadfinderin (-nen) *nf*
guide book – Reiseführer (-) *nm*
guided tour – Führung (-en) *nf*

guided tour – (by coach, etc)
  Rundfahrt (-en) *nf*
guilty – schuldig *adj*
guinea-pig – Meerschweinchen (-)
  nnt
guitar – Gitarre (-n) *nf*
gun – (handgun) Pistole (-n) *nf*
gun – (rifle) Gewehr (-e) *nnt*
guy – Typ (-en) *nm*
gym(nasium) – Turnhalle (-n) *nf*
gym(nastics) – Turnen *nnt*
  do gymnastics – turnen *v reg*

H

habit – Gewohnheit (-en) *nf*
  I am in the habit of – Ich habe
  die Gewohnheit
  get into the habit of – sich
  gewöhnen an (+ acc) *v reg refl* †
had – *see haben*
had to – *see müssen*
hail – Hagel *nm*
  it is hailing – es hagelt
hair – Haar (-e) *nnt*
hairbrush – Haarbürste (-n) *nf*
haircut – Haarschnitt (-e) *nm*
  have a haircut – sich die Haare
  schneiden lassen *v irreg dat refl*
hairdresser – (male) Friseur (-) *nm*
hairdresser – (female) Friseuse (-n)
  nf
hair dryer – Fön (-e) *nm*
hairstyle – Frisur (-en) *nf*
half – halb *adj*
  half an hour – eine halbe Stunde
  half-price – zum halben Preis
half – Halb~ *pref*
  half board – Halbpension *nf*
  half-brother – Halbbruder
  (-brüder) *nm*

half-sister – Halbschwester (-n) *nf*
half – Hälfte (-n) *nf*
half back – Läufer (-) *nm*
half past – halb
  half past two – halb drei
  half past six – halb sieben
  at half past three – um halb vier
half term holiday – (Autumn)
  Herbstferien *npl*
half term holiday – (February)
  Halbjahresferien *npl*
half term holiday – (Whitsuntide)
  Pfingstferien *npl*
half way – halbwegs *adv*
hall – (domestic) Hausflur (-e) *nm*,
  Diele (-n) *nf*
hall – (public) Halle (-n) *nf*
hall – (public, smart) Saal (Säle) *nm*
hall – (school) Aula (Aulen) *nf*
Halt! – Halt! *excl*
halt – Halt machen *v reg*
ham – Schinken (-) *nm*
  ham sandwich – Schinkenbrot (-e)
  nnt
hamburger – Hamburger (-) *nm*
hammer – Hammer (-) *nm*

---

hamster – Hamster (-) *nm*
hand – Hand (Hände) *nf*
  on the one hand – einerseits *adv*
  on the other hand – andererseits *adv*
  give s.o. a hand – helfen (+ dat) *v irreg*
handbag – Handtasche (-n) *nf*
handball – Handball (-bälle) *nm*
handicapped – behindert *adj*
hand in – abgeben *v irreg sep*
handkerchief – Taschentuch (̈tücher) *nnt*
handle – Griff (-e) *nm*
hand luggage – Handgepäck *nnt*
handmade – handgemacht *adj*
handsome – gutaussehend *adj*
handwriting – Handschrift (-en) *nf*
handwritten – handgeschrieben *adj*
handy – (useful) praktisch *adj*
handyman – Heimwerker (-) *nm*
hang – hängen *v irreg*
hang gliding – Drachenfliegen *nnt*
hang up – (phone) auflegen *v reg sep*
happen – geschehen* *v irreg*, passieren* *v reg* †
happiness – Glück *nnt*
happy – glücklich *adj*
Happy Birthday! – Herzlichen Glückwunsch zum Geburtstag! *excl*
Happy Christmas! – Frohe/Fröhliche Weihnachten! *excl*
Happy New Year! – Ein glückliches neues Jahr! *excl*
happy with – zufrieden mit (+ dat) *adj*
harbour – Hafen (Häfen) *nm*
hard – (difficult) schwer *adj*
hard – hart *adj*
hard disk – Festplatte (-n) *nf*
hardly – kaum *adv*
hard of hearing – schwerhörig *adj*

hardware shop – Eisenwarengeschäft (-e) *nnt*
hardworking – fleißig *adj*
harsh – streng *adj*
harvest – Ernte (-n) *nf*
harvest – ernten *v reg* †
has – *see haben*
has to – *see müssen*
hassle – Ärger *nm*
hassle – schikanieren *v reg* †
haste – Eile *nf*
hasten – sich beeilen *v reg refl* †
hasty – eilig *adj*
hat – Hut (Hüte) *nm*
hate – hassen *v reg*
have – haben *v irreg*
have a bath – sich baden *v reg refl* †
have a cold – erkältet sein* *v irreg*
have a flair for – eine Begabung haben *v irreg*
Have a good journey! – Gute Fahrt! *excl*
Have a good journey home! – Gute Heimreise! *excl*
Have a good time! – Viel Spaß! *excl*
Have a good trip! – Gute Reise! *excl*
Have a good weekend! – Schönes Wochenende! *excl*
have a headache – Kopfschmerzen haben *v irreg*
have a holiday – Urlaub haben *v irreg*
have a meal – essen *v irreg*
Have a nice day! – Einen schönen Tag! *excl*
Have a nice evening! – Einen schönen Abend! *excl*
have a temperature – Fieber haben *v irreg*
Have a safe journey home! – Kommen Sie gut nach Hause! *excl*

---

have a sore throat – Halsschmerzen haben *v irreg*

have a walk – spazieren gehen* *v irreg*, einen Spaziergang machen *v reg*

have breakfast – frühstücken *v reg*

have difficulty – Schwierigkeiten haben *v irreg*

have dinner – zu Abend essen *v irreg*

have friends round – Freunde einladen *v irreg sep*

have lunch – zu Mittag essen *v irreg*

have on – (clothes) anhaben *v irreg sep*

have something cleaned – etwas reinigen lassen *v irreg*

have something repaired – etwas reparieren lassen *v irreg*

have stomach ache – Magenschmerzen haben *v irreg*

have the opportunity to – die Gelegenheit haben *v irreg*

have to – (must) müssen *v irreg*

have toothache – Zahnschmerzen haben *v irreg*

hay fever – Heuschnupfen *nm*

hazard – Gefahr (-en) *nf*

hazard warning lights – Warnblinkanlage *nf*

hazelnut – Haselnuß (-nüsse) *nf*

he – er *pron nom*

head – Kopf (Köpfe) *nm*

headache – Kopfschmerzen *npl*

heading – Titel (-) *nm*

headlight – Scheinwerfer (-) *nm*

headline – Schlagzeile (-n) *nf*

headmaster – Direktor (-en) *nm*

headmistress – Direktorin (-nen) *nf*

headphones – Kopfhörer (-) *nm*

Heads or tails? – Kopf oder Zahl?

headteacher – (male) Direktor (-en) *nm*

headteacher – (female) Direktorin (-nen) *nf*

health – Gesundheit *nf*

health food – Reformkost *nf*

healthy – gesund *adj*

heap – Haufen *nm*

hear – hören *v reg*

hear from – von (+ dat) hören *v reg*

heart – Herz (en) *nnt wk*
  by heart – auswendig *adj*

heat – Hitze *nf*

heat – heizen *v reg*

heater – Heizgerät (-e) *nnt*

heating – Heizung (-en) *nf*

heatwave – Hitzewelle (-n) *nf*

heavy – schwer *adj*

hedge – Hecke (-n) *nf*

heel – (foot) Ferse (-n) *nf*

heel – (shoe) Absatz (-sätze) *nm*

height – (geographical) Höhe *nf*

height – (person) Größe *nf*

helicopter – Hubschrauber (-) *nm*

heliport – Hubschrauberlandeplatz (-plätze) *nm*

Hello! – Hallo! *excl*

helmet – Helm (-e) *nm*

Help! – Hilfe! *excl*

help – Hilfe *nf*

help – helfen (+ dat) *v irreg*

helpful – hilfsbereit *adj*

helpless – hilflos *adj*

help oneself – sich bedienen *v reg refl* †

hen – Henne (-n) *nf*

her – sie *pron acc*

her – ihr *pron dat*

her – ihr *poss adj*

herbal tea – Kräutertee (-s) *nm*

herd – Herde (-n) *nf*

here – hier *adv*

hero – Held (-en) *nm wk*

heroin – (drug) Heroin *nnt*

---

adj - adjective	*v reg* - verb regular	*v sep* - verb separable	† - see verb info
prep - preposition	*v irreg* - verb irregular	*v refl* - verb reflexive	* - takes sein

heroine – (heroic) Heldin (-nen) *nf*
herring – Hering (-e) *nm*
herself – sich *pron refl*
hesitate – zögern *v reg*
HGV – LKW (-s)(Lastkraftwagen) *nm*
Hi! – Hallo! *excl*
hidden – versteckt *adj*
hide – verstecken *v reg* †
hide o.s. – sich verstecken *v reg refl* †
hi-fi system – Stereoanlage (-n) *nf*
high – hoch *adj*
higher – höher *adj*
highest – höchst *adj*
high speed train – Schnellzug (züge) *nm*
high street – Hauptstraße (-n) *nf*
high temperature – (body) Fieber *nnt*
high tide – Flut (-en) *nf*
highway – (road) Straße (-n) *nf*
highway code – Straßenverkehrsordnung (StVO) *nf*
high wind – Sturm (Stürme) *nm*
hike – Wanderung (-en) *nf*
  go for a hike – wandern* *v reg*
hiker – (male) Wanderer (-) *nm*
hiker – (female) Wanderin (-nen) *nf*
hiking boots – Wanderschuhe *npl*
hill – Hügel (-n) *nf*
him – ihn *pron acc*
him – ihm *pron dat*
himself – sich *pron refl*
Hindu – hindu *adj*
Hindu person – Hindu (-s) *nm*
hip – Hüfte (-n) *nf*
hire – (rent) Miete (-n) *nf*
hire – mieten *v reg* †
  for hire – (taxi, etc) frei
his – sein *poss adj*
historic – historisch *adj*
history – Geschichte *nf*
hit – schlagen *v irreg*

hit song – (in English) Hit (-s) *nm*
hit song – (in German) Schlager (-) *nm*
hobby – Hobby (-s) *nnt*
hockey – Hockey *nnt*
hold – halten *v irreg*
hold back – zurückhalten *v irreg sep*
Hold the line please! – Bleiben Sie am Apparat, bitte! *excl*
holdall – Reisetasche (-n) *nf*
holdup – (traffic) Stau (-s) *nm*
holdup – (robbery) Überfall (-fälle) *nm*
hold tight – festhalten *v irreg sep*
hole – Loch (Löcher) *nnt*
holiday – (school) Ferien *npl*
holiday – Urlaub *nm*
  be on holiday – auf Urlaub sein* *v irreg*
  go on holiday – in Urlaub fahren* *v irreg*
holiday – (day) Feiertag (-e) *nm*
  Easter holidays – Osterferien *npl*
  summer holidays – Sommerferien *npl*
holiday cottage – Ferienhaus (-häuser) *nnt*
holiday maker – (male) Urlauber (-) *nm*
holiday maker – (female) Urlauberin (-nen) *nf*
holiday plans – Urlaubspläne *npl*
Holland – Holland *nnt*
hollow – hohl *adj*
holly – Stechpalme (-n) *nf*
holy – heilig *adj*
home – Haus (Häuser) *nnt*
  at the home of – bei (+ dat) *prep*
  be at home – zu Hause sein* *v irreg*
  go home – nach Hause gehen* *v irreg*
home area – Heimat *nf*

---

nm - noun masculine   *nf* - noun feminine   *nnt* - noun neuter   *npl* - noun plural
nom - nominative   *acc* - accusative   *gen* - genitive   *dat* - dative

home economics – Hauswirtschaftslehre *nf*

home game – Heimspiel (-e) *nnt*

home-made – selbstgemacht *adj*

homesickness – Heimweh *nnt*
  I'm homesick – Ich habe Heimweh

homework – Hausaufgaben *npl*

honest – ehrlich *adj*

honey – Honig (-e) *nm*

hook –Haken (-) *nm*

hooligan – Rowdy (-s) *nm*

hope – Hoffnung (-en) *nf*

hope – hoffen *v reg*

hopefully – hoffentlich *adv*

Hoping to see you soon! – Bis bald! *excl*

horizon – Horizont (-e) *nm*
  on the horizon – am Horizont

horn – (car) Hupe (-n) *nf*

horn – (music) Horn (Hörner) *nnt*

horrible – fürchterlich *adj*, furchtbar *adj*

horrified – entsetzt *adj*

horrifying – entsetzlich *adj*

horror – Horror *nm*

horror film – Horrorfilm (-e) *nm*

horror story – Horrorgeschichte (-n) *nf*

horse – Pferd (-e) *nnt*

horse riding – Reiten *nnt*
  go horse riding – reiten gehen* *v irreg*

hospital – Krankenhaus (-häuser) *nnt*

hospitality – Gastfreundschaft *nf*

host – Gastgeber (-) *nm*

hostel – Herberge (-n) *nf*
  youth hostel – Jugendherberge (-n) *nf*

hostess – Gastgeberin (-nen) *nf*

hot – heiß *adj*
  I am hot – Mir ist warm
  It is hot – Es ist warm

hot water – warmes Wasser

hotel – Hotel (-s) *nnt*

hour – Stunde (-n) *nf*

hourly – stündlich *adj*

house – Haus (Häuser) *nnt*
  at my house – bei mir
  detached house – Einfamilienhaus (-häuser) *nnt*
  semi-detached house – Doppelhaus (-häuser) *nnt*

household – Haushalt (-e) *nm*

househusband – Hausmann (-männer) *nm*

house number – Hausnummer (-n) *nf*

housewife – Hausfrau (-en) *nf*

housework – Hausarbeit *nf*

housing estate – Siedlung (-en) *nf*

hovercraft – Luftkissenboot (-e) *nnt*

how – wie *adv*

How are things? – Wie geht's?

How are you? – (formal) Wie geht es Ihnen?

How are you? – (informal) Wie geht es dir?

How do you say ... in German? – Wie sagt man ... auf deutsch?

How do you spell that? – Wie schreibt man das?

how long? – seit wann?

How long have you been learning German? – Seit wann lernst du Deutsch?

how many? – wieviele?

how much? – wieviel?

How much is it? – Was kostet das?

How much is that altogether? – Was macht das?

however – jedoch *adv*

huge – riesig *adj*

humanities – Geisteswissenschaften *npl*

humour – Humor *nm*

hundred – hundert *adj*

---

hundredth – hundertste *adj*
hunger – Hunger *nm*
hungry – hungrig *adj*
  be hungry – Hunger haben *v irreg*
  I am hungry – Ich habe Hunger
hunt – auf die Jagd gehen* *v irreg*
hunt for – suchen *v reg*
hurdle – Hürde (-n) *nf*
hurried – eilig *adj*
hurry – Eile *nf*

I am in a hurry – Ich habe es
  eilig
hurry – sich beeilen *v reg refl* †
Hurry up! – Beeil dich! *excl*
hurt oneself – sich verletzen *v reg*
  refl †
husband – Mann (Männer) *nm*
hydrofoil – Tragflügelboot (-e) *nnt*
hygienic – hygienisch *adj*
hyphen (-) – Bindestrich (-e) *nm*

I

I – ich *pron*
  I would like – Ich möchte
ice – Eis *nnt*
ice – Eis- *pref*
ice-cream – Eis *nnt*
  chocolate ice-cream –
  Schokoladeneis *nnt*
  strawberry ice-cream –
  Erdbeereis *nnt*
  vanilla ice-cream – Vanilleeis *nnt*
Iceland – Island *nnt*
Icelandic – isländisch *adj*
ice-rink – Eisbahn (-en) *nf*
ice-skating – Schlittschuhlaufen *nnt*
icy – eisig *adj*
icy – (road) vereist *adj*
ID – Ausweis (-e) *nm*
idea – Idee (-n) *nf*
  Good idea! – Gute Idee! *excl*
No idea! – Keine Ahnung!
ideal – ideal *adj*
identify – identifizieren *v reg* †
identity – Identität (-en) *nf*
identity card – Personalausweis (-e)
  nm
idiot – Idiot (-en) *nm wk*
idiotic – idiotisch *adj*

i.e. – d.h. (das heißt)
if – (whenever) wenn *sub conj*
if – (whether) ob *sub conj*
ill – krank *adj*
illness – Krankheit (-en) *nf*
illustration – Illustration (-en) *nf*
imaginary – vermeintlich *adj*
imagination – Einbildung (-en) *nf*
imagine – sich vorstellen *v reg dat*
  refl sep
immediate – (instant) sofortig *adj*
immediately – sofort *adv*
immense – enorm *adj*
impatience – Ungeduld *nf*
impatient – ungeduldig *adj*
imperfect tense – Imperfekt *nnt*
important – wichtig *adj*
impossibility – Unmöglichkeit (-en)
  nf
impossible – unmöglich *adj*
impractical – unpraktisch *adj*
impression – Eindruck (-e) *nm*
impressive – eindrucksvoll *adj*
in – in (+ acc/dat) *prep*
  in autumn – im Herbst
  in capital letters – in
  Druckbuchstaben

---

in case – falls *sub conj*
in English – auf englisch
in fact – in der Tat *adv*
in fashion – modisch *adj*
in front of – vor (+ acc/dat) *prep*
in future – in Zukunft
in general – im allgemeinen
in German – auf deutsch
in good condition – in gutem
  Zustand
in Malvern – in Malvern
in my opinion – meiner Meinung
  nach
in order to – um ... zu
in poor condition – in schlechtem
  Zustand
in spite of – trotz (+ gen) *prep*
in spring – im Frühling
in summer – im Sommer
in the 20th century – im 20.
  Jahrhundert
in the afternoon – am Nachmittag
in the country – auf dem Lande
in the east – im Osten
in the end – schließlich *adv*
in the evening – abends *adv*
in the middle of – in der Mitte
  von (+ dat)
in the morning – morgens *adv*
in the mountains – in den Bergen
in the name of Fidler – im
  Namen Fidler
in the north – im Norden
in the open air – im Freien
in the past – früher *adv*
in the process of – dabei sein*
  v irreg
in the rain – im Regen
in the south – im Süden
in the suburbs – in den Vororten
in the west – im Westen
in the world – auf der Welt
in this case – in diesem Fall
in town – in der Stadt

in turn – der Reihe nach
in winter – im Winter
included – inklusive *adv*
  service included – Bedienung
    inbegriffen
including – einschließlich *adv*
incorrect – falsch *adj*
incredible – unglaublich *adj*
indeed – tatsächlich *adv*
independent – selbständig *adj*
India – (Asia) Indien *nnt*
Indian – indisch *adj*
Indian person – (male) Inder (-) *nm*
Indian person – (female) Inderin
  (-nen) *nf*
Indian – (American) indianisch *adj*
Indian – (male) Indianer (-) *nm*
Indian – (female) Indianerin (-nen) *nf*
indicator – (car) Blinker (-) *nm*
individual – individuell *adj*
individual – Individuum (Individuen)
  nnt
indoors – drinnen *adv*
  to go indoors – ins Haus gehen
industrial – industriell *adj*
industrial area – Industriegebiet (-e)
  nnt
industry – Industrie (-n) *nf*
infection – Infektion (-en) *nf*
inform – informieren *v reg* †
information – Auskunft (-en) *nf*
  ask for information – um
    Auskunft bitten *v irreg*
information office –
  Informationsbüro (-s) *nnt*
information super highway –
  Datenautobahn (-en) *nf*
information technology –
  Informatik *nf*
ingredients – Zutaten *npl*
inhabitant – Einwohner (-) *nm*
injection – Spritze (-n) *nf*
injure – verletzen *v reg* †

---

injured – verletzt *adj*
injury – Verletzung (-en) *nf*
ink – Tinte (-n) *nf*
ink jet printer – Tintenstrahldrucker (-) *nm*
in line skates – Inline Skates *npl*
insect – Insekt (-en) *nnt*
inside – Innere *nnt* ‡
inside – drinnen *adv*
  to go inside – ins Haus gehen* *v irreg*
inside out – auf links *adv*
inspect tickets – kontrollieren *v reg* †
inspector – (male) Schaffner (-) *nm*
inspector – (female) Schaffnerin (-nen) *nf*
install – installieren *v reg* †
instant – Augenblick (-e) *nm*
instant coffee – Pulverkaffee *nm*
instantly – sofort *adv*
instead of – statt (+ gen) *prep*
instead of – (an)statt *conj*
instructor – (male) Lehrer (-) *nm*
instructor – (female) Lehrerin (-nen) *nf*
instrument – Instrument (-e) *nnt*
insurance – Versicherung (-en) *nf*
insure – versichern *v reg* †
intelligence – Intelligenz *nf*
intelligent – intelligent *adj*
intention – Absicht (-en) *nf*
intentionally – absichtlich *adv*
interest – Interesse (-n) *nnt*
  be interested in – sich interessieren für (+ acc) *v reg refl* †
interesting – interessant *adj*
international – international *adj*
internet – Internet *nnt*
  surf the internet – das Internet surfen *v reg*
interview – Interview (-s) *nnt*
into – in (+ acc) *prep*

introduce – vorstellen *v reg sep*
introduce o.s. – sich vorstellen *v reg refl sep*
in vain – umsonst
invent – erfinden *v irreg*
investigate – untersuchen *v reg insep*
invitation – Einladung (-en) *nf*
invite – einladen *v irreg sep*
Ireland – Irland *nnt*
Irish – irisch *adj*
Irishman – Ire (-n) *nm wk*
  I am Irish – Ich bin Ire
Irish Republic – die Republik Irland *nf*
Irishwoman – Irin.(-nen) *nf*
  I am Irish – Ich bin Irin
iron – (clothes) Bügeleisen (-) *nnt*
iron – (metal) Eisen- *pref*
iron – (clothes) bügeln *v reg*
irritable – reizbar *adj*
irritate – reizen *v reg*
irritated – gereizt *adj*
is – ist
  isn't it? – nicht wahr?
  It is – Es ist (+ nom)
  It is about... – Es geht um (+ acc)
  There is – Es gibt (+ acc)
Islamic – islamisch *adj*
island – Insel (-n) *nf*
isolated – einsam *adj*
IT – Informatik *nf*
it – er (nom) *pron m*
it – sie (nom/acc) *pron f*
it – es (nom/acc) *pron nt*
it – ihn (acc) *pron m*
it – ihm (dat) *pron m, nt*
it – ihr (dat) *pron f*
It depends – Es kommt drauf an
  It depends upon the weather – Es hängt vom Wetter ab
it is – es ist
It is a pity! – Schade! *excl*

---

nm - noun masculine   nf - noun feminine   nnt - noun neuter   npl - noun plural
nom- nominative   acc - accusative   gen - genitive   dat - dative

It is cold – Es ist kalt
It was – Es war
Italian – italienisch *adj*
Italian – (language) Italienisch *nnt*
Italian – (male) Italiener (-) *nm*
Italian – (female) Italienerin (-nen) *nf*

italic – Kursivschrift *nf*
Italy – Italien *nnt*
item – Gegenstand (-stände) *nm*
its – sein *poss adj m, nt,* ihr *poss adj f*
itself – selbst *pron*

J

jack – (car) Wagenheber (-) *nm*
jack – (cards) Bube (-n) *nm wk*
jacket – Jacke (-n) *nf*
jam – Marmelade (-n) *nf*
  a jar of jam – ein Glas Marmelade *nnt*
jam – (traffic) Stau (-s) *nm*
January – Januar *nm*
  in January – im Januar
Japan – Japan *nnt*
Japanese – japanisch *adj*
Japanese person – (male) Japaner (-) *nm*
Japanese person – (female) Japanerin (-nen) *nf*
jar – (jam, etc) Glas (Gläser) *nnt*
jazz – Jazz *nm*
jazz band – Jazzgruppe (-n) *nf*
jealous of – eifersüchtig auf (+ acc) *adj*
jeans – Jeans (-) *nf*
  a pair of jeans – eine Jeans
jelly – (dessert) Wackelpudding *nm*
jelly – Gelee *nnt*
jet – Düsenflugzeug (-e) *nnt*
jewel – Edelstein (-e) *nm*
jeweller – (male) Juwelier (-) *nm*
jeweller – (female) Juwelierin (-nen) *nf*
jeweller's shop – Juweliergeschäft (-e) *nnt*
jewellery – Schmuck *nm*

Jew – Jude (-n) *nm wk*
Jewess – Jüdin (-nen) *nf*
Jewish – jüdisch *adj*
job – Stelle (-n) *nf,* Job (-s) *nm*
  What's your job? – Was sind Sie von Beruf?
  do odd jobs – aushelfen (+ dat) *v irreg sep*
job offer – Stellenangebot (-e) *nnt*
jog – joggen *v reg*
jogging – Joggen *nnt*
join – (together) verbinden *v irreg*
join – (club) beitreten* (+ dat) *v irreg sep*
joint – (meat) Braten *nm*
joke – Witz (-e) *nm*
jotter – Heft (-e) *nnt*
journalist – (male) Journalist (-en) *nm wk*
journalist – (female) Journalistin (-nen) *nf*
journey – Reise (-n) *nf*
joy – Freude (-n) *nf*
joystick – (IT) Joystick (-s) *nm*
judge – (male) Richter (-) *nm*
judge – (female) Richterin (-nen) *nf*
judo – Judo *nnt*
jug – Krug (Krüge) *nm*
juice – Saft (Säfte) *nm*
  apple juice – Apfelsaft *nm*
  fruit juice – Fruchtsaft *nm*

---

adj - adjective	*v reg* - verb regular	*v sep* - verb separable	† - see verb info
prep - preposition	*v irreg* - verb irregular	*v refl* - verb reflexive	* - takes sein

orange juice – Orangensaft *nm*
July – Juli *nm*
 in July – im Juli
jumbo jet – Jumbojet (-s) *nnt*
jump – springen* *v irreg*
jumper – Pullover (-) *nm*
June – Juni *nm*
 in June – im Juni

jungle – Dschungel (-) *nm*
junior school – Grundschule (-n) *nf*
junk room – Rumpelkammer (-n) *nf*
just – (fair) gerecht *adj*
just – (only) nur *adv*
just – (recently) gerade, eben *adv*
 I have just arrived – Ich bin
 gerade angekommen

K

karate – Karate *nnt*
kebab – Schaschlik (-s) *nnt*
keen – begeistert *adj*
 be keen on – gern machen *v reg*
 be keen on sport – gern Sport
 treiben *v irreg*
keep – behalten *v irreg*
keep an eye on – beobachten *v reg* †
keep fit – trimmen *v reg*
Keep the change! – Das stimmt so!
Keep to the right! – Rechts halten!
 excl
ketchup – Ketchup *nm*
key – Schlüssel (-) *nm*
 bunch of keys – Schlüsselbund
 (-e) *nm*
key ring – Schlüsselring (-e) *nm*
keyhole – Schlüsselloch (-löcher) *nnt*
key – (keyboard) Taste (-n) *nf*
keyboard – (IT) Tastatur (-en) *nf*
keyboard – (piano) Klaviatur (-en) *nf*
kick – treten *v irreg*
kid – (child) Kind (-er) *nnt*
kidnap – entführen *v reg* †
kidnapper – (male) Entführer (-) *nm*
kidnapper – (female) Entführerin
 (-nen) *nf*
kill – töten *v reg* †
kilo(gram) – Kilo *nnt*

kilometre – Kilometer *nm*
 10 kilometres from – zehn
 Kilometer von ... entfernt
kind – nett *adj*
Kind regards – mit freundlichen
 Grüßen
kind to animals – gut zu Tieren
kind – Art (-en) *nf*
kind – (brand) Sorte (-n) *nf*
 What kind of car? – Was für
 einen Wagen?
kindergarten – Kindergarten
 (-gärten) *nm*
kindly – freundlich *adj*
kindness – Freundlichkeit (-en) *nf*
king – König (-e) *nm*
kiosk – Kiosk (-e) *nm*
kiss – Kuß (Küsse) *nm*
kiss – küssen *v reg*
kitchen – Küche (-n) *nf*
kite – Drachen (-) *nm*
kitten – Kätzchen (-) *nnt*
kiwi fruit – Kiwi (-s) *nf*
knee – Knie (-) *nnt*
kneel – knien *v reg*
knickers – Slip (-s) *nm*
knife – Messer (-) *nnt*
knit – stricken *v reg*
knock – klopfen *v reg*

There's a knock at the door –
Es klopft
knock on the door – an die Tür
klopfen *v reg*
knock s.o. over – (car) anfahren
v irreg sep
know – (fact) wissen *v irreg*

I don't know – Ich weiß es nicht
know – (person) kennen *v irreg*
get to know – kennenlernen *v reg*
sep
known – bekannt *adj*
Koran – Koran *nm*

L

laboratory – Labor (-s) *nnt*
lad – Junge (-n) *nm wk*
ladder – Leiter (-n) *nf*
Ladies' toilets – Damen
lady – Dame (-n) *nf*
  cleaning lady – Putzfrau (-en) *nf*
lady's suit – Kostüm (-e) *nnt*
lake – See (-n) *nm*
lamb – (animal) Lamm (Lämmer) *nnt*
lamb – (meat) Lammfleisch *nnt*
lamp – Lampe (-n) *nf*
land – (country) Land (Länder) *nnt*
land – (earth) Erde (-n) *nf*
  plot of land – Grundstück
  (-stücke) *nnt*
land – landen* *v reg* †
landing – (plane) Landung (-en) *nf*
landing – (house) Treppenflur (-e) *nm*
language – Sprache (-n) *nf*
  foreign language – Fremdsprache
  (-n) *nf*
  modern language – Neusprache
  (-n) *nf*
language laboratory – Sprachlabor
(-s) *nnt*
lantern – Laterne (-n) *nf*
laptop – Laptop (-s) *nm*
large – groß *adj*
laser printer – Laserdrucker (-) *nm*
last – letzt *adj*

  at last – endlich *adv*
last night – gestern abend
last week – letzte Woche
last year – letztes Jahr
last – dauern *v reg*
late – spät *adj*
later – später *adj*
  See you later! – Bis später!
latest – neuest *adj*
Latin – lateinisch *adj*
Latin – Latein *nnt*
laugh – lachen *v reg*
laundrette – Münzwäscherei (-en) *nf*
law – Gesetz (-e) *nnt*
lawn – Rasen (-) *nm*
  mow lawn – den Rasen mähen
  v reg
lawyer – (male) Rechtsanwalt
(-anwälte) *nm*
lawyer – (female) Rechtsanwältin
(-nen) *nf*
lay down – sich hinlegen *v wk refl sep*
laze about – faulenzen *v reg*
lazy – faul *adv*
lead – (dog) Leine (-n) *nf*
lead – (metal) Blei *nnt*
  leaded – verbleit *adj*
  lead free – bleifrei *adj*
lead – führen *v reg*
  in the lead – in Führung
leader – (male) Führer (-) *nm*

---

leader – (female) Führerin (-nen) *nf*
leaf – Blatt (Blätter) *nnt*
leaflet – Broschüre (-n) *nf,* Prospekt (-e) *nm*
league – Liga (Ligen) *nf*
lean – lehnen *v reg*
lean over – sich hinüberbeugen *v reg refl sep*
Do not lean out! – Nicht hinauslehnen! *excl*
learn – lernen *v reg*
least – wenigste *adj*
leather – Leder (-) *nnt*
made of leather – aus Leder
leather goods – Lederwaren *npl*
leave – (depart) abfahren* *v irreg sep*
leave – (house, etc) verlassen *v irreg*
leave ... lying around – liegenlassen *v irreg (sep)*
leave the table – den Tisch verlassen *v irreg*
left – linke *adj*
on the left – links *adv*
on the left hand side – auf der linken Seite
left-handed – linkshändig *adj*
I am left handed – (male) Ich bin Linkshänder
I am left handed – (female) Ich bin Linkshänderin
left luggage locker – Gepäckschließfach (-fächer) *nnt*
left luggage office – Gepäckaufbewahrung (-en) *nf*
left luggage ticket – Gepäckzettel (-) *nm*
left winger – Linksaußen (-) *nm*
leg – Bein (e) *nnt*
leggings – Leggings *npl*
leisure – Freizeit (-en) *nf*
leisure centre – Freizeitszentrum (-zentren) *nnt*
lemon – Zitrone (-n) *nf*

lemon tea – Zitronentee *nm*
lemonade – Limonade (-n) *nf*
lend – leihen *v irreg*
lend a hand – helfen (+ dat) *v irreg*
length – (measurement) Länge (-n) *nf*
length – (time) Dauer *nf*
at length – (finally) endlich *adv*
lens – Linse (-n) *nf*
contact lens – Kontaktlinse (-n) *nf*
Leo – (horoscope) Löwe
less – weniger *adv*
less than – weniger als
less than two kilos – weniger als zwei Kilo
lesson – Stunde (-n) *nf*
let – lassen *v irreg*
let – (allow) erlauben (+ dat) *v reg* †
let s.o. know – informieren *v reg* †
let – (rent out) vermieten *v reg* †
to let – zu vermieten
letter – (alphabet) Buchstabe (-n) *nm wk*
letter – (post) Brief (-e) *nm*
registered letter – Einschreibebrief (-e) *nm*
letter box – Briefkasten (-kästen) *nm*
lettuce – Salat (-e) *nm*
level – flach *adj*
level – (school) Niveau (-s) *nnt*
level crossing – Bahnübergang (-gänge) *nm*
liar – (male) Lügner (-) *nm*
liar – (female) Lügnerin (-nen) *nf*
Libra – (horoscope) Waage
librarian – (male) Bibliothekar (-e) *nm*
librarian – (female) Bibliothekarin (-nen) *nf*
library – Bibliothek (-en) *nf*
licence – Genehmigung (-en) *nf*
driving licence – Führerschein (-e) *nm*
lick – lecken *v reg*

---

lid – (top) Deckel (-) *nm*
lie – (be situated) liegen *v irreg*
lie – (untruth) lügen *v irreg*
lie down – sich hinlegen *v reg refl sep*
  have a lie in – (sich) ausschlafen
  v irreg (refl) sep
Liège – Lüttich *nnt*
life – Leben *nnt*
  daily life – das tägliche Leben *nnt*
  lose one's life – ums Leben
  kommen* *v irreg*
lifebelt – Rettungsring (-e) *nm*
lifeguard – Rettungsschwimmer (-)
nm
lifejacket – Schwimmweste (-n) *nf*
lifelong – lebenslänglich *adj*
lift – Lift *nm,* Aufzug (-züge) *nm,*
Fahrstuhl (-stühle) *nm*
lift – heben *v irreg*
  Can I have a lift? – Kannst du
  mich mitnehmen?
lift up – hochheben *v irreg sep*
light – (not heavy) leicht *adj*
light – (not dark) hell *adj*
light blue – hellblau *adj*
light – Licht (-er) *nnt*
light – (lamp) Lampe (-n) *nf*
  put the light on – das Licht
  anmachen *v reg sep*
light bulb – Glühbirne (-e) *nf*
light pen – Lichtstift (-e) *nm*
lighthouse – Leuchtturm (-türme) *nm*
lightning – (flash) Blitz (-e) *nm*
like – (similar) ähnlich *adj*
like – wie *prep*
  What does he look like? – Wie
  sieht er aus?
like that – auf diese Weise
like – mögen *v irreg*
  I like dancing – Ich tanze gern
  I like fish – Ich esse gern Fisch
  I like the trousers – Die Hose
  gefällt mir

I would like – Ich möchte
I would very much like – Ich
möchte gern
likeable – sympathisch *adj*
likely – wahrscheinlich *adv*
  Not likely! – Ich denke nicht
  daran!
limit – (border) Grenze (-n) *nf*
limit – (restriction) Beschränkung
(-en) *nf*
  speed limit –
  Geschwindigkeitsbeschränkung
  (-en) *nf*
line – (queue) Schlange (-n) *nf*
line – (tram, bus) Linie (-n) *nf*
line – (writing) Zeile (-n) *nf*
linen – (household) Wäsche *nf, no pl*
  dirty linen – schmutzige Wäsche
  nf
lion – Löwe (-n) *nm wk*
lip – Lippe (-n) *nf*
lip-read – von den Lippen ablesen
v irreg sep
lipstick – Lippenstift (-e) *nm*
liquid – Flüssigkeit (-en) *nf*
list – Liste (-n) *nf*
listen (to) – (zu)hören *v reg (sep)*
listen to tapes – Kassetten hören
v reg
literature – Literatur *nf*
litre – Liter *nm*
litter – Abfall *nm*
little – klein *adj*
  a little – ein bißchen
  a little more – ein bißchen mehr
live – (alive) lebendig *adj*
live – (radio, TV) live *adj*
live broadcast – Live-Sendung (-en)
nf
live – (be alive) leben *v reg*
live – (inhabit) wohnen *v reg*
  Where do you live? – Wo
  wohnst du?

---

adj - adjective	*v reg* - verb regular	*v sep* - verb separable	† - see verb info
prep - preposition	*v irreg* - verb irregular	*v refl* - verb reflexive	* - takes sein

lively – lebhaft *adj*
lively – lebendig *adj*
liver – Leber (-n) *nf*
liver sausage – Leberwurst *nf*
living – lebend *adj*
  earn one's living – (sich) seinen Lebensunterhalt verdienen *v reg (dat refl)* †
living room – Wohnzimmer (-) *nnt*
load – laden *v irreg*
loaded – beladen *adj*
loads of – eine Menge
loaf – Brot (-e) *nnt*
local – örtlich *adj*
lock – (door) Schloß (Schlösser) *nnt*
lock – abschließen *v irreg sep*
locker – Schließfach (-fächer) *nnt*
lodge with – bei (+ dat) wohnen *v reg*
lodger – (male) Untermieter (-) *nm*
lodger – (female) Untermieterin (-nen) *nf*
lodging – Mietwohnung (-en) *nf*
loft – Dachboden (-böden) *nm*
lollipop – Lutscher (-) *nm*
lonely – einsam *adj*
long – lang *adj*
  all day long – den ganzen Tag
  a long way – weit *adj*
  Don't be long! – Beeil dich! *excl*
  for a long time – lange *adv*
long ago – vor langer Zeit
longer – länger *adj*
  no longer – nicht länger *adv*
long-sighted – weitsichtig *adj*
long walk – Wanderung (-en) *nf*
look – schauen *v reg*
look – sehen *v irreg*
look – (appearance) aussehen *v irreg sep*
look after – (watch) aufpassen auf (+ acc) *v reg sep*
look after – (take care of) sich kümmern um (+ acc) *v reg refl*

look at – ansehen *v irreg sep*
look for – suchen *v reg*
look forward to – sich freuen auf (+ acc) *v reg refl*
look like – aussehen wie *v irreg sep*
Look out! – Achtung! *excl*
look round – sich umsehen *v irreg sep*
lorry – Lastwagen (-) *nm*
lorry – (HGV) LKW (-s) *nm*
lorry driver – (male) Lastwagenfahrer (-) *nm*
lorry driver – (female) Lastwagenfahrerin (-nen) *nf*
lose – verlieren *v irreg*
  lose a match – ein Spiel verlieren *v irreg*
lose one's way – (on foot) sich verlaufen *v irreg refl*
lose one's way – (by car, etc) sich verfahren *v irreg refl*
lose weight – abnehmen *v irreg sep*
lost – verloren *adj*
lost property – Fundsachen *npl*
lost property office – Fundbüro (-s) *nnt*
lot (of) – viel *adv*
  quite a lot – ganz viel
  the lot – alles
lottery – Lotterie (-n) *nf*
loud – laut *adj*
loudspeaker – Lautsprecher (-) *nm*
lounge – Wohnzimmer (-) *nnt*
lousy – mies *adj coll*
love – Liebe (-n) *nf*
love – lieben *v reg*
  I'd love to – Ich möchte gern
  be in love with s.o. – verliebt in jdn sein* *v irreg*
  I'm in love with you – Ich bin in dich verliebt
love from – Alles Gute
love story – Liebesroman (-e) *nm*

---

lovely – schön *adj*
low – niedrig *adj*
LP – Langspielplatte (-n) *nf*
luck – Glück *nnt*
  Bad luck! – Pech! *excl*
  bad luck – Pech *nnt*
  be lucky – Glück haben *v irreg*
  Good luck! – Viel Glück! *excl*
luggage – Gepäck *nnt, no pl*
  piece of luggage – Gepäckstück
  (-e) *nnt*
luggage rack – Gepäcknetz (-e) *nnt*
luggage trolley – Kofferkuli (-s) *nm*

luggage carousel –
  Gepäckausgabe (-n) *nf*
lunch – Mittagessen (-) *nnt*
lunch box – Brotdose (-n) *nf*
lunch hour – Mittagspause (-n) *nf*
have lunch – zu Mittag essen
  v irreg
Luxembourg – Luxemburg *nnt*
Luxembourger – (male)
  Luxemburger (-) *nm*
Luxembourger – (female)
  Luxemburgerin (-nen) *nf*
luxurious – luxuriös *adj*
lyrics – Worte *npl*

M

machine – Maschine (-n) *nf*
mad – verrückt *adj*
magazine – Zeitschrift (-en) *nf*
  glossy magazine – Illustrierte *nf* ‡
  women's magazine –
  Frauenzeitschrift (-en) *nf*
magic – Zauber *nm*
  The Magic Flute – Die Zauberflöte
magician – Zauberer (-) *nm*
magnificent – wunderbar, großartig
adj
maiden name – Mädchenname (-n)
  nm wk
mail – Post *nf*
main – Haupt- *pref*
  main course – Hauptgericht (-e)
  nnt
  main street – Hauptstraße (-n) *nf*
  main station – Hauptbahnhof
  (-höfe) *nm*
majestic – majestätisch *adj*
Majorca – Mallorca *nnt*
major road – Hauptstraße (-n) *nf*
make – Marke (-n) *nf*

make – machen *v reg*
make fun of – sich lustig machen
  über (+ acc) *v reg refl*
make money – Geld verdienen *v reg* †
make up one's mind – sich
  entscheiden *v irreg refl*
make-up – Make-Up *nnt*
make-up bag – Kosmetiktäschchen
  (-) *nnt*
put on make-up – sich schminken
  v reg refl
male – (person) Mann (Männer) *nm*
male – männlich *adj*
male nurse – Krankenpfleger (-) *nm*
malicious – böswillig *adj*
man – (male) Mann (Männer) *nm*
man – (person) Mensch (-en) *nm wk*
manage – zurechtkommen* *v irreg*
  sep
manage – (as boss) leiten *v reg* †
manage to do sthg – etwas schaffen
  v reg
manager – Geschäftsführer (-) *nm*

---

adj - adjective	*v reg* - verb regular	*v sep* - verb separable	† - see verb info
prep - preposition	*v irreg* - verb irregular	*v refl* - verb reflexive	* - takes sein

manageress – Geschäftsführerin (-nen) *nf*

manner – Weise (-n) *nf,* Art (-en) *nf*
  in this manner – auf diese Art und Weise

manners – Manieren *npl*

mansion – Herrenhaus (-häuser) *nnt*

manual – Hand~ *pref*

manufacture – herstellen *v reg sep*

many – viele *adj*

map – (area) Landkarte (-n) *nf*

map – (town) Stadtplan (-pläne) *nm*

March – März *nm*
  in March – im März

margarine – Margarine (-n) *nf*

mark – (school) Note (-n) *nf*

mark – (money) Mark (-) *nf*

mark – (stain) Fleck (-e) *nm*

mark – (books) korrigieren *v reg* †

mark with a cross – ankreuzen *v reg sep*

market – Markt (Märkte) *nm*

market hall – Markthalle (-n) *nf*

market place – Marktplatz(-plätze) *nm*

marmalade – Orangenmarmelade (-n) *nf*

marriage – Ehe (-n) *nf*

marriage – (ceremony) Hochzeit (-en) *nf*

married – verheiratet *adj*

married couple – Ehepaar (-e) *nnt*

marry – heiraten *v reg* †
  get married – heiraten *v reg* †

marvellous – wunderbar *adj*

masculine – männlich *adj*

mashed potato – Kartoffelpüree *nnt*

massive – riesig *adj*

master – Herr (-en) *nm wk*

master – (teacher) Lehrer (-) *nm*

match – (sport) Spiel (-e) *nnt*

match – Streichholz (-hölzer) *nnt*

matchbox – Streichholzschachtel (-n) *nf*

materials – Materialien *npl*

mathematics – Mathematik *nf*

maths – Mathe *nf*

matron – Hausmutter (-mütter) *nf*

matter – wichtig sein* *v irreg*
  It does not matter (to me) – Es macht (mir) nichts aus
  What is the matter? – Was ist los?

mattress – Matratze (-n) *nf*

mauve – lila *adj inv*

maximum – Höchst~ *pref*

maximum speed – Höchstgeschwindigkeit (-en) *nf*

maximum temperature – Höchsttemperatur (-en) *nf*

May – Mai *nm*
  in May – im Mai

may – (be allowed to) dürfen *v irreg*

may – (be able) können *v irreg*

maybe – vielleicht *adv*

mayonnaise – Mayonnaise *nf*

mayor – Bürgermeister (-) *nm*

mayoress – Bürgermeisterin (-nen) *nf*

me – mich *pron acc,* mir *pron dat*

meadow – Wiese (-n) *nf*

meal – Mahlzeit (-en) *nf*
  evening meal – Abendessen (-) *nnt*
  midday meal – Mittagessen (-) *nnt*

mean – bedeuten *v reg* †
  What does... mean? – Was bedeutet...?

mean – (nasty) gemein *adj*

mean – (money) geizig *adj*

meanwhile – inzwischen *adv*

measure – messen *v irreg*

meat – Fleisch *nnt*
  type of meat – Fleischsorte (-n) *nf*

mechanic – (male) Mechaniker (-) *nm*

mechanic – (female) Mechanikerin (-nen) *nf*

---

medal – Medaille (-n) *nf*
  gold medal – Goldmedaille *nf*
  silver medal – Silbermedaille *nf*
  bronze medal – Bronzemedaille *nf*
media – Medien *npl*
medicine – (science) Medizin *nf*
medicine – (remedy) Medikament (-e) *nnt*
medieval – mittelalterlich *adj*
Mediterranean – Mittelmeer *nnt*
medium – Mittel- *pref*
medium length – mittellang *adj*
medium size – mittelgroß *adj*
meet – (arranged) sich treffen *v irreg refl*
meet – (chance) begegnen* (+ dat) *v reg* †
meet – (get to know) kennenlernen *v reg sep*
meet – (fetch) abholen *v reg sep*
meeting – Treffen (-) *nnt*
melon – Melone (-n) *nf*
member – Mitglied (-er) *nnt*
membership card – Mitgliedskarte (-n) *nf*
memory – Gedächtnis (-se) *nnt*
memory – (computer) Speicher (-) *nm*
mend – reparieren *v reg* †
  have mended – reparieren lassen *v irreg*
Men's toilets – Herren
menu – Speisekarte (-n) *nf*
  fixed price menu – Menü (-s) *nnt*
menu of the day – Tageskarte (-n) *nf*
merchandise – Ware (-n) *nf*
merry – fröhlich *adj*
Merry Christmas! – Fröhliche Weihnachten! *excl*
mess – Durcheinander *nnt*
  in a mess – durcheinander *adv*
mess about – herumalbern *v reg sep*
message – Mitteilung (-en) *nf*
messy – unordentlich *adj*

metal – Metall (-e) *nnt*
method – Methode (-n) *nf*
metre – Meter *nm*
microchip – Mikrochip (-s) *nm*
micro-computer – Mikrocomputer (-) *nm*
microphone – Mikrophon (-e) *nnt*
microscope – Mikroskop (-e) *nnt*
microwave oven – Mikrowellenherd (-e) *nm*
midday – Mittag *nm*
  at midday – um Mittag
midday meal – Mittagessen *nnt*
  have midday meal – zu Mittag essen *v irreg*
middle – Mitte *nf*
  in the middle of – in der Mitte von (+ dat)
middle aged – mittleren Alters
Midlands – Mittelengland *nnt*
midnight – Mitternacht *nf*
  at midnight – um Mitternacht
might – könnte *see können*
mild – mild *adj*
mile – Meile (-n) *nf*
milk – Milch *nf*
milkman – Milchmann (-männer) *nm*
milk shake – Milkshake *nm*
millennium – Jahrtausend *nnt*
million – Million (-en) *nf*
mince – Hackfleisch *nnt*
mind – (look after) aufpassen auf (+ acc)_ *v reg sep*
  make up one's mind – sich entschließen *v irreg refl*
  I don't mind – Das macht mir nichts aus
  Mind the step – Vorsicht Stufe
  Never mind – Es macht nichts
mine – mein *poss adj*
  It's mine – Es gehört mir
  a friend of mine – ein Freund/eine Freundin von mir

---

adj - adjective   *v reg* - verb regular   *v sep* - verb separable   † - see verb info
prep - preposition   *v irreg* - verb irregular   *v refl* - verb reflexive   * - takes sein

miner – Bergarbeiter (-) *nm*
mineral water – Mineralwasser *nnt*
minibus – Kleinbus (-se) *nm*
minimum – Minimum (Minima) *nnt*
minimum – Mindest- *pref*
minimum temperature –
Mindesttemperatur (-en) *nf*
minor – minderjährig *adj*
minor – (under 18) Minderjährige *nmf* ‡
mint – Pfefferminzbonbon (-s) *nnt*
mint tea – Pfefferminztee *nm*
minus – (maths) minus *prep*
minute – Minute (-n) *nf*
mirror – Spiegel (-) *nm*
miserable – unglücklich *adj*
misfortune – Unglück *nnt*
Miss – Fräulein (-) *nnt*
miss – (person) vermissen *v reg* †
miss – (train, etc) verpassen *v reg* †
mist – Nebel (-) *nm*
mistake – Fehler (-) *nm*
misty – nebelig *adj*
misunderstanding – Mißverständnis
(-se) *nnt*
mix – mischen *v reg*
mixed – gemischt *adj*
mixed cold meats – Aufschnitt *nm*
mixed salad – gemischter Salat *nm*
moan – stöhnen *v reg*
moan about – (complain) sich
beklagen über (+ acc) *v reg refl* †
model – (fashion) Mannequin (-s) *nnt*
model – Modell (-e) *nnt*
a scale model – ein
maßstabgerechtes Modell *nnt*
do model-making – basteln *v reg*
modem – Modem (-s) *nnt*
moderate – mäßig *adj*
modern – modern *adj*
modern languages – Neusprachen
npl
moment – Augenblick (-e) *nm*

at the moment – zur Zeit
at this moment – im Augenblick
in a moment – gleich *adv*
Monday – Montag (-e) *nm*
on Monday – am Montag
money – Geld *nnt*
change money – Geld wechseln
v reg
monkey – Affe (-n) *nm wk*
monster – Ungeheuer (-) *nnt*
month – Monat (-e) *nm*
per month – im Monat
monthly – monatlich *adj*
monument – Denkmal (-mäler) *nnt*
mood – Laune (-n) *nf*
in a bad mood – schlechter Laune
in a good mood – guter Laune
moon – Mond (-e) *nm*
moped – Moped (-s) *nnt*
more – mehr *adv*
more and more – immer mehr *adv*
more or less – mehr oder weniger
adv
more than – mehr als
There is no more – Es ist nichts
mehr da
morning – Morgen (-) *nm*
next morning – am nächsten
Morgen
tomorrow morning – morgen
früh
Moselle – Mosel *nf*
mosque – Moschee (-n) *nf*
mosquito – Moskito (-s) *nm*
most – am meisten *adv*
most – (people) die meisten
MOT – TÜV *nm*
mother – Mutter (Mütter) *nf*
mother-in-law – Schwiegermutter
(-mütter) *nf*
motherly – mütterlich *adj*
motor – Motor (-en) *nm*
motorbike – Motorrad (-räder) *nnt*

---

nm - noun masculine   *nf* - noun feminine   *nnt* - noun neuter   *npl* - noun plural
nom- nominative   *acc* - accusative   *gen* - genitive   *dat* - dative

motor boat – Motorboot (-e) *nnt*
motorcyclist – (male) Motorradfahrer (-) *nm*
motorcyclist – (female) Motorradfahrerin (-nen) *nf*
motor home – Campingbus (-se) *nm*
motorist – (male) Autofahrer (-) *nm*
motorist – (female) Autofahrerin (-nen) *nf*
motorway – Autobahn (-en) *nf*
mountain – Berg (-e) *nm*
mountain bike – Mountainbike (-s) *nnt*, Bergrad (-räder) *nnt*
mountain climbing – Bergsteigen *nnt*
mountaineer – (male) Bergsteiger (-) *nm*
mountaineer – (female) Bergsteigerin (-nen) *nf*
mountain range – Gebirge *nnt*
mouse – Maus (Mäuse) *nf*
moustache – Oberlippenbart (-bärte) *nm*
mouth – Mund (Münder) *nm*
mouthful – Mundvoll (-) *nm*
mouth organ – Mundharmonika (-harmoniken) *nf*
move – bewegen *v reg* †
move house – umziehen* *v irreg sep*
movement – Bewegung (-en) *nf*
mow the lawn – den Rasen mähen *v reg*
Mr, Sir – Herr
Mrs, Ms – Frau
much – viel *adv*
  so much – so viel *adv*
mud – Schlamm *nm*
muddy – schlammig *adj*

muddy shoes – schmutzige Schuhe *npl*
mug – (cup) Becher (-) *nm*
mug – (attack) überfallen *v irreg insep*
multi-coloured – bunt *adj*
multiple crash – Karambolage (-n) *nf*
multi-storey car park – Parkhaus (-häuser) *nnt*
mum(my) – Mutti (-s) *nf*
Munich – München
museum – Museum (Museen) *nnt*
mushroom – Pilz (-e) *nm*
music – Musik *nf*
  pop music – Popmusik *nf*
music centre – Stereoanlage (-n) *nf*
music department – Musikabteilung (-en) *nf*
music room – Musikraum (räume) *nm*
musician – (male) Musiker (-) *nm*
musician – (female) Musikerin (-nen) *nf*
Muslim – mohammedanisch *adj*
Muslim – (male) Mohammedaner (-) *nm*
Muslim – (female) Mohammedanerin (-nen) *nf*
must – *see müssen*
must not – *see dürfen*
mustard – Senf *nm*
mutton – Hammelfleisch *nnt*
my – mein *poss adj*
myself – mich *pron acc*, mir *pron dat*
mysterious – geheimnisvoll *adj*
mystery – Geheimnis (-se) *nnt*
myth – Märchen (-) *nnt*

N

nail – Nagel (Nägel) *nm*
naked – nackt *adj*
name – Name (-n) *nm wk*
  in the name (of) – im Namen
  (+ gen)
  My name is – Ich heiße
  What is your name? – Wie heißt
  du?/Wie heißen Sie?
name – nennen *v irreg*
nanny – Kindermädchen (-) *nnt*
narrow – eng *adj*
nasty – unangenehm *adj*
nation – Volk (Völker) *nnt*
national – national *adj*
national – (German) Bundes~ *pref*
nationalist – nationalistisch *adj*
nationality – Staatsangehörigkeit
  (-en) *nf*
native – gebürtig *adj*
native language – Muttersprache *nf*
native town – Heimatstadt *nf*
natural – natürlich *adj*
natural gas – Erdgas *nnt*
natural history – Naturkunde *nf*
natural sciences –
  Naturwissenschaften *npl*
naturally – natürlich *adv*
nature – Natur *nf*
nature reserve – Naturschutzgebiet
  (-e) *nnt*
naughty – unartig *adj*
navy – Kriegsmarine (-n) *nf*
navy blue – marineblau *adj*
near (to) – in der Nähe (von + dat)
nearby – in der Nähe
nearest – nächst *adj*
nearly – fast *adv*
near sighted – kurzsichtig *adj*
neat – ordentlich *adj*
necessary – nötig, notwendig *adj*

necessity – Notwendigkeit (-en) *nf*
neck – (throat) Hals (Hälse) *nm*
  back of neck – Nacken (-) *nm*
necklace – Halskette (-n) *nf*
nectarine – Nektarine (-n) *nf*
need – brauchen *v reg*
  I need to do it – Ich muß es tun
needle – Nadel (-n) *nf*
needlework – Handarbeit *nf*
negative – negativ *adj*
neglect – vernachlässigen *v reg* †
neglected – vernachlässigt *adj*
neighbour – (male) Nachbar (-en) *nm
  wk*
neighbour – (female) Nachbarin
  (-nen) *nf*
neighbourhood – Nachbarschaft
  (-en) *nf*
neighbouring – benachbart *adj*
neither – auch nicht *adv*
neither...nor – weder ... noch *adv*
nephew – Neffe (-n) *nm wk*
nervous – nervös *adj*
netball – Korbball *nm*
Netherlands – Niederlande *npl*
neuter – Neutrum *nnt*
never – nie *adv*
never mind – es macht nichts
nevertheless – trotzdem *adv*
new – neu *adj*
New Year – Neujahr (-e) *nnt*
New Year's Day – Neujahrstag (-e)
  nm
New Year's Eve – Silvester *nnt*
New Zealand – Neuseeland *nnt*
news – (radio, TV) Nachrichten *npl*
newsagent – (male) Zeitungshändler
  (-) *nm*
newsagent – (female)
  Zeitungshändlerin (-nen) *nf*

---

newspaper – Zeitung (-en) *nf*
next – nächst *adj*
    Who's next? – Wer ist dran?
next – dann *adv*
next door – nebenan *adv*
next to – neben (+ acc/dat) *prep*
next week – nächste Woche
next year – nächstes Jahr
nice – (person) nett *adj*
nice – (weather) schön *adj*
nice-looking – gutaussehend *adj*
nickname – Spitzname (-n) *nm wk*
niece – Nichte (-n) *nf*
night – Nacht (Nächte) *nf*
    Good night! – Gute Nacht! *excl*
night club – Nachtklub (-s) *nm*
last night – gestern abend
nightdress – Nachthemd (-en) *nnt*
nightmare – Alptraum (-träume) *nm*
nil – null *adj*
    two - nil (2:0) – zwei zu null
nine – neun *adj*
nineteen – neunzehn *adj*
ninety – neunzig *adj*
ninety-one – einundneunzig *adj*
ninth – neunte *adj*
no – nein *adv*
no – kein *adj*
    no thank you – (nein) danke
    no entry – (on foot) kein Zutritt
    no entry – (vehicles) keine Einfahrt
    no good at – nicht gut in (+ dat)
    no longer – nicht länger
    no more – nicht mehr
    no-one – niemand *pron*
    no-one else – sonst niemand
    no parking – Parken verboten
    no smoking – Rauchen verboten
    no vacancies – belegt *adj*
nobody – niemand *pron*
noise – (quiet) Geräusch (-e) *nnt*
noise – (loud) Lärm *nm*

noisy – laut *adj*
non-drinking water – kein Trinkwasser
non-smoking – Nichtraucher
none the less – nichtsdestoweniger *adv*
nonsense – Unsinn *nm,* Blödsinn *nm*
noodles – Nudeln *npl*
noon – Mittag (-e) *nm*
normal – normal *adj*
normally – normalerweise *adv*
north – Nord~ *pref*
north – Norden *nm*
North America – Nordamerika *nnt*
northerly – nördlich *adj*
Northern Ireland – Nordirland *nnt*
Northern Irish – nordirisch *adj*
Northern Irishman – Nordire (-n) *nm wk*
Northern Irishwoman – Nordirin (-nen) *nf*
north Germany – Norddeutschland *nnt*
north of – nördlich von (+ dat) *adj*
North Sea – Nordsee *nf*
Norway – Norwegen *nnt*
Norwegian – norwegisch *adj*
nose – Nase (-n) *nf*
nosebleed – Nasenbluten (-) *nnt*
nosy – neugierig *adj*
not – nicht
    He's not German – Er ist kein Deutscher
    not allowed – nicht erlaubt
    not any – kein *adj*
    not at all – gar nicht
    not far from here – nicht weit von hier
    not included – nicht inbegriffen
    not likely – auf keinen Fall
    not much – nicht viel
    not only – nicht nur
    not yet – noch nicht

---

adj - adjective	*v reg* - verb regular	*v sep* - verb separable	† - see verb info
prep - preposition	*v irreg* - verb irregular	*v refl* - verb reflexive	* - takes sein

note – (money) Schein (-e) *nm*
  50 mark note –
  Fünfzigmarkschein (-e) *nm*
note – (message) Zettel (-) *nm*
note – (message) Notiz (-en) *nf*
notebook – Notizbuch (-bücher) *nnt*
note down – notieren *v reg* †
notepad – Notizblock (-blöcke) *nm*
note paper – Briefpapier (-e) *nnt*
nothing – nichts
  nothing at all – gar nichts
  nothing else – nichts anderes
  nothing much – nicht viel
  nothing new – nichts Neues
notice – (information)
  Bekanntmachung (-en) *nf*
notice – (dismissal) Kündigung (-en)
  nf
notice – bemerken *v reg* †
noticeable – bemerkbar *adj*
notice board – Anschlagbrett (-er)
  nnt, das schwarze Brett
nought – Null *nf*

noun – Substantiv (-e) *nnt*
novel – Roman (-e) *nm*
  detective novel – Krimi (-s) *nm coll*
November – November *nm*
  in November – im November
now – jetzt *adv*
nowadays – heutzutage *adv*
nowhere – nirgendwo *adv*
nuclear power – Kernenergie *nf*
number – (house, etc) Nummer (-n) *nf*
number – (numeral) Zahl (-en) *nf*
  page number – Seite (-n) *nf*
number plate – Kennzeichen (-) *nnt*
numerous – zahlreich *adj*
nurse – (female) Krankenschwester
  (-n) *nf*
nurse – (male) Krankenpfleger (-) *nm*
nursery school – Kindergarten
  (-gärten) *nm*
nut – Nuß (Nüsse) *nf*
nylon – Nylon *nnt*
  made of nylon – aus Nylon

O

oak tree – Eiche (-n) *nf*
OAP – (male) Rentner (-) *nm*
OAP – (female) Rentnerin (-nen) *nf*
obedient – gehorsam *adj*
obey – gehorchen (+ dat) *v reg* †
object – Gegenstand (-stände) *nm*
obligatory – obligatorisch *adj*
obliged – verpflichtet *adj*
oboe – Oboe (-n) *nf*
observe – bemerken *v reg* †
obstacle – Hindernis (-se) *nnt*
obstinate – stur *adj*
obtain – bekommen *v irreg*
obtain – kriegen *v reg coll*

obvious – offensichtlich *adj*
occasion – Gelegenheit (-en) *nf*
occasion – (special) Ereignis (-se) *nnt*
occasion – (time) Mal (-e) *nnt*
occasional – gelegentlich *adj*
occasionally – hin und wieder *adv*
occupant – (male) Bewohner (-) *nm*
occupant – (female) Bewohnerin
  (-nen) *nf*
occupation – Beruf (-e) *nm*
  What is your occupation? –
  Was sind Sie von Beruf?
occupational – Berufs- *pref*
occupied – (busy) beschäftigt *adj*
occupied – (table, seat) besetzt *adj*

---

nm - noun masculine   *nf* - noun feminine   *nnt* - noun neuter   *npl* - noun plural
nom- nominative   *acc* - accusative   *gen* - genitive   *dat* - dative

ocean – Ozean (-e) *nm*
o'clock – Uhr
  at six o'clock – um sechs Uhr
October – Oktober *nm*
  in October – im Oktober
odd – (strange) seltsam *adj*
odd – (number) ungerade
odd jobs – Gelegenheitsarbeiten *npl*
  do odd jobs –
  Gelegenheitsarbeiten verrichten
  v reg †
of – von (+ dat) *prep*
of – (made of) aus (+ dat) *prep*
  a pot of tea – ein Kännchen Tee
  a bottle of wine – eine Flasche
  Wein
  a pound of cheese – ein Pfund
  Käse
  two kilos of apples – zwei Kilo
  Äpfel
  12th of November – (letter
  heading) den 12. November
of course – natürlich *adv*
off – (bad food) schlecht *adj*
off – (electrical) aus *adv*
off – (not here) weg *adv*
off – (tap) zu *adv*
get off the bus – aus dem Bus
  aussteigen* *v irreg sep*
10% off – 10% Ermäßigung
offence – Straftat (-en) *nf*
commit an offence – ein
  Verbrechen begehen *v irreg*
offend – (insult) beleidigen *v reg* †
offended – beleidigt *adj*
offer – Angebot (-e) *nnt*
  special offer – Sonderangebot (-e)
  nnt
offer – bieten *v irreg*, anbieten *v irreg*
  sep
office – Büro (-s) *nnt*
official – offiziell *adj*
official – (male) Beamte *nm* ‡

official – (female) Beamtin (-nen) *nf*
often – oft *adv*
how often? – wie oft?
Oh! – Ach! *excl*
oil – Öl *nnt*
oil painting – Ölgemälde *nnt*
OK! – in Ordnung! *excl*
old – alt *adj*
  How old are you? – Wie alt sind
  Sie/Wie alt bist du?
  I am 16 years old – Ich bin 16
  Jahre alt
old age – Alter (-) *nnt*
old fashioned – altmodisch *adj*
olive oil – Olivenöl *nnt*
the Olympic games – die
  Olympischen Spiele *npl*
omelette – Omelett (-s) *nnt*
on – (horizontal) auf (+ acc/dat) *prep*
on – (vertical) an (+ acc/dat) *prep*
on and off – (occasionally) ab und zu
  adv
on behalf of – im Auftrag von (+ dat)
on board – an Bord *adv*
on foot – zu Fuß *adv*
on Friday – am Freitag *adv*
on Fridays – freitags *adv*
on purpose – absichtlich *adv*
on the bus – im Bus
  get on the bus – in den Bus
  einsteigen* *v irreg sep*
  go on the bus – mit dem Bus
  fahren* *v irreg*
on the ground floor – im
  Erdgeschoß
on the left – links *adv*
on the left hand side – auf der
  linken Seite
on the other side – auf der anderen
  Seite
on the point of – im Begriff sein*
  v irreg

---

he was on the point of phoning – er wollte gerade anrufen

on the Rhine – (afloat) auf dem Rhein

on the right – rechts *adv*

on the Thames – (afloat) auf der Themse

on the top floor – im obersten Geschoß

on the train – im Zug

on time – pünktlich *adj*

on top of – oben auf (+ dat) *adv*

and so on – und so weiter (usw.)

later on – später *adv*

What's on? – (cinema) Was läuft?

once – einmal *adv*

once more – noch einmal *adv*

one – ein *indef art m, nt*

one – eine *indef art f*

one off – einmalig *adj*

one way ticket – einfache Fahrkarte

one way street – Einbahnstraße (-n) *nf*

oneself – selbst *pron*

oneself – sich *pron refl*

onion – Zwiebel (-n) *nf*

only – einzig *adj*

only – nur *adv*

only – (time) erst *adv*

only child – Einzelkind (-er) *nnt*

onwards – vorwärts *adv*

open – offen *adj*, geöffnet *adj*
in the open air – im Freien

open air swimming pool – Freibad (-bäder) *nnt*

open – öffnen *v reg* †, aufmachen *v reg sep*

opening – Öffnung (-en) *nf*

opening hours – Öffnungszeiten *npl*

opera – Oper (-n) *nf*

opera house – Opernhaus (-häuser) *nnt*

operation – Operation (-en) *nf*

have an operation – sich operieren lassen *v irreg refl*

opinion – Meinung (-en) *nf*
in my opinion – meiner Meinung nach

opinion poll – Meinungsumfrage (-n) *nf*

opportunity – Gelegenheit (-en) *nf*

opposite – gegenüber (+ dat) *prep*

opposite – Gegenteil (-e) *nnt*

opt for – sich entscheiden für (+ acc) *v irreg refl*

optician – (male) Optiker (-) *nm*

optician – (female) Optikerin (-nen) *nf*

optimist – Optimist (-en) *nm wk*

optimistic – optimistisch *adj*

optional – auf Wunsch

optional subject – Wahlfach (-fächer) *nnt*

or – oder *coord conj*

oral – mündlich *adj*

oral question – mündliche Frage (-n) *nf*

oral test – mündliche Prüfung (-en) *nf*

orange – orange *adj*

orange – Apfelsine (-n) *nf*

orange juice – Orangensaft *nm*

orchestra – Orchester (-) *nnt*

order – (command) Befehl (-e) *nm*

order – (restaurant) Bestellung (-en) *nf*

order – (sequence) Folge (-n) *nf*

order – (tidiness) Ordnung (-en) *nf*
in alphabetical order – in alphabetischer Reihenfolge

in order to – um ... zu *conj*

order – (command) befehlen *v irreg*

order – (restaurant) bestellen *v reg* †

orderly – ordentlich *adj*

ordinal number – Ordinalzahl (-en) *nf*

ordinary – normal *adj*, gewöhnlich *adj*

organise – organisieren *v reg* †

---

nm - noun masculine   *nf* - noun feminine   *nnt* - noun neuter   *npl* - noun plural
nom- nominative   *acc* - accusative   *gen* - genitive   *dat* - dative

organised – organisiert *adj*
original – original *adj*
orphan – Waise (-n) *nf*
other – andere *adj*
   the other day – neulich *adv*
otherwise – sonst *adv*
Ouch! Ow! – Autsch! *excl*
ought – sollen *v irreg*
   I ought to do it – Ich sollte es tun
our – unser *poss adj*
ourselves – uns *pron refl*
out – (finished) zu Ende
   School's out – Die Schule ist aus
   The light is out – Das Licht ist aus
out – (outside) draußen *adv*
outdoors – draußen *adv*, im Freien
out of – aus (+ dat) *prep*
   six out of ten – sechs von zehn
out of breath – atemlos *adj*
out of date – altmodisch *adj*
out of order – (not working) außer
   Betrieb
out of season – außerhalb der Saison
outfit – (clothes) Kleidung (-en) *nf*
outside – draußen *adv*
   outside the door – draußen vor
   der Tür
outside – außerhalb von (+ dat) *prep*
outside – Außenseite (-n) *nf*
outskirts – Rand (Ränder) *nm*
outstanding – (very good)
   hervorragend *adj*
oval – oval *adj*
oven – Herd (-e) *nm*

microwave oven –
   Mikrowellenherd (-e) *nm*
over – (across, away from speaker)
   hinüber *adv*
over – (across, towards speaker)
   herüber *adv*
over – (finished) vorbei *adv*
over – (left) übrig *adv*
over – (above) über (+ acc/dat) *prep*
all over – (everywhere) überall *adv*
over and over – (again) immer
   wieder *adv*
over there – da drüben *adv*
overalls – Overall (-s) *nm*
overcoat – Mantel (Mäntel) *nm*
overdose – Überdosis (-dosen) *nf*
overhead projector –
   Tageslichtprojektor (-en) *nm*
overnight stay – Übernachtung (-en)
   nf
overseas – Übersee~ *pref*
overtake – überholen *v reg insep*
overturn – (boat) umkippen [*] *v reg*
   sep
overturn – (car) sich überschlagen
   v irreg refl insep
owe – (money) schulden *v reg* †
owe s.o. sthg – (thanks) jdm etwas
   verdanken *v reg* †
own – eigen *adj*
own – besitzen *v irreg*
owner – (male) Besitzer (-) *nm*
owner – (female) Besitzerin (-nen) *nf*
oxygen – Sauerstoff *nm*
ozone layer – Ozonschicht (-en) *nf*

P

pack – (case) packen *v reg*
pack of cards – Spiel (e) *nnt*
package – Paket (-e) *nnt*
package tour – Pauschalreise (-n) *nf*
packed lunch – Lunchpaket (-e) *nnt*
pad – (writing) Schreibblock (-blöcke) *nm*
paddock – Koppel (-n) *nf*
page – Seite (-n) *nf*
  at the bottom of the page – unten auf der Seite
  on page 51 – auf Seite 51
paid – bezahlt *adj*
pain – Schmerz (-en) *nm*
  be in pain – Schmerzen haben *v irreg*
painful – schmerzhaft *adj*
paint – (art) malen *v reg*
  paint the wall – die Wand streichen *v irreg*
painter – (male) Maler (-) *nm*
painter – (female) Malerin (-nen) *nf*
painter – (decorator) Anstreicher (-) *nm*
pair (of) – Paar *nnt*
  a pair of jeans – Jeans *nf*
  a pair of pyjamas – Schlafanzug *nm*
  a pair of shoes – ein Paar Schuhe
  a pair of shorts – eine kurze Hose *nf*
  a pair of trousers – eine Hose *nf*
Pakistan – Pakistan *nnt*
Pakistani – pakistanisch *adj*
Pakistani person – (male) Pakistaner (-) *nm*
Pakistani person – (female) Pakistanerin (-nen) *nf*
palace – Schloß (Schlösser) *nnt*
pale – (complexion) blaß *adj*
pale – hell~ *pref*

pale blue – hellblau *adj*
pan – (cooking) Topf (Töpfe) *nm*
pancake – Pfannkuchen (-) *nm*
pants – (male) Unterhose (-n) *nf*
pants – (female) Slip (-s) *nm*
paper – Papier (-e) *nnt*
  made of paper – aus Papier
paper – (exam) Testbogen (-bögen) *nm*
  newspaper – Zeitung (-en) *nf*
paperback – Taschenbuch (-bücher) *nnt*
paperclip – Büroklammer (-n) *nf*
papers – (ID) Ausweis (-e) *nm*
paragraph – Absatz (-sätze) *nm*
parcel – Paket (-e) *nnt*
parents – Eltern *npl*
park – Park (-s) *nm*
park – parken *v reg*
parking – Parken *nnt*
parking lot – Parkplatz (-plätze) *nm*
parking meter – Parkuhr (-en) *nf*
parking space – Abstellplatz (-plätze) *nm*
parking ticket – Strafzettel (-) *nm*
parliament – (national) Parlament (-e) *nnt*
parliament – (regional) Landtag (-e) *nm*
parrot – Papagei (-en) *nm*
part – Teil (-e) *nm*
  spare part – Ersatzteil (-e) *nnt*
part – (acting) Rolle (-n) *nf*
  for the most part – meistens *adv*
  part of town – Stadtteil (-e) *nm*
  part-time – Teilzeit~ *pref*
  take part in – teilnehmen an (+ dat) *v irreg sep*
participate – teilnehmen *v irreg sep*
participle – Partizip (-ien) *nnt*
particular – besondere *adj*

particularly – besonders *adv*
partner – (male) Partner (-) *nm*
partner – (female) Partnerin (-nen) *nf*
party – (celebration) Party (-s) *nf*
party – (political) Partei (-en) *nf*
pass – (an exam) bestehen *v irreg*
pass – (at table) reichen *v reg*
pass – (in car) vorbeifahren* an (+ dat) *v irreg sep*
pass – (on foot) vorbeigehen* an (+ dat) *v irreg sep*
pass – (overtake) überholen *v reg insep*
pass – (time) verbringen *v irreg*
passage – (book) Stelle (-n) *nf*
passage – (corridor) Gang (Gänge) *nm*
passenger – (male) Passagier (-e) *nm*
passenger – (female) Passagierin (-nen) *nf*
passer-by – (male) Passant (-en) *nm wk*
passer-by – (female) Passantin (-nen) *nf*
Passover – Passahfest (-e) *nnt*
passport – Paß (Pässe) *nm*
past – (beyond) hinter (+ acc/dat) *prep*
past – (time) nach (+ dat) *prep*
  five past four – fünf nach vier
  half past six – halb sieben
  quarter past three – Viertel nach drei
past – (travelling) an (+ dat) vorbei *prep*
  I'm going past school – Ich gehe an der Schule vorbei
pasta – Nudeln *npl*
paste – (glue) kleben *v reg*
pastime – Zeitvertreib (-e) *nm*
pastry – Teig (-e) *nm*
past tense – Vergangenheit (-en) *nf*
pâté – Pastete (-n) *nf*
path – Weg (-e) *nm*
pathetic – erbärmlich *adj*
patience – Geduld *nf*
patient – geduldig *adj*

patient – (male) Patient (-en) *nm wk*
patient – (female) Patientin (-nen) *nf*
patio – Terrasse (-n) *nf*
pause – Pause (-n) *nf*
pavement – Bürgersteig (-e) *nm*
paw – Pfote (-n) *nf*
pay – (salary) Gehalt (Gehälter) *nnt*
pay – (wages) Lohn (Löhne) *nm*
pay (for) – bezahlen *v reg* †
pay attention (to) – achten (auf + acc) *v reg* †
pay a visit to – (people) besuchen *v reg* †
pay a visit to – (sights) besichtigen *v reg* †
payment – Bezahlung (-en) *nf*
pay phone – Münzfernsprecher (-) *nm*
pay rise – Gehaltserhöhung (-en) *nf*
PC – PC (-s) *nm*
PE – Sport *nm*
peace – Frieden (-) *nm*
  Leave me in peace! – Laß mich in Ruhe! *excl*
peaceful – friedlich *adj*
peach – Pfirsich (-e) *nm*
peanut – Erdnuß (nüsse) *nf*
pear – Birne (-n) *nf*
pea – Erbse (-n) *nf*
peculiar – seltsam *adj*
pedestrian – (male) Fußgänger (-) *nm*
pedestrian – (female) Fußgängerin (-nen) *nf*
pedestrian crossing – Fußgängerüberweg (-e) *nm*
pedestrian precinct – Fußgängerzone (-n) *nf*
peel – schälen *v reg*
pen – (fountain) Füller (-) *nm*
pen – (ballpoint) Kuli (-s) *nm*, Kugelschreiber (-) *nm*
pencil – Bleistift (-e) *nm*
pencil case – Federmäppchen (-) *nnt*

---

adj - adjective   *v reg* - verb regular   *v sep* - verb separable   † - see verb info
prep - preposition   *v irreg* - verb irregular   *v refl* - verb reflexive   * - takes sein

pencil sharpener – Bleistiftspitzer (-) *nm*

pendant – Anhänger (-) *nm*

pen-friend – (male) Brieffreund (-e) *nm*

pen-friend – (female) Brieffreundin (-nen) *nf*

penknife – Taschenmesser (-) *nnt*

pensioner – (male) Rentner (-) *nm*

pensioner – (female) Rentnerin (-nen) *nf*

people – Leute *npl*

pepper – (spice) Pfeffer *nm*

pepper – (vegetable) Paprika (-s) *nm*

per – pro (+ acc) *prep*

  per cent – Prozent *nnt*

  per day – pro Tag

  per hour – pro Stunde

  per kilo – pro Kilo

  per month – pro Monat

  per person – pro Person

  per week – pro Woche

percussion instrument – Schlagzeug (-e) *nnt*

perfect – perfekt *adj*

performance – (drama) Vorstellung (-en) *nf*

performance – (sport, etc) Leistung (-en) *nf*

performer – (male) Künstler (-) *nm*

performer – (female) Künstlerin (-nen) *nf*

performing arts – (school) Theaterkunde *nf*

perfume – Parfüm *nnt*

perhaps – vielleicht *adv*

period – (lesson) Stunde (-n) *nf*

period – (time) Zeit (-en) *nf*

period – (in time) Zeitpunkt (-e) *nm*

period – (menstrual) Tage *npl,* Periode (-n) *nf*

  I've got my period – Ich habe meine Tage

permission – Erlaubnis (-se) *nf*

permit – erlauben *v reg* †

permitted – gestattet, erlaubt *adj*

person – (male or female) Person (-en) *nf*

  in person – persönlich *adv*

personal – persönlich *adj*

personal stereo – Walkman® (Walkmen) *nm*

persuade – überreden *v reg insep* †

pet – Haustier (-e) *nnt*

petrol – Benzin *nnt*

  4-star leaded petrol – Super verbleit *nnt*

  unleaded petrol – bleifrei *adj*

petrol pump – Zapfsäule (n) *nf*

petrol pump attendant – Tankwart (-e) *nm*

petrol station – Tankstelle (-n) *nf*

pharmacy – Apotheke (-n) *nf*

phone – Telefon (-e) *nnt*

  on the phone – am Telefon

phone – anrufen *v irreg sep,* telefonieren mit (+ dat) *v reg* †

phone book – Telefonbuch (-bücher) *nnt*

phone box – Telefonzelle (-n) *nf*

phone call – Anruf (-e) *nm*

phone card – Telefonkarte (-n) *nf*

phone number – Telefonnummer (-n) *nf*

photo – Foto (-s) *nnt*

  take a photo – fotografieren *v reg* †

photocopy – Fotokopie (-n) *nf*

photocopier – Fotokopiergerät(-e) *nnt*

photocopy – fotokopieren *v reg* †

photograph – Foto (-s) *nnt*

photographer – (male) Fotograf (-en) *nm wk*

photographer – (female) Fotografin (-nen) *nf*

photography – Fotografie *nf*

physical – körperlich *adj*

physical education – Sport *nm*

---

physics – Physik *nf*
physiotherapist – (male)
Physiotherapeut (-en) *nm wk*
physiotherapist – (female)
Physiotherapeutin (-nen) *nf*
piano – (upright) Klavier *nnt*
piano – (grand) Flügel (-) *nm*
I play the piano – ich spiele
Klavier
pick (out) – (choose) auswählen *v reg
sep*
pickpocket – Taschendieb (-e) *nm*
pick up – (collect) abholen *v reg sep*
pick up – (lift) aufheben *v irreg sep*
pick up phone – den Hörer
abnehmen *v irreg sep*
picnic – Picknick (-s) *nnt*
picnic – picknicken *v reg*
picnic area – Rastplatz (-plätze) *nm*
picture – Bild (-er) *nnt*
picturesque – malerisch *adj*
pie chart – Kreisdiagramm (-e) *nnt*
piece (of) – Stück (-) *nnt*
a piece of chocolate – ein Stück
Schokolade
piece of information – Auskunft *nf*
pig – Schwein (-e) *nnt*
piggy bank – Sparschwein (-e) *nnt*
pile – Haufen (-) *nm*
pill – Tablette (-n) *nf*
pill – (contraceptive) Pille (-n) *nf*
pillow – Kopfkissen (-) *nnt*
pillowcase – Kissenbezug (-züge) *nm*
pilot – (air) Pilot (-en) *nm wk*
pineapple – Ananas (-) *nf*
pink – rosa *adj inv*
pipe – (for tobacco) Pfeife (-n) *nf*
Pisces – (horoscope) Fische
pitch – Platz (Plätze) *nm*
pitch the tent – das Zelt aufbauen
v reg sep
pity – schade

What a pity! – Wie schade! *excl*
pizza – Pizza (-s) *nf*
placard – Plakat (-e) *nnt*
place – (spot) Stelle (-n) *nf*
place – (square) Platz (Plätze) *nm*
place – (town, etc) Ort (-e) *nm*
place of birth – Geburtsort (-e) *nm*
take place – stattfinden *v irreg sep*
at my place – bei mir
place – (vertical) stellen *v reg*
place – (horizontal) legen *v reg*
place – (insert) stecken *v reg*
place on – setzen auf (+ acc) *v reg*
plain – (no pattern) uni *adj inv*
plait – Zopf (Zöpfe) *nm*
plan – Plan (Pläne) *nm*
career plans – Berufspläne *npl*
future plans – Zukunftspläne *npl*
holiday plans – Urlaubspläne *npl*
plan – planen *v reg*
as planned – wie geplant
plan sthg – (intend) etwas vorhaben
v irreg sep
plane – Flugzeug (-e) *nnt*
by plane – mit dem Flugzeug
plant – Pflanze (-n) *nf*
plant – pflanzen *v reg*
plaster – (sticking) Pflaster *nnt*
plaster – (broken arm) Gips (-e) *nm*
plastic – Kunststoff (-e) *nm*
made of plastic – aus Kunststoff
plastic bag – Plastiktüte (-n) *nf*
plate – Teller (-) *nm*
platform – Bahnsteig (-e) *nm*
from platform 8 – auf Gleis 8
play – Theaterstück (-e) *nnt*
play – spielen *v reg*
play a trick on – veräppeln *v reg* †
play chess – Schach spielen *v reg*
play football – Fußball spielen
v reg

---

adj - adjective   *v reg* - verb regular   *v sep* - verb separable   † - see verb info
prep - preposition   *v irreg* - verb irregular   *v refl* - verb reflexive   * - takes sein

play the guitar – Gitarre spielen
v reg

player – (male) Spieler (-) *nm*

player – (female) Spielerin (-nen) *nf*

playground – Spielplatz (-plätze) *nm*

playing card – Spielkarte (-n) *nf*

playing field – Sportplatz (plätze) *nm*

pleasant – angenehm *adj*

please – bitte *adv*
    please do not... – bitte nicht

pleased – (satisfied) zufrieden *adj*
    be pleased about – sich freuen
    über (+ acc) *v reg refl*

Pleased to meet you! – Angenehm!
excl

pleasure – Freude (-n) *nf*, Vergnügen
nnt
    It's a pleasure! – Bitte sehr! Gern
    geschehen! *excl*
    with pleasure – mit Vergnügen

pluck – pflücken *v reg*

plug – (electric) Stecker (-) *nm*

plug – (bath) Stöpsel (-) *nm*

plug in – anschließen *v irreg sep*

plum – Pflaume (-n) *nf*

plumber – (male) Klempner (-) *nm*

plumber – (female) Klempnerin
(-nen) *nf*

plump – mollig *adj*

pluperfect – Plusquamperfekt *nnt*

plural – Plural (-e) *nm*
    in the plural – im Plural

p.m. – nachmittags *adv*

pocket – Tasche (-n) *nf*

pocket money – Taschengeld *nnt*

point – Punkt (-e) *nm*
    There's no point – Es hat keinen
    Zweck

pointed – spitz *adj*

pointless – zwecklos *adj*

poison – Gift (-e) *nnt*

poisonous – giftig *adj*

Poland – Polen *nnt*

police – Polizei *nf*

policeman – Polizist (-en) *nm wk*

police station – Polizeiwache (-n) *nf*

police woman – Polizistin (-nen) *nf*

policy – Politik *nf*

polish – polieren *v reg* †

polite – höflich *adj*

politeness – Höflichkeit (-en) *nf*

politician – (male) Politiker (-) *nm*

politician – (female) Politikerin (-nen)
nf

polluted – verschmutzt *adj*

pollution – Umweltschmutz *nm*,
Umweltverschmutzung *nf*

pond – Teich (-e) *nm*

pony – Pony (-s) *nnt*

pony tail – Pferdeschwanz
(-schwänze) *nm*

poodle – Pudel (-) *nm*

pool – Schwimmbad (-bäder) *nnt*

pool – (open air) Freibad (-bäder) *nnt*

pool – (indoor) Hallenbad (-bäder) *nnt*

poor – (bad) schlecht *adj*

poor – (not rich) arm *adj*

poorly – (ill) krank *adj*

pop music – Popmusik *nf*

popular – beliebt *adj*

pork – Schweinefleisch *nnt*
    roast pork – Schweinebraten *nm*

pork chop – Schweinekotelett (-s) *nnt*

port – Hafen (Häfen) *nm*

portion – Portion (-en) *nf*

Portugal – Portugal *nnt*

Portuguese – portugiesisch *adj*

Portuguese person – (male)
Portugiese (-n) *nm wk*

Portuguese person – (female)
Portugiesin (-nen) *nf*

posh – vornehm *adj*

position – Lage (-n) *nf*

positive – positiv *adj*

---

possess – besitzen *v irreg*
possibility – Möglichkeit (-en) *nf*
possible – möglich *adj*
possibly – möglicherweise *adv*
post – einwerfen *v irreg sep*
  post a letter – einen Brief
  einwerfen *v irreg sep*
postage stamp – Briefmarke (-n) *nf*
postal order – Zahlkarte (-n) *nf*
postcard – Postkarte (-n) *nf*
post code – Postleitzahl (-en) *nf*
poster – Poster (-) *nnt*
post office – Post *nf*
postman – Briefträger (-) *nm*
postpone – verschieben *v irreg*
postwoman – Briefträgerin (-nen) *nf*
pot – (cooking) Topf (Töpfe) *nm*
  a pot of coffee – ein Kännchen
  Kaffee *nnt*
potato – Kartoffel (-n) *nf*
pot plant – Topfpflanze (-n) *nf*
pottery – (workshop) Töpferei (-en) *nf*
poultry – Geflügel *nnt*
pound – Pfund *nnt*
pour a drink – einschenken *v reg sep*
powder – Pulver (-) *nnt*
powder – (cosmetic) Puder (-) *nm*
power – Kraft (Kräfte) *nf*
powerful – mächtig *adj*
power point – Steckdose (-n) *nf*
practical – praktisch *adj*
practical work – praktische Arbeit *nf*
practice – Übung (-en) *nf*
  practice makes perfect – Übung
  macht den Meister
practice – (doctor) Praxis (Praxen) *nf*
practise – üben *v reg*
praise – loben *v reg*
precaution – Vorsichtsmaßnahme
  (-n) *nf*
precious – wertvoll *adj*
precise – genau *adj*

prefer – vorziehen *v irreg sep*
  I prefer tea to coffee – Ich trinke
  lieber Tee als Kaffee
prep – (homework) Hausaufgaben *npl*
preparation – Vorbereitung (-en) *nf*
preparatory – Vor- *pref*
prep(aratory) school – private
  Grundschule (-n) *nf*
prepare – vorbereiten *v reg sep* †
prescribe – verschreiben *v irreg*
prescription – Rezept (-) *nnt*
presence – Anwesenheit (-en) *nf*
present – (not absent) anwesend *adj*
present – (current) gegenwärtig,
  im Moment *adj*
present – (gift) Geschenk (-e) *nnt*
  give as a present – schenken
  v reg
present – (tense) Präsens *nnt*
present – (introduce) vorstellen *v reg*
  sep
present – (radio, TV) moderieren
  v reg †
presenter – (TV) (male) Moderator
  (-en) *nm wk*
presenter – (TV) (female)
  Moderatorin (-nen) *nf*
press – (media) Presse *nf*
press – drücken *v reg*
press on – (continue) weitermachen
  v reg sep
pretend – tun so, als ob *v irreg*
pretty – hübsch *adj*
prevent – verhindern *v reg* †
previous – vorig, ehemalig *adj*
previously – früher *adv*
price – Preis (-e) *nm*
price list – Preisliste (-n) *nf*
priest – (RC) Priester (-) *nm*
primary school – Grundschule (-n) *nf*
primary school teacher – (male)
  Grundschullehrer (-) *nm*

---

primary school teacher – (female) Grundschullehrerin (-nen) *nf*
principal – (male) Direktor (-) *nm*
principal – (female) Direktorin (-nen) *nf*
principle – Prinzip (-ien) *nnt*
print – drucken *v reg*
printed – gedruckt *adj*
printer – Drucker (-) *nm*
priority – (traffic) Vorfahrt
prison – Gefängnis (-se) *nnt*
private – privat *adj*
private school – Privatschule (-n) *nf*
prize – Preis (-e) *nm*
probable – vermutlich *adj*
probably – wahrscheinlich *adj*
problem – Problem (-e) *nnt*
process – Prozeß (Prozesse) *nm*
  be in the process of – gerade dabei sein* *v irreg*
procession – Zug (Züge) *nm*
product – Produkt (-e) *nnt*
profession – Beruf (-e) *nm*
  What's your profession? – Was sind Sie von Beruf?
programme – (TV) Sendung (-en) *nf*
programme – Programm (-e) *nnt*
programmer – (male) Programmierer (-) *nm*
programmer – (female) Programmiererin (-nen) *nf*
progress – Fortschritt (-e) *nm*
  make progress – Fortschritte machen *v reg*
project – Projekt (-e) *nnt*
promise – Versprechen (-) *nnt*
promise s.o. sthg – jdm etwas versprechen *v irreg*
pronoun – Pronomen (-) *nnt*
pronounce – aussprechen *v irreg sep*
proper – (correct) richtig *adj*
proper – (decent) anständig *adj*
proper noun – Eigenname (-n) *nm wk*

propose – (suggest) vorschlagen *v irreg sep*
protect from – schützen vor (+ dat) *v reg*
protection – Schutz (-e) *nm*
protest – protestieren *v reg* †
Protestant – evangelisch *adj*
Protestant – Protestant (-en) *nm wk*
Protestant – Protestantin (-nen) *nf*
proud (of) – stolz (auf + acc) *adj*
prove – beweisen *v irreg*
province – Provinz (-en) *nf*
PSE – Lebenskunde *nf*
PTO – bitte wenden (b.w.)
pub – Kneipe (-n) *nf*
public – öffentlich *adj*
public holiday – Feiertag (-e) *nm*
public school – (UK) Privatschule (-n) *nf*
public transport – öffentliche Verkehrsmittel *npl*
publicity – Werbung (-en) *nf*
pudding – (dessert) Nachtisch (-e) *nm*
pull – ziehen *v irreg*
pull a face – ein Gesicht ziehen *v irreg*
pullover – Pullover (-) *nm*
pump up tyres – aufpumpen *v reg sep*
pun – Wortspiel (-e) *nnt*
punctual – pünktlich *adj*
punctuation – Zeichensetzung (-en) *nf*
puncture – Reifenpanne (-n) *nf*
punish – bestrafen *v reg* †
punishment – Strafe (-n) *nf*
pupil – (male) Schüler (-) *nm*
pupil – (female) Schülerin (-nen) *nf*
puppy – ein junger Hund *nm*
purchase – Kauf (Käufe) *nm*
purchase – kaufen *v reg*
purple – purpur *adj inv*
purpose – Zweck (-e) *nm*, Absicht (-en) *nf*
  on purpose – absichtlich *adv*

---

nm - noun masculine   *nf* - noun feminine   *nnt* - noun neuter   *npl* - noun plural
nom - nominative   *acc* - accusative   *gen* - genitive   *dat* - dative

purr – schnurren *v reg*
purse – Portemonnaie (-s) *nnt*
push – (a car) schieben *v irreg*
push – (door) drücken *v reg*
put – (vertical) stellen *v reg*
put – (insert) stecken *v reg*
put – (horizontal) legen *v reg*
put away – weglegen *v reg sep*
put back – zurückstellen *v reg sep,*
zurücklegen *v reg sep*
put down – (vertical) hinstellen *v reg*
sep
put down – (horizontal) hinlegen
v reg sep

put in the right order – ordnen
v reg †
put on – (clothes) anziehen *v irreg sep*
put on headlights – die
Scheinwerfer einschalten *v reg sep* †
put on light – das Licht anmachen
v reg sep
put on make-up – sich schminken
v reg refl
put on – (play) aufführen *v reg sep*
put out – (light) ausmachen *v reg sep*
put up – (guest) unterbringen *v irreg*
sep
put up with – aushalten *v irreg sep*
pyjamas – Schlafanzug (-züge) *nm*
puzzle – Rätsel (-) *nnt*

Q

qualification – Qualifikation (-en) *nf*
quality – Qualität (-en) *nf*
  good quality – guter Qualität
  poor quality – schlechter Qualität
quantity – Menge (-n) *nf*
quarrel – Streit (-e) *nm*
quarrel – sich streiten *v irreg refl*
quarry – Steinbruch (-brüche) *nm*
quarter – Viertel (-) *nnt*
  quarter of an hour – eine
  Viertelstunde *nf*
  quarter past one – Viertel nach
  eins
  quarter to two – Viertel vor zwei
  three quarters – Dreiviertel (-) *nnt*
  three quarters of an hour –
  Dreiviertelstunde (-n) *nf*
quarter – (town) Stadtteil (-e) *nm*
quay – Kai (-s) *nm*
queen – Königin (-nen) *nf*
question – Frage (-n) *nf*

  ask a question – eine Frage stellen
v reg
  out of the question – das kommt
  nicht in Frage
question mark (?) – Fragezeichen
nnt
question – fragen *v reg*
question s.o. – befragen *v reg* †
queue – Schlange (-n) *nf*
queue up – Schlange stehen *v irreg*
quick – schnell *adj*
  be quick – sich beeilen *v reg refl* †
quiet – (peaceful) still, ruhig *adj*
quiet – (without noise) leise *adj*
quilt – Steppdecke (-n) *nf*
quite – (fairly) ziemlich *adv*
quite – (totally) ganz *adv*
quiz – Quiz (-) *nnt*
quotation – Zitat (-e) *nnt*
quote – zitieren *v reg* †

R

rabbit – Kaninchen (-) *nnt*
race – (nationality) Rasse (-n) *nf*
race – (sport) Rennen (-) *nnt*
races – Pferderennen *nnt*
racket – (tennis) Schläger (-) *nm*
radiator – (in building) Heizkörper (-) *nm*
radiator – (in car) Kühler (-) *nm*
radio – Radio (-s) *nnt*
  be on the radio – im Radio sein* *v irreg*
radio cassette player – Radiokassettenrekorder (-) *nm*
railway – Eisenbahn (-en) *nf,* Bahn (-en) *nf*
railway carriage – Wagon (-s) *nm*
railway station – Bahnhof (-höfe) *nm*
  main railway station – Hauptbahnhof (-höfe) *nm*
rain – Regen *nm*
  in the rain – im Regen
rain – regnen *v reg* †
  It is raining – Es regnet
  It was raining – Es regnete
  It will rain – Es wird regnen
  It rained – Es hat geregnet
rainbow – Regenbogen (-bögen) *nm*
raincoat – Regenmantel (-mäntel) *nm*
rainy – regnerisch *adj*
Ramadan – Ramadan *nm*
rapid – schnell *adj*
rare – selten *adj*
raspberry – Himbeere (-n) *nf*
  raspberry tart – Himbeertorte (-n) *nf*
rat – Ratte (-n) *nf*
rate of exchange – Wechselkurs (-e) *nm*
rather – (fairly) ziemlich *adv*

I'd rather play tennis – Ich würde lieber Tennis spielen
raw – roh *adj*
razor – Rasierapparat (-e) *nm*
RE – Religion (-en) *nf*
reach – erreichen *v reg* †
read – lesen *v irreg*
reader – (male) Leser (-) *nm*
reader – (female) Leserin (-nen) *nf*
reading – Lesen *nnt*
reading matter – Lektüre *nf*
ready – fertig *adj*
  ready-made meal – Fertiggericht (-e) *nnt*
ready – (willing) bereit *adj*
real – (genuine) echt *adj*
real – (true) wirklich *adj*
realise – merken *v reg*
reality – Wirklichkeit (-en) *nf*
really – wirklich *adv*
reason – Grund (Gründe) *nm*
receipt – Quittung (-en) *nf*
receive – bekommen *v irreg,* erhalten *v irreg*
recent – neu *adj*
recently – neulich *adv*
reception – Empfang (Empfänge) *nm*
reception desk – (hotel) Rezeption *nf*
receptionist – Empfangsdame (-n) *nf*
recipe – Rezept (-e) *nnt*
reckon – (calculate) rechnen *v reg* †
reckon – (judge) meinen *v reg*
reckon – (think) denken *v irreg*
recognise – erkennen *v irreg*
recommend – empfehlen *v irreg*
recommended – empfohlen *adj*
record – (sport, etc) Rekord (-e) *nm*
record – (pop, etc) Schallplatte (-n) *nf*

---

record – (on tape) aufnehmen *v irreg sep*
recorder – (flute) Blockflöte (-n) *nf*
record player – Plattenspieler (-) *nm*
recount – erzählen *v reg* †
recover – (get back) zurückbekommen *v irreg sep*
recover – (get better) sich erholen *v reg refl* †
rectangular – viereckig *adj*
recycle – recyceln *v reg* †
red – rot *adj*
redcurrant – rote Johannisbeere (-n) *nf*
red haired – rothaarig *adj*
red wine – Rotwein (-e) *nm*
re-do – wiederholen *v reg insep* †
reduce – reduzieren *v reg* †
reduced – reduziert *adj*
reduction – (price) Ermäßigung (-en) *nf*
reel – (spool) Rolle (-n) *nf*
referee – (male) Schiedsrichter (-) *nm*
referee – (female) Schiedsrichterin (-nen) *nf*
refill – auffüllen *v reg sep*
reflexive verb – Reflexivverbum (-verben) *nnt*
refreshment bar – Imbißstube (-n) *nf*
refreshments – Erfrischungen *npl*
refuse – (rubbish) Müll *nm*
refuse – (to do sthg) sich weigern *v reg refl*
refuse – (permission) verweigern *v reg* †
region – Region (-en) *nf*
registered letter – Einschreibebrief (-e) *nm*
registration number – (car) Kennzeichen (-) *nnt*
regret – bedauern *v reg* †
regular – regelmäßig *adj*
rehearsal – Probe (-n) *nf*
relationship – Verhältnis (-se) *nnt*

relative – Verwandte *nmf* ‡
relatively – relativ *adv*
relax – sich entspannen *v reg refl* †
relaxation – Entspannung *nf*
relaxed – entspannt *adj*
reliable – zuverlässig *adj*
religion – Religion (-en) *nf*
remain – (stay) bleiben* *v irreg*
remain – (left over) übrigbleiben* *v irreg sep*
remainder – Rest *nm*
remarkable – merkwürdig *adj*
remedy for – Mittel gegen (+ acc) *nnt*
remember – sich erinnern an (+ acc) *v reg refl* †
remind of – erinnern an (+ acc) *v reg* †
remote control – (TV) Fernbedienung *nf*
removal van – Möbelwagen (-) *nm*
remove – entfernen *v reg* †
renew – erneuern *v reg* †
rent – Miete (-n) *nf*
rent – mieten *v reg* †
renting – Vermietung (-en) *nf*
repair – Reparatur (-en) *nf*
repair – reparieren *v reg* †
I have had my camera repaired – Ich habe meinen Fotoapparat reparieren lassen
repeat – wiederholen *v reg insep* †
repeat a year – (at school) sitzen bleiben* *v irreg*
replace – ersetzen *v reg* †
reply – antworten *v reg* †
reply to s.o – beantworten *v reg* †
report – Bericht (-e) *nm*
report – (school) Zeugnis (-se) *nnt*
mid-year report – Halbjahreszeugnis (-se) *nnt*
reporter – (male) Reporter (-) *nm*
reporter – (female) Reporterin (-nen) *nf*
represent – vertreten *v irreg*

---

adj - adjective	*v reg* - verb regular	*v sep* - verb separable	† - see verb info
prep - preposition	*v irreg* - verb irregular	*v refl* - verb reflexive	* - takes sein

representative – (male) Vertreter (-) *nm*
representative – (female) Vertreterin (-nen) *nf*
reputation – Ruf (-e) *nm*
request – Bitte (-n) *nf*
rescue – retten *v reg* †
resemble – ähneln (+ dat) *v reg*
reservation – Reservierung (-en) *nf*
reserve – reservieren *v reg* †
reserved – reserviert *adj*
resident – (male) Einwohner (-) *nm*
resident – (female) Einwohnerin (-nen) *nf*
resit exam – eine Prüfung wiederholen *v reg insep* †
respect – Respekt *nm*
respectable – anständig *adj*
responsibility – Verantwortung *nf*
responsible – verantwortlich *adj*
rest – sich ausruhen *v reg refl sep*
have a rest – Pause machen *v reg*
the rest – Rest *nm*
restaurant – Restaurant (-s) *nnt*
restrict – einschränken *v reg sep*
result – Ergebnis (-se) *nnt*
retire – in den Ruhestand treten* *v irreg*
retired – im Ruhestand
retired person – (male) Rentner (-) *nm*
retired person – (female) Rentnerin (-nen) *nf*
return – zurückkommen* *v irreg sep*
return journey – Rückfahrt (-en) *nf*
return ticket – Rückfahrkarte (-n) *nf*
a return ticket to Dresden – einmal nach Dresden, hin und zurück
Many happy returns! – Herzlichen Glückwunsch zum Geburtstag! *excl*
reunification – Wiedervereinigung *nf*
reverse – (car) rückwärts fahren* *v irreg*
revolver – Revolver (-) *nm*

reward – Belohnung (-en) *nf*
Rhine – Rhein *nm*
rhinoceros – Nashorn (-hörner) *nnt*
rib – Rippe (-n) *nf*
rice – Reis *nm*
rich – reich *adj*
ride – (bike) radfahren* *v irreg sep*
ride – (horse) reiten (*) *v irreg*
ridiculous – lächerlich *adj*
riding hat – Reitkappe (-n) *nf*
right – (not wrong) richtig *adj*
be right – recht haben *v irreg*
That's right – Das stimmt
the right answer – die richtige Antwort
You are right – Du hast recht
right! – also! *excl*
right – rechts *adv*
keep to the right – rechts fahren* *v irreg*
on the right – auf der rechten Seite
to the right – rechts *adv*
right-handed – rechtshändig *adj*
right now – sofort *adv*
right winger – (sport) Rechtsaußen (-) *nm*
ring – Ring (-e) *nm*
ring – (bell) klingeln *v reg*
ring the doorbell – klingeln *v reg*
ring binder – Ordner (-) *nm*
ring road – Umgehungsstraße (-n) *nf*
ring up – (phone) anrufen *v irreg sep*
rink – (skating) Eisbahn (-en) *nf*
rip – (clothes) zerreißen *v irreg*
ripe – reif *adj*
rise – (get up) aufstehen* *v irreg sep*
rise – (mountain) sich erheben *v irreg refl*
rise – (sun) aufgehen* *v irreg sep*
risk – Risiko (Risiken) *nnt*
river – Fluß (Flüsse) *nm*
road – Straße (-n) *nf*

---

nm - noun masculine	nf - noun feminine	nnt - noun neuter	npl - noun plural
nom- nominative	acc - accusative	gen - genitive	dat - dative

country road – Landstraße (-n) *nf*
major road – Bundesstraße (-n) *nf*
road map – Straßenkarte (-n) *nf*
road sign – Straßenschild (-er) *nnt*
road user – (male)
Verkehrsteilnehmer (-) *nm*
road user – (female)
Verkehrsteilnehmerin (-nen) *nf*
roadworks – Baustelle (-n) *nf*
roast – braten *v irreg*
roast – Braten (-) *nm*
roast beef – Rinderbraten (-) *nm*
roast chicken – Brathähnchen (-) *nnt*
roast pork – Schweinebraten (-) *nm*
roast potatoes – Bratkartoffeln *npl*
rock climbing – Bergsteigen *nnt*
rocking chair – Schaukelstuhl
(-stühle) *nm*
rock music – Rockmusik *nf*
rock – schaukeln *v reg*
role – Rolle (-n) *nf*
role play – Rollenspiel (-e) *nnt*
roll – (bread) Brötchen (-) *nnt,* Semmel
(-n) *nf*
roller blades – Inline Skates *npl*
rollercoaster – Achterbahn (-en) *nf*
roller skate – Rollschuh fahren*
v irreg
roller skates – Rollschuhe *npl*
romantic – romantisch *adj*
roof – Dach (Dächer) *nnt*
room – Zimmer (-) *nnt*
double room – Doppelzimmer (-)
nnt
room with twin beds –
Zweibettzimmer (-) *nnt*
rose – Rose (-n) *nf*
rosé wine – Roséwein (-e) *nm*
Rosh Hashanah – das jüdische
Neujahr *nnt*
rotten – (awful) mies *adj coll*
rotten – (food) faul *adj*
rough book – Schmierheft (-e) *nnt*

rough draft – Entwurf (Entwürfe) *nm*
round – rund *adj*
go round a corner – um die Ecke
gehen* *v irreg*
go round to a friend's house –
einen Freund/eine Freundin
besuchen *v reg* †
round about – um ... herum (+ acc)
prep
roundabout – (fair) Karussell (-s) *nnt*
roundabout – (traffic)
Verkehrskreisel (-) *nm*
round here – hier in der Gegend
route – (bus) Linie (-n) *nf*
routine – Routine (-n) *nf*
row – (argument) Streit *nm*
row – (cinema) Rang (Ränge) *nm*
row – (loud noise) Krach *nm*
row – (argue) sich streiten *v irreg refl*
row – (boat) rudern *v reg*
rowdy – laut *adj*
royal blue – königsblau *adj*
RS – Religion *nf*
rub – reiben *v irreg*
rubber – (eraser) Radiergummi (-s) *nm*
rubber band – Gummiband
(-bänder) *nnt*
rubbish – Müll *nm,* Abfall *nm*
rubbish bin – Abfalleimer (-) *nm*
rucksack – Rucksack (-säcke) *nm*
rude – (impolite) unhöflich *adj*
rude – (very) ungezogen *adj*
rug – Teppich (-e) *nm*
rugby – Rugby *nnt*
ruin – kaputt machen *v reg*
rule – Regel (-n) *nf*
as a rule – in der Regel
ruler – Lineal (-e) *nnt*
run – laufen* *v irreg*
run away – weglaufen* *v irreg sep*
run down – hinunterlaufen* *v irreg sep*

---

adj - adjective   *v reg* - verb regular   *v sep* - verb separable   † - see verb info
prep - preposition   *v irreg* - verb irregular   *v refl* - verb reflexive   * - takes sein

She ran down the street – Sie ist die Straße hinuntergelaufen

run into – (meet) begegnen* (+dat) *v reg* †

run into – (car) zusammenstoßen* mit (+ dat) *v irreg sep*

run out of – (building) hinauslaufen* aus (+ dat) *v irreg sep*

run out of petrol – eine Benzinpanne haben *v irreg*

We've run out of sugar – Der Zucker ist alle

I have run out of time – Ich habe keine Zeit mehr

run over – (accident) überfahren *v irreg insep*

run up – hinauflaufen* *v irreg sep*

He ran up the stairs – Er ist die Treppe hinaufgelaufen

runner up – (sport) Zweite *nmf* ‡

runway – Startbahn (-en) *nf*

rural – ländlich *adj*

rush – sich beeilen *v reg refl* †

I am in a rush – Ich habe es eilig

rush hour – Hauptverkehrszeit (-en) *nf*

Russia – Rußland *nnt*

Russian – russisch *adj*

Russian person – (male) Russe (-n) *nm wk*

Russian person – (female) Russin (-nen) *nf*

S

sack – Sack (Säcke) *nm*

sad – traurig *adj*

saddle – Sattel (Sättel) *nm*

sadly – leider *adv*

sadness – Traurigkeit *nf*

safe – sicher *adj*

safe – Tresor (-e) *nm*

safety – Sicherheit *nf*

safety belt – Sicherheitsgurt (-e) *nm*

Sagittarius – Schütze

said – *see sagen*

sail – Segel (-) *nnt*

sail – segeln *v reg*

sailboard – Surfbrett (-er) *nnt*

sailing dinghy – Segelboot (-e) *nnt*

sailing ship – Segelschiff (-e) *nnt*

sailor – (navy) Matrose (-n) *nm wk*

sailor – (civilian) Seemann (-männer) *nm*

saint – Sankt *adj inv*

saint – Heilige *nmf* ‡

salad – Salat (-e) *nm*

salad – (green) grüner Salat *nm*

salad – (mixed) gemischter Salat *nm*

salad – (potato) Kartoffelsalat *nm*

salad – (tomato) Tomatensalat *nm*

salami – Salami *nf*

salary – Gehalt (Gehälter) *nnt*

sale – Verkauf (Verkäufe) *nm*

for sale – zu verkaufen

on sale – zu verkaufen

sale – Schlußverkauf (-verkäufe) *nm*

in the sales – im Schlußverkauf

sales assistant – (male) Verkäufer (-) *nm*

sales assistant – (female) Verkäuferin (-nen) *nf*

salmon – Lachs (-e) *nm*

salt – Salz *nnt*

salty – salzig *adj*

same – gleich *adj*

at the same time – gleichzeitig *adv*

---

nm - noun masculine	*nf* - noun feminine	*nnt* - noun neuter	*npl* - noun plural
nom- nominative	*acc* - accusative	*gen* - genitive	*dat* - dative

sand – Sand *nm*
sandal – Sandale (-n) *nf*
sand castle – Sandburg (-en) *nf*
sandwich – Butterbrot (-e) *nnt*
  an open sandwich – ein belegtes
  Brot
sanitary towel – Damenbinde (-n) *nf*
Santa Claus – Weihnachtsmann *nm*
sardine – Sardine (-n) *nf*
satellite – Satellit (-en) *nm wk*
satellite dish – Satellitenschüssel (-n)
  nf
satisfactory – befriedigend *adj*
satisfied – zufrieden *adj*
satisfy – befriedigen *v reg* †
Saturday – Samstag (-e) *nm,*
  Sonnabend (-e) *nm*
  on Saturday – am Samstag
  See you on Saturday! –
  Bis Samstag!
sauce – Soße (-n) *nf*
saucepan – Topf (Töpfe) *nm*
saucer – Untertasse (-n) *nf*
sausage – Wurst (Würste) *nf*
  boiled sausage – Bockwurst
  fried sausage – Bratwurst
save – retten *v reg* †
save – (computer) speichern *v reg*
save money – Geld sparen *v reg*
save up for – sparen für (+ acc) *v reg*
savings – Ersparnisse *npl*
saxophone – Saxophon (-e) *nnt*
say – sagen *v reg*
say goodbye – sich verabschieden
  v reg †
scarcely – kaum *adv*
scarf – (long) Schal (-s) *nm*
scarf – (square) Tuch (Tücher) *nnt*
scary – beängstigend *adj*
scene – (crime) Tatort (-e) *nm*
scene – (play) Szene (-n) *nf*
scenery – Landschaft (-en) *nf*

scenic – landschaftlich *adj*
school – Schule (-n) *nf*
  in school – in der Schule
  I walk to school – Ich gehe zu
  Fuß zur Schule
school – (boarding) Internat (-e) *nnt*
school – (comprehensive)
  Gesamtschule (-n) *nf*
  I go to a comprehensive school
  – Ich besuche eine Gesamtschule
school – (grammar) Gymnasium
  (Gymnasien) *nnt*
school – (nursery) Kindergarten
  (-gärten) *nm*
school – (primary) Grundschule (-n) *nf*
school – (private) Privatschule (-n) *nf*
school – (secondary modern)
  Realschule (-n) *nf*
school – (secondary modern)
  Hauptschule (-n) *nf*
school bag – Schultasche (-n) *nf*
school bus – Schulbus (-busse) *nm*
schoolboy – Schüler (-) *nm*
schoolgirl – Schülerin (-nen) *nf*
school holidays – Schulferien *npl*
school report – Zeugnis (-se) *nnt*
school rule – Schulregel (-n) *nf*
school student – (male) Schüler (-) *nm*
school student – (female) Schülerin
  (-nen) *nf*
school trip – Klassenfahrt (-en) *nf*
school uniform – Schuluniform (-en)
  nf
school year – Schuljahr (-e) *nnt*
science – Naturwissenschaft (-en) *nf*
science fiction – Science Fiction *nf*
science fiction film – Science-
  Fiction-Film (-e) *nm*
science fiction story – Science-
  Fiction-Roman (-e) *nm*
scientific – wissenschaftlich *adj*
scientist – (male) Wissenschaftler (-)
  nm

adj - adjective	*v reg* - verb regular	*v sep* - verb separable	† - see verb info
prep - preposition	*v irreg* - verb irregular	*v refl* - verb reflexive	* - takes sein

scientist – (female) Wissenschaftlerin (-nen) *nf*

scissors – (pair of) Schere (-n) *nf*

scold – ausschimpfen *v reg sep*

scooter – Roller (-) *nm*

score a goal – ein Tor schießen *v irreg*

score a point – einen Punkt gewinnen *v irreg*

Scorpio – (horoscope) Skorpion

Scotland – Schottland *nnt*

Scotsman – Schotte (-n) *nm wk*

Scotswoman – Schottin (-nen) *nf*

Scottish – schottisch *adj*

scout – Pfadfinder (-) *nm*

scream – schreien *v irreg*

screen – (cinema) Leinwand (-wände) *nf*

screen – (TV) Bildschirm (-e) *nm*

screwdriver – Schraubenzieher (-) *nm*

scrum – Gedränge *nnt*

scuba diving – Tiefseetauchen *nnt*

sea – Meer (-e) *nnt,* See (-n) *nf*
  at the seaside – an der Küste
  by the sea – an der Küste

seafood – Meeresfrüchte *npl*

seagull – Möwe (-n) *nf*

seasick – seekrank *adj*

search – durchsuchen *v reg insep*

seaside resort – Badeort (-e) *nm*

season – (of year) Jahreszeit (-en) *nf*

season – (football, etc) Saison (-s) *nf*
  out of season – außerhalb der Saison

season ticket – Dauerkarte (-n) *nf*

seat – (train) Platz (Plätze) *nm*

seat belt – Sicherheitsgurt (-e) *nm*

second – zweite *adj*

second – (time) Sekunde (-n) *nf*

secondary school – *see school*

second class – (ticket) zweiter Klasse

second-hand – aus zweiter Hand, gebraucht

secret – geheim *adj*

secret – Geheimnis (-se) *nnt*

secretary – (male) Sekretär (-e) *nm*

secretary – (female) Sekretärin (-nen) *nf*

security – Sicherheit *nf*

see – sehen *v irreg*
  see again – wiedersehen *v irreg sep*
  see over – bitte wenden (b.w.)
  See you later! – Bis später!
  See you on Saturday! – Bis Samstag!
  See you soon! – Bis bald!
  See you this evening! – Bis heute abend!
  See you tomorrow! – Bis morgen!

seem – scheinen *v irreg*

seize – ergreifen *v irreg*

seldom – selten *adv*

select – wählen *v reg*

selection – Auswahl *nf*

self-confident – selbstbewußt *adj*

self-employed – selbständig *adj*

selfish – egoistisch *adj*

self-service – SB (Selbstbedienung) *nf*

self-service restaurant – Selbstbedienungsrestaurant (-s) *nnt*

sell – verkaufen *v reg* †

sellotape® – Tesafilm® *nm*

semi-colon (;) – Semikolon (-s) *nnt*

semi-detached house – Doppelhaus (-häuser) *nnt*

semi-final – Halbfinale (-n) *nnt*

send – schicken *v reg*

send for the doctor – den Arzt kommen lassen *v irreg*

senior citizen – (male) Rentner (-) *nm*

senior citizen – (female) Rentnerin (-nen) *nf*

sensational – sensationell *adj*

sensible – (practical) praktisch *adj*

sensible – (wise) vernünftig *adj*

sensitive – sensibel *adj*
sentence – Satz (Sätze) *nm*
a separable verb – ein trennbares
Verb *nnt*
separate – sich trennen *v reg*
separated – getrennt *adj*
separately – getrennt *adv*
**Do you want to pay
separately?** – Geht das getrennt
oder zusammen?
separation – Trennung (-en) *nf*
September – September *nm*
in September – im September
serial – Serie (-n) *nf*
serious – ernst *adj*
it's not serious – es ist nichts
Ernstes
serve – bedienen *v reg* †
serve oneself – sich bedienen *v reg
refl* †
service – (maintenance) Dienst (-e) *nm*
in the services – beim Militär
service – (restaurant) Bedienung *nf*
service – (tennis) Aufschlag (-schläge)
nm
service area – Raststätte (-n) *nf*
service (not) included – Bedienung
(nicht) inklusive
serviette – Serviette (-n) *nf*
session – (film) Vorführung (-en) *nf*
set – (put) setzen *v reg*
set – (school) Leistungsgruppe (-n) *nf*
set off – losfahren* *v irreg sep*
set out – sich auf den Weg machen
v reg refl
set price menu – Menü (-s) *nnt*
set the alarm clock – den Wecker
stellen *v reg*
set the table – den Tisch decken *v reg*
settee – Sofa (-s) *nnt*
settle – (bill) zahlen *v reg*
settle down – sich einleben *v reg refl
sep*

seven – sieben *adj*
seventeen – siebzehn *adj*
seventh – siebte *adj*
seventy – siebzig *adj*
seventy-one – einundsiebzig *adj*
several – mehrere *adj*
severe – (injury) schwer *adj*
sew – nähen *v reg*
sewing – Nähen *nnt*
sewing machine – Nähmaschine (-n)
nf
sexist – sexistisch *adj*
shade – Schatten (-) *nm*
in the shade – im Schatten
shake – (tremble) zittern *v reg*
shake hands with s.o. – jdm die
Hand geben *v irreg*
Shall we go? – Gehen wir?
shame – schade
What a shame! – Wie schade!
excl
shameful – beschämend *adj*
shampoo – Shampoo (-s) *nm*
shampoo one's hair – sich die
Haare waschen *v irreg dat refl*
shape – Form (-en) *nf*
share – teilen *v reg*
sharp – scharf *adj*
shave – sich rasieren *v reg refl* †
she – sie *pron nom*
shed – Gartenhäuschen (-) *nnt*
sheep – Schaf (-e) *nnt*
sheet – (bed) Laken (-) *nnt*
sheet of paper – Blatt Papier *nnt*
shelf – Regal (-e) *nnt*
shellfish – Meeresfrüchte *npl*
shelter – Schutz *nm*
sheltered from – geschützt von
(+ dat) *adj*
sherry – Sherry (-s) *nm*
shine – scheinen *v irreg*
shiny – glänzend *adj*

---

ship – Schiff (-e) *nnt*
shirt – Hemd (-en) *nnt*
shiver – zittern *v reg*
shoe – Schuh (-e) *nm*
  a pair of shoes – ein Paar Schuhe *nnt*
shoe shop – Schuhgeschäft (-e) *nnt*
shoe size – Schuhgröße (-n) *nf*
shoot – schießen *v irreg*
shoot dead – erschießen *v irreg*
shooting – Schießen *nnt*
shop – Geschäft (-e) *nnt*, Laden (Läden) *nm*, Handlung (-en) *nf*
  go round the shops – einen Einkaufsbummel machen *v reg*
shop assistant – (male) Verkäufer (-) *nm*
shop assistant – (female) Verkäuferin (-nen) *nf*
shopkeeper – Händler (-) *nm*
shoplifter – Ladendieb (-e) *nm*
shopping – Einkaufen *nnt*
  do the shopping – einkaufen gehen* *v irreg*
  go window shopping – einen Schaufensterbummel machen *v reg*
shopping bag – Einkaufstasche (-n) *nf*
shopping centre – Einkaufszentrum (-zentren) *nnt*
shopping list – Einkaufsliste (-n) *nf*
shop window – Schaufenster (-) *nnt*
short – (not long) kurz *adj*
short – (not tall) klein *adj*
shortly – bald *adv*
short-sighted – kurzsichtig *adj*
shorts – Shorts *npl*
  a pair of shorts – eine kurze Hose
should – sollte *see sollen*
shoulder – Schulter (-n) *nf*
shout – Schrei (-e) *nm*
shout – (scream) schreien *v irreg*
shout – (call) rufen *v irreg*

show – Aufführung (-en) *nf*
show – (variety) Show (-s) *nf*
show – zeigen *v reg*
shower – Dusche (-n) *nf*
  have a shower – sich duschen *v reg refl*
shower – (rain) Regenschauer (-) *nm*
  There will be showers – Es wird Schauer geben
showing – (film) Vorführung (-en) *nf*
show-off – (male) Angeber (-) *nm*
show-off – (female) Angeberin (-nen) *nf*
show off – angeben *v irreg sep*
shrewd – schlau *adj*
shrimp – Krabbe (-n) *nf*
Shrove Tuesday – Faschingsdienstag *nm*
shut – schließen *v irreg*
shut in – einschließen *v irreg sep*
shutter – Rolladen (Rolläden) *nm*
shy – schüchtern *adj*
sick bay – (school) Lazarett (-e) *nnt*
sick person – Kranke *nmf* ‡
  feel sick – sich übel fühlen *v reg refl*
  I feel sick – Mir ist übel
side – Seite (-n) *nf*
  on the other side – auf der anderen Seite
side – (team) Mannschaft (-en) *nf*
sideboard – Anrichte (-n) *nf*
side by side – nebeneinander *adv*
sight – (view) Blick (-e) *nm*
sight – (tourist) Sehenswürdigkeit (-en) *nf*
sight – (visibility) Sicht *nf*
  in sight – in Sicht
  out of sight – außer Sicht
sightseeing – Tourismus *nm*
sign – Schild (-er) *nnt*
sign – (post) Wegweiser (-) *nm*
sign – unterschreiben *v irreg insep*
signal – Signal (-e) *nnt*

---

signature – Unterschrift (-en) *nf*
signpost – Wegweiser (-) *nm*
silence – Stille (-n) *nf*
silent – still *adj*
be silent – schweigen *v irreg*
silently – leise *adv*
silk – Seide (-n) *nf*
made of silk – aus Seide
silly – dumm *adj*
silly mistake – Dummheit (-en) *nf*
silver – silbern *adj*
silver – Silber *nnt*
similar – ähnlich *adj*
simple – einfach *adj*
since – seit (+ dat) *prep*
since – seitdem, da *sub conj*
sincere – herzlich *adj*
Yours sincerely – mit freundlichen Grüßen
since then – seither *adv*
sing – singen *v irreg*
singer – (male) Sänger (-) *nm*
singer – (female) Sängerin (-nen) *nf*
single – (one/only) einzig *adj*
single – (unmarried) unverheiratet *adj*
single – Einzel~ *pref*
single parent – Alleinerziehende *nmf* ‡
single person – (male) Junggeselle (-n) *nm wk*
single person – (female) Ledige *nf* ‡
single room – Einzelzimmer (-) *nnt*
single ticket – einfache Fahrkarte *nf*
a single to Hamburg – einmal einfach nach Hamburg
singular – (grammar) Singular *nm*
in the singular – im Singular
sink – Spülbecken (-) *nnt*
Sir – mein Herr
sister – Schwester (-n) *nf*
sister-in-law – Schwägerin (-nen) *nf*
sit – sitzen *v irreg*
sit down – sich hinsetzen *v reg refl sep*

Sit down! – (informal) Setz dich!
Sit down! – (formal) Setzen Sie sich!
sit down at table – zu Tisch kommen* *v irreg*
site – (camp) Platz (Plätze) *nm*
site – (building) Baustelle (-n) *nf*
sitting room – Wohnzimmer (-) *nnt*
situated – gelegen *adj*
Malvern is situated in the Midlands – Malvern liegt in Mittelengland
situation – Situation (-en) *nf*
situation – (case) Fall (Fälle) *nm*
six – sechs *adj*
sixteen – sechzehn *adj*
sixteenth – sechzehnte *adj*
sixth – sechste *adj*
sixth form college – Oberstufenkolleg (-kollegien) *nnt*
sixth form student – (male) Abiturient (-en) *nm wk*
sixth form student – (female) Abiturient (-nen) *nf*
sixty – sechzig *adj*
sixty-one – einundsechzig *adj*
size – Größe (-n) *nf*
size – (shoes) Schuhgröße (-n) *nf*
skate – Schlittschuh (-e) *nm*
skate – Schlittschuh laufen* *v irreg*
skateboard – Rollbrett (-er) *nnt*
skateboard – Rollbrett fahren* *v irreg*
skating rink – Eisbahn (-en) *nf*
ski – Ski fahren* *v irreg*
ski – Ski (-er) *nm*
ski boot – Skistiefel (-) *nm*
skid – ins Schleudern geraten* *v irreg*
ski lift – Skilift (-s) *nm*
ski-run – Piste (-n) *nf*
skiing – Skilaufen *nnt*
skilfully – geschickt *adv*
skilled – geschickt *adj*
skin – Haut *nf*

---

adj - adjective	*v reg* - verb regular	*v sep* - verb separable	† - see verb info
prep - preposition	*v irreg* - verb irregular	*v refl* - verb reflexive	* - takes sein

skinny – dünn *adj*
skirt – Rock (Röcke) *nm*
skive – schwänzen *v reg*
sky – Himmel (-) *nm*
sky blue – himmelblau *adj*
skyscraper – Wolkenkratzer (-) *nm*
sledge – Schlitten (-) *nm*
sleep – schlafen *v irreg*
  fall asleep – einschlafen* *v irreg sep*
sleep – Schlaf *nm*
sleeper car – Schlafwagen (-) *nm*
sleep in – ausschlafen *v irreg sep*
sleeping bag – Schlafsack (-säcke) *nm*
sleepy – schläfrig *adj*
sleeve – Ärmel (-) *nm*
slice – Scheibe (-n) *nf*
slice – schneiden *v irreg*
slicing sausage – Wurst (Würste) *nf*
slide – ausrutschen* *v reg sep*
slide – (playground) Rutschbahn (-en) *nf*
slide – (transparency) Dia (-s) *nnt*
slightly – ein bißchen
slim – schlank *adj*
slim – abnehmen *v irreg sep*
slip – ausrutschen* *v reg sep*
slip of paper – Zettel (-) *nm*
slipper – Hausschuh (-e) *nm*,
  Pantoffel (-n) *nm*
slippery – glitschig *adj*
slope – Hang (Hänge) *nm*
sloping – schräg *adj*
slot machine – Automat (-en) *nm wk*
slot machine – Münzautomat (-en)
  nm wk
slow – langsam *adj*
slow down – langsamer werden*
  v irreg
slow train – Personenzug (-züge) *nm*,
  Bummelzug (-züge) *nm coll*
small – klein *adj*
small ad – Kleinanzeige (-n) *nf*
small change – Kleingeld *nnt*

small shop – Tante-Emma-Laden
  (-Läden) *nm*
smart – (clever) intelligent *adj*
smart – (fashionable) modisch *adj*
smart card – Chipkarte (-n) *nf*
smell – Geruch (Gerüche) *nm*
smell – (stink) stinken *v irreg*
smell (of) – riechen (nach + dat) *v irreg*
smelly – stinkig *adj*
smile – Lächeln (-) *nnt*
smile – lächeln *v reg*
smiling – lächelnd *adj*
smoke – Rauch *nm*
smoke – rauchen *v reg*
smoker – (male) Raucher (-) *nm*
smoker – (female) Raucherin (-nen) *nf*
smoking – (area) Raucher~ *pref*
  non smoking – (area)
  Nichtraucher~ *pref*
smooth – glatt *adj*
snack – Imbiß (Imbisse) *nm*
snack bar – Imbißstube (-n) *nf*,
  Schnellimbiß *nm*
snail – Schnecke (-n) *nf*
sneeze – niesen *v reg*
snobbish – eingebildet *adj*
snooker – Snooker *nnt*
snore – schnarchen *v reg*
snow – schneien *v reg*
snow – Schnee *nm*
snowball – Schneeball (-bälle) *nm*
snowfall – Schneefall (-fälle) *nm*
snowman – Schneemann (-männer) *nm*
snowstorm – Schneesturm (-stürme) *nm*
snuggle – schnuggeln *v reg*
so – (therefore) also *adv*
so many – so viele
so much – so viel
So what? – Na und?
soaked – durchnäßt *adj*
soaked to the skin – völlig
  durchnäßt *adj*

---

nm - noun masculine   *nf* - noun feminine   *nnt* - noun neuter   *npl* - noun plural
nom - nominative   *acc* - accusative   *gen* - genitive   *dat* - dative

soap – Seife (-n) *nf*
soap opera – Seifenoper (-n) *nf*
social studies – Sozialkunde *nf*
soccer – Fußball *nm*
society – Gesellschaft (-en) *nf*
sock – Socke (-n) *nf*
socket – Steckdose (-n) *nf*
sofa – Sofa (-s) *nnt*
soft – weich *adj*
  a soft drink – ein alkoholfreies
  Getränk *nnt*
software – Software *nf*
sold – verkauft *adj*
  sold out – ausverkauft *adj*
soldier – Soldat (-en) *nm wk*
solemn – feierlich *adj*
solicitor – (male) Rechtsanwalt
  (-anwälte) *nm*
solicitor – (female) Rechtsanwältin
  (-nen) *nf*
solid – solide *adj*
solution – Lösung (-en) *nf*
solve – lösen *v reg*
some – (countable) einige *adj*
some – (uncountable) etwas *adj inv*
some – (unspecified) irgend~ *pref*
somebody – jemand *pron nom, acc*
somebody – jemandem *pron dat*
some day – eines Tages
somehow – irgendwie
some ideas – ein paar Ideen
someone else – jemand anders *pron*
something – etwas
something bad – etwas Schlechtes
something else – etwas anderes
something good – etwas Gutes
sometime – irgendwann *adv*
sometimes – manchmal *adv*
somewhere – irgendwo *adv*
somewhere else – irgendwo anders
son – Sohn (Söhne) *nm*

son-in-law – Schwiegersohn (-söhne)
  nm
song – Lied (-er) *nnt*
soon – bald *adv*
  as soon as possible – so bald wie
  möglich
sore throat – Halsschmerzen *npl*
Sorry! – Entschuldigung!
I'm sorry! – Es tut mir leid!
sort – Sorte (-n) *nf*
sort of – Art (-en) *nf*
  What sort? – Welche Sorten?
  What sort of...? – Was für (+ acc)
sound – (excellent) prima *adj*
sound – (loud) Lärm *nm*
sound – (quiet) Geräusch (-e) *nnt*
soup – Suppe (-n) *nf*
sour – sauer *adj*
source – Quelle (-n) *nf*
south – Süden *nm*
  in South Germany – in
  Süddeutschland
  in the south – im Süden
South Africa – Südafrika *nnt*
South America – Südamerika *nnt*
southern – südlich *adj*
south of – südlich von (+ dat)
souvenir – Andenken (-) *nnt*,
  Souvenir (-s) *nnt*
soya – Soja~ *pref*
space – (universe) All *nnt*
space – (room) Platz (Plätze) *nm*
spade – Spaten (-) *nm*
spaghetti – Spaghetti *nf*
Spain – Spanien *nnt*
Spaniard – (male) Spanier (-) *nm*
Spaniard – (female) Spanierin (-nen) *nf*
Spanish – spanisch *adj*
Spanish – (language) Spanisch *nnt*
spare part – Ersatzteil (-e) *nnt*
spare time – Freizeit *nf*
spare wheel – Ersatzrad (-räder) *nnt*

---

adj - adjective	*v reg* - verb regular	*v sep* - verb separable	† - see verb info
prep - preposition	*v irreg* - verb irregular	*v refl* - verb reflexive	* - takes sein

sparkling wine – Schaumwein (-e) *nm*
sparkling water – Sprudel (-) *nm*
speak – sprechen *v irreg*
speak German – Deutsch sprechen *v irreg*
speak German fluently – fließend Deutsch sprechen *v irreg*
speaking test – mündliche Prüfung (-en) *nf*
speak loudly – laut sprechen *v irreg*
speak to s.o. – jdm sprechen *v irreg*
special – besondere *adj*
specialist – (doctor, male) Facharzt (-ärzte) *nm*
specialist – (doctor, female) Fachärztin (-nen) *nf*
speciality – Spezialität (-en) *nf*
specially – besonders *adv*
special offer – Sonderangebot (-e) *nnt*
special price – Sonderpreis (-e) *nm*
spectacle – (show) Aufführung (-en) *nf*
spectacles – (pair of glasses) Brille (-n) *nf*
spectacular – einmalig *adj*
spectator – (male) Zuschauer (-) *nm*
spectator – (female) Zuschauerin (-nen) *nf*
speech – (in public) Rede (-n) *nf*
speechless – sprachlos *adj*
speech marks („...") – Anführungszeichen *npl*
speed – Geschwindigkeit (-en) *nf*
at high speed – mit hoher Geschwindigkeit
speed limit – Geschwindigkeitsbegrenzung (-en) *nf*
speedboat – Rennboot (-e) *nnt*
spell – buchstabieren *v reg* †
How do you spell that? – Wie schreibt man das?
spelling – Rechtschreibung *nf*
spend – (money) ausgeben *v irreg sep*
spend – (time) verbringen *v irreg*

spend one's holiday – die Ferien verbringen *v irreg*
spider – Spinne (-n) *nf*
spinach – Spinat *nm*
spirits – (alcohol) Spirituosen *npl*
spiteful – gehäßig *adj*
splendid – großartig *adj*
spoil – kaputt machen *v reg*
spoil – (child) verwöhnen *v reg* †
spoilt – (child) verwöhnt *adj*
sponge – Schwamm (Schwämme) *nm*
spoon – Löffel (-) *nm*
spoonful – Löffel (-) *nm*
sport – Sport (Sportarten) *nm*
do sport – Sport treiben *v irreg*
sports car – Sportwagen (-) *nm*
sports centre – Sportzentrum (-zentren) *nnt*
sports club – Sportverein (-e) *nm*
sports facilities – Sportmöglichkeiten *npl*
sports ground – Sportplatz (-plätze) *nm*
sporty – sportlich *adj*
spot – (place) Stelle (-n) *nf*
spot – (zit) Pickel (-) *nm*
spotless – blitzsauber *adj*
spotty – (zits) pickelig *adj*
spotty – (fabric) gepunktet *adj*
sprain one's ankle – sich das Fußgelenk verstauchen *v reg dat refl* †
spray – (can) Sprühdose (-n) *nf*
spray – spritzen *v reg*
spread – (with butter, etc) schmieren *v reg*, buttern *v reg*
spring – Frühling *nm*
in spring – im Frühling
springboard – Sprungbrett (-er) *nnt*
sprout – Rosenkohl *nm, no pl*
spy – (male) Spion (-e) *nm*
spy – (female) Spionin (-nen) *nf*
spy film – Spionagefilm (-e) *nm*

---

spying – Spionage *nf*
spy story – Spionagegeschichte (-n) *nf*
square – (in town) Platz (Plätze) *nm*
square – (on paper) Feld (-er) *nnt*
square – (shape) viereckig *adj*
squash – (drink) Saft (Säfte) *nm*
squash – (sport) Squash *nnt*
squash – zerquetschen *v reg* †
squeeze – quetschen *v reg*
stable – Pferdestall (-ställe) *nm*
stadium – Stadion (Stadien) *nnt*
staff room – Lehrerzimmer (-) *nnt*
stage – Bühne (-n) *nf*
  be on the stage – auf der Bühne
  sein* *v irreg*
stain – Fleck (-en) *nm*
stain – beflecken *v reg* †
stairs – (staircase) Treppe (-n) *nf*
stall – Stand (Stände) *nm*
stalls – (theatre) Parkett *nnt*
stamp – Briefmarke (-n) *nf*
  collect stamps – Briefmarken
  sammeln *v reg*
stand – (on feet) stehen (*) *v irreg*
stand – (put up with) ertragen *v irreg*
  I can't stand her – Ich kann sie
  nicht ausstehen
stand up – aufstehen* *v irreg sep*
standard – (school achievement)
  Niveau *nnt*
standard lamp – Stehlampe (-n) *nf*
standard of living – Lebensstandard
  nm
staple – Heftklammer (-n) *nf*
stapler – Heftmaschine (-n) *nf*
star – (show business) Star (-s) *nm*
star – (sky) Stern (-e) *nm*
start – (beginning) Beginn *nm*
  at the start – am Anfang
start – beginnen *v irreg*, anfangen
  v irreg sep
start – (vehicle) anspringen* *v irreg sep*

start of school year –
  Schuljahresanfang (-anfänge) *nm*
start up – (turn key) anlassen *v irreg*
  sep
starter – (food) Vorspeise (-n) *nf*
startled – erschrocken *adj*
startling – erschreckend *adj*
state – (nation) Staat (-en) *nm*
stately home – Schloß (Schlösser) *nnt*
statement – Aussage (-n) *nf*
station – Bahnhof (-höfe) *nm*
  bus station – Busbahnhof (-höfe) *nm*
stationer's shop –
  Schreibwarenhandlung (-en) *nf*
stay – bleiben* *v irreg*
stay – Aufenthalt (-e) *nm*
stay – (hotel) Übernachtung (-en) *nf*
stay at a hotel – in einem Hotel
  übernachten *v reg insep* †
stay at home – zu Hause bleiben*
  v reg
steady – (job) fest *adj*
  I have a steady
  boyfriend/girlfriend – Ich habe
  einen festen Freund/eine feste
  Freundin
steak – Steak (-s) *nnt*
steal – stehlen *v irreg*, klauen *v reg*
  coll
steam – Dampf *nm*
steamer – Dampfer (-) *nm*
steep – (hill) steil *adj*
steering wheel – Lenkrad (-räder) *nnt*
step – Schritt (-e) *nm*
step – (on stairs) Stufe (-n) *nf*
stepbrother – Stiefbruder (-brüder) *nm*
stepdaughter – Stieftochter (-töchter)
  nf
stepfather – Stiefvater (-väter) *nm*
stepmother – Stiefmutter (-mütter) *nf*
stepsister – Stiefschwester (-n) *nf*
stepson – Stiefsohn (-söhne) *nm*
stereo – Stereoanlage (-n) *nf*

---

personal stereo – Walkman® (Walkmen) *nm*

stew – Eintopf *nm*

stewardess – Stewardeß (Stewardessen) *nf*

stick – Stock (Stöcke) *nm*

stick – (glue) kleben *v reg*

sticker – Aufkleber (-) *nm*

sticky tape – Tesafilm® *nm*

stiff – steif *adj*

still – (not moving) still *adj*
 stand still – stillstehen *v irreg sep*

still – (yet) noch *adv*

sting – Stich (-e) *nm*

sting – stechen *v irreg*

stocking – Strumpf (Strümpfe) *nm*

stocky – untersetzt *adj*

stomach – Bauch (Bäuche) *nm,* Magen (-) *nm*

stomach ache – Magenschmerzen *npl,* Bauchschmerzen *npl*

stone – Stein (-e) *nm*
 built of stone – aus Stein

stool – Hocker (-) *nm*

stop – Haltestelle (-n) *nf*
 bus stop – Bushaltestelle (-n) *nf*

stop – (doing sthg) aufhören *v reg sep*

stop – (halt) anhalten* *v irreg sep*

stop – (prevent) verhüten *v reg* †

stop smoking –zu rauchen aufhören *v reg sep*

storey – Stockwerk (-e) *nnt*
 on the fifth storey – im fünften Stock

storm – Sturm (Stürme) *nm*

stormy – stürmisch *adj*

story – Geschichte (-n) *nf*
 horror story – Horrorgeschichte (-n) *nf*
 science fiction story – Science-Fiction-Roman (-e) *nm*

storyteller – (male) Erzähler (-) *nm*

storyteller – (female) Erzählerin (-nen) *nf*

stove – (hob) Herd (-e) *nm*

stove – (oven) Ofen (Öfen) *nm*

straight – gerade, direkt *adj*

straight – (hair) glatt *adj*

straightaway – sofort *adv*

straight on – geradeaus *adv*

strange – seltsam *adj*

stranger – Fremde *nmf* ‡

strangle – erdrosseln *v reg* †

strawberry – Erdbeere (-n) *nf*

stream – Bach (Bäche) *nm*

street – Straße (-n) *nf*
 along the street – die Straße entlang
 at the corner of street – an der Straßenecke
 in the street – auf der Straße

stressed out – gestreßt *adj*

stressful – stressig *adj coll*

strict – streng *adj*

strike – (hit) schlagen *v irreg*

strike – (walk-out) Streik (-s) *nm*

strike – streiken *v reg*

striker – (on strike) Streikende *nmf* ‡

striker – (football) Stürmer (-) *nm*

string – (piece of) Schnur (Schnüre) *nf*

string – (violin, racket) Saite (-n) *nf*

stringed instrument – (with bow) Streichinstrument (-e) *nnt*

string orchestra – Streichorchester (-) *nnt*

striped – gestreift *adj*

stroll – schlendern* *v reg*

strong – stark *adj*

stubborn – stur *adj*

student – (male) Student (-en) *nm wk*

student – (female) Studentin (-nen) *nf*
 sixth form student – (male) Abiturient (-en) *nm wk*
 sixth form student – (female) Abiturientin (-nen) *nf*

studies – Studium (Studien) *nnt*
studio – (workshop) Atelier (-s) *nnt*
studio – (TV) Studio (-s) *nnt*
studious – fleißig *adj*
study – (room) Arbeitszimmer (-) *nnt*
study – (at school) lernen *v reg*
study – (at university) studieren *v reg* †
stupid – dumm, blöd *adj*
  do something stupid – eine
  Dummheit begehen *v irreg*
sturdy – stark *adj*
style – Stil (-e) *nm*
sub~ – unter~ *pref*
subject – (school) Fach (Fächer) *nnt*
  A Level subject – Leistungsfach
  (-fächer) *nnt*
  compulsory subject – Pflichtfach
  (-fächer) *nnt*
  optional subject – Wahlfach
  (-fächer) *nnt*
subscription – Abonnement (-s) *nnt*
substitute – Ersatz *nm*
subtitled – mit Untertiteln
suburb – Vorort (-e) *nm*
  in a suburb – in einem Vorort
subway – (under road) Unterführung
  (-en) *nf*
succeed – gelingen* *v irreg*
  I've succeeded – Es ist mir
  gelungen
success – Erfolg (-e) *nm*
successful – erfolgreich *adj*
such – solche
such a – ein solcher
sudden – plötzlich *adj*
suddenly – plötzlich *adv*
suede – Wildleder *nnt*
suffer – leiden *v irreg*
sugar – Zucker *nm*
suggest – vorschlagen *v irreg sep*
suit – (man's) Anzug (-züge) *nm*
suit – (woman's) Kostüm (-e) *nnt*

suit – stehen *v irreg*
  It suits me – Es steht mir
suitable – passend *adj*
suitcase – Koffer (-) *nm*
sulk – schmollen *v reg*
sum – (arithmetic) Rechnung (-en) *nf*
summer – Sommer *nm*
  in summer – im Sommer
summer holidays – Sommerferien
  npl
summery – sommerlich *adj*
summit – Gipfel (-) *nm*
sun – Sonne (-n) *nf*
sunbathe – sich sonnen *v reg refl*
sunburn – Sonnenbrand *nm*
sun cream – Sonnencreme (-n) *nf*
sun-glasses – (pair) Sonnenbrille (-n)
  nf
sunshine – Sonnenschein *nm*
sun-stroke – Sonnenstich *nm*
sun-tanned – gebräunt *adj*
sun-tan oil – Sonnenöl *nnt*
Sunday – Sonntag *nm*
  on Sunday – am Sonntag
sunny – sonnig *adj*
sunrise – Sonnenaufgang (-gänge) *nm*
sunset – Sonnenuntergang (-gänge) *nm*
sunshade – Sonnenschirm (-e) *nm*
super – super *adj inv*
superior – überlegen *adj*
supermarket – Supermarkt (-märkte)
  nm
super unleaded petrol – Super
  bleifrei *nm*
supervise – überwachen *v reg insep*
supper – (cold) Abendbrot (-e) *nnt*
supper – (hot) Abendessen (-) *nnt*
  eat supper – zu Abend essen *v irreg*
support – unterstützen *v reg insep*
sure – sicher *adj*
surely – sicherlich *adv*
surfboard – Surfbrett (-er) *nnt*

surfing – Surfen (-) *nnt*
surf – Brandung *nf*
surf the net – das Internet benutzen
  v reg †
surgery – (time) Sprechstunde (-n) *nf*
surgery – (doctor's) Praxis (Praxen) *nf*
surname – Familienname (-n) *nm wk*
surprise – Überraschung (-en) *nf*
surprise – überraschen *v reg insep*
surprised – überrascht *adj*
surprising – überraschend *adj*
surrounded by – umgeben von
  (+ dat) *adj*
surroundings – Umgebung *nf*
survey – Meinungsumfrage (-n) *nf*
suspect – verdächtigen *v reg* †
suspicion – Verdacht *nm*
swallow – verschlucken *v reg* †
swallow – (bird) Schwalbe (-n) *nf*
swap – tauschen *v reg*
sweater – Pullover (-) *nm*
sweatshirt – Sweatshirt (-s) *nnt*
Sweden – Schweden *nnt*
Swedish – schwedisch *adj*
Swedish person – (male) Schwede
  (-n) *nm wk*
Swedish person – (female)
  Schwedin (-nen) *nf*
sweep – kehren *v reg*
sweet – Bonbon (-s) *nnt*
sweet – (cute) niedlich *adj*
sweet – (nice) nett *adj*

sweet – (tasting) süß *adj*
sweet shop – Konditorei (-en) *nf*
sweet-smelling – wohlriechend *adj*
swiftness – Geschwindigkeit (-en) *nf*
swim – schwimmen (*) *v irreg*
swimming – Schwimmen *nnt*
swimming pool – Schwimmbad
  (-bäder) *nnt*
  indoor pool – Hallenbad (-bäder)
  nnt
  outdoor pool – Freibad (-bäder) *nnt*
swimsuit – Badeanzug (-züge) *nm*
swing – schaukeln *v reg*
swing – (child's) Schaukel (-n) *nf*
Swiss – schweizerisch *adj*
Swiss person – (male) Schweizer (-)
  nm
Swiss person – (female) Schweizerin
  (-nen) *nf*
switch off – ausschalten *v reg sep* †
switch on – (light, radio) einschalten
  v reg sep †
switch on – (gas) anzünden *v reg sep* †
Switzerland – Schweiz *nf*
  in Switzerland – in der Schweiz
swollen – geschwollen *adj*
swot – (male) Streber (-) *nm coll*
swot – (female) Streberin (-nen) *nf coll*
swot – pauken *v reg*, büffeln *v reg coll*
synagogue – Synagoge (-n) *nf*
syrup – (medicine) Saft (Säfte) *nm*
system – System (-e) *nnt*

---

table 193 **technical**

T

table – Tisch (-e) *nm*
  to lay the table – den Tisch
  decken *v reg*
tablecloth – Tischdecke (-n) *nf*
tablet – Tablette (-n) *nf*
table tennis – Tischtennis *nnt*
table wine – Tafelwein (-e) *nm*
tactful – taktvoll *adj*
tactless – taktlos *adj*
tail – Schwanz (Schwänze) *nm*
tailor – (male) Schneider (-) *nm*
tailor – (female) Schneiderin (-nen) *nf*
take – nehmen *v irreg*
take – (person) bringen *v irreg*
take an exam – eine Prüfung machen
  v reg
take away – mitnehmen *v irreg sep*
take away – (food) zum Mitnehmen
take back – zurücknehmen *v irreg*
  sep
take drugs – Drogen nehmen *v irreg*
take hold of – greifen *v irreg*
take notes – Notizen machen *v reg*
take off – (aircraft) starten* *v reg* †
take off – (coat, etc) ausziehen *v irreg*
  sep
take one's driving test – den
  Führerschein machen *v reg*
take one's place – Platz nehmen
  v irreg
take part in – teilnehmen an (+ dat)
  v irreg sep
take photos – Fotos machen *v reg*
take place – stattfinden *v irreg sep*
take the dog for a walk – mit dem
  Hund spazieren gehen* *v irreg*
Take the first on the left! –
  Nehmen Sie die erste Straße links!
talk – sprechen *v irreg*
talk to – sich unterhalten mit (+ dat)

talkative – gesprächig *adj*
tall – groß *adj*
tame – zahm *adj*
tampon – Tampon (-s) *nm*
tanned – gebräunt *adj*
tap – Wasserhahn (-hähne) *nm*
tape – Kassette (-n) *nf*
tape – (record) aufnehmen *v irreg sep*
tape recorder – Kassettenrekorder
  (-) *nm*
tart – (cake) Kuchen (-) *nm*
tartan – Schottenmuster *nnt*
task – Aufgabe (-) *nf*
taste – Geschmack (Geschmäcke) *nm*
taste – probieren *v reg* †
  It tastes good – Es schmeckt
Taurus – (horoscope) Stier
tax – Steuer (-n) *nf*
taxi – Taxi (-s) *nnt*
taxi driver – (male) Taxifahrer (-)*nm*
taxi driver – (female) Taxifahrerin
  (-nen) *nm*
taxi rank – Taxistand (-stände) *nm*
tea – Tee *nm*
  lemon tea – Zitronentee *nm*
tea – (meal, cold) Abendbrot(-e) *nnt*
tea – (meal, hot) Abendessen (-) *nnt*
teabag – Teebeutel (-) *nm*
teach – unterrichten *v reg insep* †
teacher – (male) Lehrer (-) *nm*
teacher – (female) Lehrerin (-nen) *nf*
teaching – (lesson) Unterricht *nm*
tea cup – Teetasse (-n) *nf*
team – Mannschaft (-en) *nf*
teapot – Teekanne (-n) *nf*
tease – necken *v reg*
teaspoon – Kaffeelöffel (-) *nm*
tea towel – Geschirrtuch (-tücher) *nnt*
technical – technisch *adj*

---

technical drawing – technisches Zeichnen *nnt*

technical secondary school – Realschule (-n) *nf*

technician – (male) Techniker (-) *nm*

technician – (female) Technikerin (-nen) *nf*

technology – Technologie (-n) *nf*

teddy bear – Teddybär (-en) *nm wk*

teenager – Jugendliche *nmf* ‡

telegram – Telegramm (-e) *nnt*

telephone – Telefon (-e) *nnt*

by telephone – telefonisch

telephone s.o – telefonieren mit (+ dat) *v reg* †

telephone – anrufen *v irreg sep*

telephone box – Telefonzelle (-n) *nf*

telephone directory – Telefonbuch (-bücher) *nnt*

telephone number – Telefonnummer (-n) *nf*

television – Fernsehen *nnt*

television set – Fernseher (-) *nm*

on television – im Fernsehen

watch television – fernsehen *v irreg sep*

tell – jdm sagen *v reg*

tell lies – lügen *v irreg*

tell off – ausschimpfen *v reg sep*

telly – Glotze *nf coll*

temperature – Temperatur (-en) *nf*

maximum temperature – Höchsttemperatur (-en) *nf*

minimum temperature – Tiefsttemperatur (-en) *nf*

have a high temperature – Fieber haben *v irreg*

ten – zehn *adj*

ten out of ten – zehn Punkte haben *v irreg*

tenant – (male) Mieter (-) *nm*

tenant – (female) Mieterin (-nen) *nf*

tender – zart *adj*

tennis – Tennis *nnt*

game of tennis – Tennisspiel (-e) *nnt*

tennis ball – Tennisball (-bälle) *nm*

tennis court – Tennisplatz (-plätze) *nm*

tennis racket – Tennisschläger (-) *nm*

tennis shoe – Tennisschuh (-e) *nm*

tense – nervös *adj*

tent – Zelt (-e) *nnt*

pitch a tent – ein Zelt aufbauen *v reg sep*

take down a tent – ein Zelt abbauen *v reg sep*

tenth – zehnte *adj*

term – (school) Trimester (-) *nnt*

term – (university) Semester (-) *nnt*

autumn half-term holiday – Herbstferien *npl*

February half-term holiday – Halbjahresferien *npl*

summer half-term holiday – Pfingstferien *npl*

terminus – Endstation (-en) *nf*

terrace – Terrasse (-n) *nf*

terraced house – Reihenhaus (-häuser) *nnt*

terrible – schrecklich, furchtbar *adj*

terrific – wunderbar *adj*

terrify – erschrecken *v irreg*

be terrified – große Angst haben *v irreg*

test – Test (-s) *nm*

driving test – Fahrprüfung (-en) *nf*

speaking test – mündliche Prüfung (-en) *nf*

text book – Schulbuch (-bücher) *nnt*

Thames – Themse *nf*

by the Thames – an der Themse

on the Thames – (afloat) auf der ' Themse

than – als *sub conj*

less ... than – weniger ... als

---

more ... than – mehr ... als

thank – danken (+ dat) *v reg*

thank s.o. – sich bedanken *v reg refl* †

thank you – danke *adv*

thank you very much – vielen Dank

no thank you – (nein) danke *adv*

thanks to – dank (+ gen/dat) *prep*

that – daß *subord conj*

that – jener *dem pron*

that – das *pron*

That comes to ten marks – Das macht zehn Mark

That depends – Es kommt darauf an

That is to say – Das heißt

That's all – Das wär's

That's enough – Das reicht

That's right – Das stimmt

thatched roof – Strohdach (-dächer) *nnt*

that one – dieser *dem pron*

the – der, die, das, die, etc *pron*

theatre – Theater (-) *nnt*

theft – Diebstahl *nm*

their – ihr *poss adj*

it's theirs – das gehört ihnen

them – sie *pron acc*

them, to them – ihnen *pron dat*

themselves – sich *pron refl*

then – dann, danach, darauf *adv*

there – (motion) dahin *adv*

I am going there – Ich gehe dahin

there – (position towards) dort *adv*

there are, there is – es gibt (+ acc)

there are – es gibt

There are no ... – Es gibt keine ...

There is no ... – Es gibt keinen/keine/kein ...

There was, there were – Es gab

There will be – Es wird. .. geben

There would be – Es gäbe

therefore – also, deshalb *adv*

thermometer – Thermometer (-) *nnt*

thermometer – (medical) Fieberthermometer (-) *nnt*

these – diese *dem pron*

they – sie *pron nom*

they – (people in general) man *pron nom sing*

thick – (not clever) dumm *adj*

thick – (not thin) dick *adj*

thief – (male) Dieb (-e) *nm*

thief – (female) Diebin (-nen) *nf*

thigh – Schenkel (-) *nm*

thin – dünn *adj*

thing – Ding (-e) *nnt*, Sache (-n) *nf*

thingamajig – Dingsbums *nnt*

think – denken *v irreg,* glauben *v reg*

think – (have opinion) meinen *v reg*

think about – nachdenken über (+ acc) *v irreg sep*

think of – denken an (+ acc) *v irreg*

third – (fraction) Drittel (-) *nm*

third – (in order) dritte *adj*

thirst – Durst *nm*

be thirsty – Durst haben *v irreg*

I am thirsty – Ich habe Durst

thirteen – dreizehn *adj*

thirtieth – dreißigste *adj*

thirty – dreißig *adj*

this – dieser *dem pron*

This is Anne speaking – Anne am Apparat

this way – hier entlang *adv*

those – jene *dem pron*

thought – Gedanke (-n) *nm wk*

thousand – tausend *adj*

thousands of – Tausende von (+ dat)

threaten – bedrohen *v reg* †

three – drei

throat – Hals (Hälse) *nm*

have a sore throat – Halsschmerzen haben *v irreg*

throat pastille – Halstablette (-n) *nf*

---

through – durch (+ acc) *prep*
through train – Durchgangszug (-züge) *nm,* D-Zug (-Züge) *nm*
throw – werfen *v irreg*
thumb – Daumen (-) *nm*
thunder – Donner *nm*
thunder – donnern *v reg*
thunderstorm – Gewitter (-) *nnt*
  There will be thunderstorms – Es wird Gewitter geben
Thursday – Donnerstag *nm*
  on Thursday – am Donnerstag
tick – (✓) ankreuzen *v reg sep*
ticket – (bus, train) Fahrkarte (-n) *nf*
ticket – (plane) Ticket (-s) *nnt*
  book of tickets – Streifenkarte (-n) *nf*
  return ticket – Rückfahrkarte (-n) *nf*
  single ticket – einfache Fahrkarte (-n) *nf*
  weekly ticket – Wochenkarte (-n) *nf*
ticket inspector – (male) Schaffner (-) *nm*
ticket inspector – (female) Schaffnerin (-nen) *nf*
ticket machine – Fahrkartenautomat (-en) *nm wk*
ticket office – Schalter (-) *nm*
  at the ticket office – am Schalter
tide – (high) Flut (-en) *nf*
  at high tide – bei Hochwasser
tide – (low) Ebbe (-n) *nf*
  at low tide – bei Tiefwasser
tidy – ordentlich *adj*
tidy up – aufräumen *v reg sep*
tie – Krawatte (-n) *nf,* Schlips (-e) *nm*
tie – anbinden *v irreg sep*
tiger – Tiger (-) *nm*
tight – eng *adj*
tights – (pair of) Strumpfhose (-n) *nf*
till – (cash) Kasse (-n) *nf*

till – bis (+ acc) *prep*
time – (occasion) Mal (-e) *nnt*
time – Zeit (-en) *nf*
  dinner time – (school) Mittagspause (-n) *nf*
  free time – Freizeit *nf*
  a long time ago – vor vielen Jahren
  every time – jedes Mal
  for a long time – für eine lange Zeit
  for the first time – zum ersten Mal
  for the last time – zum letzten Mal
  from time to time – ab und zu *adv,* dann und wann *adv*
  have a good time – sich amüsieren *v reg refl* †
  Have a good time! – Viel Spaß! *excl*
  many, many times – sehr oft
  on time – pünktlich *adj*
  three times – dreimal *adv*
time – (by clock) Uhr
  At what time? – Um wieviel Uhr?
  What time is it? – Wie spät ist es?
time – (on clock) Uhrzeit (-en) *nf*
time off – (work) Urlaub *nm*
time off – (leisure) Freizeit *nf*
timetable – (school) Stundenplan (-pläne) *nm*
timetable – (transport) Fahrplan (-pläne) *nm*
tin – Dose (-n) *nf*
tin opener – Dosenöffner (-) *nm*
tiny – winzig *adj*
tip – (end) Ende (-n) *nnt*
tip – (hint) Tip (-s) *nm*
tip – (money) Trinkgeld (-er) *nnt*
tip – (rubbish) Müllhalde (-n) *nf*
tip – (summit) Gipfel (-) *nm*
tired – müde *adj*
tiring – ermüdend *adj*

tissue – Papiertaschentuch (-tücher) *nnt*
title – (homework) Überschrift (-en) *nf*
title – (book, play) Titel (-) *nm*
to – (in order to) um. .. zu *conj*
to – in (+ acc) *prep*
  to the cinema – ins Kino
  to the church – in die Kirche
  to the hotel – ins Hotel
to – nach (+ dat) *prep*
  to Berlin – nach Berlin
to – zu (+ dat) *prep*
  to the post office – zur Post
  to the shops – zu den Geschäften
  to the school – zur Schule
  to the station – zum Bahnhof
  from 4th to 10th July – vom vierten bis zum zehnten Juli
to – (clock time) vor (+ dat) *prep*
  it's quarter to four – es ist Viertel vor vier
  at quarter to four – um Viertel vor vier
toast – (bread) Toast *nm*
tobacco – Tabak (-e) *nm*
tobacconist – (male) Tabakhändler (-) *nm*
tobacconist – (female) Tabakhändlerin (-nen) *nf*
tobacconist's shop – Tabakhandlung (-en) *nf*
today – heute *adv*
today – (nowadays) heutzutage *adv*
toe – Zeh (-en) *nm*
together – zusammen *adv*
toilet – Toilette (-n) *nf*
toilet block – Sanitäranlage (-n) *nf*
toilet paper – Toilettenpapier *nnt*
token – Münze (-n) *nf*
told – gesagt *see sagen*
tolerate – tolerieren *v reg* †
toll – Zoll *nm*

tomato – Tomate (-n) *nf*
tomorrow – morgen *adv*
  day after tomorrow – übermorgen *adv*
  from tomorrow – ab morgen
  See you tomorrow! – Bis morgen! *excl*
tomorrow evening – morgen abend
tomorrow morning – morgen früh
ton – Tonne (-n) *nf*
tone – Ton (Töne) *nm*
tone – (on phone) Signal (-e) *nnt*
tongue – Zunge (-n) *nf*
  mother tongue – Muttersprache (-n) *nf*
tonight – (evening) heute abend
tonight – (night-time) heute nacht
too – (as well) auch *adv*
too – (excessively) zu *adv*
Too bad – Pech!
too many – zu viele
too many people – zu viele Leute
too much – zu viel
tool – Werkzeug (-e) *nnt*
tooth – Zahn (Zähne) *nm*
toothache – Zahnschmerzen *npl*
  have toothache – Zahnschmerzen haben *v irreg*
toothbrush – Zahnbürste (-n) *nf*
toothpaste – Zahnpasta *nf*
top – (summit) Gipfel (-) *nm*
top – oben *adv*
  at the top – oben *adv*
  at the top of the page – oben auf der Seite *prep*
topic – Thema (Themen) *nnt*
torch – Taschenlampe (-n) *nf*
torn – zerrissen *v irreg*
tortoise – Schildkröte (-n) *nf*
total – Endsumme (-n) *nf*
totally – total *adv*
touch – berühren *v reg* †

---

tough – (meat) zäh *adj*
tough – (resilient) widerstandsfähig *adj*
Tough luck! – Pech! *excl*
tour – Tour (-en) *nf*
tourism – Tourismus *nm*
tourist – (male) Tourist (-en) *nm wk*
tourist – (female) Touristin (-nen) *nf*
tourist centre – Touristenstadt (-städte) *nf*
tourist information office – Informationsbüro (-s) *nnt*
tourist office – Verkehrsamt (-ämter) *nnt*
tournament – Tournier (-e) *nnt*
tow – schleppen *v reg*
towards – (time) gegen (+ acc) *prep*
towards midday – gegen Mittag
towards – (place) in Richtung
towards Berlin – in Richtung Berlin
towards – (in relation to) gegenüber (+ dat) *prep*
towards – entgegen *adv*
towel – (bath) Badetuch (-tücher) *nnt*
towel – (hand) Handtuch (-tücher) *nnt*
tower – Turm (Türme) *nm*
tower block – Wohnblock (-s) *nm*
town – Stadt (Städte) *nf*
  into town –in die Stadt
  in town – in der Stadt
town centre – Stadtmitte (-n) *nf*
  in the town centre – in der Stadtmitte
town hall – Rathaus (-häuser) *nnt*
town plan – Stadtplan (-pläne) *nm*
toy – Spielzeug (-e) *nnt*
track – Bahn (-en) *nf*
tracksuit – Trainingsanzug (-anzüge) *nm*
tractor – Traktor (-en) *nm*
trade – (profession) Beruf (-e) *nm*
trade – (business) Handel *nm*

tradition – Tradition (-en) *nf*
traditional – traditionell *adj*
traffic – (drugs) Handel *nm*
traffic – (vehicles) Verkehr *nnt*
traffic jam – Stau (-s) *nm*
traffic lights – Ampel (-n) *nf*
trailer – Anhänger (-) *nm*
train – Zug (Züge) *nm*
  by train – mit dem Zug
  catch the train – den Zug nehmen *v irreg*
  get on the train – in den Zug einsteigen* *v irreg sep*
  get off the train – aus dem Zug aussteigen* *v irreg sep*
  through train – Durchgangszug (-züge) *nm*
train – (animal) dressieren *v reg* †
train – (sport) trainieren *v reg* †
trainer – (person) Trainer (-) *nm*
trainer – (shoe) Turnschuh (-e) *nm*
training – (vocational) Ausbildung (-en) *nf*
tram – Straßenbahn (-en) *nf*
trampoline – Trampolin (-e) *nnt*
trampoline – Trampolin springen* *v irreg*
transform – verwandeln *v reg* †
transistor – (radio) Kofferradio (-s) *nnt*
translate – (in writing) übersetzen *v reg insep*
translate – (interpret) dolmetschen *v reg*
translation – Übersetzung (-en) *nf*
transport – Transportmittel (-) *nnt*
travel – fahren* *v irreg*, reisen* *v reg*
travel agency – Reisebüro (-s) *nnt*
travel by bus – mit dem Bus fahren* *v irreg*
travel by car – mit dem Wagen fahren* *v irreg*
travel by coach – mit dem Reisebus fahren* *v irreg*

---

travel by train – mit dem Zug
fahren* *v irreg*
traveller – Reisende *nmf* ‡
travellers' cheque – Reisescheck
(-s) *nm*
tray – Tablett (-s) *nnt*
treasure – Schatz (Schätze) *nm*
treat – (medical) behandeln *v reg* †
treatment – Behandlung (-en) *nf*
trend – Tendenz (-en) *nf*, Trend (-s)
nm
tree – Baum (Bäume) *nm*
  fruit tree – Obstbaum (-bäume) *nm*
tremble – zittern *v reg*
trembling – zitternd *adj*
tremendously – furchtbar *adv*
trendy – in *adj inv*
triangle – Dreieck (-e) *nnt*
trip – (outing) Ausflug (Ausflüge) *nm*
trip – (journey) Reise (-n) *nf*
trip over – (fall) hinfallen* *v irreg*
sep
trolley – (supermarket)
Einkaufswagen (-) *nm*
trolley – (luggage) Kofferkuli (-s) *nm*
trombone – Posaune (-n) *nf*
trouble – Problem (-e) *nnt*
  be in trouble – Probleme haben
v irreg
trousers – (pair of) Hose (-n) *nf*
trout – Forelle (-n) *nf*
truant – schwänzen *v reg*
truck – Lastwagen (-) *nm*
true – richtig, wahr *adj*
trumpet – Trompete (-n) *nf*
trunk road – Bundesstraße (-n) *nf*
trunks – (swimming) Badehose (-n) *nf*
trust – Vertrauen *nnt*
trust – trauern *v reg*
truth – Wahrheit (-en) *nf*
try – versuchen *v reg* †
try – (food) probieren *v reg* †

try on – (clothes) anprobieren *v reg*
sep †
try to – versuchen *v reg* †
  I tried to phone – Ich habe
versucht anzurufen
T-Shirt – T-Shirt (-s) *nnt*
tube – (toothpaste, etc) Tube (-n) *nf*
tube – (London) U-Bahn *nf*
tube station – U-Bahnstation (-en) *nf*
Tuesday – Dienstag *nm*
  on Tuesday – am Dienstag
tulip – Tulpe (-n) *nf*
tumble drier – Wäschetrockner (-)
nm
tuna – Thunfisch (-e) *nm*
tune – (music) Melodie (-n) *nf*
tune – (instrument) stimmen *v reg*
tunnel – Tunnel (-) *nm*
  Channel Tunnel – Kanaltunnel
nm
turkey – Truthahn (-hähne) *nm*
Turkey – die Türkei *nf*
turn – drehen *v reg*
turn – (off road) abbiegen *v irreg sep*
turn off – (light) ausschalten *v reg sep* †
turn off – (tap) zudrehen *v reg sep*
turn on – (light) anmachen *v reg sep*
turn on – (tap) andrehen *v reg sep*
turn pale – blaß werden* *v irreg*
turn round – sich umdrehen *v reg*
refl sep
turquoise – türkis *adj inv*
TV news – Nachrichten *npl*
twelfth – zwölfte *adj*
twelve – zwölf *adj*
twelve o'clock – (mid-day) Mittag
nm
twelve o'clock – (midnight)
Mitternacht *nf*
twentieth – zwanzigste *adj*
twenty – zwanzig *adj*
twenty-one – einundzwanzig *adj*

---

adj - adjective   *v reg* - verb regular   *v sep* - verb separable   † - see verb info
prep - preposition   *v irreg* - verb irregular   *v refl* - verb reflexive   * - takes sein

twenty-first – einundzwanzigste *adj*
twice – zweimal *adv*
twins – Zwillinge *npl*
twin brother – Zwillingsbruder
(-brüder) *nm*
twin sister – Zwillingsschwester (-n)
nf
twin town – Partnerstadt (-städte) *nf*
twist an ankle – sich das Fußgelenk
verrenken *v reg dat refl* †
two – zwei *adj*
type – (sort) Art (-en) *nf*
type – Typ (-en) *nm*

type – tippen *v reg*
typewriter – Schreibmaschine (-n) *nf*
typical – typisch *adj*
typist – (male) Stenotypist (-en) *nm wk*
typist – (female) Stenotypistin (-nen)
nf
tyre – Reifen (-) *nm*
  to have a flat tyre – eine
  Reifenpanne haben *v irreg*
tyre pressure – Reifendruck *nm*
  check the tyre pressure – den
  Reifendruck kontrollieren *v reg* †

U

ugly – häßlich *adj*
UK – das Vereinigte Königreich *nnt*
umbrella – Regenschirm (-e) *nm*
un~ – un~ *pref*
unaccustomed – ungewohnt *adj*
unavoidable – unvermeidlich *adj*
unbearable – unerträglich *adj*
unbelievable – unglaublich *adj*
uncertain – ungewiß *adj*
uncle – Onkel (-) *nm*
uncomfortable – unbequem *adj*
unconscious – bewußtlos *adj*
under – unter (+ acc/dat) *prep*
underclothes – Unterwäsche *nf, no pl*
underground – U-Bahn (-en) *nf*
underground station –
  U-Bahnstation (-en) *nf*
underground ticket –
  U-Bahnfahrkarte (-n) *nf*
underline – unterstreichen *v irreg*
  insep
underneath – unter (+ acc/dat) *prep*
underpants – (pair of) Unterhose (-n)
nf

understand – verstehen *v irreg*
understanding – verständnisvoll *adj*
understanding – Verständnis (-se)
nnt
understood – verstanden *adj*
  I have not understood – ich
  habe nicht verstanden
undertake – unternehmen *v irreg*
  insep
underwear – Unterwäsche *nf, no pl*
undress – sich ausziehen *v irreg refl*
  sep
unemployed – arbeitslos *adj*
unemployed person – Arbeitslose
  nmf ‡
unemployment – Arbeitslosigkeit *nf*
uneven – ungleich *adj*
unexpected – unerwartet *adj*
unfair – unfair *adj*
unfavourable – ungünstig *adj*
unfit – unfit *adj*
unfold – entfalten *v reg* †
unforgettable – unvergeßlich *adj*
unfortunate – unglücklich *adj*

---

nm - noun masculine   *nf* - noun feminine   *nnt* - noun neuter   *npl* - noun plural
nom- nominative   *acc* - accusative   *gen* - genitive   *dat* - dative

unfortunately – leider,
 unglücklicherweise *adv*

unfriendly – unfreundlich *adj*

ungrateful – undankbar *adj*

unhappy – unglücklich *adj*

unhurt – unverletzt *adj*

unification – Vereinigung *nf*

uniform – Uniform (-en) *nf*

unify – vereinigen *v reg* †

unimportant – unwichtig *adj*

unique – einmalig *adj*

unit – Einheit (-en) *nf*

  the Day of German Unity – der
Tag der deutschen Einheit *nm*

United Kingdom – Vereinigtes
Königreich *nnt*

universal – allgemein *adj*

universal – Universal~ *pref*

universe – Universum (Universen)
nnt

university – Universität (-en) *nf*

unjust – ungerecht *adj*

unknown – unbekannt *adj*

unleaded – bleifrei *adj*

unleaded petrol – bleifreies Benzin
nnt

unlucky – unglücklich *adj*

unmarried – ledig *adj*

unnecessary – unnötig *adj*

unpack – auspacken *v reg sep*

unpleasant – unangenehm *adj*

untidy – unordentlich *adj*

until – bis (+ acc) *prep*

  until Sunday – bis Sonntag

  not until Sunday – erst am
Sonntag

untruthful – unehrlich *adj*

unusual – ungewöhnlich *adj*

unwell – krank, unwohl *adj*

  I am unwell – Mir ist unwohl

up – oben *adv*

  be up – (out of bed) aufgestanden
sein* *v irreg*

uphill – bergauf *adv*

up there – dort oben *adv*

upon – auf (+ acc/dat) *prep*

upper – ober~ *pref*

upside down – auf den Kopf gestellt
adj

upstairs – oben *adv*

  go upstairs – nach oben gehen*
v irreg

urban – städtisch *adj*

urgency – Dringlichkeit *nf*

urgent – dringend *adj*

us – uns *pers pron acc/dat*

USA – Vereinigte Staaten *npl*

use – (custom) Brauch (Bräuche) *nm*

use – Gebrauch *nm, no pl*

use – Benutzung *nf*

use – (make use of) benutzen *v reg* †

use – (need) brauchen *v reg*

useful – nützlich *adj*

useless – nutzlos *adj*

user – (male) Benutzer (-) *nm*

user – (female) Benutzerin (-nen) *nf*

usherette – Platzanweiserin (-nen) *nf*

usual – normal, gewöhnlich *adj*

  as usual – wie gewöhnlich *adv*

usually – normalerweise *adv*

V

vacancies – Zimmer frei
  no vacancies – belegt *adj*
vacuum cleaner – Staubsauger (-) *nm*
vacuum – staubsaugen *v reg*
vague – ungenau *adj*
vain – (conceited) eitel *adj*
  in vain – vergebens *adv*
valid – gültig *adj*
valley – Tal (Täler) *nnt*
valuable – wertvoll, kostbar *adj*
valuables – Wertsachen *npl*
value – Wert (-e) *nm*
van – Lieferwagen (-) *nm*
vanilla – Vanille *nf*
vanilla ice cream – Vanilleeis *nnt, no pl*
vanish – verschwinden* *v irreg*
vanity – Eitelkeit (-en) *nf*
varied – verschieden *adj*
vary – verschieden sein* *v irreg*
VAT – MWSt (Mehrwertsteuer) *nf*
VCR – Videokassettenrekorder (-) *nm*
veal – Kalbfleisch *nnt*
vegan – vegan *adj*
vegan – (male) Veganer (-) *nm*
vegan – (female) Veganerin (-nen) *nf*
vegetable – Gemüse *nnt no pl*
vegetarian – vegetarisch *adj*
vegetarian – (male) Vegetarier (-) *nm*
vegetarian – (female) Vegetarierin (-nen) *nf*
vehicle – Fahrzeug (-e) *nnt*
velvet – Samt *nm*
verb – Verb (-en) *nnt*
version – Ausführung (-en) *nf*
  in the original version – (soundtrack) im Originalton
very – sehr *adv*
vest – Unterhemd (-en) *nnt*

vet – (male) Tierarzt (-ärzte) *nm*
vet – (female) Tierärztin (-nen) *nf*
vicar – (protestant, male) Pastor (-en) *nm*
vicar – (protestant, female) Pastorin (-nen) *nf*
victim – Opfer (-) *nnt*
victorious – siegreich *adj*
victory – Sieg (-e) *nm*
video – Video~ *pref*
video camera – Videokamera (-s) *nf*
video cassette – Videokassette (-n) *nf*
video game – Videospiel (-e) *nnt*
video recorder – Videokassettenrekorder (-) *nm*
video – auf Video aufnehmen *v irreg sep*
Vienna – Wien
view – Blick (-e) *nm*, Aussicht (-en) *nf*
viewer – (male) Zuschauer (-) *nm*
viewer – (female) Zuschauerin (-nen) *nf*
vigorous – lebhaft *adj*
vile – (person) ekelhaft *adj*
vile – (weather) scheußlich *adj*
village – Dorf (Dörfer) *nnt*
vine – Rebstock *nm*
vinegar – Essig *nm*
vine grower – (male) Weinbauer (-n) *nm wk*
vine grower – (female) Weinbäuerin (-nen) *nf*
vineyard – Weinberg (-e) *nm*
viola – Bratsche (-n) *nf*
violence – Gewalt *nf*
violent – (person) gewalttätig *adj*
violent – (storm) gewaltig *adj*
violin – Geige (-n) *nf*, Violine (-n) *nf*
Virgo – Jungfrau
visa – Visum (Visen) *nnt*

nm - noun masculine	*nf* - noun feminine	*nnt* - noun neuter	*npl* - noun plural
nom- nominative	*acc* - accusative	*gen* - genitive	*dat* - dative

visibility – Sicht *nf, no pl*
visible – sichtbar *adj*
visit – Besuch (-e) *nm*
visit – (person) besuchen *v reg* †
visit – (tourist attraction) besichtigen
  v reg †
visitor – (guest) Gast (Gäste) *nm*
  We have visitors – Wir haben
  Besuch
visitor – (tourist, male) Besucher (-)
  nm
visitor – (tourist, female) Besucherin
  (-nen) *nf*

vital – unbedingt notwendig *adj*
vocabulary – (individual items)
  Vokabel (-n) *nf*
vocabulary – (complete list)
  Wortschatz *nm*
voice – Stimme (-n) *nf*
volleyball – Volleyball *nm*
voluntary – freiwillig *adj*
volunteer – Freiwillige *nmf* ‡
vomit – sich erbrechen *v irreg refl,*
  sich übergeben *v irreg insep,* kotzen
  v reg coll
voyage – Reise (-n) *nf*

W

waffle – (edible) Waffel (-n) *nf*
wages – Lohn (Löhne) *nm*
waist(line) – Taille (-n) *nf*
waistcoat – Weste (-n) *nf*
wait – warten *v reg* †
wait (for) – warten auf (+ acc) *v reg* †
waiter – Kellner (-) *nm*
Waiter! – Herr Ober! *excl*
waiting room – Wartesaal (-säle) *nm*
waitress – Kellnerin (-nen) *nf*
Waitress! – Fräulein! *excl*
wake s.o. – wecken *v reg*
wake up – aufwachen* *v reg sep*
Wales – Wales *nnt*
walk – gehen* *v irreg*
walk – (stroll) Spaziergang (-gänge)
  nm
walk the dog – den Hund ausführen
  v reg sep
  go for a walk – spazierengehen*
  v irreg sep
walkman® – Walkman® (Walkmen)
  nm
wall – (exterior) Mauer (-n) *nf*
wall – (interior) Wand (Wände) *nf*

wallet – Brieftasche (-n) *nf*
wallpaper – Tapete (-n) *nf*
wallpaper – tapezieren *v reg* †
want – wollen *v irreg*
war – Krieg (-e) *nm*
warden – (youth hostel, male)
  Herbergsvater (-väter) *nm*
warden – (youth hostel, female)
  Herbergsmutter (-mütter) *nf*
warden – (traffic, male) Hilfspolizist
  (-en) *nm wk*
warden – (traffic, female) Politesse
  (-n) *nf*
wardrobe – Kleiderschrank
  (schränke) *nm*
warm – warm *adj*
  It is warm – (weather) Es ist warm
  I am warm – Mir ist warm
warm up – sich aufwärmen *v reg refl*
  sep
warn about – warnen vor (+ dat)
  v reg
warning – Warnung (-en) *nf*
was – war *see sein*
  It was – Es war

---

adj - adjective   *v reg* - verb regular   *v sep* - verb separable   † - see verb info
prep - preposition   *v irreg* - verb irregular   *v refl* - verb reflexive   * - takes sein

was able to – konnte *see können*
was obliged to – mußte *see müssen*
wash – (clothes etc) waschen *v irreg*
have a wash. – sich waschen *v irreg refl*
I have washed – Ich habe mich gewaschen
wash basin – Waschbecken (-) *nnt*
wash one's hair – sich die Haare waschen *v irreg dat refl*
I'm washing my hair – Ich wasche mir die Haare
washing – (clothes) Wäsche *nf*
do the washing – die Wäsche machen *v reg*
washing machine – Waschmaschine (-n) *nf*
washing powder – Waschpulver *nnt*
washing up liquid – Spülmittel *nnt*
do the washing up – spülen *v reg*
wasp – Wespe (-n) *nf*
waste – verschwenden *v reg* †
a waste of time – Zeitverschwendung *nf, no pl*
wasted – (useless) nutzlos *adj*
wasted – (time, effort) verloren *adj*
wasteful – verschwenderisch *adj*
waste paper basket – Papierkorb (-körbe) *nm*
watch – Armbanduhr (-en) *nf*
watch – zusehen *v irreg sep*, zuschauen *v reg sep*, gucken *v reg coll*
watch TV – fernsehen *v irreg sep*
water – Wasser *nnt, no pl*
water – (plants) begießen *v irreg*
waterproof – wasserdicht *adj*
water sports – Wassersport *nm*
do watersports – Wassersport treiben *v irreg*
water skiing – Wasserskifahren *nnt*
water-ski – Wasserski laufen* *v irreg*
wave – (hand) winken *v reg*
wave – (sea) Welle (-n) *nf*

way – (method) Art (-en) *nf*
way – (route) Weg (-e) *nm*
a long way off – weit weg
by the way – übrigens
in this way – auf diese Weise
on the way – unterwegs *adv*
the right way – der richtige Weg
way in – (on foot) Eingang (-gänge) *nm*
way in – (by car) Einfahrt (-en) *nf*
way out – (on foot) Ausgang (-gänge) *nm*
way out – (by car) Ausfahrt (-en) *nf*
WC – WC (-s) *nnt*
we – wir *pers pron*
weak – schwach *adj*
wear – tragen *v irreg*
wear out – verschleißen *v irreg*
weather – Wetter *nnt, no pl*
in bad weather – bei schlechtem Wetter
in good weather – bei gutem Wetter
weather forecast – Wettervorhersage (-n) *nf*
wedding – Hochzeit (-en) *nf*
wedding dress – Hochzeitskleid (-er) *nnt*
Wednesday – Mittwoch *nm*
on Wednesday – am Mittwoch
weeds – Unkraut *nnt, no pl*
week – Woche (-n) *nf*
during the week – in der Woche
last week – letzte Woche
next week – nächste Woche
per week – pro Woche
weekdays – wochentags *adv*
weekend – Wochenende (-n) *nnt*
weekly – wöchentlich *adj*
weep – weinen *v reg*
weigh – wiegen *v irreg*
weight – Gewicht (-e) *nnt*
welcome – willkommen *adj*
Welcome! – Herzlich willkommen!

You're welcome! – Nichts zu danken!

welcome – willkommen heißen *v irreg*

welcoming – freundlich *adj*

well – (water) Brunnen (-) *nm*

well – gut *adj*
  all is well – alles geht bestens
  as well – auch *adv*
  I am well – Mir geht es gut
  Get well soon! – Gute Besserung!

well-behaved – artig *adj*

well brought up – guterzogen *adj*

well-built – (person) stark gebaut *adj*

well-cooked – (steak) gut durchgebraten *adj*

Well done! – Gut gemacht! *excl*

well-known – bekannt *adj*

well-paid – gut bezahlt *adj*

Welsh – walisisch *adj*

Welsh – (language) Walisisch *nnt*

Welshman – Waliser (-) *nm*

Welsh woman – Waliserin (-nen) *nf*

went – *see gehen*

west – Westen *nm*
  in the west – im Westen
  west of – westlich von (+ dat)

western – (film) Western (-) *nm*

West Indian – westindisch *adj*

West Indian – (male) Westinder (-) *nm*

West Indian – (female) Westinderin (-nen) *nf*

the West Indies – die Westindischen Inseln *npl*

wet – naß *adj*

wet paint – frisch gestrichen

wet through – durchnäßt *adj*

what? – was? *adv*

What is that? – Was ist das?

What did you say? – Was hast du gesagt?

What's going on? – Was ist los?

What's the matter? – Was ist los?

What else? – Was sonst?

What's new? – Was gibt's neues?

what – was *sub conj*

what? – (how) wie? *adv*

What is ...like? – Wie ist ...? *adv*

What is your name? – Wie heißt du? Wie heißen Sie?

What (did you say)? – Wie bitte?

What does... mean? – Wie heißt ...?

What is the time? – Wie spät ist es?

What is it in German? – Wie heißt das auf deutsch?

What is the way to...? – (+ town name) Wie kommt man nach ...?

What is the best way to ...? – (+ building) Wie kommt man am besten zum/zur...?

what? – (which) welche *adj*

What colour? – Welche Farbe?

What a pity! – Schade! *excl*

What is it about? – Worum handelt es sich?

whatsit – Dingsbums *nnt coll*

wheel – Rad (Räder) *nnt*

wheelbarrow – Schubkarre (-n) *nf*

wheelchair – Rollstuhl (-stühle) *nm*

when – (in past) als *sub conj*

when – (whenever) wenn *sub conj*

when? – (question) wann *adv*

where – wo *sub conj*

where? – wo *adv*

where (from)? – woher *adv*

Where do you come from? – Woher kommst du?

(to) where? – wohin *adv*

Where are you going (to)? – Wohin gehst du?

whether – ob *sub conj*

which – der, die, das *rel pron*

which? – welche *adj*

while – während *sub conj*
  a long while – lange *adv*

---

adj - adjective	*v reg* - verb regular	*v sep* - verb separable	† - see verb info
prep - preposition	*v irreg* - verb irregular	*v refl* - verb reflexive	* - takes sein

whilst – während *sub conj*
whipped cream – Schlagsahne (-n) *nf*
whisky – Whisky *nm, no pl*
whisper – flüstern *v reg*
whistle – pfeifen *v irreg*
white – weiß *adj*
white coffee – Kaffee mit Sahne
white wine – Weißwein (-e) *nm*
Whitsun – Pfingsten *npl*
who? – wer?
Who is coming with us? – Wer kommt mit?
Who(m) did you see? – Wen hast du gesehen?
Who did you give the book to? – Wem hast du das Buch gegeben?
whose – wessen *rel pron*
whose? – wessen?
whole – ganz *adj*
on the whole – im großen und ganzen
the whole time – die ganze Zeit
wholemeal bread – Vollkornbrot (-e) *nnt*
why? – warum? *adv*
wide – breit *adj*
widely known – weit verbreitet *adj*
widow – Witwe (-n) *nf*
widowed – verwitwet *adj*
widower – Witwer (-) *nm*
width – Breite (-n) *nf*
wife – Frau (-en) *nf*
wild – wild *adj*
will – *see future tenses*
will – (want to) wollen *v irreg*
win – gewinnen *v irreg*
wind – Wind (-e) *nm*
windy – windig *adj*
window – Fenster (-) *nnt*
window – (shop) Schaufenster (-) *nnt*
window shopping – einen Schaufensterbummel machen *v reg*

windscreen – Windschutzscheibe (-n) *nf*
windscreen wiper – Scheibenwischer (-) *nm*
windsurf – windsurfen *v reg*
I went windsurfing – Ich bin windsurfen gegangen
wine – Wein (-e) *nm*
wine bar – Weinstube (-n) *nf*
wine list – Getränkekarte (-n) *nf*
winger – (sport) Außen (-) *nm*
winner – (male) Sieger (-) *nm*
winner – (female) Siegerin (-nen) *nf*
winter – Winter *nm*
in winter – im Winter
winter sports – Wintersport *nm, no pl*
wipe – wischen *v reg*
wise – weise *adj*
wish – Wunsch (Wünsche) *nm*
wish – wünschen *v reg*
Best wishes – alles Gute *excl*
wish (to) – wollen *v irreg*
wish to – Lust haben zu *v irreg*
with – mit (+ dat) *prep*
With best wishes from – (male, formal) Ihr *poss adj*
With best wishes from – (male, informal) Dein *poss adj*
With best wishes from – (female, formal) Ihre *poss adj*
With best wishes from – (female, informal) Deine *poss adj*
with pleasure – mit Vergnügen
with success – mit Erfolg
without – ohne (+ acc) *prep*
without doubt – zweifellos *adv*
witness – (male) Zeuge (-n) *nm wk*
witness – (female) Zeugin (-nen) *nf*
woman – Frau (-en) *nf*
wonder – sich fragen *v reg refl*
wonderful – wunderbar, wunderschön *adj*

---

wood – Holz *nnt*
wooden – aus Holz
woodwork – Werken *nnt*
wool – Wolle (-n) *nf*
woollen – aus Wolle
word – Wort (Worte) *nnt*
word processing – Textverarbeitung *nf*
word processing program – Textverarbeitungsprogramm (-e) *nnt*
work – Arbeit (-en) *nf*
  on working days – werktags
  out of work – arbeitslos *adj*
  part-time work – Teilzeitarbeit (-en) *nf*
work – (person) arbeiten *v reg* †
  work hard – fleißig arbeiten *v reg* †
  work part-time – halbtags arbeiten *v reg* †
work – (machine) funktionieren *v reg* †
worker – (male) Arbeiter (-) *nm*
worker – (female) Arbeiterin (-nen) *nf*
work experience – Berufspraktikum (-praktika) *nnt*
workshop – Werkstatt (-stätten) *nf*
world – Welt (-en) *nf*
world championship – Weltmeisterschaft (-en) *nf*
worldwide – weltweit *adj*
worm – Wurm (Würmer) *nm*
worn out – verschlissen *adj*
worried – ängstlich *adj*
worry – sich Sorgen machen (über + acc) *v reg dat refl*
  Don't worry! – Keine Angst! *excl*

worse – schlimmer *adj*
worse and worse – immer schlimmer *adv*
worth – Wert (-e) *nm*
  It's worth DM 2 000 – Es ist DM 2 000 wert
  It's not worth it – Es lohnt sich nicht
worthless – wertlos *adj*
worth seeing – sehenswert *adj*
worthwhile – sinnvoll *adj*
wound – Wunde (-n) *nf*
wrap up – (present) einpacken *v reg sep*
wrist – Handgelenk (-e) *nnt*
wrist watch – Armbanduhr (-en) *nf*
write – schreiben *v irreg*
write back – beantworten *v reg* †
write down – aufschreiben *v irreg sep*
write to – schreiben an (+ acc) *v irreg*
writer – (male) Schriftsteller (-) *nm*
writer – (female) Schriftstellerin (-nen) *nf*
writing paper – Schreibpapier *nnt*
  in writing – schriftlich *adj*
written test – schriftliche Prüfung *nf*
wrong – falsch *adj*
  be wrong – unrecht haben *v irreg*
  I am wrong – Ich habe unrecht
  What's wrong? – Was ist los?
wrong number – falsch verbunden
wrong side – Kehrseite (-n) *nf*
wrong way round – falsch 'rum

X

Xmas – Weihnachten *npl*
X-ray – Röntgenbild *nnt*
X-ray – röntgen *v reg*

to be X-rayed – sich röntgen lassen *v irreg refl*

Y

yacht – Jacht (-en) *nf*
yacht marina – Jachthafen (-häfen) *nm*
yard – (place) Hof (Höfe) *nm*
yawn – gähnen *v reg*
year – Jahr (-e) *nnt*
   be X years old – X Jahre alt sein*
   in Year 7 – im sechsten Schuljahr
   in Year 8 – im siebten Schuljahr
   in Year 9 – im achten Schuljahr
   in Year 10 – im neunten Schuljahr
   in Year 11 – im zehnten Schuljahr
   in Year 12 – in der Oberstufe
   in Year 13 – (male) Abiturient
   in Year 13 – (female) Abiturientin
   last year – letztes Jahr
   next year – nächstes Jahr
   school year – Schuljahr (-e) *nnt*
yearly – jährlich *adj*
yell – grölen *v reg*
yellow – gelb *adj*
yes – ja *adv*
yes, really – doch *adv*
yesterday – gestern *adv*
   the day before yesterday – vorgestern *adv*
yesterday evening – gestern abend *adv*
yet – noch *adv*
   not yet – noch nicht *adv*
yoga – Joga *nm, no pl*
yoghurt – Joghurt (-s) *nm*

you – (informal) du *pron nom sing*
you – (informal) dich *pron acc sing*
you – (informal) dir *pron dat sing*
you – (formal) Sie *pron nom/acc sing or pl*
you – (formal) Ihnen *pron dat sing or pl*
you – (informal) ihr *pron nom pl*
you – (informal) euch *pron acc/dat pl*
you – (persons unspecified) man *pron nom sing*
you – (persons unspecified) einen *pron acc sing*
you – (persons unspecified) einem *pron dat sing*
young – jung *adj*
young people – Jugend *nf, no pl*
young person – Jugendliche *nmf* ‡
younger – jünger *adj*
youngest – jüngste *adj*
your – (formal) Ihr *poss adj*
your – (informal sing) dein *poss adj*
your – (informal pl) euer *poss adj*
yourself – selbst *adv*
Yours – (informal) Alles Gute
Yours faithfully – (very formal) Hochachtungsvoll *adv*
Yours sincerely – (formal) mit freundlichen Grüßen
youth – Jugend *nf, no pl*
youth club – Jugendklub (-s) *nm*
youth hostel – Jugendherberge (-n) *nf*

Z

zebra – Zebra (-s) *nnt*
zebra crossing – Zebrastreifen *nm*
zero – Null (-en) *nf*
zip – Reißverschluß (-verschlüsse) *nm*
zit – Pickel (-) *nm*
zither – Zither (-n) *nf*
zone – Zone (-n) *nf*

industrial zone – Industriegebiet (-e) *nnt*
pedestrian zone – Fußgängerzone (-n) *nf*
zoo – Zoo (-s) *nm*, Tiergarten (-gärten) *nm*

Verbs with separable or inseparable prefixes and with the prefixes be-, ent-, er-, ge- and ver- should be looked up without their prefix. * denotes verb with *sein* in perfect and other compound tenses.

Infinitive	3rd Person Present	Imperfect	Perfect	Meaning
backen	**bäckt**	backte	gebacken	to bake
befehlen	**befiehlt**	befahl	befohlen	to command
begießen	begießt	begoß	begossen	to water (plants)
beginnen	beginnt	begann	begonnen	to begin
beißen	beißt	biß	gebissen	to bite
bersten	**birst**	barst	geborsten*	to burst
beschließen	beschließt	beschloß	beschlossen	to decide
beschreiben	beschreibt	beschrieb	beschrieben	to describe
biegen	biegt	bog	gebogen	to bend
bieten	**bietet**	bot	geboten	to offer
binden	**bindet**	band	gebunden	to fasten
bitten (um)	**bittet (um)**	bat (um)	gebeten	to ask (for)
blasen	**bläst**	blies	geblasen	to blow
bleiben	bleibt	blieb	geblieben*	to stay
braten	**brät**	briet	gebraten	to roast
brechen	**bricht**	brach	gebrochen	to break
brennen	brennt	brannte	gebrannt	to burn
bringen	bringt	brachte	gebracht	to bring

Infinitive	3rd Person Present	Imperfect	Perfect	Meaning
denken	denkt	dachte	gedacht	*to think*
dürfen	**darf**	durfte		*to be allowed to*
empfehlen	**empfiehlt**	empfahl	empfohlen	*to recommend*
erschrecken	**erschrickt**	erschrak	erschrocken	*to terrify*
essen	**ißt**	aß	gegessen	*to eat*
fahren	**fährt**	fuhr	gefahren*	*to travel*
fallen	**fällt**	fiel	gefallen*	*to fall*
fangen	**fängt**	fing	gefangen	*to catch*
finden	**findet**	fand	gefunden	*to find*
fliegen	fliegt	flog	geflogen*	*to fly*
frieren	friert	fror	gefroren	*to freeze*
geben	**gibt**	gab	gegeben	*to give*
gehen	geht	ging	gegangen*	*to go*
gelingen	gelingt	gelang	gelungen*	*to succeed*
genießen	genießt	genoß	genossen	*to enjoy*
geschehen	**geschieht**	geschah	geschehen*	*to happen*
gewinnen	gewinnt	gewann	gewonnen	*to win*
greifen	greift	griff	gegriffen	*to grasp*
haben	**hat**	hatte	gehabt	*to have*
halten	**hält**	hielt	gehalten	*to stop, to hold*
hängen	hängt	hing	gehangen	*to hang*

Infinitive	3rd Person Present	Imperfect	Perfect	Meaning
heben	hebt	hob	gehoben	to lift
heißen	heißt	hieß	geheißen	to be called
helfen	**hilft**	half	geholfen	to help
kennen	kennt	kannte	gekannt	to know
kommen	kommt	kam	gekommen*	to come
können	**kann**	konnte		to be able to
laden	lädt	lud	geladen	load
lassen	läßt	ließ	gelassen	to leave
laufen	**läuft**	lief	gelaufen*	to run
leiden	**leidet**	litt	gelitten	suffer
leihen	leiht	lieh	geliehen	to lend
lesen	**liest**	las	gelesen	to read
liegen	liegt	lag	gelegen	to lie
liegenlassen	läßt liegen	ließ liegen	liegenlassen	to leave lying around
messen	**mißt**	maß	gemessen	to measure
mögen	**mag**	mochte		to like to
müssen	**muß**	mußte		to have to
nehmen	**nimmt**	nahm	genommen	to take
nennen	nennt	nannte	genannt	to name
pfeifen	pfeift	pfiff	gepfiffen	whistle
raten	**rät**	riet	geraten	to guess

Infinitive	3rd Person Present	Imperfect	Perfect	Meaning
reiben	reibt	rieb	gerieben	to rub
reißen	reißt	riß	gerissen	to tear
reiten	reitet	ritt	geritten*	to ride
riechen	riecht	roch	gerochen	to smell
rufen	ruft	rief	gerufen	to call
scheiden	scheidet	schied	geschieden	to part
scheinen	scheint	schien	geschienen	to shine, to seem
schießen	schießt	schoß	geschossen	to shoot
schieben	schiebt	schob	geschoben	to push
schlafen	schläft	schlief	geschlafen	to sleep
schlagen	schlägt	schlug	geschlagen	to hit
schleichen	schleicht	schlich	geschlichen*	to creep
schließen	schließt	schloß	geschlossen	to shut
schneiden	schneidet	schnitt	geschnitten	to cut
schreiben	schreibt	schrieb	geschrieben	to write
schreien	schreit	schrie	geschrieen	to shout
schweigen	schweigt	schwieg	geschwiegen	to be silent
schwimmen	schwimmt	schwamm	geschwommen(*)	to swim
sehen	sieht	sah	gesehen	to see
sein	ist	war	gewesen*	to be
singen	singt	sang	gesungen	to sing

Infinitive	3rd Person Present	Imperfect	Perfect	Meaning
sinken	sinkt	sank	gesunken*	to sink
sitzen	sitzt	saß	gesessen	to sit
sollen	**soll**	sollte		to be supposed to, to ought to
sprechen	**spricht**	sprach	gesprochen	to speak
springen	springt	sprang	gesprungen*	to jump
stechen	**sticht**	stoch	gestochen	sting
stehen	steht	stand	gestanden	to stand
stehlen	**stiehlt**	stahl	gestohlen	to steal
sterben	**stirbt**	starb	gestorben*	to die
steigen	steigt	stieg	gestiegen*	to climb
stinken	stinkt	stank	gestunken	to smell
stoßen	**stößt**	stieß	gestoßen*	to bump
streichen	streicht	strich	gestrichen	to cancel
sich streiten	**streitet**	stritt	gestritten	to argue
tragen	**trägt**	trug	getragen	to carry, wear
treffen	**trifft**	traf	getroffen	to meet, to hit
treiben	treibt	trieb	getrieben	to do (sport)
treten	**tritt**	trat	getreten*	to step
trinken	trinkt	trank	getrunken	to drink
tun	**tut**	tat	getan	to do

Infinitive	3rd Person Present	Imperfect	Perfect	Meaning
verbringen	verbringt	verbrachte	verbracht	to spend time
vergessen	**vergißt**	vergaß	vergessen	to forget
vergleichen	vergleicht	verglich	verglichen	to compare
verlassen	**verläßt**	verließ	verlassen	to leave
verlieren	verliert	verlor	verloren	to lose
vermeiden	**vermeidet**	vermied	vermieden	to avoid
verschleißen	verschleißt	verschliß	verschlissen	to wear out
verschwinden	**verschwindet**	verschwand	verschwunden*	to promise
wachsen	**wächst**	wuchs	gewachsen*	to grow
waschen	**wäscht**	wusch	gewaschen	to wash
weisen	weist	wies	gewiesen	to show
werben	wirbt	warb	geworben	to attract
werden	**wird**	wurde	geworden*	to become
werfen	**wirft**	warf	geworfen	to throw
wiegen	wiegt	wog	gewogen	weigh
wissen	**weiß**	wußte	gewußt	to know
wollen	**will**	wollte		to want to
ziehen	zieht	zog	gezogen	to pull
zwingen	zwingt	zwang	gezwungen	to force

GRAMMAR INFORMATION

ADJECTIVES

Adjectives followed by a noun

Adjectives followed by a noun agree with ("match") the noun by taking an ending which depends on four factors:

(a) the article (determiner) or lack of one in front of the adjective
(b) the gender of the noun - masculine, feminine, or neuter
(c) the case of the noun - nominative, accusative, genitive or dative
(d) whether the noun is singular or plural

There are three tables (sets) of adjective endings. The one to use depends on which article (determiner) is used:

Table 1:

After *der/die/das, etc* (the); *dieser* (this); *jener* (that); *jeder* (each); *welcher* (which); *solcher* (such a), *mancher* (many a) and *alle* (all, which is, of course, plural)

	Masculine Singular	Feminine Singular	Neuter Singular	Plural (all genders)
Nom:	der kleine Mann	die kleine Frau	das kleine Kind	die kleinen Leute
Acc:	den kleinen Mann	die kleine Frau	das kleine Kind	die kleinen Leute
Gen:	des kleinen Mannes	der kleinen Frau	des kleinen Kindes	der kleinen Leute
Dat:	dem kleinen Mann	der kleinen Frau	dem kleinen Kind	den kleinen Leuten

Remember:

- All Genitive and Dative Singular and all Plural endings are *-en*.
- Masculine and Neuter nouns in the Genitive singular have *-es* or *-s* added. If they are single syllable nouns they usually add *-es*.
- You need to add *-n* to nouns which do not already have one in the Dative Plural of all genders.

Table 2:

After *ein/eine/ein* (a), kein (no), *and the Possessive Adjectives, mein* (my), *dein* (your, familiar singular), *sein* (his/its), *ihr* (her/its), *unser* (our), *euer* (your, familiar plural), *Ihr* (your, polite singular or plural) and *ihr* (their) the adjective has the following endings:

	Masculine Singular	Feminine Singular	Neuter Singular	Plural (all genders)
Nom:	ein kleiner Mann	eine kleine Frau	ein kleines Kind	keine kleinen Leute
Acc:	einen kleinen Mann	eine kleine Frau	ein kleines Kind	keine kleinen Leute
Gen:	eines kleinen Mannes	einer kleinen Frau	eines kleinen Kindes	keiner kleinen Leute
Dat:	einem kleinen Mann	einer kleinen Frau	einem kleinen Kind	keinen kleinen Leuten

Remember:
- For reasons of logic, *ein* itself has no plural. If "a" is plural (i.e. "some"), adjectives follow the plural pattern for Table 3 given below.
- All Genitive and Dative Singular and all Plural endings are *-en*.
- Masculine and Neuter nouns in the Genitive singular have *-es* or *-s* added. If they are single syllable nouns they usually add *-es*.
- You need to add *-n* to nouns which do not already have one in the Dative Plural of all genders.

Table 3:
Adjectives which are used alone before the noun have the following endings:

	Masculine Singular	Feminine Singular	Neuter Singular	Plural (all genders*)
Nom:	guter Wein	gute Milch	gutes Bier	gute Getränke
Acc:	guten Wein	gute Milch	gutes Bier	gute Getränke
Gen:	guten Weins	guter Milch	guten Biers	guter Getränke
Dat:	gutem Wein	guter Milch	gutem Bier	guten Getränken

(*also after non-specific numbers: *viele* (many), *mehrere* (several), *einige* (a few), *ein paar (*a few) and numbers)

Remember:
- Masculine and Neuter nouns in the Genitive singular have or -*s* added. If they are single syllable nouns they usually add -*es*.
- You need to add -*n* to nouns which do not already have one in the Dative Plural of all genders.

Adjectives not followed by a noun

Adjectives which stand alone - usually after *sein, werden* and *scheinen* - do not have an adjective ending.

      Example: Der Mann ist klein   *The man is small*

CASES

The four cases in German can seem difficult to understand. In fact, the rules for their use are relatively straightforward.

Nominative

The Nominative case is used:

  1. for the subject of a verb

      Example: Heute scheint **die Sonne**   *Today the sun is shining*

      Remember: The subject is not always the first idea in a sentence. (see **word order**)

  2. after the verbs *sein, werden, bleiben, heißen* and *scheinen*

Accusative

The Accusative case is used:

  1. for the direct object (the thing that suffers the action of the verb) of most verbs.

      Example: Ich habe **einen Kuli** gekauft   *I bought a biro*

  2. after certain prepositions. (See **prepositions**).

Dative

The Dative case is used:

  1. after certain prepositions. (See **prepositions**)

  2. after certain verbs which always take the Dative.

The most frequent are *helfen (to help)*, *folgen (to follow)* and *danken (to thank)*.

Example: Ich helfe **meinem Vater** in der Küche
                  I help my father in the kitchen

3. for the indirect object of a verb
   Example: Er gibt **seiner** Mutter das Buch
                     He gives the book to his mother

Genitive
The Genitive case is used:

1. to show "of" or possession. You may find it easier to use von + Dative.

   Example: ein Foto **meiner Schwester**   *a photo of my sister*
                     ein Foto **von meinem Bruder**   *a photo of my brother*

2. An alternative form similar to English usage (but with no apostrophe) is used with the names of people, towns or countries.

   Example: Barbaras Kuli   *Barbara's biro*

3. after certain prepositions. (See **prepositions**).

CONJUNCTIONS

Conjunctions are words which join two clauses, such as "and", "but", "because" and "while". There are two kinds of conjunction in German, known as co-ordinating conjunctions and subordinating conjunctions.

Co-ordinating conjunctions
These join two clauses which could otherwise stand as two German sentences in their own right without any changes being made to them. Most of them can also link single words or phrases in lists. There are five common ones.

They have NO effect on word-order. They are:

    und *and*   aber *but*   oder *or*   sondern *but not*   denn *for*

    Example: Er wohnt in Lübeck, **und** er hat dort viele Freunde
                     He lives in Lübeck and has many friends there

Subordinating conjunctions

These are conjunctions which add a subordinate clause (i.e. one which could not stand on its own as a German sentence without any changes being made to it) on to a main clause. They affect the word order by sending the verb to the end of the clause.

Example: **Wenn** es heute regnet, bleibe ich zu Hause
Ich bleibe zu Hause, **wenn** es heute regnet
I shall stay at home if it rains today

If a separable verb is the last word in the clause it does not separate.

Example: Wenn er heute **ankommt**, bleibe ich zu Hause
If he arrives today I shall stay at home

The common subordinating conjunctions are listed below:

als	*when (single occasion in* past)
nachdem	*after (she had done* that)
ob	*whether*
weil	*because*
wenn	*if, when, whenever (repeated* occasion)

NOUNS

German nouns always start with a capital letter.

All German nouns belong to one of three grammatical genders, masculine (der), feminine (die), or neuter (das).

Plural forms are difficult in German, and the only way to make real headway in learning plural forms is to learn them with each new word.

Singular:	der Stadtplan *map*	die Schule *school*	das Buch *book*
Plural:	die Stadtpläne *maps*	die Schulen *schools*	die Bücher *books*

Adjectival nouns ‡

All adjectives and participles can be used as nouns in German. They are then written with a capital letter.

Example: Deutsche *nmf* ‡   *German person*

Adjectival nouns take the same endings as they would if they were followed by a noun of the appropriate gender.

Like Table 1:	Masculine Singular	Feminine Singular	Plural
Nom:	der Deutsche	die Deutsche	die Deutschen
Acc:	den Deutschen	die Deutsche	die Deutschen
Gen:	des Deutschen	der Deutschen	der Deutschen
Dat:	dem Deutschen	der Deutschen	den Deutschen

Like Table 2:	Masculine Singular	Feminine Singular	Plural (Like Table 3)
Nom:	ein Deutscher	eine Deutsche	Deutsche
Acc:	einen Deutschen	eine Deutsche	Deutsche
Gen:	eines Deutschen	einer Deutschen	Deutscher
Dat:	einem Deutschen	einer Deutschen	Deutschen

Weak nouns *nm wk, nnt wk*

These nouns are slightly irregular. They are **masculine** with the exception of *das Herz*.

The majority have *-en* throughout the plural and in all cases of the singular except the Nominative. They do not usually have an *-s* in the Genitive singular. However, the following **do** add an *-s* in the Genitive singular: *der Name, der Buchstabe, der Gedanke* and *das Herz*.

Example:	Singular	Plural
Nominative:	der Franzose	die Franzosen
Accusative:	den Franzosen	die Franzosen
Genitive:	des Franzosen	der Franzosen
Dative:	dem Franzosen	den Franzosen
Nominative:	der Mensch	die Menschen
Accusative:	den Menschen	die Menschen
Genitive:	des Menschen	der Menschen
Dative:	dem Menschen	den Menschen

PREPOSITIONS

Prepositions are words which are used to show a relationship between one noun and another. This word often shows the position of one thing in relation to another. Prepositions in German are followed by different cases.

Prepositions which take the Accusative

bis	*as far as; until*	ohne	*without*
durch	*through*	um	*at + clock times, about*
für	*for*	pro	*per*
gegen	*against*	wider	*against*

Example:	**für** meinen Vater	*for my father*
	durch die Aula	*through the school hall*

Prepositions which take the Dative

aus	*out of, made of*
außer	*except for*
bei	*at the house of*
gegenüber*	*opposite*
mit	*with, by*
nach	*to, after + time*
seit	*since, for*
von	*from, of*
zu	*to, at, at + price*

* may come before or after the noun

Example: **mit** meinem Freund   *with my (boy)friend*
              seit zwei Jahren   *for two years*
              der Kirche **gegenüber** *opposite the church*

Remember:

- Even though *aus* and *zu* imply motion, they **ALWAYS** take the Dative.
- Most nouns add an *-n* in the Dative plural if they do not already have one. This is often forgotten.

Example: Ich sehe meine alten Freunde mit meinen neuen Freunde**n**
              I see my old friends with my new friends

Prepositions which take either Dative or Accusative

Nine common prepositions can take either Accusative or Dative. These can best be learnt in related groups.

in	*in, inside*
an	*on (the side of), at, of*
auf	*on (top of), at, in*
hinter*	*behind*
vor*	*in front of, before*
über	*over*
unter*	*under*
neben*	*next to*
zwischen*	*between*

* usually with Dative

Remember:
If the preposition is about position, then the Dative is used. If it is about motion towards, then the Accusative is used.

Example: Ich gehe **in die** Schule   (in + Accusative - motion)
I go to **school**
Ich arbeite **in der** Schule   (in + Dative - position)
I work in school

Prepositions which take the Genitive
These are listed with the three most common ones first, then related pairs.

trotz	*despite, in spite of*
während	*during*
wegen	*because of*
außerhalb	*outside (of)*
innerhalb	*within*
anstatt	*instead of*
statt	*instead of*

Example: **während** der Ferien   *during the holidays*
trotz der Hitze   *despite the heat*

Tip: Remember that masculine and neuter nouns add an *-s* in the Genitive singular.

Example: **wegen** des schlechten Wetter**s**
because of the bad weather

PERSONAL PRONOUNS AND POSSESSIVES

Nominative	Accusative	Dative	Possessive
ich	mich	mir	mein
du	dich	dir	dein
Sie	Sie	Ihnen	Ihr
er	ihn	ihm	sein
sie	sie	ihr	ihr
es	es	ihm	sein
wir	uns	uns	unser
ihr	euch	euch	euer (eure)
Sie	Sie	Ihnen	Ihr
sie	sie	ihnen	ihr

Sie or du?

Germans are very concerned to use the correct form for "you". Getting it wrong is impolite. The following are the main rules concerning choice of "you":

1. *du/dich/dir/dein* is used for speaking to a child (up to about 15) or an animal, and between children, students, relatives and close friends.

2. *ihr/euch/euch/euer/* is used to address a group of two or more people in which at least some would be addressed as "*du*".

3. *Sie/Sie/Ihnen/Ihr* is used in all other instances, particularly if addressing one or more strangers.

Er, sie and es

Remember that "it" may refer to a masculine or feminine noun in German, and that *er* or *sie, ihn* or *sie, ihm* or *ihr* may be needed in preference to *es*, which is reserved for neuter nouns. *Er* and *sie* do not refer solely to biological gender.

> Example: Hier ist die Tasche. Ich habe **sie** gestern gekauft
> *Here is the bag. I bought it yesterday*
> Hier ist der neue Stuhl. Ich habe **ihn** gestern bekommen
> *Here is the new chair. I got it yesterday.*

Man

The word *man* takes third person singular endings and means literally in English 'one'.

> Example: **Man** muß die Hausaufgaben machen
> *One must do the homework*

WORD ORDER

1. In a simple sentence, the verb is the second idea. It may come after the subject, after another idea, or after a subordinate clause.

In compound tenses such as the perfect tense, the auxiliary (*haben* or *sein*) occupies the position of second idea in the sentence, while the past participle is at the end of the sentence. The rest of the sentence is sandwiched between the two. In the same way the main part of a separable verb occupies the position of the second idea in the sentence and the prefix is at the end of the sentence. A modal verb takes the second position in the sentence. If there is an infinitive it goes to the end of the sentence.

Our preference is to call this rule the "1 - 2 - 3 rule".

	VERB		
1st idea	**2nd idea**	**3rd idea**	
Ich	**gehe**	heute in die Stadt	
Heute	**gehe**	ich in die Stadt	
In die Stadt	**gehe**	ich heute	
Wenn es sonnig ist,	**gehe**	ich in die Stadt	
Ich	**bin**	in die Stadt	gegangen
Ich	**habe**	ein Buch	gekauft
Der Bus	**kommt**	um neun Uhr	an
Ich	**will**	eine Banane	essen
Er	**muß**	ins Bett	gehen

2. Adverbs in German are usually in the order Time - Manner - Place.

Time	Manner	Place
Ich fahre heute	mit dem Bus	nach Worcester

3. If two sentences are joined by a co-ordinating conjunction such as *und, aber,* or *oder,* the conjunction does NOT count in the word order for the 1 - 2 - 3 rule and has no effect on it.

Example: Ich **mag** Mathe, aber ich **mag** lieber Chemie
                I like Maths but I prefer Chemistry

4. If a clause is joined to the rest of the sentence by a subordinating conjunction, the verb (or the auxiliary) goes to the end of that clause. The past participle comes before the auxiliary.

Example: Ich fahre mit dem Bus zur Schule, wenn es um 8 Uhr **regnet**
                I travel to school by bus if it is raining at 8 o'clock
                Renate weiß, daß sie zu spät abgefahren **ist**
                Renate knows that she has set off too late

VERBS

When a verb is listed in a dictionary or word list, it is given in the **Infinitive**.
Example: wohnen   *live*
             gehen   *go, walk*

The infinitive will normally be the starting point in describing how tenses are formed.

Regular and irregular verbs

There are two main sorts of verbs in German:

Regular which follow a rule. Regular verbs are often called **weak** verbs in German (because they do not have a "mind of their own"). They are marked *v reg*. Some regular verbs have minor variations. They are marked *v reg†*. See page 229.

Irregular which do not always follow a rule and therefore have to be learnt. Irregular German verbs are often called **strong** verbs (because they are "strong-minded"). They are marked *v irreg*.

Both regular and irregular verbs can fall into the following categories:

Reflexive marked *v reg refl* or *v irreg refl*. If the reflexive pronoun is dative, they are marked *v reg dat refl* or *v irreg dat refl*.

Separable with prefixes which separate and go to the end of the clause. They are marked *v reg sep* or *v irreg sep*.

Inseparable with prefixes which do not separate. They are marked *v reg insep* or *v irreg insep*.

Regular Verbs *v reg*

Infinitive/ Command	Present	Perfect
spielen *to play* Spiel! Spielt! Spielen Sie!	ich spiele du spielst Sie spielen er/sie/es spielt wir spielen ihr spielt Sie spielen sie spielen	ich habe gespielt du hast gespielt Sie haben gespielt er/sie/es hat gespielt wir haben gespielt ihr habt gespielt Sie haben gespielt sie haben gespielt

Irregular Verbs *v irreg*

Infinitive/ Command	Present	Perfect
sehen *to see* Sieh! Seht! Sehen Sie!	ich sehe du siehst Sie sehen er/sie/es sieht wir sehen ihr seht Sie sehen sie sehen	ich habe gesehen du hast gesehen Sie haben gesehen er/sie/es hat gesehen wir haben gesehen ihr habt gesehen Sie haben gesehen sie haben gesehen

Irregular Verbs with 'sein' *v irreg*

Infinitive/ Command	Present	Perfect
gehen* *to go* Geh! Geht! Gehen Sie!	ich gehe du gehst Sie gehen er/sie/es geht wir gehen ihr geht Sie gehen sie gehen	ich bin gegangen du bist gegangen Sie sind gegangen er/sie/es ist gegangen wir sind gegangen ihr seid gegangen Sie sind gegangen sie sind gegangen

Reflexive Verbs *v refl*

Infinitive/ Command	Present	Perfect
sich waschen *to wash (oneself)* Wasch dich! Wascht euch! Waschen Sie sich!	ich wasche mich du wäschst dich Sie waschen sich er/sie/es/wäscht sich wir waschen uns ihr wascht euch Sie waschen sich sie waschen sich	ich habe mich gewaschen du hast dich gewaschen Sie haben sich gewaschen er/sie/es hat sich gewaschen wir haben uns gewaschen ihr habt euch gewaschen Sie haben sich gewaschen sie haben sich gewaschen

Separable Verbs *sep*

Infinitive/ Command	Present	Perfect
aufstehen* *to get up, to stand up* Steh auf! Steht auf! Stehen Sie auf!	ich stehe auf du stehst auf Sie stehen auf er/sie/es/steht auf wir stehen auf ihr steht auf Sie stehen auf sie stehen auf	ich bin aufgestanden du bist aufgestanden Sie sind aufgestanden er/sie/es/ist aufgestanden wir sind aufgestanden ihr seid aufgestanden Sie sind aufgestanden sie sind aufgestanden

Haben or sein?

The choice of *haben* or *sein* as auxiliary in the perfect tense can cause some difficulty. In this dictionary verbs which require *sein* are marked with *.
A simple rule of thumb is:

Verbs of motion, plus *bleiben, sein* and *werden* require *sein* as an auxiliary.

sein	*to be*	haben	*to have*
ich bin	*I am*	ich habe	*I have*
du bist	*you are*	du hast	*you have*
Sie sind	*you are*	Sie haben	*you have*
er/sie/es ist	*he/she/it is*	er/sie/es hat	*he/she/it has*
wir sind	*we are*	wir haben	*we have*
ihr seid	*you are*	ihr habt	*you have*
sie sind	*they are*	sie haben	*they have*
Sie sind	*you are*	Sie haben	*you have*

Modal Verbs

The Plural forms follow the pattern of the regular verbs. Note, however, the singular forms:

können *to be able to*	wollen *to want to*	müssen *to have to*	mögen *to like*	dürfen *to be allowed to*	sollen *ought to, to be supposed to*
ich kann	ich will	ich muß	ich mag	ich darf	ich soll
du kannst	du willst	du mußt	du magst	du darfst	du sollst
er/sie/es kann	er/sie/es will	er/sie/es muß	er/sie/es mag	er/sie/es darf	er/sie/es soll
wir können	wir wollen	wir müssen	wir mögen	wir dürfen	wir sollen
ihr könnt	ihr wollt	ihr müßt	ihr mögt	ihr dürft	ihr sollt
sie können	sie wollen	sie müssen	sie mögen	sie dürfen	sie sollen
Sie können	Sie wollen	Sie müssen	Sie mögen	Sie dürfen	Sie sollen

The modal verbs are often followed by another verb. This second verb will be in the infinitive form and will be the last word in a main sentence.

Ich will heute abend ins Kino **gehen,** aber ich muß die Hausaufgaben **machen**
I want to go to the cinema tonight, but I have to do my homework

Imperfect

The Imperfect is the past tense most commonly used in formal writing such as books and newspapers. Here are some common imperfect forms you might meet:

ich war	*I was*	ich kaufte	*I bought*
ich hatte	*I had*	es regnete	*it rained*
ich ging	*I went*	es schneite	*it snowed*
ich fuhr	*I went*		

Regular verbs with variations †

Some regular verbs have minor variations. They are marked *v reg*†.

1. Verbs ending in *-ieren* (except *schmieren*) do not have a *ge-* on the front of the past participle in the perfect and other compound tenses.

    Example: kopieren   ich habe kopiert

Verbs in this category include:

addieren, adoptieren, akzeptieren, sich amüsieren, anprobieren, arrangieren, blockieren, buchstabieren, dekorieren, demonstrieren, diskutieren, dressieren, existieren, fotografieren, fotokopieren, funktionieren, gratulieren, identifizieren, informatisieren, informieren, installieren, sich interessieren, kontrollieren, kopieren, korrigieren, moderieren, notieren, organisieren, passieren*, polieren, probieren, protestieren, sich rasieren, reduzieren, reparieren, reservieren, schickanieren, studieren, tapezieren, telefonieren, tolerieren, trainieren, zitieren

2. Verbs starting with *be-, emp-, ent-, er-, -ge, - ver-* and *zer-* do not add a *ge*-on the front of the past participle in the perfect and other compound tenses.

      Example: beenden   ich habe ... beendet

Verbs in this category include:

sich bedanken, bedauern, bedeuten, (sich) bedienen, bedrohen, sich beeilen, beenden, beflecken, befragen, befriedigen, begegnen*, begleiten, begrüßen, behandeln, sich beklagen, beleidigen, bemerken, beneiden, benutzen, beobachten, sich beruhigen, berühren, sich beschweren, besichtigen, bestätigen, bestellen, bestrafen, besuchen, bewegen, bewundern, bezahlen, empören, entdecken, entführen, sich entschuldigen, sich entspannen, entwickeln, erforschen, sich erholen, (sich) erinnern, sich erkälten, erklären, sich erkundigen, erlauben, ermutigen, erneuern, erreichen, ersetzen, erstaunen, erwähnen, erwarten, erzählen, gehorchen, gehören, sich gewöhnen, veräppeln, verdächtigen, verdanken, verdienen, vereinigen, verfaulen, verhaften, verhindern, verhüten, verkaufen, verlangen, (sich) verletzen, verleugnen, vermieten, vernachlässigen, verpassen, verrenken, verrichten, verschlucken, verschwenden, versichern, verspäten, verstauchen, (sich) verstecken, versuchen, verursachen, verwandeln, verweigern, verwöhnen, zerquetschen, zerstören

3. Verbs whose infinitives end in *-den, -men, -nen* and *-ten* have the endings *-test* and *-tet* in the *du* and *er* forms of the present tense. In the imperfect tense, they add an extra *e* before the imperfect endings are added. In the perfect tense, they add an extra *e* before the final *-t* of the past participle.

      Example: arbeiteten   du arbei**test**, er arbei**tet**; ich arbei**te**te, etc;
                                           ich habe gearbeitet

Verbs in this category include:

abtrocknen, achten, antworten, anzünden, arbeiten, atmen, ausrichten, ausschalten, (sich) baden, beantworten, bluten, bürsten, einschalten, entfalten, entfernen, falten, flirten, husten, kosten, landen*, (sich) leisten, mieten, öffnen, ordnen, rechnen, retten, schalten, schulden, senden, starten*, töten, trocknen, übernachten, unterrichten, vollenden, vorbereiten, warten, sich wenden, wetten, zelten, züchten

WRITING LETTERS AND POSTCARDS

Pupils are often asked to write a letter or a postcard in German. It is particularly important to **carry out the tasks set in the question.** In other words, you should not write a pre-prepared letter which has only a vague resemblance to the question.

Postcards are nearly always to friends. Letters can be to friends and family (informal letters) or to businesses, hotels or public offices (formal letters).

Informal letters and postcards

Letter envelope

When you write an envelope or a card to an address in Germany:-
> Write *Herrn, Frau* or *Familie* first on a line on its own.
> Sometimes the surname is written next, followed by the first name.
> The street name comes before the house number.
> Leave a line space before writing the 5-figure postcode.
> It is written before the name of the town, on the same line.
> The town is usually written in capital letters.

The name and address of the sender are normally written on the back of the envelope, after the word *Absender:* or *Abs:* (Sender).

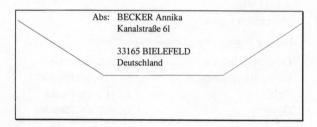

Informal Letters

Town and date   It is usual just to write the name of the town and the date.
Put this information in the **top right-hand corner** of the page.

Dear ...
Lieber Robert,	(male)
Liebe Anne,	(female)
Lieber Robert, liebe Anne,	(more than one person)
Liebe Freunde,	(plural, all male, male and female)
Liebe Freundinnen,	(plural, all female)

Punctuation   Nowadays a comma is frequently used after *Liebe(r)...*,
The first word of the letter should start with a lower case letter
unless it requires a capital letter (because it is a noun or *Sie*).
If an exclamation mark is used after *Liebe(r)....!* then the first word
of the letter should begin with a capital letter.

Du or Sie?   Informal letters and postcards to one person are usually written in
the **Du** form. **Du, Dich, Dir** and **Dein** are written with a capital
letter in informal letters.
If you are writing to more than one person, use **Ihr, Euch** and
Euer, again with capital letters.

Closing   Useful phrases include:

Das ist alles für heute.	*That's all for today.*
Jetzt muß ich meine	*Now I'm going to*
Hausaufgaben machen	*do my homework.*
Ich hoffe, bald	*I hope to hear*
von Dir zu hören.	*from you soon.*
Schreib bald.	*Write soon.*
Bis später.	*See you soon.*

Signing off   Use one of these phrases:

Alles Gute
Mit besten Grüßen

Follow it with one of these expressions:

Dein Brieffreund	(if you are male)
Deine Brieffreundin	(if you are female)
Dein	(if you are male)
Deine	(if you are female)

Finally, sign your name.

Formal letters

Your address	In the **top right-hand corner** of the page write your own address.

Recipient's Address

In the **top left-hand corner** of the page put the name and address of the person or firm you are writing to.

Date   Write the date under your address.

Dear ...

Lieber Herr Kohl,	*Dear + name*
Liebe Frau Kohl,	*Dear + name*
Sehr geehrter Herr,	*Dear Sir*
Sehr geehrte Dame,	*Dear Madam*
Sehr geehrte Damen und Herren,	*Dear Sirs*

Punctuation   Nowadays a comma is frequently used after *Liebe(r)....,*
The first word of the letter should start with a lower case letter unless it requires a capital letter (because it is a noun or *Sie*). If an exclamation mark is used after *Liebe(r)....!* then the first word of the letter should begin with a capital letter.

Du or Sie?   Formal letters are always written in the **Sie** form. Use **Sie, Ihnen** and **Ihr.** Don't forget the capital letters.

Signing off   Business letters in German usually end with

mit freundlichen Grüßen

which is the equivalent of *Yours sincerely* or *Yours faithfully*.

Hochachtungsvoll

is used nowadays only in very formal letters.

Finally, sign your name.

The envelope   Your name and address are normally written on the back of the envelope, after *Absender/Abs*. (See page 231).

Sample informal letter

Malvern, den 6.Mai 1998

Lieber Klaus,

vielen Dank für Deinen Brief, der gestern hier angekommen ist...

Schreib bald wieder
Dein Brieffreund

Paul

Sample formal letter

John WHITE
32 New Street
OLDTOWN
OT6 7XY
GB

Städtisches Informationsbüro
Hauptstraße 26
64720 ERBACH
Germany   *den 14. November 1997*

Sehr geehrte Damen und Herren,

mit diesem Brief bitte ich Sie um einige Informationen über....

Vielen Dank für Ihre Mühe.

mit freundlichen Grüßen

John WHITE

INSTRUCTIONS

Note: These instructions have been given in the **du** form, which is the one used by most text books. Versions of the most frequently used command words in the **Sie** form can be found at the end of this section on page 239.

All four skills: Listening, Reading, Speaking, Writing

Sequence words

zuerst	*first*
jetzt	*now*
dann	*then*

Questions

um wieviel Uhr?	*at what time?*
wann?	*when?*
warum?	*why?*
was?	*what?*
was heißt ....?	*what does ... mean?*
was kostet	*how much does ... cost?*
was kostet das?	*how much is it?*
welchen ziehst du vor?	*which one do you prefer?*
wer hat recht?	*who is right?*
wie	*how?*
wie ist er/sie/es?	*what is he/it like?*
wo?	*where?*
wo ist...?	*where is?*
wo sind...?	*where are?*

Information

auf deutsch	*in German*
auf englisch	*in English*
bitte wenden	*turn over the page*
deiner Meinung nach	*in your opinion*
du wirst nicht alle Buchstaben brauchen	*you will not need all the letters*
einige Fragen	*some questions*
einige Sätze	*some sentences*
er spricht über	*he is talking about*
es wird zwei Pausen im Ausschnitt geben	*there will be two pauses in the extract*
es wird zwei Pausen in der Ansage geben	*there will be two pauses in the announcement*

falsch	*false, wrong*
folgende Antworten	*the following answers*
für jede Frage/für jede Person	*for each question/for each person*
für jeden Kunden	*for each customer*
hier ist ein Beispiel	*here is an example*
in Ziffern	*in numbers*
richtig	*true*
sie spricht mit...	*she is speaking to ...*
sie spricht über	*she is talking about*
zwischen zwei Personen	*between two people*

Listening and Reading

beantworte auf deutsch	*answer in German*
beantworte auf deutsch oder kreuze die Kästchen an	*answer in German or tick the boxes*
beantworte die Fragen	*answer the questions*
bitte wenden	*turn the page, turn over*
du darfst ein Wörterbuch benutzen, wenn du willst	*you may use a dictionary if you wish*
du findest Information über...	*you will find information on...*
du wirst eine Mitteilung/einen Dialog/eine Sendung/ein Interview hören	*you are going to hear a message/a dialogue/a programme/an interview*
du wirst einige Dialoge zweimal hören	*you will hear twice some short dialogues*
entscheide	*decide*
ergänze die Sätze	*complete the sentences*
erkläre, wie/erkläre, warum	*explain how/explain why*
finde das Symbol, das dem Wort entspricht	*find the symbol which matches the word*
finde den entsprechenden Satz für jedes Foto	*find the sentence which matches each photo*
finde den Fehler	*find the mistake*
finde den Text, der jedem Bild/Titel entspricht	*find the text which matches each picture/title*
finde die richtige Antwort auf jede Frage	*choose the right answer to each question*
finde die Worte, die Redewendungen	*find the words, the phrases*
finde X auf dem Plan	*find X on the plan*
fülle die Einzelheiten aus	*complete the details*
fülle die Liste/die Tabelle aus	*complete the list/table/grid*
fülle die Lücken aus	*fill in the blanks*
fülle die Vergleiche aus	*complete the comparisons*

höre das Beispiel an	*listen to the example*
höre gut zu	*listen carefully*
korrigiere die Aussage	*correct the statement*
korrigiere die Fehler	*correct the mistakes*
kreuze das Kästchen an	*tick the box*
kreuze den richtigen Satz an	*tick the appropriate sentence*
kreuze die richtigen Kästchen an	*tick the (appropriate) boxes*
kreuze nur 5 Kästchen an	*tick 5 boxes only*
lies den Artikel, den Text, die Geschichte	*read the article, the text, the story*
lies den Brief	*read the letter*
lies die Anweisungen	*read the instructions*
lies die Anzeigen	*read the adverts*
lies die Fragen	*read the questions*
lies die Information	*read the information*
lies die Liste/lies die Notizen	*read the list/look at the notes*
lies einen Ausschnitt aus einer Zeitung	*read the extract from a newspaper*
lies folgende Sätze	*read the following sentences*
lies sorgfältig	*read carefully*
mach Notizen	*make notes*
notiere die Einzelheiten	*note down the details*
ordne die Bilder richtig ein	*put the pictures into the correct order*
ordne die Wörter richtig ein	*arrange the words in the correct order*
schau dir die Tabelle an	*look at the grid*
schau dir die Bilder an	*look at the drawings*
schreibe auf englisch	*write the equivalent in English*
schreibe das Wort, das zu den anderen nicht paßt	*write the odd word out*
schreibe den Buchstaben	*write the letter*
schreibe den entsprechenden Buchstaben	*write the letter which matches*
schreibe den richtigen Buchstaben ins Kästchen	*put the correct letter in the box*
schreibe die Antworten	*write the answers*
schreibe die Nummer	*write the number*
schreibe im Kästchen die Nummer des entsprechenden Bildes	*write the number of the illustration in the box*
schreibe Notizen	*make notes*
schreibe die entsprechenden Nummern	*write the numbers which match*
sind die Sätze richtig oder falsch?	*are the sentences true or false?*
unterstreiche/verbinde	*underline/match up*
wähle die passendste Beschreibung	*choose the description which best fits*
wähle die richtige Antwort	*choose the correct answer*
wähle ja oder nein	*circle yes or no*

wenn der Satz richtig ist, kreuze das Kästchen **richtig** an	*if the sentence is true, tick the **true** box*
wenn der Satz falsch ist, kreuze das Kästchen **falsch** an	*if the sentence is false, tick the **false** box*
wenn die Aussage falsch ist, korrigiere sie	*if the statement is incorrect, write a correct one*
wenn die Aussage richtig ist, kreuze das Kästchen **richtig** an	*if the statement is true, tick the **true** box*
wenn die Aussage falsch ist, kreuze das Kästchen **falsch** an	*if the statement is true, tick the **false** box*
zeichne ein Pfeil, um zu zeigen, welches Bild sich auf welches Bild bezieht	*draw an arrow to show which picture goes with which sign*
zeig auf dem Plan/auf der Karte	*mark on the plan/map*

Speaking

beantworte diese Fragen	*answer these questions*
bedanke dich beim Ladenbesitzer	*thank the shopkeeper*
beende die Unterhaltung höflich	*end the conversation politely*
begrüße den Prüfer	*greet the examiner*
benutze die Symbole, um einen Dialog zu erfinden	*use the symbols to make up a dialogue*
beschreibe das Bild	*describe the picture*
bitte um folgende Information	*ask for the following information*
sag, was du gemacht hast	*say what you did*
schau dir dir Bilder an	*look at the pictures, the photos*
sprich	*speak*
stelle Fragen	*ask questions*

Writing

ändere	*change*
beantworte den Brief	*reply to the letter*
beantworte die Fragen, die im Brief stehen	*answer the questions asked in the letter*
bereite folgende Aufgaben auf deutsch vor	*prepare the following tasks in German*
beschreibe	*describe/write a description of*
du darfst ein Wörterbuch benutzen	*you can use a dictionary*
erfinde eine Broschüre, ein Poster	*prepare a brochure, a poster*
erkläre, wie .../ erkläre, warum ...	*explain how ... /explain why ...*
erwähne	*mention*
erzähle, was du gemacht hast	*say what you did*
frage nach folgenden Einzelheiten	*ask for the following details*
frage um Rat	*ask for advice*

fülle das Formular aus	fill in the form
gib Auskunft	give information
gib deine Eindrücke	give your impressions
gib deine Meinung und sage warum	write your opinion and the reasons for it
in deinem Brief sollst du ...	in your letter you should ...
sagen, was du gemacht hast	say what you did
schreibe die Einzelheiten	write the details
schreibe eine Antwort	write a reply
schreibe eine Kurzfassung	summarise
schreibe eine Liste	write a list
schreibe eine Postkarte/einen Brief	write a postcard/a letter
schreibe einen Artikel	write an article
schreibe etwa 100 Worte	write about 100 words
stelle dich vor	introduce yourself
stelle dir vor, daß ...	imagine that...
vergleiche	make a comparison
wähle Thema 1 oder Thema 2	choose title 1 or title 2

Common commands in the Sie form

antworten Sie	reply	einen Kreis um	
beenden Sie	finish	notieren Sie	note
begrüßen	greet	ordnen Sie	arrange
benutzen Sie	use	schauen Sie sich ...an	look at
bereiten Sie ... vor	prepare	schreiben Sie	write
beschreiben Sie	describe	setzen Sie ein	put
entscheiden Sie	decide	Sie können	you can
ergänzen Sie	complete	sprechen Sie (über)	speak (about)
erklären Sie	explain	stellen Sie sich vor	imagine
erwähnen Sie	mention	unterstreichen Sie	underline
erzählen Sie	tell (a story)	verbessern Sie	correct
finden Sie	find	wählen Sie	choose
fragen Sie	ask	wenden Sie	turn
fragen Sie	ask (questions)	zeichnen Sie	draw
füllen Sie ... aus	fill in	zeigen Sie	indicate
geben Sie	give		
hören Sie ... zu	listen to		
kreuzen Sie an	tick		
lesen Sie	read		
machen Sie	make		
machen Sie	circle		

Mitteleuropa